EMBLEMATICS
AND
SEVENTEENTH-CENTURY
FRENCH LITERATURE

EMF CRITIQUES

EDITOR
David Lee Rubin

Emblematics and Seventeenth-Century French Literature
COPY EDITOR
Marie Hertzler

PRODUCTION
Angel Applications

COVER DESIGN
Dallas Pasco

EMBLEMATICS AND SEVENTEENTH-CENTURY FRENCH LITERATURE

DESCARTES, TRISTAN, LA FONTAINE AND PERRAULT

LAURENCE GROVE

ROOKWOOD PRESS
CHARLOTTESVILLE

©2000 by ROOKWOOD PRESS, INC.
520 Rookwood Place
Charlottesville, Virginia 22903-4734, USA
All rights reserved. Published 2000
Printed in the United States of America.

This book is printed on acid-free paper.

Library of Congress Cataloguing-in-Publication Data

Grove, Laurence.
 Emblematics and seventeenth-century French literature: Descartes, Tristan, La Fontaine, and Perrault/Laurence Grove.
     p.cm.—(EMF critiques)
 Includes bibliographical references and index.
 ISBN 1-886365-19-9
 1. French literature—17th century—History and criticism. 2. Emblems in literature. I. Title. II. Series.

PQ245.G75 2001
840.9'004—dc21

00-051752

Contents

Foreword

I. Introduction 1

II. Emblematics in Seventeenth-Century France 5

III. Descartes: Traces of an Emblematic Upbringing 28
    A. The Influence of a Jesuit Education 31
    B. Descartes's Language in the Light of Emblematics 45
    C. "ceux qui suivent maintenant Aristote…sont
       comme le lierre…" 60

IV. Tristan's Emblematic Sonnets 74
    A. Glasgow University Library SMAdd.392 79
    B. Tristan and Emblematic Reading Practices 82

V. Emblematic Structures in the Work of La Fontaine 105
    A. La Fontaine and Guéroult 110
    B. Visual Interaction with La Fontaine's Texts 123
    C. La Fontaine and Fouquet 142

VI. Perrault's Debt to the Device 163
    A. Bibliothèque de l'Arsenal ms. 3328 165
    B. Charles Perrault and the Art of the Device 177

VII. Conclusion: Further Possibilities 190

Appendix A: Tristan L'Hermite:
              The GUL SMAdd.392 Manuscripts 205
Appendix B: Charles Perrault's *Discours sur l'Art des Devises* 228

Bibliography 259

LIST OF FIGURES
Figures are not to scale

Figure 1.   "Ingratitude," from Gilles Corrozet, *Hecatomgraphie* (Paris: Janot, 1540). Bibliothèque nationale de France.

Figure 2.   "Te stante virebo," from Claude Paradin, *Devises héroïques* (Lyons: J. de Tournes and G. Gazeau, 1557). Glasgow University Library.

Figure 3.   "Speculum creaturarum," from Ioannes David, *Duodecim specula* (Antwerp: Plantin, 1610). Glasgow University Library.

Figure 4.   "Praestant interna coronae," from *Devises pour les tapisseries du roy*, ms. fr. 7819, Bibliothèque nationale de France.

Figure 5.   "1610: Devises du portail de l'église de La Flèche," from *Série Qb 1*, Bibliothèque nationale de France (Département des Estampes).

Figure 6.   "Devises de la Pompe funèbre d'Henri IV," from *Série Qb 1*, Bibliothèque nationale de France (Département des Estampes).

Figure 7.   "Planche que les Iesuites ont fait graver," from *Série Qb 1*, Bibliothèque nationale de France (Département des Estampes).

Figure 8.   Frontispiece from Tristan L'Hermite, *La Folie du sage* (Paris: Toussaint Quinet, 1645). Bibliothèque nationale de France.

Figure 9.   "Reçu" (thought to be in the hand of Tristan L'Hermite), Bibliothèque nationale de France (Département de Manuscrits, Cabinet des Titres), Pièces Originales 1711.

Figure 10. "Arrousé i'augmente," from Otto Van Veen, *Amorum emblemata* (Antwerp: Verdussen, 1608). Glasgow University Library.

Figure 11. "Planche," from Tristan L'Hermite, *Poésies galantes et héroïques* (Paris: Loyson, 1662). Bibliothèque nationale de France.

Figure 12. "Plustot montrer que dire," from Otto Van Veen, *Amorum emblemata* (Antwerp: Verdussen, 1608). Glasgow University Library.

Figure 13. "En jouant," from Otto Van Veen, *Amorum emblemata* (Antwerp: Verdussen, 1608). Glasgow University Library.

Figure 14. "Cette nuit en dormant," from Glasgow University Library SMAdd.392 copy of Otto Van Veen, *Amorum emblemata* (Antwerp: Verdussen, 1608), with manuscript additions of verse by Tristan L'Hermite.

Figure 15. "Quelqu'autre d'une humour commune," from Glasgow University Library SMAdd.392 copy of Otto Van Veen, *Amorum emblemata* (Antwerp: Verdussen, 1608), with manuscript additions of verse by Tristan L'Hermite.

Figure 16. "Amours de Canante," from Glasgow University Library SMAdd.392 copy of Otto Van Veen, *Amorum emblemata* (Antwerp: Verdussen, 1608), with manuscript additions of verse by Tristan L'Hermite.

Figure 17. "Sonnet," from Glasgow University Library SMAdd.392 copy of Otto Van Veen, *Amorum emblemata* (Antwerp: Verdussen, 1608), with manuscript additions of verse by Tristan L'Hermite.

Figure 18. "Les Riches sont supportés & les povres oppressés," from Guillaume Guéroult, *Premier livre des emblemes* (Lyons: Balthazar Arnoullet, 1550). Glasgow University Library.

Figure 19. "La Grotte de Thétis," from André Félibien, *Description de la Grotte de Versailles* (Paris: Imprimerie Royale, 1676). Glasgow University Library.

Figure 20. "Le Cerf," from Horapollo, *De la signification des notes hiéroglyphiques* (Paris: Kerver, 1543). Bibliothèque nationale de France.

Figure 21. Frontispiece from Jean de La Fontaine, *A Hundred Fables of La Fontaine* with Pictures by Percy J. Billinghurst (London: John Lane, 1900). Carnegie Library of Pittsburgh copy.

Figure 22a. Opening page from Charles Perrault, *Discours sur l'art des devises*, ms. 3328 pièce 1, Bibliothèque de l'Arsenal.

Figure 22b. Folio 41 (including four additional autograph lines) from Charles Perrault, *Discours sur l'art des devises*, ms. 3328 pièce 1, Bibliothèque de l'Arsenal.

Figure 23. Opening page from Charles Perrault, *Mémoires de ma vie* (autograph manuscript), ms. fr. 23 991, Bibliothèque nationale de France.

Figure 24. "Scientia Inflat," from Georgette de Montenay, *Emblemes, ou devises chrestiennes* (Lyons: Jean Marcorelle, 1571). Glasgow University Library.

Figure 25. "Cendrillon," from Charles Perrault, *Histoires ou contes du temps passé* (Paris: Claude Barbin, 1697). Bibliothèque nationale de France.

Figure 26. "Le Corbeau et le Renard," from Gabriel Faene, trans. Charles Perrault, *Cent Fables* (London: Darres et Du Bosc, 1743). Glasgow University Library.

Figure 27. "Le Coc et le Renard," from Charles Perrault, *Le Labyrinthe de Versailles* (Paris: Imprimerie Royale, 1677). Glasgow University Library.

Figure 28. "Consilium pravæ mulieris," from Hernando de Soto, *Emblemas moralizades* (Madrid: Por los Herederos de Iuan Iniguez de Lequerica, 1599). Glasgow University Library.

To Mungo and Dad

Foreword

Many thanks are due to Drs Alison Adams and Stephen Rawles for their unfailing help and friendship in matters both general and emblematic. They have also given permission for chapter III and appendix A to be reproduced, some of this material having first appeared in volume 2 of the Glasgow Emblem Studies series. Professor Peter Daly and Professor Daniel Russell have allowed me to reissue in chapter VI and appendix B material that first appeared in *Emblematica* 7.1 (1993).

I am indebted to Professor Noël Peacock for his encouragement and support, to Mrs Eila Smyth for her unflagging help and good humour and to the University of Glasgow's Faculty of Arts for financial assistance.

The work as it stands owes much to the editorial skills of Professor David Lee Rubin, Dr Marie Hertzler and the two readers, Professors Hugh M. Davidson and David Graham. Their suggestions and comments have resulted in the initial manuscript, a version of my 1994 University of Pittsburgh doctoral dissertation, being vastly improved and expanded, in many instances beyond recognition.

I am especially grateful to Professor Daniel Russell. This book would not have been possible without his constant advice and encouragement at every stage of its development. Above all I would like to thank Jane, my sister and my parents.

Emblematics
and
Seventeenth-Century
French Literature

I
INTRODUCTION

Emblems and devices played a central rôle in the cultural life of seventeenth-century France. Demand was enough to allow over one hundred editions of the Père Claude-François Menestrier's various emblematically concerned writings. Emblems and devices were used as an essential component of royal entries, ballets and funerals. They were often the subject of discussion among the *salonistes* or could be used for the purposes of religious propaganda. Only recently, thanks to scholars such as Mario Praz, Peter Daly and Daniel Russell have we been able to appreciate the importance of this phenomenon within the culture of the reign of Louis XIV.[1]

The aim of this study is to apply such relatively new perspectives to improve our understanding of French literature of the period in context. The work is not, therefore, an analysis of emblematics per se, but rather an attempt at a reconsideration of our attitude towards major writings of the seventeenth century in the light of information that until recently had been unavailable or grossly neglected.

There are of course some models in the field. Recent critical approaches to seventeenth-century French literature have thrown new light on important parallel issues such as that of text/image interaction or the influence of emblem-related forms. Raymond LePage has considered methods of reading the illustrations of La Fontaine's *Fables*[2] and Boris Donné, Jean-Pierre Collinet and Françoise Charpentier have discussed the influence of Francesco Colonna's *Songe de Poliphile* upon La Fontaine's *Psyché*,[3] to cite but four examples. More generally, Françoise Siguret's *L'Œil surpris*[4] considers questions of visual perception and the interpretation of images in the early seventeenth century. She takes specific examples from Descartes's *Dioptrique*, Corneille's *Illusion comique* and Etienne Binet's *Merveilles de la nature*.

With direct reference to the emblem and device Kurt Weinberg, Margaret McGowan, Patrick Dandrey and Leonard Johnson have produced excellent articles that apply a knowledge of emblematics to works of Mme. de La Fayette, Jean de La Fontaine and Tristan L'Hermite.[5] Daly has worked on English and German literature and Russell upon French poetry of the sixteenth century.[6] However, whereas the latter examples do not concern French seventeenth-century literature, the former have the limited scope of the short article. Georges Couton too can be classed in this category; his work on La Fontaine and emblems forms part of his research on seventeenth-century allegory, but in reference to his *Écritures codées*[7] he openly admits that "On aimerait que ce petit livre, qui n'a aucune prétention à l'exhaustivité, aidât, au moins dans ses débuts, celui qui entreprendrait une recherche d'ensemble" (8). Such, in part, is precisely the aim of this work.

We shall approach this task through the vehicle of four precise, representative, but by no means unique, case studies of specific authors; these are intended to be of interest per se, but also as an indication of the possibilities for applying a specific method to other authors and works.

Our chosen authors are René Descartes, Tristan L'Hermite, Jean de La Fontaine and Charles Perrault. While all are major writers and thereby fit one of the requirements I set, they are perhaps as different each from the other as possible. Descartes, a *moderne* active in the first half of the century, was a philosopher generally writing in prose. He would have been influenced by the religious emblematics of the Jesuits of La Flèche. Tristan L'Hermite's poetry is also from the beginning of the century, but the particular influence we shall discuss, the love emblems of Otto Van Veen, is decidedly secular. La Fontaine, similarly a poet of importance but late in the reign of Louis XIV, was greatly influenced by the *anciens*. His salon circles were closely associated with much of the court emblematics of the time. Charles Perrault was a fellow member of the Académie Française in the latter part of the century, but a leading *moderne*. With him we return to prose compositions and consider the theory of emblematics.[8]

Emblematics can improve our understanding of literature on several levels. Only specific examples can demonstrate this amply, allowing conclusions to be drawn while going beyond mere generalities. On a primary, most precise level, Charles Perrault's *Discours sur l'art des devises* represents the author's own theory of emblematics, a subject he considered important enough to mention in his *Mémoires de ma vie*.[9]

In other cases a knowledge of emblematics can help us seize specific aspects of a text hitherto not in evidence. Following Leonard Johnson's example, we will show how certain of Tristan's poems operate as direct references to the emblems of Van Veen. In the case of La Fontaine, H. Gaston Hall has analysed the notion of *contaminatio* using the example of "La Grenouille qui veut se faire aussi grosse que le boeuf" (*Fable* I, III) and borrowings from Jean Baudoin and Terence.[10] In chapter V of the present study we will show that the final line of La Fontaine's *Fable* II, XVI ("Le Corbeau voulant imiter l'aigle"), "Où la Guêpe a passé le Moucheron demeure," refers directly to Guillaume Guéroult's emblem 9, "De l'Araigné, de la guespe, & de la mouche." In such cases it is only when we are able to pick up the emblematic reference that we can fully appreciate the significance of the text in question.

On a broader level, understanding the structure of the emblem and the mentality that allowed it such a success can help us to understand the structure of literary texts composed under such influence. Tristan's poetry, for example, in the specific context of manuscripts now in Glasgow University Library, can be seen to operate as a single element in an amalgamized composition that functions through the bringing together of texts and images from multiple sources. Similarly, visual elements can be read as part of a text (e.g. the decorative arts of Vaux-le-Vicomte with respect to La Fontaine's *Songe de Vaux*[11]) or textual images evoking pictures (e.g. Descartes's reference to the climbing ivy in the *Discours de la méthode*) could be seen as forming an

Introduction

emblematic *imago*, requiring the reader of the time to approach the text via a global image rather than through the 'linear' reading that would probably be automatic to us today. Understanding the cultural phenomenon of emblematics can, in this way, bring us closer to the literary mentality of the age and thereby help us avoid anachronistic readings as we approach the texts themselves today.

Emblematic influence in its most general form involves the cultural context of the authors in question as well as the very nature of their works; Joan DeJean,[12] David Lee Rubin,[13] Jürgen Grimm,[14] Jean-Pierre Collinet,[15] John D. Lyons[16] and Amédée Carriat[17] are among those who have offered much insight in this field; nonetheless it is a notion that has often been overlooked by critics. Much of this context can be reconstructed from materials like those to be found in the Bibliothèque de l'Arsenal's *Recueil Conrart*. This collection, consisting essentially of manuscript pieces from the literary circles of the seventeenth century, shows, among other things, that much of the pro-Fouquet propaganda came in the form of *Recueils de devises*; in chapter V of this study we shall demonstrate how the same series of manuscripts shows the closeness of the fable and emblem forms in La Fontaine's time. Descartes's education at La Flèche included the study of Jesuit emblems whose clarity and concision to pedagogical purposes would later be the hallmarks of the Cartesian method. These kinds of knowledge of a major prevalent cultural influence are essential if we are to understand the basic workings of the seventeenth-century literary mind.

To repeat, our study will aim to demonstrate this hypothesis through the examples of four specific authors. In the case of Descartes and La Fontaine our studies will work from the specific to the general while relating to the authors' published works. Our chapters on Tristan and Perrault will concentrate on the presentation and analysis of little-known manuscript texts that are directly concerned with emblematics. Our conclusions are obviously intended to be of particular interest to scholars of these authors; however the implications of the study's method go far beyond such specific cases. We should constantly bear in mind that the same sort of approach can also be applied to such other authors of the period as Jean Racine, Blaise Pascal or Mme. de Scudéry. Applied to other writers in similar fashion, the study's method should help put a new, more accurate perspective on our reading of seventeenth-century French literature in general.

NOTES

[1] Mario Praz, *Studies in Seventeenth-Century Imagery*, 2nd ed., 2 vols. (Rome: Edizione di Storia et Letteratura, 1975). Peter M. Daly, *Literature in the Light of the Emblem: Structural Parallels Between the Emblem and Literature in the Sixteenth and Seventeenth Centuries* (Toronto: U of Toronto P, 1979). Daniel Russell, *The Emblem and Device in France* (Lexington: French Forum, 1985). A new edition is forthcoming.

[2] Raymond G. LePage, "The 1668 Edition of the *Fables*: An Iconographic Interpretation," *L'Esprit Créateur* 21.4 (1981), 66-77.

[3] Boris Donné, *La Fontaine et la poétique du songe: Récit, rêverie et allégorie dans* Les Amours de Psyché (Paris: Champion, 1995), especially pages 162-80. Jean-Pierre Collinet, *Le Monde*

littéraire de La Fontaine (Paris: PUF, 1970; Geneva: Slatkine, 1989), especially pages 95-106 and 435-38. Francoise Charpentier, "De Colonna à La Fontaine: Le Nom de Poliphile," *L'Intelligence du passé: Les Faits, l'écriture et les sens: Mélanges offerts à Jean Lafond*, eds. Pierre Aquilon, Jacques Chupeau and others (Tours: Universtité François Rabelais, 1988), 369-78

[4] *L'Œil surpris: Perception et représentation dans la première moitié du XVIIe siècle* (1985; Paris: Klincksieck, 1993).

[5] Kurt Weinberg, "The Lady and the Unicorn, or M. de Nemours à Coulomiers: Enigma, Device, Blazon and Emblem in La Princesse de Clèves," *Euphorion* 71 (1977), 306-55. Margaret M. McGowan, "Moral Intention in the Fables of La Fontaine," *Journal of the Warburg and Courtauld Institutes* 29 (1966), 264-81. Patrick Dandrey, "De l'Art des devises à la poétique de l'apologue: La Préface des *Fables* de La Fontaine (1668) à la lumière du traité des *Devises* du P. Le Moyne (1666)," *Le Fablier* 7 (1995), 105-23. Leonard Johnson, "*Amorum emblemata*: Tristan L'Hermite and the Emblematic Tradition," *Renaissance Quarterly* 21 (1968), 429-41.

[6] Daniel Russell, "Emblematic Structures in Sixteenth-Century French Poetry," *Jahrbuch für Internationale Germanistik* 14 (1982), 54-100, and *Emblematic Structures in Renaissance French Culture* (Toronto: U of Toronto P, 1995).

[7] *Écritures codées: Essais sur l'allégorie au XVIIe siècle* (Paris: Aux Amateurs de Livres, 1990).

[8] For an overview of recent critical approaches to the study of our four primary authors, see the introductory sections to chapters III to VI respectively.

[9] See chapter VI for full references and further explanation.

[10] H. Gaston Hall, "*Contaminatio* in a Fable by La Fontaine (1,3)," *PFSCL* 11 (1979), 91-106.

[11] On the rôles and interaction of the four Allegories in the *Songe de Vaux*, see specifically Robert N. Nicolich's "The Triumph of Language: The Sister Arts and Creative Activity in La Fontaine's *Songe de Vaux*," *L'Esprit Créateur* 21.4 (1981), 10-21.

[12] "La Fontaine's *Psyché*: The Reflecting Pool of Classicim," *L'Esprit Créateur* 21.4 (1981), 99-109. This and the remainder of the works cited in this introduction will be discussed further in the chapters that follow.

[13] *A Pact with Silence: Art and Thought in the* Fables *of Jean de La Fontaine* (Columbus: Ohio State UP, 1991).

[14] "Stratégies de désorientation dans les 'Fables' de La Fontaine," *Ouverture et dialogue: Mélanges offerts à Wolfgang Leiner à l'occasion de son soixantième anniversaire*, eds. Ulrich Döring, Antiopy Lyroudias and Rainer Zaiser (Tübingen: Narr, 1988), 175-91.

[15] *Le Monde littéraire de La Fontaine*.

[16] "*Camera Obscura*: Image and Imagination in Descartes's *Méditations*," *Convergences: Rhetoric and Poetic in Seventeenth-Century France*, eds. David L. Rubin and Mary B. McKinley (Columbus: Ohio State UP, 1989), 179-95.

[17] *Tristan ou l'éloge d'un poète* (Limoges: Rougerie, 1955).

II
EMBLEMATICS IN SEVENTEENTH-CENTURY FRANCE

An emblem, broadly speaking, is a combination of text and image whose whole is formed by the interaction of the component parts; this whole purveys a message, moral lesson or observation of general import. This can best be demonstrated by a specific example; figure 1 shows Gilles Corrozet's ivy emblem taken from the *Hecatomgraphie* of 1540.[1] The picture or *imago* shows a tree covered with the ivy. This scene in itself delivers no specific message. The message is to be gleaned from the title or *motto*, "Ingratitude." Again, on its own "Ingratitude" is a wide concept; coupled with the picture of ivy, we understand the reference as being to the ingratitude of one who neglects his benefactor as the ivy strangles its sustainer. The four-line verse text, or *subscriptio*, makes this clear, but again without the adjoining *motto* and *imago* it would lose the effect that the context assures.

There are of course variations upon this general process. In some cases the *subscriptio* can be several pages long, in others no more than a quatrain. Many emblems include a fourth element, an adjoining commentary. Indeed, in the case of Corrozet the facing page bears a 26-line poem on the subject of ingratitude and ivy, although it can be argued that the commentary is very much an integral part of the emblem rather than a supplementary addition. It is also possible for the *motto* to be a statement or proverb rather than a title (as in this particular case), thereby further increasing the artfulness of the interaction. Questions of definition are therefore contested, but for our purposes the general terminology of an interaction of *motto*, *imago* and *subscriptio* will suffice.[2]

The other major emblematic form was the device. A device does not carry the emblem's general import, but rather is applicable to a particular individual, organisation or community. An example of a device that employs the ivy theme is that of the Cardinal de Lorraine, as given in Claude Paradin's *Devises héroïques* of 1557 (see figure 2).[3] Again, the motto, "Te stante virebo," is meaningless without the picture, as is the ivy without the motto. Together, however, they form a statement of the Cardinal's dependence on, and loyalty to, the king; like the ivy, he will always flourish, providing he has support (here the king's).[4] In Paradin's edition, the device is followed by a commentary; however in general the *imago* and *motto* alone (or on occasion just one of the two parts) suffice to evoke the bearer. The device, unlike the emblem, would more often than not be seen outside of printed collections. Notable examples are Louis XII's porcupine device with the motto "de près et de loin" or "eminus et

Figure 1. "Ingratitude," from Gilles Corrozet, *Hecatomgraphie* (Paris: Janot, 1540).

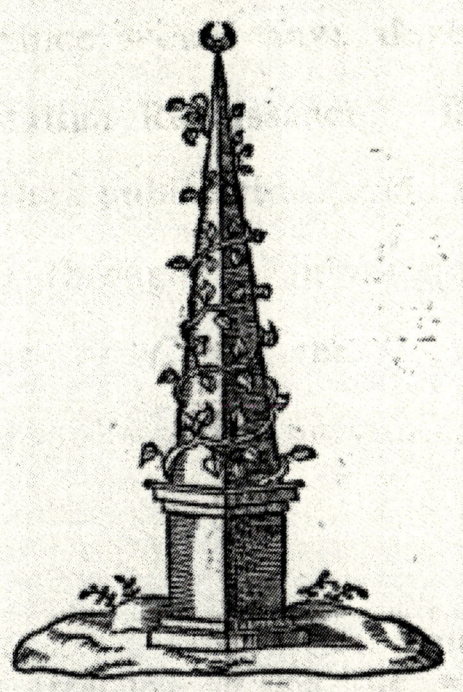

Figure 2.   "Te stante virebo," from Claude Paradin, *Devises héroïques* (Lyons: J. de Tournes and G. Gazeau, 1557).

cominus,"[5] François Ier's "Nutrisco et extinguo" and salamander device[6] (both of which adorn the walls of the royal château at Blois) and Nicolas Fouquet's squirrel with the motto "quo non ascendet?"[7]

Michel Pastoureau[8] claims the origin of the device can be traced back to the heraldry of the Middle Ages. Less debatable is the idea that the device in France would have developed under influence from the *imprese* of the Italian Renaissance. The fifteenth and early sixteenth centuries saw the publication and popularity of various works operating essentially through an interaction of text and image. These included the *Tablet of Cebes*, the *Dream of Poliphile* and Renaissance editions of Horapollo's *Hieroglyphics*.[9]

The first work to call itself an emblem book was Andrea Alciato's *Emblematum liber* of 1531, published in Augsburg by Heinrich Steyner. The work's 104 emblems follow the basic format of a title/*motto*, a woodcut engraving and a verse *subscriptio*. Subjects include such topics as the wisdom of remaining silent when one is ignorant and the comparison of the miserly accumulation of riches with the ass who carries fine foods but eats only thistles. The work was popular enough to go to well over one hundred editions between 1531 and the end of the seventeenth century, including that of Chrestien Wechel of Paris in 1536 with its French translation/adaptation by Jean Le Fevre.[10]

The first French emblem book was Guillaume de La Perrière's *Le Théâtre des bons engins* of 1540 ns.[11] According to Greta Dexter,[12] this was an extended version of the emblems La Perrière had composed for Marguerite de Navarre's 1533 entry into Toulouse ("Introduction," vi). In this edition each of the one hundred emblems consists of a picture and accompanying *dizain*, but by the 1545 De Tournes edition a motto-like title had been added. As with Alciato, the subjects are general and varied; La Perrière's work includes such titles as "Nous serons tous egaux en la fin," "En tous endroits flatteurs sont danguereux" and "Force n'ha lieu, ou Prudence domine." In total the work went to thirteen editions. One of La Perrière's last works, *La Morosophie* of 1553,[13] is considered by some to be an updated version of the *Théâtre* (Dexter, "Guillaume de La Perrière"[14]).

The ivy emblem with which we opened the discussion was taken from another early French collection, the *Hecatomgraphie* of Gilles Corrozet. The title, woodblock engraving and accompanying *quatrain* were surrounded by a decorative frame that Janot had used a little earlier for an edition of La Perrière's *Théâtre*. The facing page of each of the *Hecatomgraphie*'s one hundred emblems bore a lengthier verse text on the theme of the emblem. Again the emblems' subjects (e.g. "Vertu domine sur les astres," "La force de l'amour," "La guerre doulce aux inexpérimentez") cover a variety of topics giving moral advice and food for contemplation.[15]

In the middle years of the sixteenth century both Barthélemy Aneau and Guillaume Guéroult authored descriptions of animals that resembled emblem books.[16] In these the woodcut and title are followed by a rhyming description of the animal in question. In both cases the *recueil* as a whole aims by successive stages to show the superiority of man over the animals and the magnificence of God, creator of all things. The same two authors also produced emblem books proper. Aneau's *Picta poesis* of

1552,[17] which he translated into French in the same year under the title of *Imagination poétique*,[18] claims that the adding of texts to the pictures will render them "parlantes" (6). The work follows the tripartite structure with the stated aim, broadly speaking, of adding vivacity through the interaction of poetry and image.[19] Subjects are varied (e.g. "Raison d'esprit avec travail de corps," "Rien ne fault sans bon conseil entreprendre," "Les vieux soient supportez par les ieunes") with the vague common link being that of the conveyance of moral learning, in practice often based on the works of Ovid. Moral learning is also the stated aim of Guillaume Guéroult's *Premier livre des emblemes*, published in Lyons by Balthazar Arnoullet in 1550. This work will be discussed at some length in chapter V.

Pierre Coustau's *Le Pegme* of 1555[20] gives an early example of a work whose emblems are extended by the addition of lengthy explanatory commentaries, each labelled as a "Narration philosophique."[21] The *Pegme* follows the usual format of *motto*, *imago* and *subscriptio*, and covers a general selection of moral and philosophical lessons (e.g. "Contre ceux qui vivent sous l'Empire de leurs femmes," "Vertu surmonte tout," "Contre les iuges corrumpus"). These are then supplemented by the prose commentary joined to each emblem, explaining and expanding the general message with the help of ample quotation from the ancients. The general format of Coustau's innovation was to become popular with seventeenth-century emblem authors such as Jean Baudoin and Marin Le Roy de Gomberville (see below).

Georgette de Montenay's *Emblemes, ou devises chrestiennes* of 1571[22] was the first Protestant emblem book.[23] As such it was innovative in a domain—the dissemination of religious ideas—in which the emblem form was to play an important rôle. Montenay promotes her faith through a hundred emblems with subjects such as faith in God to conquer fear ("Quem timebo"), to unite peoples ("Foedere perfecto") and to offer peace after death ("Desiderans dissolvi"). A peculiarity of the collection is that these titles, which function as the motto of each emblem, feature not above the engraving but within it, carried in a scroll or *bandereau*. The *subscriptio* then takes the form of an *huitain*.

These are just a sampling of some of the early French emblem books. Other French authors merit discussion (e.g. Maurice Scève, Jean-Jacques Boissard, Théodore de Bèze) as do other works and editions of works by the authors we have mentioned. We should also remember that the emblem books of such foreign authors as Ioannes Sambucus, Hadrianus Junius, Nicolas Reusner, Joachim Camerarius and Julius Wilhelm Zincgref would have been read in France. Finally, works not labelled as emblem books could, in practice, represent perfect cases of the emblematic mentality regarding text/image interaction. Two examples, the animal collections of Aneau and Guéroult, have already been cited. Others include the various editions of the *Ovide moralisée* (also known as the *Ovide figurée*), Jean de Vauzelles's *Les Simulachres & historiees faces de la Mort*[24] and Blaise de Vigenère's editions of Philostratus's *Les Images ou tableaux de platte peinture*.[25]

Our survey has up to now dealt with the beginnings of the emblem form and its growth through the sixteenth century. The relevance of such background material to our study lies in the fact that a good many of the emblem books circulating in seventeenth-century France were in fact sixteenth-century emblem books. These were sometimes reeditions, but not always, as the lifespan of books was generally much longer than it is today. As Russell points out in "Emblems and Devices in Seventeenth-Century French Culture," of the hundred or so emblem books that constituted seventeenth-century France's cultural tissue, fewer than a dozen originated in seventeenth-century France (9).

Two such examples, however, are Jean Baudoin's *Recueil d'emblèmes divers*, published in Paris by Jacques Villery (1638-39), and Marin Le Roy de Gomberville's *La Doctrine des mœurs*[26] of 1646. Both works are marked by detailed copperplate engravings and an exhaustive commentary in the tradition of Coustau's "narrations philosophiques." Each of Baudoin's emblems consists of a full-page engraving on the left-hand page, with the motto/title (e.g. "Que l'honneste Amour, l'Honneur & la Verité sont inseparables," "Que les vrais thresors sont dans les bons Livres"), the number of the "Discours" (e.g. "Discours III," "Discours XXVIII," etc.) and the start of the commentary on the facing page. The commentary describes the emblem, then discusses points raised with ample references to the ancients. Gomberville's work gives the engraving and motto (e.g. "fuir le vice, c'est suivre la vertu," "l'argent corrompt tout," "La Mort nous égale tous") on the left-hand page, with the number of the "Explication" (e.g. "Explication de la cinquième figure" etc.) followed by a short poem and the start of the commentary on the facing page. Gomberville's "Explication" is somewhat shorter than Baudoin's and tends to be limited to a commentary on the engraving and its immediate implications.[27]

It is particularly interesting to note that both works draw inspiration from other emblem books. Gomberville's emblems are based on the *Emblemata horatiana*[28] by the Dutch artist Otto Van Veen. Baudoin's come largely from Alciato. By the beginning of the seventeenth century, therefore, the emblem was already a recognised form attracting anthologisers. As such, it is fair by this time to talk of a well-established tradition.

It is harder to draw conclusions about the popular devices known within seventeenth-century France because, as Vladimir Jurèn has demonstrated,[29] they were mainly to be found outside of printed collections. However, the fact that one of the main printed *recueils* of the sixteenth century—Paradin's *Devises héroïques*—was reedited several times in the seventeenth century does suggest that the devices of the Renaissance were still playing an important rôle in the society of the Grand Siècle. On the other hand, the seventeenth century did see a new flourish of theoretical works debating at length the criteria for a perfect emblem or device, often with the author in question adding a few examples of his own invention. These treatises were new to France, even if they were largely inspired by earlier Italian works on the *impresa*. Their very existence reinforces the idea that by the reign of Louis XIV a literary form that a century earlier had been spontaneous and sporadic was now meeting with attempts at official definition. The institutionalisation of emblematics in this way was to be reflected by the use of emblems and devices within the most important cultural institutions of seventeenth-century France: the schools, the churches and the court. The remainder of this chapter will largely be given to outlining such usage.

The rôle of emblems in education is one of the best indications of the phenomenon's institutionalisation. As the case of René de Bruc, Marquis de Montplaisir, shows, emblems could well have been used for private secular education.[30] More certain is the fact that in England, emblem books were used as part of the Latin Grammar school curriculum, as Ayers Bagley points out.[31] In France it was in the domain of religious, specifically Jesuit, education that their use was most marked.

The *Ratio atque institutio studiorum societatis Iesu*[32] of 1603 (updated from a Rome 1586 version) gives us a detailed account of the teaching curriculum in Jesuit schools. Emblematics figure fairly prominently, above all in the classes of rhetoric and humanities. The principles of the *Ratio studiorum* are largely confirmed by Joseph de Jouvancy's *De Ratione discendi et dociendi*.[33] Although published in France in 1711 (a Frankfurt 1706 edition also exists), it seems likely that this work reflects accurately the teaching practices in Jesuit schools throughout the seventeenth century. The *De Ratione discendi et dociendi* also emphasises the teaching of emblems, devices, and other related forms.

Various other works, such as published or manuscript collections of students' compositions or descriptions of ceremonies within Jesuit schools confirm the importance of emblematics within Jesuit education.[34] Judi Loach, in "Emblematics Within Mainstream Education,"[35] summarises this importance when she points out that,

> A *Cours dicté* for rhetorique classes given at the Jesuit-run town college in Vienne (south of Lyons) in 1649 contains extensive sections on symbolic images, and in particular on emblems. From their tone and context it becomes apparent that emblematics often appeared in the school curriculum, and thus formed part of mainstream education—at least in mid-17th century France.

Beyond the domain of education, emblems played an important rôle in the diffusion of religious doctrine in general throughout seventeenth-century France. Indeed the height of the celebrations for the Jesuits' centenary in 1640 was marked by the publication of an emblem book, the lavish *Imago primi saeculi Societatis Iesu*.[36] Jesuit emblem books came to flourish in seventeenth-century France, the form being particularly suited to the attractive presentation of essential eternal truths; Richard Dimler[37] estimates that the corpus consists of approximately two thousand editions of which the vast majority are from the seventeenth century. Although most of these are not the work of French printers, the international nature of the movement meant that many of the works would have been known in France.

A popular example was Hermann Hugo's *Pia desideria*, published by Heinrich Aertssen in Antwerp in 1624. It was rapidly translated into all the main European languages, starting with French—the first of two translations—in 1629. Each emblem consists of an *imago*, a *motto* taken from the Bible and a *subscriptio* in the form of a meditational poem. The fourth element of each emblem is a long prose commentary containing frequent references to the Holy Scriptures. These inspire the reader to reflect upon the limited nature of our earthly condition, the aspirations of the soul and the true path to God. The exact references are given in the margin, thereby allowing the reader to find the original source and continue his meditation beyond the bounds of the emblem. The work as a whole has a tripartite structure comprised of sections of fifteen emblems: "Gemitus animae poenitentis" ["The Cry of the Penitent Soul"], "Desideria animae sanctae" ["The Desires of the Sacred Soul"] and "Suspiria animae amantis" ["The Sighs of the Loving Soul"]. On a linear level, therefore, the reader can follow the progress of the emblems' evolution as they trace the soul's path from desperation to its pure exaltation in the love of God. On a general level, the dynamics of interaction through which the *Pia desideria* functions involve a physical image (the engraving) and a virtual image—man's vision of the soul and of God—to be combined with a physical text—that of the emblem—and a virtual text (the Scriptures to which the emblem refers).

This process of interaction can be found throughout the lively tradition of Jesuit emblem books. Roger Paultre[38] cites the interesting examples of Ioannes David's *Typus occasionis*[39] and *Duodecim specula*.[40] Both these works boast a thematic unity; the first is almost a récit of the Christian's path through Temptation on to the Good, with Evil being punished at the end; the second presents twelve emblems based, as the title suggests, on the image of the mirror. In both cases the emblems are composed of a title, an engraving whose various features are labelled "A," "B," "C" and so on, and a *subscriptio* glossing these various features. The gloss could be a label to an object/person in the picture, an explanation of the object/person's significance, a moral drawn from the object/person's significance, or a short extract of speech to accompany the object/person.[41]

Such a layout suggests a particularly evolved stage of the text/image interaction that was already apparent in early emblem collections. The picture, although containing several distinct elements, has a unifying central theme, and, above all, a background décor that places the various elements within a single plane of action. Distinctive features, such as elements of the background décor, expression on the characters' faces or "freeze-frame action" (e.g. a personification of Time fleeing), create a static global image, a frozen piece of action that can easily be memorised by the reader.

The use of labelling letters ("A," "B," "C," etc.) points explicitly to a phenomenon essential to emblematic expression: the *subscriptio* interacts with the *imago* so as to provide the linear movement that the global image lacks. The text, referring to specific parts of the picture with the aid of the labelling letters, recounts the events or draws moralising conclusions. For the complete sense of the emblem—as summed up in the *motto*—to be obtained, the two distinct features have to be melded together. This is a notion often lost to the modern reader as modern engravings/photographs do not interact with the text, they illustrate it. A modern illustration represents a single aspect of its text, adding no further nuance of meaning to the work as a whole. A modern illustration could not meaningfully label its parts "A" to "F" in reference to a narrative or moralising text.

It is not by pure chance that such a method of expression should have appealed so distinctly to the Jesuits. Their goal of clear and memorable teaching undoubtedly

Figure 3. "Speculum creaturarum," from Ioannes David, *Duodecim specula* (Antwerp: Plantin, 1610).

favoured the use of global images to be retained in the mind. The nature of the subject taught, namely the mysteries of the divine, favoured a method whereby the message was not stated clearly; the reader was to induce the overall message following the interaction of the emblem's parts. In similar fashion, the Jesuits' message was to be gleaned by the believer who would combine and apply different individual aspects of personal faith. Furthermore, David's choice of the mirror as subject was far from fortuitous: just as the mirror allows us to see by reflection, so the teachings of the church and Scriptures reflected an image of the invisible truth that was God, thereby allowing man to visualise truths normally unavailable to the naked eye. In the same way, the mixing of the emblem's very different elements created an overall message that could not be seen in the individual parts. Understanding the mentality behind Jesuit emblem books is an important step towards understanding the now-lost reading habits of the emblematic age.

Our conclusions concerning Hugo and David could be supplemented by analysis of the works of Jeronimo Nadal, Pedro Bivero and other Jesuits too numerous for this introductory survey to accommodate. The sheer volume of their production, as indicated by Dimler, is evidence enough of their major importance in seventeenth-century France. Furthermore, although the beliefs and teaching style of the Jesuits were particularly suited to emblematic expression, they had by no means monopolised the phenomenon of the religious emblem book. The popularity of Montenay's Protestant *Emblemes, ou devises chrestiennes*, a work reedited three times in the early seventeenth century (Heidelberg 1602, Frankfurt 1619 and La Rochelle 1620), bears witness to this fact. Jean Martin's *Le Paradis terrestre,* published in Paris in 1655, on the other hand, follows, through emblems, the journey of conversion from Protestantism to Catholicism. These works are typical examples of a widespread phenomenon. A considerable amount of critical attention has already been given to the subject, with the overall conclusion being that the religious emblem book was an essential part of seventeenth-century France's cultural composition.[42]

Religion and emblematics did not only interact, however, by way of the printed word and image. The fashion for religious emblem books was matched by certain manifestations of the phenomenon in everyday life. We have already made brief mention of Le Jay's *Le Triomphe de la religion* in reference to education; this work describes the devices and decorations used to underline the oratory on the occasion of a sermon by the Père Quartier. Le Jay points out that the devices "furent faites pour estre placées dans la Salle où se prononça la Harangue, & pour l'orner d'une maniere proportionnée au dessein du Discours" (sig. A-vi). It is not hard to imagine the Père Quartier (and indeed others like him) referring to the room's decoration as an integral part of his sermon, with the result effectively being emblems composed of images interacting with an oral text. Presumably the hanging decorations would have served as memory devices functioning in much the same manner as the global image of the Jesuit emblem books.[43]

Peter Bayley's research[44] supports the hypothesis that the Père Quartier was not the only one to use emblematics in the structuring of his sermons. He gives the examples of Jean Bertaut who chooses emblems "in order to illustrate or clinch an argument" (75-76), Jean Suffren who refers to a pelican emblem to explain why Christ died on a cross (84) and Gaspar de Seguiran who uses Alciato's candle emblem in reference to good works (84). Nor was the Père Quartier's sermon the only occasion for which a church was physically decorated with devices. Claude-François Menestrier, to whom we shall return later, describes this practice with reference to funerals in his *Lettre sur l'usage d'exposer des devises dans les églises pour les décorations funèbres*.[45] To take one specific example, in another work[46] he describes the devices that decorate the nave, choir, altar and even the chairs in the Basilica of Saint Denis for the funeral of Queen Marie-Thérèse. In short, the rôle of emblematics in the religious culture of seventeenth-century France was not limited to the multifarious publications of the time; emblems and devices were present before the very eyes and ears of churchgoers. Judi Loach comes to a similar conclusion in her "Jesuit Emblematics and the Opening of the School Year at the Collège Louis-Le-Grand":

> At the time of their conception and use, were emblems *primarily* seen—as scholars tend to see them when they look back from the twentieth century, their ideas moulded by the materials extant today—as the subject of publication, and therefore as a literary genre? Or were they rather constituent elements of dramatic performances, or other multi-media events? Were emblems thus concrete, perhaps even three-dimensional, objects? And could they even be amalgams or hybrids, actually constituted, at least in part, by performance? Such entities would, obviously, be ephemeral, and therefore merely recorded in subsequent publications, as opposed to owing their existence uniquely to these two-dimensional media. (171-72)

Moving therefore from the divine to the secular, emblematics—in particular devices—were constantly present in seventeenth-century French court life. Charles Perrault in his *Courses de testes et de bagues*[47] describes the Carrousel of 1662 that took place in front of the Tuileries. The king and members of the court paraded in various troupes, each donning an extravagant costume, masquerading as Americans, Persians or Egyptians. The parade would be followed by games and mock battles. Throughout, prominent display was made of the participants' devices. In Perrault's printed account each double page illustrating a troupe or a procession is followed by a page giving the devices of those involved. This is a typical example of the show made of devices at the Carrousels and fêtes that composed an important part of court celebrations. Other notable examples include the 1612 Carrousel on the Place Royale (now Place des Vosges) in honour of the Franco-Spanish marriages, or the "Plaisirs de l'Isle Enchantée" given at Versailles in 1664.[48]

Ceremonious royal entries, a court fashion that had grown in the sixteenth century, continued to be popular in the seventeenth century. The 1600s saw, among others, the entries of Marie de Médicis into Lyons and Avignon (both 1600), those of Louis XIII into Lyons (1622) and Paris (1628) and that of Louis XIV and Marie-

Thérèse into Paris (1660). In the case of Louis XIII's triumphal entry into Paris in 1628 in celebration of victory at the siege of La Rochelle (Mourey, 116-20), the ceremony was based on a series of twelve triumphal arches, each representing one of the king's qualities. Thus the king would pass through a representation of his "Piété," "Amour du peuple," "Prudence," "Magnificence" and so on. In each case the arch was decorated with devices, emblems, iconographic statues and *tableaux allégoriques* representing the virtue in question. Mourey describes the arch representing "Force," positioned beneath the vaults of the Châtelet, as follows:

> Seize peintures s'étalent aux murs, au-dessus des statues, huit de chaque côté, touchant la nature et les symboles du feu; sans oublier d'innombrables devises latines.
> A la voûte se déploie un ciel d'or bruni semé d'étoiles d'or, parmi les splendeurs duquel planent les 4 vertus cardinales, sur un nuage, avec leurs symboles et trois anges soutenant une couronne de France. (120)

Also featuring strongly in the procession were chariots representing scenes such as a Roman circus. The last of these was the "navire de la ville de Paris." The procession was closed, therefore, by a three-dimensional enactment of the town's "fluctuat nec mergitur" ["it floats and it does not sink"] device.

It was normal for triumphal arches to be constructed for a ceremonial entry; these could be adorned with iconographical representations of virtues or directly with the device of the king and with others relevant to the occasion. The display of banners, often bearing devices, would play an important rôle in the procession itself. Indeed not just royal entries, carrousels and fêtes, but court ceremonies of all kinds gave a prominent position to the display of emblematic compositions. Menestrier describes these compositions in particular reference to the funeral of Queen Marie-Thérèse, but the display of devices would also have played an important rôle in marriages and christenings.

Outside of the pomp of the different ceremonies various other channels existed for emblematic court propaganda. Religious emblem books were more numerous than court emblem books, but the latter were nonetheless common. Martinet's *Emblemes royales a Louis le Grand*, published in Paris in 1673, consists of sixty emblems in praise of Louis XIV regarding his deeds and his personality. The labelling of the collection as "emblemes" suggests there is a general moral lesson to be learned from the king's example. An example of negative propaganda is to be found in the *Emblemes Politiques: Presenté a son Eminence*.[49] This work, whose images are described rather than drawn, was essentially a pamphlet attacking Mazarin. The emblems' themes are commonplaces, such as "les choses qui viennent tost, sont de peut [sic] de durée," which in the context of advice to Mazarin take on a scathing new sense.

The seventeenth century also saw a fashion for collections of biographies. These would typically give a portrait of the subject (e.g. Richelieu, Condé) with his name (and sometimes the motto of his device) as title, accompanied by a description of his personality and achievements on the facing page. This format effectively gave the tripartite image/text structure of the emblem. Examples included Marc de Vulson's *Les Portraits des hommes illustres*[50] and the *Abregé de l'histoire des Roys de France avec leurs effigies, depuis Pharamond jusques au Roy Louys XIII à present regnant.*[51]

In the case of *Les Portraits des hommes illustres*, the main engraving of each subject is encased in a frame bearing various vignettes. These vignettes tell of the principle deeds of the person in question by a mixture of illustrations and accompanying captions. The portrait of Richelieu, for example, is surrounded by scenes showing, among others, "prise de La Rochelle 1628," "La prise de Nancy 1633" and "La prise de la Ville de Treves." Most interesting is the fact that such scenes are interspersed with devices. Richelieu's include three *fleurs-de-lys* with the motto "sola mihi redolent" ["theirs is my only scent"], and an eagle with a lightning bolt and the motto "Expertus Fidelem Iupiter" ["Jupiter knows fidelity through experience"]. Four pages of text then tell of the Cardinal's achievements. Although the portraits start in the Middle Ages with such subjects as Abbé Suger and Joan of Arc, about a third of the work is concerned with seventeenth-century subjects. The collection ends with six pages describing and explaining "Les devises heroyques peintes dans la Galerie du palais Cardinal."

Indeed seventeenth-century editions of Paradin's *Devises héroïques*, mentioned briefly above, and publications such as the lists of devices in Perrault's *Courses de testes et de bagues* indicate that the device was an important part of every courtier's cultural identity. Paradin's work had first appeared in 1551, preceding even the various Italian treatises by writers on the device like Paolo Giovio and Girolamo Ruscelli.[52] By the mid seventeenth century twelve editions had appeared, including that of 1622 in which the devices are "Reveuës & augmentées de moitié par messire Francois d'Amboise."[53] In that edition each device consists of the *motto* in Latin or Greek, the *imago*, a French translation of the *motto* and a commentary of generally between one and three pages in length. This gives information on the device's bearer, explains the *motto*'s provenance and, if necessary, the meaning of the picture,[54] as well as on occasions explaining the reasons for the bearer's choice of the device. The devices, whose bearers belong to various periods of history, are mainly those of royalty and nobles of France and elsewhere. Examples include Henri II, Philippe de Bourgogne, the dukes of Montmorency, the Emporer Vespasianus, Pope Clement VII and Eleonor of Spain, sister of Charles V. The collection also contains a few adaptations of Horapollo's *Hieroglyphics* and some devices devoid of any specific bearer. Three examples, the ivy of the Cardinal de Lorraine, the porcupine of Louis XII and the salamander of François Ier, have already been cited.

Having a device would naturally enough imply its prominent display. The example of the royal château of Blois has already been mentioned; one way of identifying the date of its different wings is by the adorning devices, those of Louis XII, François Ier or Henri IV. Similarly the upper terraces of the castle at Saint Germain are decorated with the salamander of François Ier. Within the castle itself an engraving of the salamander dominates the fireplace of the great hall. By the late seventeenth century, Louis XIV's sun device with the motto "nec pluribus impar" ["(it/he shines) equally for all"] was to be found inscribed on monuments throughout the kingdom.[55]

Such display, however, was not limited to royalty. Of specific concern to our study, as we shall see in chapter V, is the case of Nicolas Fouquet's device, that features prominently in the decoration of his castle at Vaux-le-Vicomte. As Louis XIV's *Surintendant des finances*, Fouquet had risen, by dint of adept financial management, to the heights of fortune and power. He had chosen to represent his success by a squirrel accompanied, audaciously in the circumstances, by the motto, "Quo non ascendet?" ["To where shall he not climb?"]. Fouquet's squirrel adorned the gateposts of Vaux-le-Vicomte; it was engraved on the castle's outer walls and painted on the interior's ceilings. So effective was the propaganda that by the 1660s the squirrel had become a synonym in court circles for Surintendant Fouquet.[56] In similar fashion Colbert was an eagle, Tellier was a lizard and Louis XIV was of course the sun.

One further interesting and unique case is that of Bussy Rabutin's castle at Bussy-le-Grand in Bourgogne (Côte-d'Or). Here the display in question is not that of his own device, but rather that of devices composed for his various mistresses. In addition, contrary to common court practice, the devices in question are far from flattering. One specific example is that of the device portraying Mme. de Montglas with the figure of Fortune accompanied by the motto "Leves Ambo, Ambo Ingratae": both fortune and Bussy's mistress are fickle and ungrateful![57]

Emblems and devices appeared therefore in court circles in the context of ceremonies, publications or architectural decoration. Naturally, given such prominent display, they also came to be used as a vehicle for salon discussion. Evidence of this is to be found in various manuscript pieces, in particular certain ones belonging to the Bibliothèque de l'Arsenal's *Recueil Conrart*.[58] Manuscript 5417, for example, contains various letters, often insulting in tone, to and from Richelieu. Piece 15 of that collection then gives a series of anonymous

> Devises par lesquelles un chacun peut connoître la vanité de Jean Armand de Plessis Cardinal de Richelieu & juger quelle sera sa fin.

These are adapted versions of the devices to be found in the Cardinal's *Cabinet* at Bois-le-Vicomte, a manuscript version of which forms part of the *Recueil Conrart* manuscript 3307. In manuscript 5417, the original version is given in the left hand column, and on the right are to be found "contre devises representant au vrai les moeurs et la conduite du Cardinal de Richelieu." On occasions, for example number 12, it is the motto that is adapted:

> (on the left:) Trois colomnes avec leurs bases & chapiteaux sur la première desquelles, il y a un rond, sur la seconde un quarré, et sur la 3e un Triangle, et un chapeau de Cardinal audessus
> Naturae virtutis et artis[59]

(on the right:) Sur la même
>Naturae parvum, virtutis nihil, artis nimium[60]

Alternatively, as in number 6, it can be the picture that would change:

(on the left:) Deux serpans enlassez elevans leurs têtes, et sifflans contre une aigle qui est dans les nuës
>Non deseret alta[61]

(on the right:) Un gibet, auquel est figuré un Card^l pendu
>Non deseret alta.

This is just one of many manuscript examples. Others include devices composed by individuals such as the "Devises de M. Clément,"[62] poems based on devices such as "A Mlle de Richelieu sur sa devise d'une Abeille—sonnet"[63] or, as we shall see in chapter V, devices composed for specific persons or events such as the "Devises tirées de l'Ecriture en faveur de Fouquet."[64] Given the abundance of such pieces, it seems highly likely that the salonists of seventeenth-century France must sometimes have centered their discussion on the informal composition of such devices. Indeed Pierre Le Moyne says as much in his *De l'Art des devises*[65] when he suggests that devices should not be hard to represent as "il se faut contenter de les dire à l'oreille, ou de les faire voir sur des Tablettes dans une Ruelle" (117).

The notion that devices had a rôle to play in the operations of the salons implies a certain level of their institutionalisation. This institutionalisation was completely formalised in 1663 with the foundation of the *Académie des devises et inscriptions*. Set up at the instigation of Colbert, this body was better known as the *Petite académie* because it was composed of a select group of four members of the Académie Française who met on a weekly basis. One of its main achievements was the composition of a series of *Devises pour les tapisseries du Roy*. The tapestries in question, praising the king for securing peace, were executed in the 1660s by the Gobelins manufactory. Charles Perrault had created the majority of the sixteen "Devises des Elements" and the sixteen "Devises des Quatre Saisons" which decorated the tapestries' borders. These appeared in various forms, including luxury manuscripts (see fig. 4 for an example), with painted miniatures by Jacques Bailly, that in themselves attested to the heights of elegance, craftsmanship and expenditure to which the art of the device had risen.[66]

Another proof of the institutionalisation of emblematics by the end of the seventeenth century—or indeed perhaps a direct result of such institutionalisation—was the lively current of literary debate that had arisen on the subject. Furthermore, the leading protagonists of the debate were very much the figureheads of the officialdom. In his *Discours sur l'art des devises*, the main subject of our chapter VI, Charles Perrault describes how a "sçavant homme" addressed the Académie Française at length purely to criticise a device of Perrault's composition. The implication is that a debate on such a topic was very much in keeping with the preoccupations of the literary elite of the time.

Figure 4. "Praestant interna coronae," from *Devises our les tapisseries du roy*, ms. fr. 7819, Bibliothèque nationale de France.

Perrault's justification of his device then leads to a discussion of the criteria necessary for the composition of devices in general: a device should be a comparison of two things of which one is represented and one understood, with a motto applicable to both; the subject of the *imago* should not be named in the motto; simple images such as a star or a tree are better than hybrid compositions; natural images are better than artificial ones; bodiless arms or legs, even coming out of a cloud, are disagreeable; of human figures only those of mythology are acceptable, etc. Such points may seem trivial to modern eyes, but Perrault is a good deal less pedantic than many of his contemporaries. Of these particularly worthy of note are M. Clément, *Conseiller en la Cour d'Aides*, Henri Estienne, Pierre Le Moyne, whose *Art des devises* has been cited above, and the Père Bouhours, mentioned by Jouvancy in his *De Ratione discendi et dociendi*.[67]

If any single figure exemplifies the lively debate on emblem theory in seventeenth-century France, it is the Père Claude-François Menestrier. Although not invited by Colbert to take part in the founding of the *Petite académie* (much to his understandable displeasure), Menestrier was nonetheless the undisputed expert on the composition of the device. In his *Devise du roy, justifiée*,[68] in which the defence of a device gives the opening pretext for a general treatise, Menestrier discusses the theory and social implications of the device in seventeenth-century France.[69]

Menestrier's theory did not limit itself to the device, as indeed his *L'Art des emblemes* of 1662 had shown.[70] In this he gives a history of the emblem form starting from the Greek anthology, examples of possibly emblematic structures within literature, including the "Carte de Tendre" and the fables of Aesop and La Fontaine, and a classification of emblems according to their subject matter. Examples include mythology or "emblèmes fabuleux," biography or "emblèmes héroiques," and abstract notions or "emblèmes idéels." Perhaps of greatest interest is the definition he (and indeed other theorists like him) gives of the composition of the emblem and device in dualistic terms indicative of the Cartesian mentality of the time: the "signification" or "sens moral" is the "âme" of the device, whereas the "forme," the component parts, represents the "corps."

The literary theory of Menestrier's treatises on emblematics is accompanied by an underlying historical and political function, the praise of Louis XIV. The idealisation of peace in the "emblèmes idéels" alerts the reader to the *res gesta* of the king, and the great figures of antiquity and mythology ("emblèmes héroiques," "emblèmes fabuleux") are understood as precedents to Louis himself. This aspect of Menestrier's work came to be exemplified in his *Histoire du roy Louis le Grand par les médailles, emblèmes, devises, jettons, inscriptions, armoiries & autres monumens publiques, recueillis et expliquéz* of 1689.[71] Indeed, beyond his publications, Menestrier had been responsible for the composition of emblems and devices for religious and court ceremonies such as those described throughout this chapter.[72]

The example of the Père Claude-François Menestrier is a particularly suitable note upon which to conclude a survey of the rôle of emblematics in seventeenth-century France. As the leading authority on the subject, his very standing both in religious (Jesuit) and court (Académie Française) circles attests to the importance given to the emblem and the device. This importance is underlined by the fact that his various publications on the subject of emblematics totalled over one hundred editions. Nonetheless his art was not limited to the libraries and the salons of the time; it was displayed before the eyes of all: in reference to the emblems cited in his *L'Art des emblèmes*, Menestrier states that they are to be found,

> dans les pompes funèbres, dans les descriptions des entrées des Princes, dans les revers des médailles modernes, dans les salles et les galleries dont ils font les ornements, & en divers autres endroits (121).[73]

Although limited to an outline survey and an indication of further sources, this chapter should nonetheless have given an idea of the importance of emblematics as a major cultural phenomenon within the everyday lives of the educated population of seventeenth-century France. As such it is fair to suppose that emblematics would have influenced the cultural elite in much the same way that artistic and literary production of today might be influenced by cinema, radio or television. This influence came in the form of direct cultural references as well as through the existence of an emblematic mentality.

A mentality, by its very nature, is hard to define. Nonetheless, it is fair to assume that the existence of emblematics as a dominant cultural force is proof enough of the existence of a general way of thinking that enabled emblems to become a fashion. It is surely a question of an approach to texts, to the plastic arts and to the interaction of the two that was perhaps far different three hundred years ago from what it is today.

The willingness with which the minds of the seventeenth century put image and text together is exemplified in the show-piece court-castles of Vaux-le-Vicomte and Versailles. These extravagant displays of power and wealth required not only the architecture of Louis Le Vau, but also the paintings of Charles Le Brun, the gardens of André Le Nôtre and the texts of André Félibien, Molière and Jean de La Fontaine. For Louis XIV the expression of his status required all of the arts in an amalgam that is no longer second nature to us; nineteenth-century positivism and definitions have ensured the separation of the various disciplines.[74]

The emblematic mentality involves, therefore, an interaction of genres, but also an interaction of approach to genres. It is no coincidence that one of the age's main masterpieces, Poussin's *Les Bergers d'Arcadie*,[75] can only be fully appreciated when one seizes the interaction of image—the shepherds around the tomb—and text—"Et in Arcadia ego" ["I (death) am also in Arcadia"].[76] Poussin's image creates a global picture, a scene that stays in the mind. Needless to say, an image has no point of departure or ending. As such it corresponds to the eternal paradise that is Arcadia. A text, however, like mortality itself, is linear, it starts with the first line or word and ends with the last. To grasp the painting's full sense and poignancy we must be open to the concepts of global images, linear texts, and, moreover, the interaction of the two: even in ever-lasting paradise, finite death is present. Such a method of interpretation is largely alien to an age now dominated by print,[77] where all texts have a beginning and an end and illustrations just refer to specific points in the text. To understand the differences is to start to understand the nature of the emblematic mentality.

This work is concerned with the influence of the emblematic mentality within the domain of literature. Our aim is to explore the nature of such influence and then to apply our findings to better our understanding of the texts of the Grand Siècle. Such work has already been carried out by Peter Daly in respect of German and English literature.[78] Whereas he applies his findings to the works of Greiffenberg and Grimmelshausen, we shall concentrate upon Descartes, Tristan L'Hermite, La Fontaine and Perrault.

NOTES

[1] (Paris: Janot). The 1544 edition of this work is also available in facsimile reprint edited by Alison Adams (Geneva: Droz, 1997).

[2] For a book-length introduction to the early emblem books, see Alison Saunders, *The Sixteenth-Century French Emblem Book: A Decorative and Useful Genre* (Geneva: Droz, 1988). Chapters I (pages 1-28) and V (pages 141-94) are specifically concerned with questions of theory and form. For a discussion of the way in which the various parts of the emblem interact, see the following: Irene Bergal, "Discursive Strategies in Early French Emblem Books," *Emblematica* 2.2 (1987), 273-91; David Graham, "'Voiez icy en ceste histoire...': Cross-Reference, Self-Reference and Frame-Breaking in some French Emblems," *Emblematica* 7.1 (1993), 1-24; Simone Perrier, "La Circulation du sens dans les *Emblemes chrestiens* de G. de Montenay (1571)," *Nouvelle Revue du XVIe Siècle* 9 (1991), 73-89; Jerome Schwartz, "Emblematic Theory and Practice: The Case of the Sixteenth-Century French Emblem Book," *Emblematica* 2.2 (1987), 293-315.

[3] (Lyons: J. de Tournes and G. Gazeau). A facsimile edition edited by Alison Saunders (Aldershot: Scolar Press, 1989) is also available.

[4] It is interesting to note that the negative associations of the ivy theme (as shown for example in Corrozet's emblem) caused the Cardinal de Lorraine's device to backfire; opponents accused him of stifling the king as the ungrateful ivy stifles its treè. This point will be discussed further in chapter III.

[5] I.e. "From far and from near." The porcupine, supposedly by propelling its quills, or alternatively by raising them, was able to defend itself from near or from afar.

[6] I.e. "I nourish and I extinguish." The device, broadly speaking, plays upon the fact that the salamander's treatment of the fire was thus akin to François Ier's respective treatment of friends or foes. Nonetheless the wording is somewhat ambiguous, as Anne-Marie Lecoq points out in the first chapter (pages 35-53) of her *François Ier imaginaire: Symbolique et politique à l'aube de la Renaissance française* (Paris: Macula, 1987). This should be consulted for in-depth analysis of François Ier's device.

[7] "To where shall he not climb ?" The comparison is with Fouquet's rapid rise to success as Louis XIV's *Surintendant des finances*. This example will be discussed further in chapter V. A full discussion of the various manifestations of the emblem and of the device and of the distinctions between the two forms is given by Daniel Russell in *The Emblem and Device in*

France. This work represents a general but extremely thorough introduction to French emblematics, giving a view of the history and the theory of these literary forms. Chapters 1 and 2 deal with the device and the emblem respectively, including "The Idea of the Emblem in the Seventeenth Century" (89-112). Chapter 3 discusses the differences between the two forms and the final chapter deals with word/text interaction in general under the title "The Emblematic Process."

An overview of the concept and nature of the emblem and device in seventeenth-century France, followed by an analysis and bibliography of research up until 1994 is provided by Russell in "Emblems and Devices in Seventeenth-Century French Culture," *EMF: Studies in Early Modern France: Volume 1: Word and Image*, ed. David Lee Rubin (Charlottesville VA: Rookwood, 1994), 9-30.

For an analysis of emblematics in the context of Early-Modern symbolic representation and the mentality thereby implied, see Anne-Elisabeth Spica, *Symbolique humaniste et emblématique: L'Evolution et les genres (1580-1700)* (Paris: Champion, 1996).

Finally, a general study of French seventeenth-century emblematics is currently being prepared by Alison Saunders.

[8] "Aux Origines de l'emblème: La Crise de l'héraldique européenne aux XVe et XVIe siècles," *Emblèmes et devises au temps de la Renaissance*, ed. M.-T. Jones-Davies (Paris: Touxot, 1981), 129-36.

[9] Full details of studies to be consulted for information on these and other protoemblematic pieces are given in Laurence Grove and Daniel Russell's *The French Emblem: Bibliography of Secondary Sources* (Geneva: Droz, 2000). This work gives bibliographic details and a short précis of articles and books on the subject of French emblematics. As well as protoemblematics, the Bibliography also covers works on French emblematics in general and fundamental research tools such as catalogues and reference books. The final two sections deal with French emblem writers by alphabetical order of author's name and French emblematics as applied to the study of literature, art and history.

[10] This edition has been reproduced on the Glasgow Emblem Group's webpage at www.gla.ac.uk/Library/Emblems/index.html. The site also provides links to other emblem webpages.

[11] (Paris: D. Janot). This work is available in facsimile reprints edited by Greta Dexta (Gainesville: Scholars' Facsimiles & Reprints, 1964) and Alison Saunders (Aldershot: Scolar Press, 1993). Saunders's edition includes La Perrière's *Morosophie*.

[12] Introduction, *Le Théâtre des bons engins*, by Guillaume de La Perrière (Gainesville: Scholars' Facsimiles & Reprints, 1964), i-xx.

[13] (Lyons: Macé Bonhomme).

[14] Greta Dexter, "Guillaume de La Perrière," *Bibliothèque d'Humanisme et Renaissance* 17 (1955), 56-73.

[15] For an analysis of the *Hecatomgraphie*, see Alison Adams's introduction to her edition of the work.

[16] Barthélemy Aneau, *Décades de la description, forme et vertu naturelle des animaulx, tant raisonnables que brutz* (Lyons: B. Arnoullet, 1549). Guillaume Guéroult, *Second livre de la description des animaux, contenant le blason des oyseaux* (Lyons: B. Arnoullet, 1550).

[17] (Lyons: Macé Bonhomme).

[18] (Lyons: Macé Bonhomme).

[19] "Affin que les images ensevelies, & muetes, je ramenasse en lumiere & vie" (8).

[20] (Lyons: Macé Bonhomme). A facsimile reprint edited by Stephen Orgel (New York: Garland, 1979) is also available.

[21] This French version, translated by Lanteaume de Romieu, follows the *Pegma cum narrationibus philosophicis* that Macé Bonhomme had also published in 1555.
[22] (Lyons: Jean Marcorelle). A facsimile reprint edited by C. N. Smith (Menston: Scolar, 1973) is also available.
[23] The first Catholic emblem book, Benedito Arias Montano's *Humanae salutis monumenta* (Antwerp: Plantin), also appeared in 1571.
[24] *Les Simulachres & historiees faces de la Mort, autant elegamment pourtraictes, que artificiellement imaginees* (Lyons: Melchior and Gaspard Trechsel, 1538).
[25] (Paris: Veuve Abel L'Angelier, 1615).
This chapter does not aim to go beyond the limits of an introductory survey. For a lengthier introduction to the works mentioned and discussed in this section the following should be consulted: Jean-Marc Chatelain's *Livres d'emblèmes et de devises: Une Anthologie (1531-1735)* (Paris: Klincksieck, 1993); Alison Adams, Stephen Rawles and Alison Saunders's *A Bibliography of French Emblem Books to 1700* (Geneva: Droz, 1999); John Landwehr's *French, Italian, Spanish and Portuguese Books of Devices and Emblems 1534-1827: A Bibliography* (Utrecht: Haentjens Dekker & Gumbert, 1976); John Landwehr's *Emblem books in the Low Countries 1554-1949: A Bibliography* (Utrecht: Haentjens Dekker & Gumbert, 1970): John Landwehr's *German Emblem Books 1531-1888: A Bibliography* (Utrecht: Haentjens Dekker & Gumbert, 1972); Arthur Henkel and Albrecht Schöne's *Emblemata: Handbuch zur Sinnbildkunst des XVI und XVII Jahrhunderts*, 2 vols., (Stuttgart: J.B. Metzlersche, 1967).
Chatelain's anthology gives three chapters of introduction to the history and theory of emblematics before the presentation of ninety different works from the various emblematic cultures. Each entry gives publication details, an illustration and a brief commentary on the work in question. Adams, Rawles and Saunders provide full bibliogaphic details—these include precise dating details, languages used, description of layout, further remarks and lists of copies consulted—for the known corpus of French emblem books, namely those in French and those published in France. Arrangement is by author's name, volume I covering A-K and volume II (due to appear in 2002) L-Z. Landwehr's listings are not as complete, but his various publications, also arranged by author's name, allow the curious reader to locate bibliographic details of non-French works. For research by theme, *Emblemata* is indispensable. Under various categories (e.g. "Die Vier Elemente, "Planzenwelt," "Menschewelt") and subsections (e.g. "Bäume," "Rankende Gewächs," then "Weinstock," "Efeu," "Mistel," etc.) Henkel and Schöne list individual emblems from the major works of the tradition. Illustrations and German translations of the texts are provided.
[26] (Paris: Sevestre).
[27] For an analysis of plates 33 and 34 of the *Doctrine*, see Claire Pace's "'La Vie des champs est la vie des héros': Images of Landscape and Rural Life and Gomberville's *La Doctrine des moeurs*," *Emblems and Art History*, eds. Alison Adams and Laurence Grove (Glasgow: Glasgow Emblem Studies, 1996), 41-68. For a description and analysis of a manuscript version of the work, see Daniel Russell's "Thoughts on a Newly-Discovered Manuscript Version of Gomberville's *Doctrine des moeurs* (1646)," *Emblems and the Manuscript Tradition*, ed. Laurence Grove (Glasgow: Glasgow Emblem Studies, 1997), 1-18.
[28] (Antwerp: Verdussen, 1607).
[29] "Le Jeton français et la littérature emblématique," *XVIIe Siècle* 158 (1988), 21-40.
[30] See Daniel Russell, "M. de Montplaisir and his Emblems," *Neophilologus* 67 (1983), 503-16. Here Russell points to the possibility of René de Bruc using emblems for the education of his son.
[31] "Some Pedagogical Uses of the Emblem in Sixteenth- and Seventeenth- Century England,"

Emblematica 7.1 (1993), 39-60.

[32] (Tours: Claude Michael).

[33] *Magistris scholarum inferiorum societatis Jesu de ratione discendi et dociendi Congregationis Generalis XIV* (Paris: C. Jombert et J. Mongé, 1711).

[34] One such published example of a collection of students' work, the *In anniversarium Henrici Magni obitus diem lacrymæ collegii flexiensis regii societatis Iesu* [The Tears of the Jesuit College of La Flèche for the Anniversary of the Death of Henry the Great] (La Flèche: Rexe, 1611) will be discussed at some length in the next chapter. Another published collection of students' emblems is the *Typus mundi*, produced by the Jesuit college at Antwerp in 1627. Russell ("Emblems and Devices" 18) mentions two manuscript collections, mss. Lat. 10170 and 10171 at the Bibliothèque nationale. Karel Porteman's *Emblematic Exhibitions (Affixiones) at the Brussels Jesuit College (1630-1685): A Study of the Commemorative Manuscripts (Royal Library, Brussels)* (Brussels: Brepols, 1996) provides a catalogue of the Royal Library's wealthy collection of similar anthologies. Russell also mentions Gabriel-François Le Jay's *Le Triomphe de la religion sous Louis le Grand* (Paris: G. Martin, 1687) as a description of a Jesuit school ceremony involving emblematics developed around a sermon by the Père Quartier. Quartier's sermon and, more generally, emblematics as taught in Paris, are discussed by Judi Loach in "Jesuit Emblematics and the Opening of the School Year at the Collège Louis-Le-Grand," *Emblematica* 9.1 (1995), 133-76.

[35] *Abstracts* (Glasgow: Glasgow International Emblem Conference, 1990), 75.

[36] (Antwerp: Balthasar Moretus, 1640). For further information on its one hundred emblems telling of the society's history, beliefs and honours, see Mario Praz's *Studies in Seventeenth-Century Imagery*, 185-89. This work presents a study of emblems by subject matter based largely on the themes of profane and sacred love, which also gives a general history of the emblems and devices of all cultures. Praz provides a particularly thorough introduction to the theory and practice of Jesuit emblematics. The appendix on "Emblems and Devices in Literature" deals largely with English examples such as Sir William Alexander, Nashe and Shakespeare. Praz's text is followed by a bibliography of emblem books arranged alphabetically by author.

[37] "A Short Title Listing of Jesuit Emblem Books," *Emblematica* 2 (1987), 138-87.

[38] Pages 120-37 of *Les Images du livre: Emblèmes et devises* (Paris: Hermann, 1991).

[39] *Typus occasionis in quo receptae commoda neglectae vero incommoda, personato schemate propantur* (Antwerp: Plantin, 1605).

[40] *Duodecim specula Deum aliquando videre desideranti concinnata* (Antwerp: Plantin, 1610).

[41] This process is illustrated in figure 3, the "Speculum creaturarum" ["The Mirror of Creations"], emblem 8 of the *Duodecim specula*. This particular emblem will be discussed in chapter III.

[42] On Jesuit emblematic manifestations in general, see Chatelain, Dimler and Praz (170-203). For a fuller survey and bibliography of the various seventeenth-century religious emblem books, see Praz (134-68).

[43] For further discussion of Le Jay's sermon and the *Triomphe de la religion*, see Judi Loach, "Jesuit Emblematics and the Opening of the School Year at the Collège Louis-Le-Grand." On pages 158-67 Loach gives precise details of the way in which the sermon referred to the decoration of the chapel. See also chapter III section B below.

[44] *French Pulpit Oratory 1598-1650: A Study of Themes and Styles* (Cambridge: Cambridge UP, 1980).

[45] (Paris: R. Pepie, 1687).

[46] *Description de la decoration funebre de Saint Denis pour les obseques de la Reine* (Paris:

Robert de la Caille, 1683).

[47] *Courses de testes et de bagues faittes par le roy et par les princes et seigneurs de sa cour, en l'année 1662* (Paris: Imprimerie Royale, 1669).

[48] For a comprehensive and well-illustrated account of court fêtes from the Middle Ages onwards, see Gabriel Mourey, *Le Livre des fêtes françaises* (Paris: Librairie de France, 1930). See also Jacques Vanuxem, "Le Carrousel de 1612 sur la Place Royale et ses devises," *Les Fêtes de la Renaissance*, vol. 1 (Paris: CNRS, 1956), 191-203.

[49] (Paris: n.p., 1649).

[50] *Les Portraits des hommes illustres françois qui sont peints dans la galerie du palais Cardinal de Richelieu avec leurs principales actions, armes, devises, & eloges latins, desseignez & gravez par les sieurs Heince et Bignons, peintres et graveurs ordinaires du Roy* (Paris: Pepingué, De Sercy and De Luynes, 1655). A 1650 (Paris: Sara) edition also exists.

[51] (Rouen: David Ferrand, 1636).

[52] For a brief description of these as well as an introduction to the art of the *imprese*, see Chatelain, Praz (55-82) and Robert Klein's "La Théorie de l'expression figurée dans les traités italiens sur les imprese 1555-1612," *Bibliothèque d'Humanisme et Renaissance* 19 (1957), 320-42.

[53] *Devises héroïques: Reveuës & augmentées de moitié par messire Francois d'Amboise* (Paris: Rolet Boutonne, 1622).

[54] E.g. for Marguerite de Navarre's device, a heliotrope, following Ovid, is a flower that always tends towards the sun (46).

[55] Although in these cases the devices are indicative of the date of construction, this method is not always reliable: as a way of marking lineage, devices often continued to be displayed on buildings and their extensions after the original owner's death.

[56] See, for example, the sonnet "Sur la devise de M. Fouquet" (*Recueil Conrart*, Arsenal ms. 5420, piece 57), or La Fontaine's "Le Renard et l'ecureuil." Both these pieces are discussed in chapter V.

[57] This and the other devices that decorated Bussy's castle are discussed in greater detail by Christine Lorgues-Lapouge in "Banished to Bussy," *FMR* 34 (1988), 89-106.

[58] For a brief explanation of the nature and provenance of the *Recueil Conrart*, see chapter V.

[59] "Of Nature, Virtue and Art."

[60] "Of Little Nature, no Virtue and too much Art."

[61] "The Heavens are Untouched."

[62] *Recueil Conrart* manuscript 5418, piece 49. For Daniel Russell's edition of this piece, see "Two Seventeenth-Century Treatises on the Art of the Device," *Emblematica* 1 (1986), 79-106.

[63] *Recueil Conrart* manuscript 5132 piece 25.

[64] *Recueil Conrart* manuscript 4171.

[65] (Paris: Sebastien Mabre Cramoisy, 1666).

[66] The *Petite académie* is discussed at greater length in chapter VI. I will return to the *Devises pour les tapisseries du roy* in both chapters V and VI, where full bibliographic references are to be found.

[67] A clear introduction to their works and ideas, as well as to those of other theorists like them, is given by Daniel Russell in his *Emblem and Device in France*.

[68] (Paris: Michalet, 1679).

[69] For further discussion of this and other seventeenth-century works of theory in the context of Perrault's *Discours sur l'art des devises*, see chapter VI.

[70] (Lyons: B. Coral). Menestrier was also to publish another work bearing virtually the same

title, namely, *L'Art des emblèmes, où s'enseigne la morale par les figures de la fable, de l'histoire et de la nature* (Paris: La Caille, 1684). Both publications have been reproduced in facsimile form (one volume each: The Philosophy of Images volumes 15 and 18), edited by Stephen Orgel (New York: Garland, 1979).

[71] (Paris: Nolin).

[72] Fuller details on these compositions and on Menestrier's emblem theory in general are given by Russell (*Emblem and Device*, 96-108), by David Graham in "Pour une rhétorique de l'emblème: *l'Art des emblèmes* du Père Claude-François Menestrier," *PFSCL* 14.26 (1987), 13-36, and by Judi Loach in "Menestrier's Emblem Theory," *Emblematica* 2 (1987), 317-36.

[73] Menestrier then suggests other emblematic manifestations to be described later: "les Desseins emblematiques des Peintures des Eglises, Sales, Cabinets, Galleries, Palais, Maisons de Campagne, & [...] les Pompes scavantes & ingenieuses, ou la maniere de dresser les Appareils funebres, les receptions des Princes, les Carrousels, les Ballets, les Scenes des representations, & les Festes des canonizations des Saints & autres choses semblables" (122).

[74] On the interaction of the various arts (painting, architecture, literature) with respect to La Fontaine's *Songe de Vaux*, see Robert N. Nicholich's "The Triumph of Language: The Sister Arts and Creative Activity in La Fontaine's *Songe de Vaux*."

[75] (Louvre, Paris). The painting dates from c. 1638-40.

[76] For a discussion of the various possible interpretations of the painting, see Erwin Panofsky's "*Et in Arcadia Ego*: Poussin and the Elegiac Tradition," chapter 7 (pages 340-67) of *Meaning in the Visual Arts* (Harmondsworth: Penguin, 1970; originally published by Doubleday of New York, 1955).

[77] At least until recently; perhaps the daily influence of television and cinema will bring a new emblematic age. With the coming of hypertext or, as Theodor Holm Nelson puts it, "the publishing of tomorrow, which will not be on paper," it seems likely that any remaining print domination will take an increasingly visual—i.e. computerised—form. Nelson's *Literary Machines 93.1* (Sausalito CA: Mindful Press, 1993) should be consulted for further exploration of this notion. The above quotation is taken from the unnumbered Preface.

[78] Peter M. Daly, *Literature in the Light of the Emblem: Structural Parallels Between the Emblem and Literature in the Sixteenth and Seventeenth Centuries*. The opening chapter gives a general introduction and history of the emblem and related forms before the concept of the "word-emblem" is explored in chapter 2. This Daly defines as "a verbal image that has qualities associated with emblems" (55). The bulk of the study demonstrates how a knowledge of this concept and of emblematics in general can enlighten our reading of poetry (chapter 3), drama (chapter 4) and narrative prose (chapter 5). As well as Greiffenberg and Grimmelshausen, the work also discusses Crashaw, Shakespeare and Jonson.

III
Descartes:
Traces Of An Emblematic Upbringing[1]

René Descartes (1596-1650), philosopher, scientist and man of letters, expounded a method of thinking whose influence is still important today. It involves the rationalisation and logical ordering of known givens so as to facilitate the discovery of new knowledge. Using such a method Descartes progressed from the proof of our own existence (the famous "je pense donc je suis") to the proof of that of God and of the physical world. He concludes by encouraging mankind to apply his method to master the world around him. These ideas are set forth principally in two works, the *Meditationes de prima philosophia* and the *Discours de la méthode pour bien conduire sa raison et chercher la vérité dans les sciences*.

The *Discours de la méthode* was published in Leyden in 1636 together with *La Dioptrique*, *Les Météores* and *La Géométrie*. The *Meditationes de prima philosophia* appeared in Paris five years later (1641), although it had been written and circulated in manuscript form previously. Such circulation had resulted in a series of objections from prominent theologians and savants of the time. These were published, together with Descartes's replies, in the same volume as the *Meditationes*. In the Amsterdam edition of 1642 a seventh series of objections and replies, together with an *Epitre* from the Père Jacques Dinet, were added. The French translation (*Meditations métaphysiques*), by the Duc de Luynes but with Descartes's approval, was published in Paris in 1647.

Between 1627 and 1628 Descartes composed the *Regulæ ad directionem ingenii*. This unfinished piece is an early attempt to present the Cartesian method, here through the medium of a series of short rules. One of Descartes's final works, the *Passions de l'âme* of 1649, comprised of a series of paragraphs on the workings of the various passions, attempts to use the Cartesian method to explain the rational functioning of human emotions.

Descartes also made important advances in the sciences. Much of his correspondence, for example with Pierre de Fermat, Gérard Desargues and Florimond Debeaune, dealt with mathematical problems of various kinds. In his *Géométrie*, published with the *Discours*, Descartes took the first step in the development of coordinate geometry. Four years earlier he had already solved the geometrical problem of Pappus as proposed by Golius.[2] His *Dioptrique*, also published with the *Discours*, gave us the formula for refraction thereby opening the way for making spectacles.

Descartes's wide range of interests and achievements also included research on meteors, snowflake crystals and the human foetus, as well as the composition of a ballet (*La Naissance de la Paix*, 1649) for the Queen of Sweden![3]

Studies of Descartes have generally, indeed almost exclusively, been the domain of scholars of philosophy, mathematics or science. One unusual exception to this rule is William McStewart's "Descartes and Poetry,"[4] but even here no real analysis is given. McStewart contents himself (presumably for reasons of limited space?) with pointing out Descartes's more literary activities. Few major studies have addressed Descartes's use of language outside of clarifications of philosophical meaning. John D. Lyons notes as much in the introduction to "The Cartesian Reader and the Methodic Subject"[5] :

> the tendency to read the works of Descartes as if they were a content without a form, a purely transparent and innocent language without a voice is extremely tenacious. Works as recent as those of Roger Lefèvre and Peter Schouls[6] treat language in Descartes as if it were of importance only in cases of individual words—the outward form of a discrete concept—and not as the very body of the Cartesian text. (37)

Lyons's work goes on to discuss the question of Descartes's authorial 'I,' the persona which allows the reader to participate in the methodic discovery of truth. His conclusion might well evoke a comparison with the learning methods of Jesuit emblem books, such as Ioannes David's "Speculum creaturarum," cited above. In both cases the authors induce the reader to active learning through participation rather than passive acceptance of givens:[7]

> In its curious ability to contain author and reader, speaker and listener, in a single voice, the methodic subject becomes the foundation of the subsequent growth of the novel of formation, of the practice of spiritual direction in the seventeenth century. (47)

In "*Camera Obscura*: Image and Imagination in Descartes's *Méditations*" Lyons considers another subject familiar to the student of the emblem:

> For the late Renaissance and early modern period, a major tension exists between what can be seen and what can be said. [. . .] I would like to explore briefly some of the problems that Descartes encountered when he adopted, as criteria for truthfulness, terms belonging chiefly to the visual arts. Although Descartes did find ways to move from seeing to saying—or, in other words, from visual to verbal modes of truth—he had to travel a path marked with images of monsters and ghosts. (179)

Lyons discusses Descartes's testing of the boundaries between that which can be pictured and that which cannot. An important question, one to which Descartes often returns, is that of the status of the image as regards 'reality.' In the *Principia* Descartes dedicates a chapter to "Du Monde visible." His statement in the third *Méditation* that "Les idées sont en moi comme des tableaux, ou des images" (416) is well-known. As Lyons points out, "Descartes took for philosophical reflection terms more often associated with the description of images" (180). Such description of images will form the starting point for section III B of this study.

One of the most potentially promising titles regarding the question of Descartes's use of language is Noam Chomsky's *Cartesian Linguistics*.[8] However Chomsky in fact makes no attempt to discuss Descartes's style. Indeed he states that "Descartes himself devoted little attention to language" (2). It would be unfair to suggest, however, that Descartes did not know the value of words. Furthermore, if such were the case, it would be greatly out of keeping with the tone and content of his formative education. Studies on Descartes's manner of expression are, therefore, relatively limited. Although, as stated, Lyons tackles the important question of visual imagery, no reference is made to writings on the subject of the time, nor to Descartes's literary and cultural background. Given that until fairly recently strict academic boundaries have prevailed—philosophers do not study use of language, art historians do not consider metaphysics, and so on—it is perhaps not surprising that the specific question of the influence of emblematics upon Descartes is completely unexplored territory.

The main aim of this chapter is to establish a case for linking emblematics and Descartes. A substantial first section, therefore, will outline the rôle of emblematics in Descartes's education and point to direct emblematic references in Descartes's texts. Such preliminary research justifies a general analysis of Descartes's use of language in the light of the emblem tradition.

This general analysis will comprise the second section of the chapter. In many ways Descartes's method of expression has much in common with that of the emblematics of his Jesuit educators. Descartes, however, used the images that formed part of his cultural baggage in order to present a very different message. Recognition of Descartes's debt helps us appreciate the true nature and extent of his innovation. To this end we shall present a broad analysis of examples largely taken, for the sake of convenience, from the *Discours de la méthode*.

Our final section will give a precise example of how a knowledge of emblematics can add to our understanding of Descartes's text. The example to which we refer, Descartes's ivy comparison in book 6 of the *Discours*, is by no means unique in its kind. It is primarily a good indication of the extent to which the analysis of Descartes's writing in the light of emblematics can improve our understanding of his work in context.

III A

The Influence of a Jesuit Education[9]

Descartes was born and baptised at La Haye in Touraine in 1596. His father, Joachim, son of a doctor, was a Conseiller au Parlement de Bretagne. Descartes's mother, Jeanne, died a year later while giving birth to a sibling. Sometime between 1604 and 1607 René Descartes entered the Jesuit college of La Flèche. He stayed until between 1612 and 1615, going on to Poitiers where he received his Baccalauréat and *licence en droit* in 1616. Adrien Baillet tells us that Descartes entered La Flèche at the age of eight at Easter of 1604 and that he left in 1612 at the age of seventeen (1: xlvii).[10] Whatever the precise dates, it is clear that his formative years were spent at the Jesuit college of La Flèche.[11]

The college was founded in 1604 by an edict of Henri IV requiring a "séminaire general et universel auquel seroient enseignées toutes les sciences et facultés que les jésuites ont accoutumé d'enseigner aux plus grands collèges et universités de leur compagnie" (quoted in Marchant de Burbure[12] 287). Furthermore, the progress of the new college received the king's personal attention, a fact reflected in the eminent standing of early teachers. These included Noël Petau (1583-1652), teacher of rhetoric at La Flèche from 1613-1618, author of a number of historical and theological works and generally renowned figure in Christian circles of the time, and Nicolas Caussin (1583-1651), the confessor of Louis XIII and adversary of Richelieu. Descartes himself was placed under the charge of the Père Charlet, who, according to Baillet, "luy tint lieu de Père & de Gouverneur pendant huit ans" (1: 18). It was also at La Flèche that Descartes's long friendship with Mersenne was born (Baillet 1: 21).

Descartes's room was next to the *Salle des actes*.[13] This was the main assembly hall on the first floor of the *Cour des classes*, the central one of five courtyards at La Flèche. Also on the first floor was the library containing over eight thousand volumes and the *Galerie du Collège*; it was here that students' compositions, often emblematic in nature, would be displayed on the occasions of the college's various celebrations. The ground floor of the *Cour des classes* was taken up with classrooms. Opposite the *Salle des actes* was the chapel, whose first stone was laid in 1607.

Such was the setting for Descartes's early education, a formation which included the use of emblematics. This was of course the case with any Jesuit upbringing, as the vastness of the corpus of Jesuit emblem books suggests. The direct references to emblems and devices in the Jesuit teaching manuals—the *Ratio studiorum* and the *De Ratione discendi et dociendi*—make it clear that they had an important rôle to play in Jesuit education. Furthermore, certain documents specific to the early years of La Flèche give us examples directly related to the education of Descartes.

The important rôle of emblematics within the Jesuit circles of seventeenth-century France has already been discussed in chapter II. It is fair to surmise that the library of a Jesuit college would have been stocked with a fair selection of the two thousand Jesuit emblem books that were available by the end of the seventeenth century in France.[14] The Jesuits also appropriated for pedagogical purposes emblems and devices that at their origin were not specifically Jesuit. Jetons produced at the end of each year in celebration of the reigning monarch, for example, may well have inspired the decoration for fêtes in honour of Henri IV. Most importantly, as a Jesuit college of the first class,[15] the teaching curriculum at La Flèche would have been that of the *Ratio studiorum*. This was all the more certain in view of the fact that the Père Jean Chastellier, who held the office of second rector of the college from 1604-1606, had been charged with the promotion of the *Ratio studiorum* within the French provinces.

The *Ratio studiorum* is divided into eleven general sections covering the duties of the teachers of the various classes as well as those of the governors. The work suggests the study of emblematics principally for the classes of rhetoric and humanities. Section 12 of the "Regulae professoris rhetoricae" states, "Concertatio, seu exercitatio sita erit [...] in hieroglyphicis, symbolis Pythagoreis, apophthegmatis, adagiis, emblematiis aenigmatisque interpretandis."[16] A few pages later, section 15 suggests the study of hieroglyphs and emblems for the students' day-off ("die vacationis")! It was common practice for the students to display their work at regular intervals or on special occasions. Section 10 of the "Regulae professoris humanitatis" tells us that pictures could be joined to the posted poems "in the manner of emblems" ("quae emblemati"). Similarly public readings could lead to the selection of the best emblematic compositions: "Emblemata vero & carmina, que celeberrimis aliquot diebus propalam collocantur, a duobus per Rectorem designandis, legantur omnia, atque optima seligantur" ("Regulae praefecti studiorum inferiorum," § 3).[17] Section 7 of the "Regulae Academiae rhetorum et humanitarum" repeats the notion of displaying emblems as part of certain special celebrations. A few pages earlier in the same section the composition of emblems had figured as a subject for rhetorical debate: "nunc emblemata & insignia de certa aliqua materia componant; nunc inscriptiones aut descriptiones, nunc aenigmata faciant, aut dissolvant."[18]

These are just a few typical examples, the likes of which are common within the pages of the *Ratio studiorum*. The work also emphasises time and again the importance of brevity of expression and memorisation in all classes. In view of the frequency of such references, they are perhaps as important as the passages in which emblematics are mentioned directly: the *Ratio studiorum* when read as a whole gives the distinct impression of an emblematic mentality—learning through memorisation, motto-like summaries, and word/image interaction—as being at the base of a Jesuit education.

Jouvancy's *De Ratione discendi et dociendi* leaves the reader with very much the same impression. This work approaches the question of education from the angle of the subject matter of the curriculum rather than the tasks of the various teachers, but the conclusions tend to be very much those of the *Ratio studiorum*. A large section of chapter 2 of the first part is given to the question of the definition of an enigma ("Quid sit Aenigma") and other close literary forms; section II (Article IV) differentiates between an "aenigma" and "emblema," whereas section III goes on to describe rebuses and devices. In the list of works to be consulted, Jouvancy cites Buhursius (Dominique Bouhours) and Erasmus's *Adagia*. In the section on "Libri singulis in

Scholis praelegandi" ["Books to be chosen for the individual classes"] (second part, Article VII), Jouvancy gives one of the most important of the proto-emblematic pieces, the "Cebetis tabula," or the *Tablet of Cebes*. It is significant that of the few modern authors that Jouvancy mentions directly, the common link is that of emblematics or proto-emblematics. Like the *Ratio studiorum*, the *De Ratione discendi et dociendi* leaves the twentieth-century reader with the distinct impression that Jesuit education relied heavily on learning methods that involved memorisation and expression through the interaction of text and image.

It is clear, therefore, that as a student in a major Jesuit school, Descartes's education would have been influenced by the study of emblematics. The evidence of the specific case of a ceremony that Descartes attended confirms this conclusion and provides precise examples of the emblematics that would have marked his schooldays. The ceremony in question is the transfer of the heart of Henri IV, in accordance with a promise made by the king to the Jesuits, to the college of La Flèche on 4 June 1610.

The Père Jacquin, superior of the Jesuits of the *Maison professe de Saint Louis* in Paris,[19] had taken charge of the embalmed heart of Henri IV on 15 May 1610.[20] Here it was displayed to the public in a *pavillon* to the right of the altar, accompanied by the continual flame of two white wax candles, until 31 May. The ensuing journey from Paris lasted four days, culminating in the transfer of the heart to the Jesuits of La Flèche on 4 June. An engraving of the transfer shows us a long procession of candle-bearing mourners. A ceremonious parade of students, presumably including Descartes, and dignitaries from the college and town of La Flèche received the heart. The procession then passed through the main gate of the town, which was "resvestüe de deüil et d'ecussons," on to the Eglise Saint Thomas, La Flèche's main church.[21]

After a service the heart was taken to the college. Its portal was decorated as follows:

> Sur le frontispice du portail, estoit au milieu un grand tableau du nom de Jesus, audessus duquel on voyoit un coeur Rayonnant et richement couronné. a La droite on avoit représenté un phenix brulant sur un bucher, Lequel disoit similis in prole resurgo pour faire entendre qu'Henry Le grand renaist en La personne du Roy son fils qui succede a ses Vertus, et deviendra comme Luy L'obiet de L'amour des peuples. A gauche estoit un pelican Lequel avec son bec faisoit sortir de son sang pour en nourrir ses petits, et plus bas on Lisoit ces paroles mors, et Vita Iuvat natos, ce qui signifie allegoriquement que Le Roy s'estant sacrifié pendant sa Vie en s'exposant a toutes sortes de dangers pour La gloire, et L'utilité de sa famille Royale, il Luy sert encor beaucoup apres sa mort en Luy Laissant ses qualitez heroïques, et son exemple a Imiter.

Beyond the portal, in the centre of the main courtyard, had been erected an arch, 27 feet high and 26 feet wide, decorated with torches, an inscription dedicated to Henri IV, and the arms of France and Navarre. The galleries on the sides of the court-

Figure 5.   "1610: Devises du portail de l'église de La Fléche," from *Série Qb 1*, Bibliothèque nationale de France (Département des Estampes).

yard were decorated with silver "fleurs de Lys," the arms of France accompanied by "testes de mort," and torches. The rear of the courtyard was "tapissé d'affiches en tailles douces" showing Henri carried away by an eagle. Those present would undoubtedly have been reminded of Alciato's Ganymede emblem: Ganymede, the son of Jupiter, is portrayed being carried off to the heavens in glory with the message that one should rejoice in God. In view of the circumstances, Ganymede could fittingly be replaced by Henri IV, the assumption being that the emblematic reference was well-known enough for the allusion to be obvious.

The procession passed through the arch and between a column and pyramid, also situated in the courtyard. The entrance to the building was "couverte de deüil, et d'ecussons." Once inside the building mourners saw that in front of the altar had been constructed an "echaffaut" upon which the heart was initially placed. The altar was "tendu de noir avec tous les ornemens convenables" and flanked by two columns surmounted by an arch to the ceiling. This was decorated with the arms of France and Navarre. Beneath the arch was positioned the receptacle where the king's heart was ceremoniously laid to rest.

The *Mercure françois*[22] of 1610 gives the following general impression of the college's decoration:

> On ne voyoit en tout ce College qu'armes de France & de Navarre,
> & des testes de mort, des larmes et des fleurs de lys d'argent, avec
> emblèmes & tableaux où étoient plusieurs devises & disticques
> qui les expliquoient. (469)

The decoration of the college in expression of its grief was described in the *Annuæ litteræ Societatis Iesu*[23] of 1610 as follows: "luctum suum variis argumentis, atque emblematis, arcubus, machinis ingenti cum labore, tum sumptu extructis, est testificatum" (141).[24] Indeed one could assume that the majority of the emblems would have decorated the galleries of the college in keeping with the Jesuit tradition for festival days.[25]

The procession leading to the transfer of the heart of Henri IV took up the first of three days of ceremonies at La Flèche. Theses and literary exercises, recitations and ballet dominated the second and third days. A brief description of these type of activities is given in the *Annuæ litteræ Societatis Iesu*[26] of 1611.[27] This tells that on the second day the pupils took part in public philosophical debates. In the afternoon everyone gathered to witness the deciphering of the four enigmas decorating the base of the huge pyramid that had been constructed. This was to the delight of all present! The secret message was, naturally enough, in praise of Henri IV (90-91).[28] Such debates and interpretation of emblematic enigmas are of course in keeping with the tone of those described in the *Ratio studiorum*.[29]

The ceremonies in honour of Henri IV did not stop after the transfer of his heart. Quite the contrary, 4 June came to mark the date for annual celebrations, the Henriades, particular to La Flèche, and which lasted until 1792. Following in the footsteps of the transfer ceremony itself, the Henriades involved the complete decora-

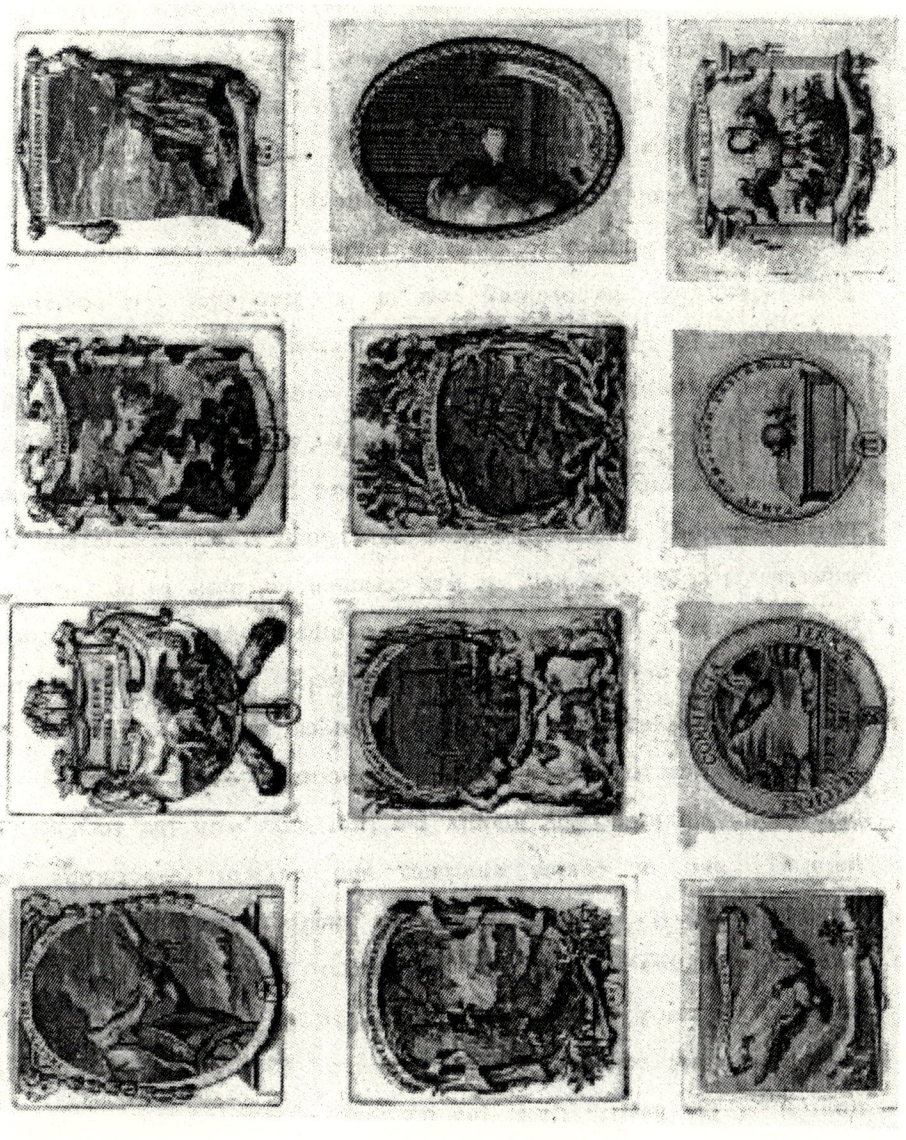

Figure 6. "Devises de la Pompe funèbre d'Henri IV," from *Série Qb1*, Bibliothèque nationale de France (Département des Estampes).

tion of the college in banners bearing enigmas, allegorical paintings and of course emblems and devices. Sermons and ceremonies would occupy mainly the first day, with the second day given to rhetorical and philosophical debates. The final day saw the ceremony's plays and ballets. The event also gave students the opportunity to display their work publicly. This would include poems, enigmas and epigrammatic compositions, often produced especially for the occasion. It was common for these to be published in an anthology marking the occasion. Such anthologies might also include a general description of events and transcriptions of sermons.

One such anthology, the *Lacrymæ collegii*[30] of 1611, is of particular interest. The work was produced as part of the celebrations in honour of the first anniversary of the transfer of the heart, effectively the opening year of the Henriades. It contains a description of events, a selection of students' work (the main bulk of the volume) and transcriptions of sermons pronounced on 4 June. The work is particularly valuable as it represents a contemporary written account of a ceremony in which Descartes took part.

The opening section of the *Lacrymæ collegii*, "Lectori benevolo" ["To the kind reader"], introduces the reader to the public display of students' work and to the notion of an annual ceremony on 4 June. The text explains that it became customary for students to display publicly writings of all kinds; that is to say "writings in Greek or Latin, with or without set rhythms, emblems, hieroglyphs and enigmas." In honour of Henri, whose gift of his heart allowed his light to continue to shine in the college, 4 June had been set as the date for such celebrations (6).[31]

The "Lectori benevolo" goes on to make it clear that the ceremony of 1611 was to boast much of the pomp and splendour of the previous year's events. The college was decorated extravagantly with "variorum emblematum picturae commendabiles" ["Pictures recommendable for emblems of all sorts"] (7), the Jesuits had constructed a pyramid with four enigmas around its base ("Basim obsidebant maiora quatuor aenigmata") (9), and much time was given to rhetorical debates, including those based on a discussion of the works that had been posted.[32] As with the previous year, the third day was dedicated to theatrical productions. The *Lacrymæ collegii* includes transcriptions of two sermons, one in Latin, one in French, pronounced on 4 June. Both are highly solemn in tone, stressing the benevolence of Henri IV and the bitter sorrow felt at his loss.

The remainder of the *Lacrymæ collegii*, nearly three hundred pages, consists of the poems written, displayed[33] and discussed as part of the celebrations of 1611.[34] These form a varied corpus, in French, Latin and Greek, focusing on different aspects of Henri's virtues, sadness at his loss and hopes for the future through the reign of Louis XIII. Although many of the poems are several pages in length, one of the most popular forms is the epigram. The *Lacrymæ collegii* opens with "Ad lectorem epigramma" ["Epigrams for the reader"] (15); on page 154 and page 161 we find more "epigramma," and a long series of Greek "EPIGRAMMA" appears on pages 182-88. One typical example reads as follows:

Henrico Magno Galliarum et Navarrae Regi,
Virtute Fortissimo
Pietate Clementissimo
Bello Invictissimo
Custudio avitæ Religionis
Virtutis & literarum fautori
Hostium domitori.[35] (23)

The use of the dative case (the poem is addressed to Henry) suggests the style of an inscription to be displayed or engraved on a plinth. Such a poem, and indeed many other epigrams of the *Lacrymæ collegii* in the same style, could reasonably have been intended for display next to a portrait (or statue) of the king. This process would effectively create an emblematic composition in the style of courtly jetons or biographies in the manner of Vulson's *Les Portraits des hommes illustres*.[36]

Another interesting but longer piece is entitled "De Henrici Magni fortuna emblema in quo varii depinguntur Heröes" (280-81).[37] The poem in question is an allegorical work demonstrating the greatness of Henri IV. The visual nature of the description brings to mind engravings of the period such as the "Embleme representant L'Estat de la famille royale au temps du mariage du roy."[38] In a similar vein is the "Tumulus virtutum Henrici Magni Galliarum et Navarrae Christianissimi" ["Mound of the virtues of the most Christian Henry the Great of France and Navarre"] (138-53). This poem is divided into various sections, each bearing the title of one of thirteen qualities of the dead king: "religio" ["religion"], "pietas" ["piety"], "iustitia" ["justice"], "fortitudo" ["strength"], et cetera. Again it is not hard to imagine the various sections of the poem being displayed in such a way as to create a physical "tumulus," or mound. This would play upon the other meaning of "tumulus"—a tomb—in honour of the dead king. It would also have been in keeping with the Jesuit tradition for the various sections to be juxtaposed with iconographical representations of the virtues in question.[39]

One final piece figuring in the *Lacrymæ collegii* deserves special attention: a sonnet "Sur la mort du Roy Henry le Grand, et sur la decouverte de quelques nouvelles Planettes, ou Estoiles errantes autour de Iupiter, faicte l'Année d'icelle par Galilee Galilee, celebre Mathematicien du Grand Duc de Florence" (163).[40] The poem suggests that the new stars discovered by Galileo are the soul of Henri IV, given by God "Pour servir aux mortels de cœleste flambeau." Since it was normal for all students to participate in the celebrations, it is perhaps possible that the piece referring to Galileo's discoveries is the contribution from the young Descartes. This would be in keeping with his apparent liking for poetry[41] and with the interest in astronomy that would come to light in his later works. Even if the piece is not by Descartes, the reference to astronomy does add to the background regarding the teachings at La Flèche and Descartes's development. It is important to note that at the time science and emblematics were not incompatible.

Although the *Lacrymæ collegii* presents the events and compositions of the first and probably grandest of the Henriades, it is fair to presume that the ceremonies of the following years, including those up to Descartes's departure, were very much in the same vein. It is worth mentioning briefly, however, two further instances of emblematic manifestations at the college. One, the ceremony for the canonisation of the Saints Ignatius and François-Xavier of 1622, postdates Descartes's graduation. It is nonetheless of interest as it represents another example of a typical ceremony of which we have a first-hand account. This comes in the form of *Le Triomphe des Saints*.[42]

The work gives a detailed description of the ceremony's procession including the devices on the banners that were carried. A typical example is the description of the presentation of a pomegranate device that was carried in procession in honour of the Virgin:

> Un grand Guidon de taffetas bleu, avec une grosse grenade d'or, de laquelle tomboient plusieurs grains pourris, les entiers paroissant au milieu avec cette devise en lettre d'or, TUTA SINU MELIORA FOVENTUR, & de l'autre un grand nom de Maria en chiffre, enrichi d'une couronne Imperialle, le tout d'or. (14)

A full account, some twenty-four pages (28-51), then describes the devices that decorated the exterior of the *Cour des classes* and of the galleries, as well as those on the inside of the classrooms and galleries. One of the most important emblems that decorated the galleries was dedicated to Saint François-Xavier. It hung opposite the one dedicated to Saint Ignatius:

> A gauche en mesme hauteur S. François Xavier, avec cet embléme à l'opposite de l'autre; un globe terrestre ouvert par le haut en deux parts, qui estoient rejointes avec une chaisne d'or, & en l'ouverture, un triangle d'or rayonnant, chargé d'une croix rouge, & sa devise, DIVISUM UTROQUE REVINXI. Ces deux SS. estoient tirez le plus au naturel qu'on avoit peu, & la face fort devote, qui regardoient vers le ciel, & N. S. Pere le Pape les regardoit d'un visage benin, ayant ce vers escrit en lettre capitale au pied destail de son throsne ECLIPSES INTER GEMINUM MIHI NASCITUR ASTRUM. (31)

The account goes on to describe the *affiches* or allegorical paintings produced by the various classes as well as the explanation of enigmas (53-59). The work of the students of Logic is described as follows:

> Les Logiciens mirent sur leurs theses le triomphe de S. Ignace, porté au ciel par les mains de la Pieté & de la Doctrine, en une planche de taille douce, large de quatorze poulces sur onze. La Pieté tenoit la droitte en un char enlevé par deux Cygnes, mais à la gauche celuy de la Doctrine estoit tiré de deux Aigles couronnez,

chacune estendoit doucement un bras pour soustenir & eslever S. Ignace tout en Gloire, & ayant sur sa teste une couronne supportee par deux Anges, chargez des symboles de l'amour de dieu & du prochain. L'heresie & l'ignorance y tombent à la renverse sous les roües des chariots, & tout ce que nous avons dit esta*n*t en l'air, la ville de Rome est au bas, & fait voir les temples, maisons de pieté, & de doctrine que le S. y avoit fait bastir.
Cet embléme estoit expliquee au bas dans un rouleau soustenu par deux Anges. Et sur le rencontre heureux de cet Anagramme fort a leur avantage.

SANCTUS IGNATIUS LOIOLA
NATA SALUS NOVIS LOGICIS[43]

Ils prirent pour tiltre,
IGNATI quantus es si te metimur ex nomine quo cu*m* salus natus est, quantum nomen, sivel nomen salutis omen est, felices novi Logici quibus tuum favet numen et nomen.[44] (56-57)

Descriptions such as this and the ones cited above comprise the essential fabric of *Le Triomphe des Saints*. In short, the vast majority of the seventy pages of the account of the festival relates to emblematics. To the modern reader such emphasis seems repetitive and completely alien. It is fair to assume, however, that for the Jesuits at La Flèche such emphasis would have seemed normal. We can conclude that fashion has changed, and emblematics were an inherent and essential part of their manner of thinking and of expression of their belief. It is unlikely that such a marked interest would have been any less ten years earlier, during Descartes's time.

Our final example of emblematic manifestations at La Flèche is the "Planche que les Iesuites ont fait graver"[45] shown in figure 7. The top and main section of the "Planche," shows the college's physical appearance (its "corps" in emblematic terms) as well as its values and aspirations (its "âme"), via an emblematic exchange between Henri IV, Saint Louis and Louis XIII.[46] Below the kings of France we see devices representing the principal disciplines studied at La Flèche: theology, philosophy, rhetoric and *belles lettres*. Theology is represented by a triangle and a ray of light with the motto "ostentat iter" ["it shows the way"]. Philosophy has the device of two globes with "novit utrumque," "it knows both," indicating that philosophy can lead to knowledge of the earthly sciences as well as of the divine and metaphysical.[47] Rhetoric is represented by lightning and bees. *Belles lettres* has a beehive and a garden device with the motto "cogit florea messis" ["the harvesting of flowers goes with it"]. Explanations and interpretations are given in the engraving's manuscript text which is also included in *Série Qb 1*. Images of this kind were undoubtedly a typical part of the cultural baggage reflected in Descartes's metaphorical language, as we shall see in the next section of this chapter. Here it suffices to note that such a "Planche," representing the very essence of La Flèche, could hardly have escaped his attention. Furthermore, the "Planche" in question was used as a frontispiece for a programme of the philosophy debates at La Flèche. These "programmes" were the printed version of

Figure 7. "Planche que les Iesuites ont fait graver," from *Série Qb 1*, Bibliothéque nationale de France (Département des Estampes).

the debates to which Descartes refers disparagingly in his *Discours de la méthode*.

The aim of this section has been to demonstrate the considerable rôle played by emblematics in Descartes's formative education. We have seen that emblems played an important part in the general curriculum, as well as in certain ceremonies and debates regarded as special events by all involved in the college. Specific examples, considered important enough to be recorded in engravings, give us precise details of the emblematic compositions in question. These include devices displayed at a ceremony in which Descartes probably took part, and those of a "Planche" that was later displayed on the cover of the programme of philosophy. Given such evidence it is fair to conclude that Descartes's formative education would have made emblematics part of his cultural baggage. This was true of any literary man of the age, as we have suggested in chapter II; it was especially important in the case of Descartes on account of the heavy reliance upon emblematics that formed part of the Jesuit training at La Flèche or indeed of any such Jesuit college.

Adrien Baillet, Descartes's biographer, confirms such conclusions. Differing notions of the concept of history over the centuries mean that his accounts should be viewed with a certain caution. Nonetheless, the fact that he was a near contemporary of Descartes does mean that he had a feeling for the mentality and priorities of the age that is now largely lost to us. For Baillet, Descartes would not only have studied and lived with the emblematics at La Flèche, he would without doubt have participated in their very composition. He gives the following description of the ceremony for the transfer of the king's heart:

> ce qu'il y avoit de particulier, outre les litres, les écussons, les têtes de morts, les larmes, & les fleurs de lys d'argent, étoient les emblêmes, les devises, & les épigrammes, à la composition desquelles on ne pourra pas croire que M. Descartes n'a point eu de part, lorsqu'on songera au talent et à l'inclination qu'il avoit pour les Vers. (1: 23)

Despite Baillet's assurance, we have no emblems that carry Descartes's signature. Nonetheless there are certain elements in his style that bear the hallmark of the emblematic mentality, a few of which merit brief consideration.

On two occasions Descartes refers to himself as having a device. In a letter to Mersenne of April 1634, in reference to Galileo's condemnation, he mentions "le desir que j'ay de vivre en repos & de continuer la vie que i'ay commencée en prenant pour ma devise: bene vixit, bene qui latuit" (1: 285-86).[48] To Chanut in a letter of 1 November 1646 Descartes refers to the belief held by certain savages that monkeys know how to speak but prefer to remain silent. He then states that likewise he should refrain from publishing,

> & ayant pris pour ma devise,
> Illi mors gravis incubat,
> Qui, notus nimis omnibus,
> Ignotus moritur sibi,
> de n'etudier plus que pour m'instruire.... (4: 535-37)[49]

These "devises" do not involve the interaction of text and image,[50] but they are examples of the epigrammatic mentality essential for the motto around which traditional devices were formed.

This epigrammatic mentality also marks one of Descartes's earliest writings, his *Cogitationes privatæ* of 1619. This work originally appeared in a notebook (now lost) mentioned in an inventory of Descartes's papers made after his death. The notebook was undoubtedly composed during his travels in the years following his departure from La Flèche. Baillet had seen the notebook and describes the jottings as divided into various sections. These included the "Praeambula," with the motto "Initium sapientæ timor Domini" ["The fear of the Lord is the beginning of wisdom"], the "Experimenta" and the "Olympica" (Baillet 1: 50). The text we have now is based upon a copy taken by Leibniz and first published as the *Cogitationes privatæ* in 1859.[51] The work consists of short reflections such as "Dicta sapientum ad paucissimas quasdam regulas generales possunt reduci" ["The sayings of the wise can be reduced to certain very limited general rules"] (10: 217). Often a general introductory phrase can serve as a heading for a longer discussion. Under the title, for example, of "Polybii Cosmopolitani Thesaurus Mathematicus" ["The Mathematical Treasure-Chest of Cosmopolitan Polybius"] (10: 214) Descartes gives us a paragraph on how mathematics can lead to human advancement. Interesting also is a reference he makes to those who are "ensnared day and night in the Gordian knot of that science [mathematics]" (10: 214):[52] the Gordian knot featured prominently in humanist culture, one example, as we have seen (figure 6), occurring in the devices at La Flèche.

Such an epigrammatic style would not be lost in Descartes's later works. The *Regulæ ad directionem ingenii*, written around 1628 (although not published until 1701), consists precisely of a series of one- or two-sentence rules upon which long commentaries and explanations are based. Similarly, the *Passions de l'âme* of 1649, published shortly before Descartes's death, is made up of 212 titles or short sentences regarding the passions, each explained by a text, generally of a paragraph's length. Indeed it is fair to say that on the whole Descartes's works are marked by a lapidary style whereby short memorable phrases are contextualised by longer explanations. The obvious model for such a technique is the *Adagia*[53] of Erasmus. Considered by many as the prime example of a protoemblematic piece, a good number of the *Adagia*'s titles (e.g. "Dulce bellum inexpertis," "Homo bulla") came to feature in emblem books. In emblematic terms, the title of the *Adage* provides the *motto*, whereas the visual nature of many of the examples in Erasmus's main text gives the *imago* as well as the explanatory *subscriptio*.[54]

Before concluding this brief overview of certain emblematic elements in Descartes's style, we should consider the central topic of the representation of the intangible through the visible. On the broad subject of Descartes and the question of representation through images, John D. Lyons's "*Camera Obscura*: Image and Imagination in Descartes's *Méditations*" should be consulted. Lyons concludes by noting that for Descartes,

> The exactness of representation which is possible in an image, even a dream image, is less important at this point than the plausible fabulation which permits the movement of figures into and out of the image. (194)

By comparison with the way in which text/image interaction functions, one might note that the picture or imagined figure provides the static, global image while a text would add the "plausible fabulation." Needless to say, the process is akin to that inherent in emblem books.

With this in mind two sections from the "Olympica" section of the *Cogitationes privatæ* are of particular interest. First,

> Ut imaginatio utitur figuris ad corpora concipienda, ita intellectus utitur quibusdam corporibus sensibilibus ad spiritualia figuranda, ut vento, lumine: unde altius philosophantes mentem cognitione possumus in sublime tollere.[55] (10: 217)

The importance of this idea can be inferred from the fact that Descartes virtually repeats himself in a second passage: "Sensibilia apta concipiendis Olympicis: ventus spiritum significat, motus cum tempore vitam, lumen cognitionem, calor amorem, activas instantania creationem"[56] (10: 218).

In both cases the gist of Descartes's argument is summed up by the phrase that acts as a title (or indeed as a motto) to the second quotation: "Sensibilia apta concipiendis Olympicis." Descartes suggests the use of visual[57] or bodily ("corpora") notions such as the wind, light, movement or heat in order to represent the purely intelligible ("spiritualia"), such as the spirit, knowledge, the passage of time or love. Analysis of Descartes's later works reveals that such a method of representation will form a crucial part of the expression of his philosophy, be it through the piece of wax in the *Meditationes* (2: 187-90), the blindman in the dark in the *Discours de la méthode* (90), or the basket of apples in the seventh set of *Objections et réponses* (2: 982-83).

The same motto, "Sensibilia apta concipiendis Olympicis," could be used to summarise the mentality behind Jesuit emblematics (see above). The teaching of the belief in God and of the miracles of the Trinity required students to seize intelligible rather than tangible notions. Using emblems, the Jesuits made the supernatural accessible to all by rendering it visual. In the teachings of Ignatius the application of the senses played an important rôle; this application could be achieved through the picture of the emblem. Furthermore, the mystic element often attributed to emblems via their association with hieroglyphics, added the nuance of sacredness[58] necessary for the earthly expression of divine truths. This mystic element was further reinforced by the very working of the emblem: the initial meanings of the individual parts are transcended by their conjunction, as the act of bringing them together turns the key to open a hidden layer, the completed sense of the emblem and the sacred truths therein expressed. The interaction of the parts makes the unreadable readable, just as the emblem itself makes the unreadable mysteries of the divine readable by expressing the intelligible through the visual. In this respect the emblem can be seen as holding up a microcosmic mirror to the macrocosm that is the world of God's creation. The whole process could well be summed up by the words "Sensibilia apta concipiendis Olympicis."

The aim of this brief discussion has been to suggest that important elements of Descartes's style—epigrammatic expression and the presentation of the intelligible through the visual—were in keeping with the emblematic mentality of the time. We have already shown that the concrete manifestations of this mentality, the Jesuit emblematics of the early seventeenth century, had played an unavoidably important, and by implication influential, rôle in Descartes's cultural formation. Such knowledge should therefore be applied so as to enhance the modern-day reader's understanding and appreciation of Descartes's writings.

III B

Descartes's Language in the Light of Emblematics

The *Discours de la méthode* contains approximately thirty-five metaphorical images. On occasions Descartes's imagery goes no further than a passing reference or references to illustrate a point:

> elles [ideas of the senses] peuvent aussi nous tromper assez souvent, sans que nous dormions: comme lorsque ceux qui ont la jaunisse voient tout de couleur jaune, ou que les astres ou autres corps fort éloignés nous paraissent beaucoup plus petits qu'ils ne sont. (65)

Some metaphorical images, such as that of the painting, appear more than once:[59]

> Mais je serai bien aise de faire voir, en ce discours, quels sont les chemins que j'ai suivis, et d'y représenter ma vie comme en un tableau. (34-35)

> Mais, tout de même que les peintres, ne pouvant également bien représenter dans un tableau plat toutes les diverses faces d'un corps solide, en choisissent une des principales qu'ils mettent seule vers le jour, et ombrageant les autres, ne les font paraître qu'en tant qu'on les peut voir en la regardant: ainsi, craignant de ne pouvoir

> mettre en mon discours tout ce que j'avais en la pensée, j'entrepris seulement d'y exposer bien amplement ce que je concevais de la lumière. (68)

Other recurring themes are the pathway or the contrast between darkness and light. Descartes also uses extended metaphors of a highly visual nature forming a key part of the exposition of philosophical argument:

> car l'obscurité des distinctions et des principes dont ils [the schoolmen] se servent est cause qu'ils peuvent parler de toutes choses aussi hardiment que s'ils les savaient, et soutenir tout ce qu'ils en disent contre les plus subtils et les plus habiles sans qu'on ait moyen de les convaincre. En quoi ils me semblent pareils à un aveugle qui, pour se battre sans désavantage contre un qui voit, l'aurait fait venir dans le fond de quelque cave fort obscure; et je puis dire que ceux-ci ont intérêt que je m'abstienne de publier les principes de la philosophie dont je me sers; car étant très simples et très évidents, comme ils sont, je ferais quasi le même, en les publiant, que si j'ouvrais quelques fenêtres, et faisais entrer du jour dans cette cave, où ils sont descendus pour se battre. (90)

The sheer quantity and variety of Descartes's use of metaphor indicates that figurative language had a central—and presumably carefully calculated—rôle to play in the expression of his philosophy.

The subject matter of at least two-thirds of Descartes's images had also formed the basis for emblems in the major works of the corpus of emblem books.[60] Sometimes the same theme had been used in much the same context but with different nuances of meaning. Roemer Visscher's emblem 36 of his *Zinnepoppen* (Amsterdam, circa 1620, originally 1614) also presents virtue entering through a newly opened window. He presents it as the "licht von Godes woordt," the light of God's word.

Other common themes such as the painter or engraver had been used to express ideas in a different way.[61] Descartes's painter copes with the limitations of two-dimensional representation, but La Perrière's engraver had symbolised optimistic ambition:

> Tout bon tailleur de tout boys fait image,
> En les bouchant par art, tant qu'il souffit:
> Semblablement, l'homme prudent et sage
> Toute fortune applicque à son proufit.
> (*Morosophie*, emblem 78)

Descartes's images of the plastic arts present success as less of a certainty. Referring to the mixture of good and bad precepts with which he had been schooled, he states "il est presque aussi malaise de les en séparer [the good precepts from the bad], que de tirer une Diane ou une Minerve hors d'un bloc de marbre qui n'est point encore ébauché" (46). Descartes's theme of the stars viewed from afar had also been treated by La Perrière in a different way. Descartes used the image to demonstrate the scientific phenomenon of our senses as fallacious. La Perrière had drawn a moral comparison:

> L'on ne peut veoir les astres clairement,
> Sans que le vent ayt déchassé les nues:
> Vertus ne sont aussi semblablement
> (Sans déchasser les vices) obtenues.
> (*Morosophie*, emblem 51)

Although the themes of the vast majority of Descartes's images had also featured in the work of emblem-writers in one form or another, we should, nonetheless, be extremely wary when drawing conclusions based upon similarities between authors of different periods. Linking themes most likely come from a third common source or sources, such as the Ancients or the Bible, rather than as a result of 'direct' influence. We are not concerned, therefore, with the originality (or lack thereof) of the themes themselves, but rather with the nature of the presentation of the themes. The evidence of Descartes's education suggests that his exposure to age-old topics such as the stars viewed from afar, the metaphor of the boat or that of the lute would largely have been through Renaissance, including emblematic, presentations of such subjects.

Accordingly, much of the skill of Descartes's use of language lay in the manipulation of the traditions of presentation with which he was familiar. The full significance of Descartes's images only becomes clear in the light of the tradition against which they were read. Descartes inevitably used his readers' knowledge of the cultural tradition of the time in order to add aspects and nuances to his own texts that are now largely lost to the modern reader.

The effectiveness of Descartes's use of language is dependent upon a careful choice of images that clarify and enhance his philosophical case. In order for the images, however well chosen, to fulfill their potential, Descartes needed to present them as effectively as possible. Accordingly, the clarity of the *Discours de la méthode* relies upon a careful interaction of concision and suggestiveness that would have been worthy of the methods of presentation taught by the schoolmasters at La Flèche.

In the *Cogitationes privatae* Descartes had already suggested that it was possible to condense vast areas of knowledge into the concision of a few phrases: "Dicta sapientum ad paucissimas quasdam regulas generales possunt reduci" ["The sayings of the wise can be reduced to certain very limited general rules"] (10: 217). A few years later "general rules" of this kind were to form the basis of the *Discours de la méthode*. Descartes presents the four rules of which the method is composed as breaking away from the complicated enumeration of precepts upon which his forerunners had based their logic: "ainsi, au lieu de ce grand nombre de préceptes dont la logique est composée, je crus que j'aurais assez des quatre suivants" (46). The four rules in question take up little more than half a page. Descartes follows a similar procedure at the beginning of book 3 of the *Discours* regarding his practical approach to the path of discovery: "je me formai une morale par provision, qui ne consistait qu'en trois ou quatre maximes" (51).

The *Discours de la méthode* as a whole consists of little more than thirty pages. Descartes suggests that even this may be too much: "Si ce discours semble trop long pour être tout lu en une fois, on le pourra distinguer en six parties" (31). Indeed the concision that marks the *Discours* is also an important feature of many of the works in which Descartes presents his ideas:[62] the *Meditationes* goes to little more than seventy pages and is again divided into six subsections; the *Passions de l'âme*, his final piece, is divided into numerous sections that generally do not exceed a page or two.

The concision of Descartes's writings results from that of his style, and his imagery is an important factor in ensuring the necessary brevity of expression. Key points to Descartes's philosophy become clear with the support of briefly presented images to which the reader can relate: the questioning of our physical existence, for example, leads to the assurance of our spiritual existence ("je pense donc je suis"); the hypothetical doubt at the base of this reasoning is an essential part of the Cartesian method. It is important for the doubt to be plausible, not ordinarily a simple task: it is not easy to convince the reader that neither he nor the book in front of him necessarily exist. In the *Discours* Descartes achieves this task by undermining the surest of senses, vision, in two different respects, through the questioning of our judgement of colour, and that of distance:

> elles [the ideas of the senses] peuvent aussi nous tromper assez souvent, sans que nous dormions: comme ceux qui ont la jaunisse voient tout de couleur jaune, ou que les astres ou autres corps fort éloignés nous paraissent beaucoup plus petits qu'ils ne sont. (65)

The images of jaundice and of the stars viewed from afar carry associations clear and common enough that two quick references suffice for the reader to understand that he cannot rely upon the "evidence" of the physical world. Descartes's imagery gives quick validation of complicated philosophical ideas.

On other occasions Descartes expands an image thereby minimising the necessary accompanying explanation:

> Et enfin, comme ce n'est pas assez, avant de commencer à rebâtir le logis où on demeure, que de l'abattre, et de faire provision de matériaux et d'architectes, ou s'exercer soi-même à l'architecture, et outre cela d'en avoir soigneusement tracé le dessin; mais qu'il faut aussi s'être pourvu de quelque autre, où on puisse être logé commodément pendant le temps qu'on y travaillera; ainsi, afin que je ne demeurasse point irrésolu en mes actions pendant que la raison m'obligerait de l'être en mes jugements, et que je ne laissasse pas de vivre dès lors le plus heureusement que je pourrais, je me

formai une morale par provision, qui ne consistait qu'en trois ou
quatre maximes, dont je veux bien vous faire part. (51)

Descartes's philosophy, one essential to our daily existence ("le logis où on demeure"), will raze old prejudices ("abattre") and start from anew ("rebâtir le logis"). The philosophy requires careful planning ("tracé le dessin"), a basis of known facts ("matériaux") and solid formulation from the basis of the facts ("l'architecture"). During the full formulation of the philosophy Descartes will follow a "morale par provision" ("[the temporary house] où on puisse être logé").

The choice of the verb "demeurer" allows Descartes to connect the metaphor of the house ("demeurer" in the sense of "inhabit") with the non-metaphorical statement of provisional philosophical intent ("que je ne demeurasse point irrésolu," "for me not to remain irresolute"). Descartes then goes on to present the "morale par provision" through "quatre maximes." He has, in effect, already provided a clear exposition of his overall philosophical intent without the need for a literal explanation. Based on the image of the house, it is a summary of his philosophy that is easy for the reader to visualise and retain in his mind.

Visualisation is at the base of the mechanics of Descartes's use of language. The house metaphor is especially effective as it is an image familiar to the reader not only through engravings or descriptions, but through daily experience. The same is true of the confusion of the town built by several architects as compared to the clarity of the one designed by a single person (41-42). Even the Biblical image of the palace built upon sand is easy to visualise (37). Indeed of the thirty-five or so metaphors featuring in the *Discours de la méthode*, the majority refer to phenomena that would have formed part of the reader's everyday visual experience: sleep and dreams (59-60), a clock (74, 80-81), a ship (81), judges and lawyers (89), ivy (90), a blindman (90), a lute (95) and so on.

In the majority of cases these everyday phenomena form a comparison with concepts or ideas rather than with other phenomena of the visual world. The clock is an exception as it represents the mechanics of man and of the animals' bodies, but the helmsman in his boat is used in a comparison with the human soul; ivy represents the limitations of the schoolmen's knowledge, the town planned by several architects impure and unfounded judgement, and the blindman ignorance. Descartes is clearly following the early principles of his *Cogitationes privatae*: "Sensibilia apta concipiendis Olympicis: ventus spiritum significat, motus cum tempore vitam, lumen cognitionem, calor amorem, activas instantania creationem" (10: 218).[63]

The nature of the presentation of Descartes's metaphors forces the reader to play an active rôle in their deciphering and, by implication, in the journey along the path of philosophical discovery. Sylvie Romanowski, in her largely structuralist reading of Descartes,[64] notes that "la fusion est totale entre le *je* de l'auteur et celui du lecteur" (174). Lyons, who also cites Romanowski, compares such an approach to "the practice of religious meditations popularized by the Ignatian *Spiritual Exercises*" ("Cartesian Reader," 37). He goes on to remind us that Descartes allows his audience to remember certain discoveries by "leading the reader through the steps of the discoveries *as if the reader were thinking for himself* (43, Lyons's italics). Indeed, Descartes himself indicates that the reader should not be content to accept passively facts presented by the author:

> Comme, pour moi, je me persuade que, si on m'eût enseigné, dès ma jeunesse, toutes les vérités dont j'ai cherché depuis les démonstrations, et que je n'eusse eu aucune peine à les apprendre, je n'en aurais peut-être jamais su aucunes autres, et du moins que jamais je n'aurais acquis l'habitude et la facilité, que je pense avoir, d'en trouver des nouvelles, à mesure que je m'applique à les chercher. (91)

Our approach to the house metaphor shows this process in action. The initial reference to the "logis où on demeure" is vague and possibilities of meaning are manifold. Descartes makes the metaphor more specific by the addition of detail: "provision de matériaux et d'architectes," "tracé le dessin." The reader now realises that Descartes is referring to careful planning and sound construction. When the inhabiting of the house doubles up with the notion of philosophical stance ("que je ne demeurasse point irrésolu") the text has become precise enough for the reader to arrive at its exact meaning.

A similar process operates in the case of the ivy metaphor of book 6: "Ils [the followers of Aristotle] sont come le lierre, qui ne tend point à monter plus haut que les arbres qui le soutiennent" (90). The reading procedure evolves from a non-specific image—that of ivy—whose relevant attributes Descartes then clarifies: the ivy climbs no higher than the tree. The metaphorical process culminates in the intended application of the image, namely that the followers of Aristotle are like the ivy, as they can go no higher than their sustainer. The reader of the *Discours* cannot learn this lesson passively. In order to understand he must follow each step as Descartes guides him from the general to the specific.

In sum, the effectiveness of Descartes's use of language relies upon the concision of his expression. Descartes achieves this concision through the careful choice of visual images whose suggestiveness gives the reader immediate access to the understanding and mental retention of abstract philosophical notions. The mechanics of such imagery allow the reader to play an active rôle in the discovery of Cartesian ideas as he progresses from a general field of reference to the specific in order to seize the metaphor's message.

Descartes's use of language owes much to that of his Jesuit masters. It was they, presumably, that inspired him to the art of concision through visual images. Much the same style of language dominates a sermon delivered by the Jesuit Philibert Quartier, the *Ludovico Magno pro extincta hæresi panegyricus dictus* ["speech delivered for Louis the Great in favour of the extinction of heresy"].[65] Quartier gave the speech in question on 17 December 1686 at the College Louis le Grand in Paris. Gabriel-François Le Jay's *Triomphe de la religion sous Louis le Grand* reproduces the devices that were used to decorate the hall for the occasion. Although the speech postdates Descartes considerably, we can assume that the mechanics of the Jesuits' use of language had not essentially changed. Evidence to support this supposition is given by certain of the engravings that decorate Le Jay's work. They are exactly those that decorated the college of La Flèche on the occasion of the transfer of Henri IV's heart (figure 6).

Quartier's speech is short compared to many religious sermons of the time. His work outlines the glories of Louis XIV, underlines the beneficial effects of the Revocation of the Edict of Nantes and expresses the joy of the "non-heretics." The opening section of Quartier's sermon concludes as follows: "verbo dicam, Hæresim LUDOVICUS MAGNUS extinxit inspirante Pietate, promovente Sapientia, Felicitate coronante. Quae tria dum oratione persequor, animis, oro vos, & lingua favete" (8-9).[66] Quartier intended that these central attributes—Piety, Wisdom and Joy—each of which provided the guiding subject for one of the three main sections of his sermon, should remain fully implanted in his audience's mind. To this end the room had been decorated as follows:

> Sous un riche Dais estoit le Portrait du Roy. Il estoit soûtenu d'un costé par la Piété, de l'autre par la Sagesse; & la Félicité le couronnoit: pour montrer que ç'a esté la Piété qui a inspiré à ce Grand Monarque le dessein d'exterminer l'Héresie de son Royaume; que la sagesse luy en a fourni les moyens, & que la Félicité a couronné cette glorieuse entreprise. C'est ce qu'esprimoit cette Inscription,
>
> EXTINXIT
> INSPIRANTE
> PIETATE,
> PROMOVENTE
> SAPIENTIA,
> FELICITATE
> CORONANTE,[67]
>
> qui répondoit à l'idée qu'on s'estoit proposée dans le Panégyrique du Roy. (Le Jay, 20-21)

In this case an iconographic portrait had condensed and rendered directly visual the concepts of Piety, Wisdom and Joy. The devices that Le Jay goes on to describe served much the same purpose. Towards the end of his sermon Quartier gives a general survey of the state of "Religio" abroad in England, Germany, Austria, Hungary, Asia and Poland (68-78). Accordingly, Le Jay's last two devices are dedicated "A la gloire de Louis le Grand pour avoir travaillé heureusement à étendre la religion dans les pays les plus eloignez après l'avoir affermie dans toute l'étendue de son royaume" (123). The first shows a plan of a solar-centric Copernican universe with the motto "Hinc totum lucet in orbem" ["From here he lights the whole world"]. The second gives the source of a great river accompanied by "Da' suoi a' remoti" ["From his own on to distant lands"].

Such representations would have allowed the audience to retain concise concrete images as a reminder and explanation of Quartier's discourse: the iconographic portrait presents Piety, Wisdom and Joy as Louis's important attributes; the images of the sun at the centre of the universe or the far-flowing river symbolise the king's extending influence. In short, Quartier uses memorial images as ways to narrativise that which is not narrative. The process can be compared to the case of the reader of the *Discours* who remembers the principles of Cartesian philosophy through the image of the well-planned and carefully-constructed house.

The emblems and devices favoured in the speeches and writings of Quartier and others like him gave, by their very nature, expression through concision. The fact that the text refers to specific visible images lessens the need for lengthy descriptions in order to convey and render memorable the potential message. Emblem writers themselves were aware of this essential attribute. Indeed David Graham points to the various markers—e.g. "voicy," "ici," "voir"—writers would use to draw the reader's attention from the text to the picture.[68] Guillaume de La Perrière, a writer very much typical of the early emblem tradition, makes concision his stated goal. In the *Morosophie*'s preface to Antoine de Bourbon, La Perrière points out that the composition of the French *quatrains* was not without difficulty, but, "ie l'ay fait, à fin qu'en petit lieu, l'artifice fust trouvé plus grand, & plus ingenieux." Another preface to the *Morosophie*, that of Jacques de Maulevant, has the same theme:

> On ne te [La Perrière] peult louer condignement
> Pour tes escritz en brefveté faciles:
> Car tous autheurs confessent franchement,
> Que brefveté les rend fort difficiles.

He concludes with an analysis of the relationship of the *quatrain*'s verses to the picture, their aim and achievement being "Pour que grand sens fust en peu d'escriture."

La Perrière is also representative of the emblem tradition in that the images he uses are ones the reader can inevitably recognise. Architectural motifs figure prominently in *La Morosophie*'s one hundred emblems; indeed approximately one third of these show some sort of structure in the background. Some emblems have structural motifs as the central theme, without exception in order to discuss abstract notions. Emblem 79 points out that buildings constructed in elevated sites, like high-placed citizens, are more at risk to life's perils:

> Les bastimentz qui sont en lieu infime,
> Tremblant la terre ont peu de detriment
> Fortune aussi, a gens d'estat sublime
> Plus qu'aux petitz donne peine & tourment.

In emblem 9 a high-perched palace represents Honour. The path leading Virtue to Honour is unfortunately blocked by "Envie." Emblem 67's structure is a statue whose high position, like that of "Grand dignite subittement acquise," results in its sudden downfall. In all of these cases, the fact that the picture's subject, be it a palace or a statue, is not abstract, makes it easy for the reader to memorise, as well as for the artist to draw.

Technical considerations were of less concern in the case of seventeenth-century Jesuit emblem books illustrated by the more advanced method of copperplate engraving. On the other hand, the difficult-to-conceive spiritual nature of matters discussed required extra clarity of visual expression. To compensate, Jesuit emblem books often expressed their message through variations on a central dominating theme, thereby reducing the subject under discussion to the domain of a single concept. Furthermore the single concept was often of a highly visual nature. Praz cites the example of Father Maximilian Van der Sandt whose sermons in their printed versions were decorated with emblems: the *Maria flos mysticus*[69] around the theme of flowers, the *Maria, gemma mystica*[70] precious stones and the *Aviariam marianum*[71] birds (195).

In a similar vein Georg Stengel's egg-shaped *Ova Paschalia sacro emblemate inscripta descriptaque*[72] bears the physical form of the guiding metaphor. Antonius Wierix's *Cor Iesu amanti sacrum* (without place or date, but probably Antwerp circa 1586, and much imitated throughout the seventeenth century) was based on the theme of the heart. Ioannes David's *Duodecim specula* of 1610 presents the discovery of God through the theme of the mirror, and his *Typus occasionis* of 1605 tells the story of the personified figure of Occasion. In all likelihood Descartes was able to consult the emblem books of the Père David in the library at La Flèche.

In all of these cases, and many others like them, visual phenomena gave access to the invisible and divine. In the case of the "Speculum creaturarum," emblem 8 of David's *Duodecim specula* (figure 3), the process in operation is twofold. The emblem book's earthly theme, through which the work's spiritual message is presented, is that of the mirror. Furthermore the emblem in question describes the very process in action: a man and a woman look into a mirror in which are represented earthly phenomena; the sea, the sky, land, ships (thus the wind) and so on. These earthly phenomena allow the couple to see the work of God, the angels and the heavens in general. The divine is to be seen and understood in the form of God's creations on earth, these creations being a mirror through which the viewers can see God himself. At the same time the couple represents the reader and the mirror represents the emblem book, the *Duodecim specula*, that he is in the act of reading. To make things clear the image is glossed with the letters "A," "B" and "C" and summed up by the words "Invisibilium per visibilia contemplatio." The notion of the "contemplation of the invisible through the visible" summarises the image of the "Speculum creaturarum," the goal of the *Duodecim specula* as a whole and the general process of Jesuit emblematic rhetoric.

In the "Speculum creaturarum," as throughout the *Duodecim specula*, the relevance of the general field of reference—the mirror—is overtly specified in each instance by the addition of the gloss. Central to the second mirror emblem, the "Speculum fallax" ["The Deceptive Mirror"], is a large shining ball with which a fox plays joyfully. At this stage the possibilities of meaning are vast, but the title has already suggested notions of deceptiveness to the reader. The central position and size of the ball indicate that the deceptiveness is of importance. The gloss clarifies the image: "Mundus speculorum fallacium fallacissimum." The world, that is to say the centrally positioned ball, is the greatest of all deceivers. The full lesson the reader will then draw is that the affairs of this world are mere vanities compared, by implication, with the eternal truth of God's paradise. In the "Speculum fallax" physical phenomena to theological and not to metaphysical ends are used to present the deceptiveness of our earthly perception.

The use of the lettered gloss clearly indicates the way from the general message to the specific message. Other emblem books do not label the process as overtly, but they nonetheless largely follow the same method. To take the example of Corrozet's ivy emblem (figure 1), the initial possibilities of meaning based on the picture are manifold: the field of interest could be the tree, the ivy as evergreen, the ivy that climbs and so on. The title specifies the theme of ingratitude and the *subscriptio* adds the final precision, namely that the ungrateful ivy strangles its sustainer. The one hundred emblems of La Perrière's *Morosophie* follow a similar uniform pattern as far as the relationship between the image, the text and the message is concerned. Of the four lines of each quatrain, the first two describe the picture, whereas the last two draw the moral. It was obviously considered important for the reader to grasp this notion as the process is described twice in the introductory prefaces; once in the preface to Antoine de Bourbon,

> en chacun de noz Cent Emblemes Moraux du present œuvre i'ay encloz aux deux premiers vers Latins la description du portrait figuré, & aux deux vers suyvantz, le sens Allegoricque & Moral dudit pourtrait

and once in the final preface by Jacques de Maulevant,

> En tes escritz sont sentences subtiles,
> Et d'abondant cest œuvre as composé
> Tout par quatrains, et si bien disposé
> Qu'aux premiers vers descrite est la peincture
> Le sens moral aux derniers est posé.

As with Corrozet, La Perrière's pictures contain a vast field of possibilities. It is the first two lines of La Perrière's *quatrain* that will define the picture's particular interest. Even at this stage the directions the reader can take are multiple. The last two verses tell us how to apply the information of the first two lines. In other words, a general set of givens (the picture) is narrowed down to a specific set of givens (the first two lines), from which the conclusion is drawn (the moral).

Descartes was, in spite of his foresight, a man of his time, a man who expressed himself through the methods of his time, and specific to his upbringing. The general trends of Descartes's use of language bear the hallmarks of a Jesuit education of which effective expression constituted an essential part. The language of Jesuit emblematics was based upon concision, visual clarification of abstract notions and methodological construction allowing the neophyte to follow the process of enlightenment step by step. Much of the essence of this expression is summed up by the *subscriptio* of David's "Speculum creaturarum," "Invisibilium per visibilia contemplatio." A few years later Descartes was to note, along similar lines, that "Sensibilia apta concipiendis Olympicis."

Nonetheless, the common ground between Descartes's use of language and that of his educators should not overshadow their very different objectives. Lyons points tellingly to,

> the major disruptive force of images in general in the Cartesian system. They are combinations and hence confusions—things joined together. ("*Camera Obscura*," 187)

Although Descartes was firmly to reject confusion, he did so through the very medium of such images. Descartes was to use the same emblematic images as did the Jesuits, often in very much the same way, but in order to express completely different ideas.

Descartes's presentation of the example of the dreaming sleeper (*Discours*, 63-65) has certain points in common with the style of Jesuit rhetoric. This may seem strange in a context criticising those whose understanding of existence is bounded by the limitations of sensory perceptions:

> ils sont tellement accoutumés à ne rien considérer qu'en l'imaginant, qui est une façon de penser particulière pour les choses matérielles, que tout ce qui n'est pas imaginable leur semble n'être pas intelligible. Ce qui est assez manifeste de ce que même les philosophes tiennent pour maxime, dans les écoles, qu'il n'y a rien dans l'entendement qui n'ait premièrement été dans le sens. (63)

Descartes nonetheless goes on to present the intangible—that the doubt of metaphysical certainties such as the existence of God and of the soul is unfounded—through an example from everyday life—the dreaming sleeper—, thereby rendering the unimaginable imaginable:

> lorsqu'il est question d'une certitude métaphysique, on ne peut nier que ce ne soit assez de sujet, pour n'en être pas entièrement assuré, que d'avoir pris garde qu'on peut, en même façon, s'imaginer, étant endormi, qu'on a un autre corps, et qu'on voit d'autres astres, et une autre terre, sans qu'il en soit rien. Car, d'où sait-on que les pensées qui viennent en songe sont plutôt fausses que les autres, vu que souvent elles ne sont pas moins vives et expresses? Et que les meilleurs esprits y étudient tant qu'il leur plaira, je ne

crois pas qu'ils puissent donner aucune raison qui soit suffisante
pour ôter ce doute, s'ils ne présupposent l'existence de Dieu. (64)

The God to which Descartes refers is a perfect, abstract God the creator. Nowhere in Descartes's major writings does he refer to the Trinity, to Jesus, to the Holy Ghost or indeed to the God of any organised religion. The importance of this distinction becomes clear when we consider the meaning of the dreaming-sleeper image to those familiar with the emblematic language of Descartes's upbringing.

In the religious emblem books of the late sixteenth or early seventeenth centuries, the awakening from the dream invariably represents the awakening to Christ. Emblem 26 of Johann Mannich's *Sacra emblemata*[73] represents the dreamer as Evil, to be awakened by a dog. The moral of the emblem is that safety lies with the light of the Gospel: "…prehende / lucem Evangelii, sic bene tutus eris" ["…Seize / the light of the Gospel, thus you will be well safe"]. The fifty-seventh emblem of Georgette de Montenay's *Emblemes, ou devises chrestiennes* portrays sleep as ignorance compared with the knowledge of Christ. The moral, "Surge, illucescet tibi Christus" ["Arise, Christ will illuminate you"], tells of the awakening to Christ, as indeed the title suggests.

The reader of the seventeenth century would have been aware that Descartes's dreamer is a far cry from this tradition. The worries brought by sleep are metaphysical and can be overcome not by an awakening to Jesus but by the application of pure and simple reason: "Car enfin, soit que nous veillons, soit que nous dormions, nous ne devrons jamais laisser persuader qu'à l'évidence de notre raison" (65). What Descartes omits is, effectively, as important as what he does say. Descartes takes an image used by his forefathers, he appropriates it and uses it in an emblematic way very much in keeping with the style of his forefathers, but the message he presents is entirely different.

Descartes achieves the same sort of subversion by a passing reference to those who desire beyond their means. The context is that of the third of the provisional maxims, namely "de tâcher toujours plutôt à me vaincre que la fortune, et à changer mes désirs que l'ordre du monde" (53). Descartes advises the reader to achieve all that he can and to accept that the impossible is indeed impossible:

> et que faisant, comme on dit, pas davantage d'être sains, étant malades, ou d'être libres, étant en prison, que nous faisons maintenant d'avoir des corps d'une matière aussi peu corruptible que les diamants, ou des ailes pour voler comme les oiseaux. (54)

In the iconography of the time, wings were often used to represent the poet's genius striving for greater heights. A stone, representing earthly concerns and attached to the poet's foot, renders the wings useless. Andreas Alciato, Hadrianus Junius, Otto Van Veen and Gabriel Rollenhagen all composed emblems along these lines. Viewed in this tradition, Descartes's text is urging stoic acceptance rather than despair before the reality of the limitations to our aspirations. His is a practical and reasonable response to the situation.

The implications of this reasoned response carry added bite when one is aware of the usage of the theme of wings in religious emblem books. One particularly telling example is that of "Religio" as presented by Théodore de Bèze in emblem 39 of his *Icones*.[74] Along with the Bible held aloft, the figure's most distinctive feature is her giant pair of wings. The *subscriptio* explains: "Cur alata? homines doceo supra astra volare" ["Why wings? I teach men to fly above the stars"] (line 7).

To the reader for whom wings are associated with religion or faith in Christ, Descartes is effectively implying that trusting oneself to Jesus does no good when faced with practical difficulties. An open statement to this effect, or indeed to the effect that applied reason, rather than an awakening to Christ, is the best response to the uncertainties of the dreamer's sleep, would have incurred the censor's wrath. By playing upon layers of meaning known to his readers through the emblem literature of the time, Descartes is possibly suggesting a subversive meaning that he could not have expressed safely otherwise.

Another of the *Discours*'s passing images suggests the same sort of process at work. In reference to the execution of his theories expounded in the *Dioptrique*, Descartes states,

> je ne m'étonnerais pas moins, s'ils [his readers] rencontraient [would succeed] du premier coup, que si quelqu'un pouvait apprendre, en un jour, à jouer du luth excellement, par cela seul qu'on lui aurait donné de la tablature qui serait bonne. (95)

Descartes could have chosen any musical instrument, or he could have chosen not to specify. The choice of the lute was surely made in full awareness of the connotations it would suggest to his readers. Alciato presents the lute, accompanied by the title "Foedera," in order to symbolise harmony among men. La Perrière takes the notion a little further by suggesting that a people can be won over with sweet words akin to the sound of the lute softening the heart:

> Ainsi q'un Luc amollist plus le cœur
> Par sa douceur, qu'un son espouventable:
> Appaiser faut d'un peuple la fureur,
> Non par menace, ains par parolle affable. (*Morosophie*, Emblem 21)

In the same collection La Perrière also compares the tuning of the lute to acting for the public good:

> C'est bien en vain quand d'accorder poursuys
> Mon Luc, voyant que ie suys phrenetique:
> Si sot & fol en ma mayson ie suys,
> Seray ie sage au fait du bien publicque? (Emblem 36)

Pierre Coustau and Florent Schoonhoven both present the lute in terms of sociability. Coustau's *Pegma* presents the Aspedian lute-player as playing only for himself (60). As such he is "contra amicos nostrates" ["Against friends and countrymen"]. Schoonhoven[75] points out that "sibi soli canere odiosum est" ["It is despicable to play for oneself alone"] (Emblem 59). Jacob Cats's[76] religious lute emblem also plays upon the theme of sociability through the representation of harmony to be found in love or friendship with God (Emblem 43). Conversely, the lute with the broken string in Hans Holbein's *The Ambassadors*[77] of 1533 clearly represents the schism between the Catholic and Protestant churches at the time of the painting.

In short, emblem literature generally portrays the lute as a symbol of harmony in society; harmony through common accord or harmony from without through the love of God. Descartes's emphasis, however, is not on society, but on the individual. Indeed the individual following a method attentively, the "tablature," with the aim of learning. There is no notion of blind faith in a religious God or magical harmony within society. The instrument is to be learnt through perseverance and method.

The newness of Descartes's method is underlined by the rejection of themes commonly associated with the images he chooses. These themes would often, but not exclusively, have been presented to Descartes through the emblem literature of the time. However we should also remember that the images to which we have referred—the lute, the sleeper, wings—appear throughout works of the Renaissance, be they the books of Commonplaces, the blason-style poems, the "contes," or the "novels" of writers such as Rabelais. Emblematics represent a mentality encompassing many of the traits of Renaissance literature. The examples cited provide good examples of a general mode of thinking rather than individual and exceptional cases. The images employed by Alciato, Montenay, La Perrière and so on are typical of those of the developing forms of emblematics, and in many ways these forms are a typical expression of Renaissance mentality.

One such image common to Renaissance culture and used by Descartes, is that of the ship and its helmsman. The theme is age-old, but Descartes was nonetheless probably aware of some of its applications in emblem literature. These could range from the boat as the *res publica* to man's hope placed in God. Under the title of "La Chose publique" Corrozet, in his *Hecatomgraphie*, explains,

> Comme en la nef chascun s'applicque
> Faire l'office, ou il est mis:
> Tout ainsi en la republicque,
> Par degré plusieurs sont commis.

Montenay's Emblem 11 shows a pilgrim-like sailor in his ship:

> Du grand peril des vens et de la mer
> Cest homme a bien cognoissance tresclaire,
> Et ne crains point de se voir abismer,
> Puis que son Dieu l'adresse et luy esclaire.

> Nul, qui en Dieu remet tout son affaire,
> Ne se verra despourveu de secours.
> Mais cestui-la, qui fera le contraire,
> Sera confus par son propre recours.

The message of the helmsman trusting his ship as the believer trusts his faith is also that of Reusner's "Christus meum asylum" in his *Emblemata* of 1581:[78]

> Seu morior, seu vivo, meum est christus asylum:
> Fortunae Christus portus, et aura meae
> Ille meae mentis spes, et fiducia sola:
> Pendet ab hoc uno iam mea certa salus.
> Anchora sit fidei signum, sub imagine Christi:
> Sistere quae tutum littore sola potest.[79]

Like the lute, the boat tends to be an image of collective aspirations, either those of men working together or working with God or Christ. It is interesting therefore that Descartes should use the image (like that of the lute) on the individual level regarding the relationship of our body to our soul:

> J'avais décrit, après cela, l'âme raisonnable [...] et comment il ne suffit pas qu'elle soit logée dans le corps humain, ainsi qu'un pilote dans son navire, sinon peut-être pour mouvoir ses membres, mais qu'il est besoin qu'elle soit jointe et unie plus étroitement avec lui pour avoir, outre cela, des sentiments et des appétits semblables aux nôtres, et ainsi composer un vrai homme. (81)

The initial basis for comparison would be purely physical, that of the body containing the soul as a ship is a vessel for its pilot. Descartes had already made a mechanical comparison of the workings of the heart to the cogs and weights of a clock (74). Similarly, in the paragraph preceding the ship metaphor, he likens the bodies of animals to "une horloge, qui n'est composé que de roues et de ressorts" (80).

In the case of man's soul, Descartes rejects the mechanical metaphor: "il ne suffit pas qu'elle soit logée dans le corps humain, ainsi qu'un pilote en son navire." Man's soul is more complex than the robotic bodies of animals, thus the purely physical metaphor of the ship will not suffice. Whereas Descartes's predecessors had been ready to compare the mechanics of a ship with the miracle of salvation in Christ, or with human interaction within a society, Descartes's uses his rhetoric to emphasise the separation between the non-mechanical (the soul) and the purely mechanic (the body).

In all of these cases it becomes clear that Descartes's choice and presentation of images is far from original, but the use to which he puts them is. Indeed the very presentation of the images forms part of the logic of their argument, often in order to reject the precepts of those whose language Descartes is imitating. Descartes uses terms of reference that are familiar to his readers; in so doing he expresses a different level of meaning by association with the message his reader would expect. The modern reader can only fully understand Descartes's texts when aware of the references that he is contradicting or unexpectedly ignoring. In short, Descartes's use of language appears far more nuanced to the reader armed with the emblematic background that was second nature to the reader of the seventeenth century. In the final section of this chapter we shall demonstrate in greater detail how a knowledge of the emblematic cultural background of La Flèche can be applied at a precise textual level.

III C

"CEUX QUI SUIVENT MAINTENANT ARISTOTE ...SONT COMME LE LIERRE..."

In the sixth and final book of the *Discours* Descartes sums up his reasons for not publishing until then. In the book's sixth paragraph he warns that hearsay can distort and that only his direct words should be taken as his. He applies the same rule to the way in which the lost writings of the pre-Socratic school have been reported to modern man. Moving on to Aristotle, he states,

> et je m'assure que les plus passionnés de ceux qui suivent maintenant Aristote se croiraient heureux, s'ils avaient autant de connaissance de la nature qu'il en a eu, encore même que ce fût à condition qu'ils n'en auraient jamais d'avantage. Ils sont comme le lierre, qui ne tend point à monter plus haut que les arbres qui le soutiennent, et même souvent qui redescend, après qu'il est parvenu jusques à leur faîte; car il me semble aussi que ceux-là redescendent, c'est-à-dire se rendent en quelque façon moins savants que s'ils s'abstenaient d'étudier, lesquels, non contents de savoir tout ce qui est intelligiblement expliqué dans leur auteur, veulent, outre cela, y trouver la solution de plusieurs difficultés, dont il ne dit rien et auxquelles il n'a peut-être jamais pensé. (90)

Descartes then compares the schoolmen's use of obscure arguments to a blindman who fights in the dark; a clear and simple philosopher, admitting to only a few evident truths, would then throw light on such a battle. He continues with the suggestion that by following such simple steps as are outlined in the *Discours*, Descartes's reader could apply his method so as to allow him to make discoveries for himself. The section then explains that Descartes was publishing at that moment to avoid obtaining a bad reputation for himself and so as to invite objections. The book ends with a final reiteration of the importance of "bon sens" and a justification for the choice of writing in French.

Descartes's reference to ivy in which he compares those who comment endlessly on the writings of Aristotle to the ivy that climbs the tree but never reaches higher, is placed in the middle of the central and longest paragraph of the concluding book of the *Discours*. Furthermore the comment forms part of the transition from the past (not publishing/study in school) to the future (publishing/discovery via experimentation) in the same way that Descartes will provide the transition from a method of thinking rooted in the past—the confused commentaries of the schoolmen—to a philosophy aimed at constructing for the future.

A page or so earlier Descartes had referred to the debates in the schools of the time:

> Et je n'ai jamais remarqué non plus que, par le moyen des disputes qui se pratiquent dans les écoles, on ait découvert aucune vérité qu'on ignorât auparavant; car, pendant que chacun tâche de vaincre, on s'exerce bien plus à faire valoir la vraisemblance, qu'à peser les raisons de part et d'autre; et ceux qui ont été longtemps bons avocats ne sont pas pour cela, par après, meilleurs juges. (89)

These debates are presumably those to which the *Ratio studiorum*, the *De Ratione discendi et dociendi* and the *Lacrymæ collegii* refer. As we have seen, they often relied on the application and discussion of emblematics. Let us consider, therefore, the precise meaning of ivy in the language of these debates, that is to say the significance of ivy for someone sharing Descartes's cultural baggage.

As well as being a common motif in writings from the Ancients onwards, the ivy was a popular theme throughout the emblem literature that served as one of the rôle models for the classes of rhetoric and the "disputiones" at La Flèche. Particularly interesting is the polarity of the topos's meanings; the ivy portrayed alone or climbing a tree or a wall could represent alternatively true friendship, or at the other extreme, perfidious ingratitude. It will also be worth considering the parallel theme of the vine, often interchangeable with ivy by dint of their physical similarity; the vine, however, normally representing fertile union, lacks the negative connotations of ivy.

The 1546 edition of Alciato's *Emblematum libellus*[80] includes a series of emblems depicting plants and trees. The evergreen ivy, a gift from Bacchus to Osiris, is compared to the poets whose brow it crowns: both are pale (the poets from study), but both will boast glory flourishing for years to come. In a 1510 engraving by Nicoletto de Moderna, entitled *The Birth of Christ*,[81] ivy is shown as climbing a column whose base is engraved with the motto "virtus ascendit" ["Virtue Climbs"]. This example is typical of the emblematic word/text interaction often to be found in works of art at the time. The *Imago primi sæculi*, although postdating Descartes's years at La Flèche, gives us the supreme example of Jesuit emblem book mentality. In the section entitled "Societatis nascens" ["The Society at Birth"], under the theme of "Renovato votorum" ["Allegiance Reaffirmed"], the engraving of the ivy clinging to the oak is given the motto, "Nexus non sufficit unus" ["One Embrace is not Enough"]. The emblem compares love, whose fire must constantly be stoked, to the ivy that covers the tree with a thousand embraces. Finally the positive use of ivy in devices was also well-known and common. A typical example, that of the Cardinal de Lorraine's "Te stante virebo" ivy device (figure 2), appears in Paradin's 1557 *Devises héroïques* (72-73).[82]

In similar fashion, the vine came to be associated with fruitful union. Peter Demetz[83] points to the tradition of the vine representing sexual union as opposed to the barren, unproductive undertones sometimes associated with ivy. Emblems by Otto Van Veen and Daniel Heinsius show the vine representing love on a spiritual level even after death (Henkel and Schöne, column 260). Andrea Alciato, Juan de Borja and Joachim Camerarius are more general: their emblems all present the vine as friendship beyond death (Henkel and Schöne, column 259).[84]

Opposed to themes of lasting friendship or loyalty to one's sovereign are certain representations of the ivy in a negative context. Our study opened with the well-known example of the sixth emblem of Corrozet's *Hecatomgraphie* (figure 1). The ivy that climbs the tree in this case strangles its sustainer and thereby bears the title "Ingratitude." Similarly in Barthélemy Aneau's *Picta poesis* an engraving showing the ivy wrapped around the full length of a tree's trunk accompanies the *motto* "noxia copulatio" ["Destructive Embrace"] (53). The emblem in question equates the ivy's strangling embrace with destruction through lustfulness. La Perrière shows an ivy climbing a tree in number 82 of his *Théâtre des bons engins*. The accompanying dizain is typical of the negative ivy tradition:

>L'Arbre soustienne le lierre en ieunesse,
>Et l'entretient tousiours par son support:
>Mais le lierre estant creu l'arbre presse,
>Et si l'estrainct par lyaisons si fort,
>Qu'en peu de temps la rendu sec & mort
>Ung homme ingrat tousiours aussi meffait,
>A celuy la qui du bien luy à fait.
>Ingratitude est ainsi sans raison,
>Le lyonneau en fin celuy deffait
>Qui le nourrit & tient en sa maison.

The negative aspect of the topos also made its mark on devices. The Cardinal de Lorraine for one found himself open to enemy propaganda on account of his device. Russell quotes the following verses by a Protestant satirist: "Lyerre semble enrichir le mur et le tenir: / Mais en la fin il le fait en ruyne venir, / S'on ne l'arrache avant que dans la pierre il mine" (*Emblem and Device*, 71). Indeed in the 1614 edition of Paradin's *Devises héroïques*,[85] the following change had been noted and added to the commentary of the Cardinal's "Te stante virebo": "Il [the Cardinal] changea depuis d'ame *Ad hæsit anima mea post te*, prenant Dieu pour la Piramide" (94). If the ivy became less and less frequent as a subject for devices, it is precisely because, by the seventeenth century, it could no longer provide the unambiguous praise the bearer required.

The emblematics with which Descartes came into direct contact at La Flèche used the ivy and vine images in the positive sense. Let us reconsider two examples already cited in the opening section of this chapter. For the ceremony of the transfer of Henri IV's heart, the college had been decorated with a series of devices (figure 6) whose "explication" may also be found in *Série Qb 1*. Of these the fifth shows a tree supporting a vine with the motto, "amplificat, fulcit, tutatur et ornat." The "explication" tells us that this represents the fact that,

> Henri IV estoit le plus grand soutien de la famille Royale, et qu'il auroit tousjours contribué pendant sa vie a son éclat, à sa grandeur et a son elevation, ce qui doit d'autant plus faire regreter la perte de ce prince.

Again, it is interesting to note that this same device would later appear in Le Jay's *Le Triomphe de la religion sous Louis le Grand* of 1687. Furthermore it is perfectly in keeping with the tone of the ivy emblem of the 1640 *Imago primi sæculi*, cited above. Such repetition suggests the existence of a whole emblematic vocabulary in the Jesuit colleges. It is not a question of ad hoc images that would largely pass unnoticed, but rather a firmly-set canon that must have been well known to all involved in the movement.

The "Planche que les Iesuites ont fait graver a lhonneur du college de la Fleche" (figure 7, see also section A above) stands as a tribute to all that the college represents: the background gives us the physical aspect of the college buildings (in emblematic terms the college's "corps") whereas the allegorical foreground shows the college's aspirations and values (its "âme"). The central figure is Saint Louis, king of France from 1226 to 1270, to whom the college is dedicated. At his side are Henri IV, founder of the college, and Louis XIII, the reigning monarch. The angel on the left bearing the arms of Henri IV reiterates his importance, while the right-hand figure, dressed in the *fleur-de-lys* of France and the arrows of La Flèche, bears the IHS of the Jesuits, the crowned heart of Henri IV and an inscription referring to the light of Jesus. Below the four principal disciplines of the college, theology, philosophy, rhetoric and humanities, are portrayed through devices.

Of specific interest is the emblematic exchange between the principle protagonists who speak through the mottoes of devices. Saint Louis, in reference to the palm tree at his side, tells Louis XIII, "hinc daphnem palmis Ludovice marita": Louis should join his laurels to Saint Louis's palm, symbols of victories, thereby continuing the Jesuit's past tradition of honours on into the present. The laurels of Louis XIII are portrayed climbing the victorious palm tree of Saint Louis. However the young king's reply, "me stante vigebat," would indicate that he himself takes the rôle of the palm of victory, standing true and allowing the college's laurels to remain strong. Whatever the assignment of rôles, the reply reminds us of the "te stante virebo" of the well-known ivy device cited above. The immediate associations are therefore those of service and loyalty.

It is the ivy itself that forms the basis of the device created by Henri IV's reply to Saint Louis: "Dive tuis hederas appendit flexia palmis tu foveas" ["O Divine One may you allow the ivy of La Flèche to cling to your palm tree"]. Indeed the engraving shows the ivy of La Flèche clinging to the palm tree of Saint Louis. The accompanying text explains that Henri IV's statement is,

> pour marquer qu'il met Le College de La fleche sous La protection de ce saint monarque dont Les palmes, c'est a dire Les Victoires n'ont pas esté moins admirables que ses Vertus et que Les jesuites, et Leurs écoliers s'attacheront tousiours autant a son culte, que Le Lierre s'attache au palmier qui Le soutient.

Not only, therefore, does ivy play a central rôle in Jesuit emblematic expression, but the topos is moreover used to represent the college of La Flèche itself ("hederas...flexia"). As such the motif must have been pregnant with meaning for the college's students.

Bearing in mind the cultural background surrounding the ivy, let us return to book 6 of the *Discours de la méthode*. The section in question contains two indirect but clear references to the style of learning practised at La Flèche. First of all, in the second of the two passages cited above, Descartes states that he himself is the best critic of his own work and backs up his argument by referring to the "disputes qui se pratiquent dans les écoles." These presumably are the debates described throughout the *Ratio studiorum*. They were staged at regular intervals, as well as for special ceremonies, largely as a way of practising and improving the students' rhetorical expression. As Descartes had noticed, the debates were minimally concerned with the search for "truth." Competitors would compose emblems, enigmas or inscriptions simply to strengthen the effect of their argument.

In the following paragraph of the *Discours*, the one in which Descartes refers to the ivy, he criticises those who pass adverse judgement on the pre-Socratics even though their writings are lost to us. The introduction to the ivy comparison follows immediately, referring to those who comment endlessly on the writings of Aristotle. Such practices were precisely those followed at La Flèche and other schools like it. The *Ratio studiorum* constantly refers to the study of Aristotle, his texts being adapted to fit the study of rhetoric, philosophy or morality, according to the needs of the circumstances in question. Moreover the texts of Aristotle were to be carefully interpreted so that they would fit in with Jesuit beliefs. Students were even warned against non-Christian readings of his works: "Aristotalis interpretes male de Christiana religione meritos [...] caveat" ["one should beware of [...] interpretations of Aristotle that disserve the Christian faith"] ("Regulæ professoris philosophiae" § 9, § 3).

Two sections implicitly criticising the curriculum followed at Jesuit schools such as La Flèche are followed therefore by the introduction of a motif known to figure strongly in the emblematics of these institutions. Following a reference to the rhetorical debates practised in the schools and to the scholastic adaptation of the texts of Aristotle, the mention of ivy would surely have created associations appropriate to the context; the ivy of the colleges in question was the ivy of loyalty or even the "hederas flexia," the evergreen ivy that symbolised La Flèche itself.

Such associations result in initial contradictions; Descartes's text is implicitly critical of the Jesuit institutions, but it then evokes a theme normally resounding with praise for these same schools. The contradiction is resolved as the text advances; it is not the ivy of honour, friendship and support, but ivy in the negative sense of the theme, a "lierre, qui ne tend point à monter plus haut que les arbres qui le soutiennent." Descartes's comparison is effective, therefore, because it backs up the implicit criticism of the Jesuit schools precisely by throwing into question and undermining the values and symbolism dearest to them. Elsewhere Descartes goes to pains to express his admiration for and debt to his teachers and their learning: "j'étais en l'une des plus célèbres écoles de l'Europe, où je pensais qu'il devait y avoir de savants hommes, s'il y en avait en aucun endroit de la terre" (35). However, the precepts upon which they base their education—precepts rooted in the past—are those that should be questioned. In the *Discours* Descartes takes the framework of their learning, but he systematically questions its contents in order to go forward to a new future based upon his method. Ivy will provide the perfect metaphor for the expression of this process, but only to those aware of the theme's implications.

Descartes's use of ivy in the tradition of La Perrière and Corrozet represents first of all, therefore, a direct contradiction of the ivy image used in Jesuit emblematics at schools such as La Flèche. As such it is in keeping with the argument followed up to now, a criticism of purely rhetorical (as opposed to empirically scientific) debates and the scholastic commentaries that use such expression to distance the truths of the Ancients. Going beyond a straightforward statement of contradiction, we should now also consider the precise textual implications of the ivy as used by Descartes.

To go back to La Perrière and Corrozet, the ivy is found to strangle the tree that supports it. La Perrière's *dizain* has been cited above. It is worth reminding ourselves of the *subscriptio* of the *Hecatomgraphie*'s ivy emblem:

> Le l'hierre croist autour d'un arbre & monte
> Iusqu'au coupeau, & ta*n*t croist sa puissance
> Que celuy arbre il offusque & surmo*n*te
> Et en la fin luy porte grand nuissance.

Within the tradition the tree is sometimes replaced by a wall, for example in *dizain* 150 of Maurice Scève's *Délie*,[86] but the result is inevitably harm or death inflicted upon the sustainer. In Descartes's comparison, the sustainer is Aristotle, upon whom the endless scholastic commentators thrive. Descartes makes it clear that the commentators can climb no higher than their model, whereas he aims to go further, allowing mankind to make itself "maîtres et possesseurs de la Nature" (84). He is surely implying, however, that they are also killing off the value of the learning of the Ancients.

Placed in the context of the emblematic cultural background of the time, Descartes's reference to ivy is therefore heavy with meaning. It is a reference that expresses a great deal in a few words through the medium of a carefully chosen image. As such the ivy reference is a stylistic microcosm of the *Discours* as a whole:

in the *Discours* Descartes presents a whole new philosophy in the vehicle of just over sixty carefully-written pages. The ivy image uses the very cultural references of a system whose foundations he will throw into doubt, just as Descartes himself will work through and within the firmly established intellectual society of his time in order to promote the method that will undermine many of the same society's beliefs.

A final, somewhat more practical factor should also be considered: in the 1630s it was normal to present the writings of Aristotle as supporting the Christian cause. To suggest, on the contrary, that the teachings of the church schools were stifling the glories of Aristotle was risky business. Descartes opens book 6 of the *Discours* by referring to Galileo who in 1633 had been placed under close surveillance and forbidden to teach because he had published his support for Copernicus. The layers of meaning and possible emblematic implications of the ivy topos, however, allowed Descartes to express himself fully without risking the wrath of the censoring authorities.

The aim of this section has been to demonstrate how a knowledge of emblematics can allow us to appreciate possible layers of meaning within areas of Descartes's text—in this case his reference to ivy—that at first glance might have seemed quite straight-forward. Other possibilities surely exist. The triangle, for example, is used to represent the clearest and simplest of geometrical truths, and the starting point for a philosophical method based upon mathematical certainties (62-63). In the "Planche" representing La Flèche discussed in this section, however, it is the triangle that composes the device for theology. The accompanying text explains that,

> c'est La Theologie qui conduit Le plus seurement a La connoissance du mystere de la Trinité ainsi que des autres Les plus importans de La religion, ce qui doit faire regarder La Theologie comme La première, et La principale des sciences.

Could Descartes be using the triangle to contrast the certainties of mathematics with the mysteries of the "science" of theology? This, and other examples such as the pathway or imagery of light and darkness,[87] are there for scholars to explore.

***

Descartes's philosophical writings are profound enough to provoke discussion irrespective of changing cultural context. In a way, therefore, it is hardly surprising that his works have generally become the domain of students of pure philosophy. The finer points of Descartes's ontological and metaphysical arguments viewed purely per se continue to provoke lively discussion in which this study is not intended to participate.

Nonetheless much is to be gained by appreciating that Descartes was very much a man of his time. Initial surprise upon learning that the author of the *Meditationes* also analysed the workings of love, studied music and composed a ballet is lessened when we appreciate that pre-Revolution France did not compartmentalise and separate fields of learning as is the case today. The emblematic mentality was a product indicative of such interdisciplinarity. As we have stated, emblems and devices were important in Descartes's cultural upbringing.

Viewed in this way, other aspects of Descartes's writings take on new light. Descartes's classification through body and soul distinctions was in keeping not only with philosophical, metaphysical and moral treatises from the Middle Ages onwards, but these were also the very terms of literary expression. One of the main points of contention for theorists such as Menestrier and Perrault was the classification of the parts of the device into notions of the "âme" and "corps." Descartes was, therefore, using the terms of contemporary literary debate, but for different purposes.

Concluding consideration could be given to an area of Descartes's skills viewed by modern commentators as amongst the most important: the field of geometry, a domain that is in an essential way an emblematic discipline.[88] In general terms we might consider geometry as pictorial whereas algebra is more concerned with text, but as Boyce Gibson has pointed out,[89] "cette distinction nette entre l'algèbre et la géométrie n'existait pas dans l'esprit de Descartes" (390). A geometrical demonstration usually begins with a visual figure or *imago*. There is also an accompanying proposition—an element not unlike the *motto* of an emblem—that briefly points to the meaning and characteristics of the image. The proof then shows the reasoning that justifies the proposition, the parallel being with the emblem's *subscriptio*, the last piece in the tripartite whole. We have in effect a striking variation on the *visibilia/invisibilia* theme: the figure is intended precisely to evoke something that is a pure object of thought since the lines and triangles, the curves and circles of geometry do not exist either in the world or on the sheets of paper where they are drawn.

To appreciate and explore such nuances is to appreciate Descartes's art in context. Such awareness allows us to understand the true nature of his innovation on a general level, but also, on occasions, to grasp more clearly the full implications of specific textual references. Unlike the works of La Fontaine,[90] those of Descartes do not immediately strike the modern reader as being more accessible in the light of emblematics. This chapter has aimed to demonstrate that emblems and devices did form a part of Descartes's cultural background, and as such can facilitate any analysis of his works that is not purely structuralist.

NOTES

[1] I am particularly grateful to David Graham who suggested this chapter title, as well as those of Chapters IV, V and VI.

[2] For an explanation of the problem as well as of Descartes's solution, see J. F. Scott, *The Scientific Work of René Descartes: (1596-1650)* (London: Taylor and Francis, 1976), pages 97-100.

[3] Descartes's complete works are edited by Ch. Adam and P. Tannery in their twelve-volume *Œuvres de Descartes* (Paris: Vrin, 1964-76). More accessible is Ferdinand Alquié's three-volume *Œuvres philosophiques* (Paris: Garnier, 1963-73). This edition contains the main philosophical texts together with informative notes. Geneviève Rodis-Lewis's edition of the *Discours*

de la méthode includes a good biographical summary, general introduction and select bibliography. The source material for this biographical introduction to Descartes has been taken from the latter.

[4] *Romanic Review* 29 (1938), 212-42.

[5] *L'Esprit Créateur* 21.2 (1981), 37-47.

[6] Roger Lefèvre, *La Strucure du cartésianisme* (Lille: Publications de l'Université de Lille III, 1978) and Peter A. Schouls, *The Imposition of Method: A Study of Descartes and Locke* (Oxford: Clarendon Press, 1980) [Lyons's note].

[7] This process will be discussed further in section III B below.

[8] *Cartesian Linguistics: A Chapter in the History of Rationalistic Thought* (New York: Harper & Row, 1966).

[9] Some of the material from this section and from section III C is to appear in my "Jesuit Emblematics at La Flèche (Sarthe) and their Influence upon René Descartes," *The Jesuits and the Emblem Tradition*, eds. Marc Van Vaeck and John Manning (Turnhout: Brepols, 1999). I am grateful to Karel Porteman and to Marc Van Vaeck for their kind permission to republish this material.

[10] *La Vie de Monsieur Descartes*, 2 vols. (Paris: Daniel Horthemels, 1691). As a near contemporary (1649-1706) and first biographer of Descartes, Baillet provides us with an invaluable historical source.

[11] Descartes's education at La Flèche provides the general theme to *René Descartes (1596-1650): Célébrations nationales du quadricentenaire de sa naissance: Actes du colloque universitaire: La Formation de Descartes*, ed. Jean Petit (La Flèche: Prytanée National Militaire, 1997). For an overview specific to Descartes's education, see Geneviève Rodis-Lewis's chapter, "Un Elève du collège jésuite de La Flèche: René Descartes" (25-36). For an overview of Jesuit education, see Lucy Giard's contribution, "Le Système éducatif des jésuites à l'époque de Descartes" (199-225).

[12] F. Marchant de Burbure, *Essais historiques sur la ville et le college de La Flèche* (Angers: Veuve Pavie, 1803).

[13] See page 109 of Jules Clère, *Histoire de l'Ecole de La Flèche* (La Flèche: E. Jourdain, 1853).

[14] A recent visit has indicated that in the case of La Flèche further research into the college's library would be rewarding. An important number of the Prytanée National Militaire's books has been handed down from the Jesuits and a very brief inspection showed emblem literature, including the *Imago primi saeculi...* to be a feature. I am very much indebted to M. Jean-Claude Ménard for his help in this respect.

[15] There were three classes of Jesuit college, the distinction being made largely on the basis of size. The differences in the teaching curriculum at the large, medium and small colleges is outlined in the Bibliothèque nationale's ms. Latin 10 981. Camille de Rochemonteix has transcribed the text of this manuscript in Appendix 3 of volume 1 of his *Un College de Jesuites au XVIIe et XVIIIe siècles*, 4 vols. (Le Mans: Leguicheux, 1889).

[16] "Discussion and exercises will be arranged [. . .] on the interpretation of hieroglyphs, Pythagoran symbols, devices, adages, emblems and enigmas."

[17] "Indeed emblems and poems shall be openly gathered together over a period of days for the most popular to be chosen by two of the Rectors. All of them shall be read and the best selected."

[18] "In some cases they compose emblems and devices from certain fixed subject matter. In others they devise or solve inscriptions, diagrams or enigmas."

[19] Now known as the Eglise Saint Paul Saint Louis, rue Saint Antoine.

[20] The source for this and for the information on the heart's journey from Paris to La Flèche is the manuscript text accompanying an engraving entitled "Transport du coeur d'Henri IV au college des Iesuites de la Flèche Le 4 Juin 1610." This piece forms part of the Bibliothèque nationale (Département des estampes) *Série Qb 1 in folio* ("Histoire de France en estampes: 1610").

[21] This, and the quotations and information given in the three following paragraphs, are taken from the text accompanying an engraving entitled "1610: Devises du portail de l'eglise de la Flèche," which is also part of *Série Qb 1*. The title is in fact misleading; the text, cited below, makes it clear that the devices in question had in reality decorated the portal of the college of La Flèche. The engraving itself is reproduced in figure 5.

[22] *Le Mercure françois ou, la suitte de l'histoire de la paix: Commençant l'an MDCV pour suitte du Septenaire du D. Cayer, & finissant au Sacre du Tres-Chrestien Roy de France & de Navarre Loys XIII* (Paris: Jean Richer, 1619).

[23] *Annuæ litteræ Societatis Iesu Anni CI>. I>C. X. Ad Patres et fratres eiusdem societatis* (Dillingen: Veuve Ioannes Mayer, 1610).

[24] "It proved its grief by various debates and by emblems, by triumphal arches and by constructions labouriously put up at great cost."

[25] See the *Ratio studiorum*, "Regulæ Academiæ rhetorum et humanitarum," section 7, mentioned above. Certain of these "Devises de la Pompe funèbre d'Henri IV au Collège de la Flèche" form part of *Série Qb 1*. The engravings in question are reproduced in figure 6. It is also interesting to note that many of these exact same devices (e.g. "Frustra tentassent alii," "Quod contra superos extructa," "Amplificat, fulcit, tutatur et ornat," "Monstrant portumque viamque") are to be found in Gabriel-François Le Jay's *Le Triomphe de la religion sous Louis le Grand*, discussed briefly in the previous chapter. The fact that a series of devices could be reproduced and referred to in works separated by a span of seventy-seven years suggests that they were not fleeting compositions quickly forgotten. On the contrary, such an occurrence might indicate the existence of a canon of Jesuit devices to be used and reused, and known by all. I have provided brief analysis of this case in "The Use and Re-Use of Jesuit Emblematics in Seventeenth-Century France," forthcoming in *Emblematica*.

[26] *Annæ litteratæ Societatis Iesu, Anni CI>. I>C. XI. Ad Patres et fratres eiusdem societatis* (Dillingen: Melchior Algeyer, 1611).

[27] This description is of a memorial ceremony held a year later (discussed below), but we can assume that the events of 1610 were, for all intents and purposes, the same.

[28] The original text appears as follows: "Die altero et Lycæo & Academia prodeuntes periti & exercitati iuvenes de Philosophiæ parte cum laude responderunt. Post meridiem explicata in cœtu maximo quatuor ænigmata basi ingentis pyramidis ante ædes Patrum erectæ inscripta, non sine magna præsentium voluptate; cum omnes animadverterunt, arcanorum sensum ad ipsius Henrici laudem ingeniosem devolvi".

[29] "Regulæ Academiæ rhetorum et humanitarum," section 7 (quoted above).

[30] *In anniversarium Henrici Magni obitus diem lacrymæ collegii flexiensis regii societatis Iesu* ["*The Tears of the Royal Jesuit College of La Flèche to Mark the Anniversary of the Death of Henry the Great*"] (La Flèche: Rexe, 1611).

[31] The original text appears as follows: "singulis annis mos invaluit, ut superiores quatuor scholae, in quibus iuventus ad humanitatem informatur, certo quodam ac statuto die varias omnis generis scriptiones, Graecas, Latinas, astrictas, solutatasque numeris, Emblemata, Hieroglyphica, Aenigmata publice proponant affigant, partim ad civitatis illicium, partim & maxime ad incitamentum adolescentiae: Ad eam celebritatem quartus Iunii selectus est, idque annis consequentibus perpetuum futurum est in honorem Henrici Magni, quod ipse licet

[32] "Dies ille reliquus, totusque sequens partim in disceptatione Philosophicarum Thesium, partim in lectione scriptionum propalem affixerum, partim denique in explicatione ænigmatum magna ingeniorum & doctrine contentione consumptus est" (12).

[33] The "Lectori benevolo" points out that each class was assigned a part of the galleries to be decorated with their works (6).

[34] This was not the only anthology of students' work of this kind. See also, for example, the *Orationes variæ funebres latinæ et gallicæ, item Poemata in Depositione Corde Henrici Magni* (La Flèche: n.p., 1612), the *Flores mei fructus honoris et honestatis* (La Flèche: n.p., 1620) or the *Musæ Flexienses Ludovico XIII regi christianissimo justo pioque principi de rebellione et perfidia triumphanti canunt: Epicinium* (La Flèche: n.p., 1629), to name but three.

[35]   "To Henry the Great King of France and of Navarre
         To him who is strongest in virtue
         Most clement in piousness
         Most invincible in war
         Guardian of the religion of our ancestors
         Upholder of virtue and of letters
         Conqueror of enemies."

[36] For examples, see chapter II. Pierre Laurens in his *L'Abeille dans l'ambre: Célébration de l'épigramme alexandrine à la fin de la Renaissance* (Paris: Belles Lettres, 1989) gives further examples of such jetons and biographies, as well as an in-depth analysis of the dynamics of the epigram with respect to these and other emblematic forms (424-61).

[37] "De Henrici Magni fortuna emblema in quo varii depinguntur Heröes quorum licet infantia fuerat abiecta & a belluis aut volucribus educata tamen ad Regie magnitudinis fastigium aspirarunt ex quo deinde precipiti morte rapti fuerunt" ["Emblem on the fortune of Henry the Great in which various heroes are depicted; despite their childhood being taken away and despite them being brought up by beasts or birds, they nonetheless reached the heights of the king's magnanimity and so were snatched from imminent death"].

[38] "Embleme representant l'estat de la famille royale au temps du mariage du roy, et la victoire de l'amour sur le coeur de ce prince." This piece, again from *Série Qb 1*, shows Louis XIII as Jupiter and his queen as Junon being carried to the heavens in an eagle-drawn chariot. Various objects, such as a lightning bolt for power, or a sceptre for political force, represent the sovereigns' attributes. This "embleme" gives a good example of the *tableau allégorique* of the kind popular at La Flèche.

[39] Four such iconographical representations of the virtues—strength, justice, prudence and temperance—adorned the base of the monument for Henri's heart. The engraving of this monument is part of *Série Qb 1*.

[40] The sonnet appears as follows:
         La France avoit des-ia respandu tant de pleurs
         Pour la mort de son Roy, que l'Empire de l'onde
         Gros de flots ravageoit à la Terre ses fleurs
         D'un Deluge second menaçàt tout le monde,
         L'ors que l'Astre du iour, qui va faisant la ronde
         Autour de l'univers, meu des proches malheurs
         Qui hastoient devers nous leur course vagagabonde [sic]

> Luy parla de la sorte, au fort de ses douleurs.
> FRANCE, de qui les pleurs, pour la mort de ton Prince,
> Nuisent par leur excez à toute autre Province,
> Cesse de t'affliger sur son vuide tombeau,
> Car Dieu l'ayant tiré tout entier de la Terre,
> Au Ciel de Iupiter maintenant il esclaire,
> Pour servir aux mortels de cœleste flambeau.

[41] "Il aimait les vers beaucoup, plus que ne pourroient l'imaginer ceux qui ne le considèrent que comme un Philosophe qui auroit renoncé à la bagatelle. Il avoit même du talent pour la Poësie, aux douceurs de laquelle il a déclaré qu'il n'étoit pas insensible, & dont il a fait voir qu'il n'ignoroit pas les délicatesses" (Baillet 1: 19). See also William McStewart, "Descartes and Poetry."

[42] *Le Triomphe des Saints Ignace et François Xavier, au College Royal de la Flèche, contenant le Sommaire de ce qui s'y est est faicte, en la solemnité de leur canonization: Depuis le Dimanche 24 Juillet 1622 iusques au dernier jour dudit mois* (La Flèche: Louis Hebert, 1622).

[43] "Saint Ignatius Loyola
    The Wellbeing of the Students of Logic is Destined."

[44] "Ignatius, whether we believe that our well-being comes as a result of your name, or that your name is an omen for our well-being, the Students of Logic are fortunate to be favoured by divine will *numen* and by your name *nomen*."

[45] "Planche que les Iesuites ont fait graver a lhonneur du college de la Fleche sur sa fondation faite par Henri IV." This piece is also to be found in *Série Qb 1*.

[46] See section III C below for fuller discussion of this aspect of the "Planche."

[47] This device therefore has certain points in common with Descartes's philosophical writings; he too considers the physical sciences in works such as *La Dioptrique* or *Les Météores*, as well as the metaphysical in the *Meditationes*.

[48] The "devise" ("He lived well who lived well apart") is based upon Ovid, *Tristia*, III IV 25. Ovid's actual words are "Crede mihi, bene qui latuit bene vixit." It is interesting to note that Baillet's frontispiece consists of an engraving of Frans Hals's portrait of Descartes surmounted on a base bearing the words "bene vixit, bene qui latuit." A similar emblematic frontispiece opens the 1635 Camusat edition of Montaigne's *Essais*. In this case the author's portrait is accompanied by his well-known "Que sais-je?" device. The fact that Baillet, or at least his publisher, should use the same technique in reference to Descartes clearly situates him, albeit unconsciously, in the contemporary cultural context of representation through emblematics.

[49] The "devise" ("A terrible death waits for him / Who, too well-known to all / Dies without knowing himself") is taken from Seneca, *Thyestes*, lines 401-03.

[50] Although in the case of the second "devise" one might suggest that the *imago* is provided by the monkeys to which Descartes refers.

[51] Adam and Tannery give the *Cogitationes privatæ* on pages 213-19 of volume X.

[52] "huius scientiae nodis Gordiis noctes diesque irretiti."

[53] *Adagiorum opus* (Basle: Froben, 1528).

[54] On the similarities between Erasmus's works and those of emblem writers, see Jean-Michel Massing, "Erasmus and the Origin of the Emblem," *Abstracts* (Glasgow: Glasgow International Emblem Conference, 1990), 76. See also Irene M. Bergal, "Word and Picture: Erasmus' *Parabolae* in La Perrière's *Morosophie*," *Bibliothèque d'Humanisme et Renaissance* 47.1 (1985), 113-23. In his "Some Pedagogical Uses of the Emblem in Sixteenth- and Seventeenth-Century England," Ayers Bagley points to the emblematic contents of certain of Erasmus's *Colloquia* (45-50). In reference to *The Godly Feast*, for example, "Erasmus had his Eusebius

create a house and garden of devices and emblematic images" (11). The style of the *Colloquia* is also to be found in Descartes's *La Recherche de la verité par la lumière naturelle*, although the work's ideas are radically opposed to those of the Renaissance. *La Recherche de la verité*, an unfinished and posthumously published piece, takes the form of a philosophical discussion between Poliandre, Epistemon and Eudoxe. On the general relationship between the emblem and the epigram, Pierre Laurens should be consulted.

[55] "Just as the imagination uses figures in order to conceive bodily matters *corpora*, so the intellect uses certain sensory bodies in order to represent spiritual matters, such as the wind, the light: thus philosophising to a higher degree *altius philosophantes* we can raise the mind to the highest level by applying our intelligence *cogitatione*."

[56] "Matters that can be perceived by the senses *sensibilia* are suitable for conceiving of those of the heavens *Olympicis*: the wind signifies the spirit, movement with time signifies life, light signifies knowledge, heat signifies love, instantaneous activity signifies creation."

[57] Visual in so much as the direct effect can be perceived by the senses.

[58] See, for example, the full title of the Kerver 1543 edition of the *Hieroglyphics*: *De la signification des notes hiéroglyphiques des Ægyptiens, c'est à dire des figures par les quelles ilz escripvoient leurs mystères secretz et les choses sainctes et devines*.

[59] For painting imagery and the *Méditations*, see pages 189-93 of Lyons's "*Camera Obscura*: Image and Imagination in Descartes's *Méditations*."

[60] This calculation is based on a thematic survey of the emblems cited in Henkel and Schöne's *Emblemata*. As this work by no means covers all the works of the emblem-book corpus, the total is "at least" two-thirds.

[61] For a general survey and analysis of images of the painter in emblems, see Judith Dundas's "Emblems and the Art of Painting: *Pictura* and Purpose" in *Emblems and Art History*, eds. Alison Adams and Laurence Grove (Glasgow: Glasgow Emblem Studies, 1996), 69-96.

[62] I.e. as opposed to works such as the *Objections et réponses* in which he defends his ideas, or the appendices to the *Discours* (*La Géométrie*, *La Dioptrique* and *Les Météores*) in which he gives a practical demonstration of the ideas presented.

[63] See note 151 of section III A above for a translation.

[64] *L'Illusion chez Descartes: La Structure du discours cartésien* (Paris: Klincksieck, 1974).

[65] (Paris: G. Martin, 1687).

[66] "In short, Louis the Great extinguished Heresy by inspiring Piety, advancing Wisdom and crowning Joy. I shall tell you more about these three attributes, and pray your silence and kind attention."

[67] "Inspired with Piety, admonished with Wisdom and crowned by Joy, he crushed (heresy)."

[68] See "'Voiez icy en ceste histoire…': Cross-Reference, Self-Reference and Frame-Breaking in some French Emblems."

[69] (Mainz: G. Schonwetterus, 1629).

[70] (Mainz: J. T. Schonwetterus, 1631).

[71] (Mainz: J. T. Schonwetterus, 1627).

[72] (Munich: n.p., 1634).

[73] (Nuremberg: J. F. Sartorius, 1625).

[74] (Geneva: J. Laon, 1580).

[75] *Emblemata* (Gouda: Andreas Burier, 1618).

[76] *Proteus* (Rotterdam: Pieter Van Waesberge, 1627).

[77] (National Gallery, London).

[78] (Frankfurt: Joannus Feyer).

[79] "Whether I die or live, let Christ be my shelter:
Christ is the haven and guiding wind of my fortune
He is my hope, and only ally:
My true salvation depends upon him alone.
Let my anchor be the sign of faith in the image of Christ:
It alone can hold me in safe shores."

[80] (Venice: Aldus, 1546).

[81] (National Museum, Vienna).

[82] I cite further examples in my "Reading Scève's *Délie*: The Case of the Emblematic Ivy," *Emblematica* 6.1 (1992), 1-15. Of particular interest are Hampton Court Palace's *History of Abraham* tapestries in which centrally located ivy appears in all scenes whose main themes are victory and virtue.

[83] "The Elm and the Vine: Notes towards the History of a Marriage Topos," *Publications of the Modern Language Association* 73 (1958), 521-32.

[84] Emblem 41 of the *Morosophie*, however, gives us an interesting exception to the general trend. Here La Perrière promotes a cause that Descartes would surely have approved:
Laisser ne faut la Vigne en son ramage,
Sans la couper, quand est temps et saison:
Semblablement, tout engin trop volage
Faut reprimer et soumetre à raison.

[85] *Devises héroïques et emblêmes de M. Claude Paradin, reveuës & augmentées de moytie* (Paris: J. Millet, 1614).

[86] (Lyons: Sabon, 1544). A facsimile edition has been edited by D. Wilson (Menston: Scolar, 1972).

[87] For an introduction to the question of Descartes's light imagery, see Claire Gaudini, "La Lumière cartésienne: Métaphore et phénomène optique," *Biblio 17: Actes de New Orleans*, ed. Francis L. Lawrence (Paris: Biblio 17, 1982), 319-36.

[88] I am grateful to Hugh M. Davidson for these suggestions on the emblematic nature of geometry.
For a consideration of the way in which Descartes's philosophical method is underpinned by the principles of geometry, see Boyce Gibson, "La «Géométrie» de Descartes au point de vue de sa méthode," *Revue de Métaphysique et de Morale* 4 (1896), 386-98. Despite its age, this article still appears incisive and clear.

[89] See the preceding footnote for full reference.

[90] See chapter V.

IV
Tristan's Emblematic Sonnets[1]

Known chiefly for his plays, François Tristan L'Hermite du Solier (1601-1655) had for much of this century been classified through N.-M. Bernadin's label of "précurseur de Racine."[2] The greatest success was enjoyed by *La Mariane* (1636), a tragedy which provides a psychological portrait of Herod and his mixture of love and hate towards his wife. Tristan's other tragedies, such as *Panthée* (1639) and *La Mort de Senèque* (1644) were less successful, but *Le Parasite*, a comedy of 1654, played for some time.

In more recent years the worth of Tristan's lyric poetry has received greater recognition. His poetic *œuvre* is varied, ranging from commissioned love poetry—often strongly influenced by Petrarch and Marino—and weighty political pieces, to compositions of a more personal tone—of these "La Mer" and "Le Promenoir des deux amants" are most often cited—to short and witty libertine ballads or descriptions of places. In the latter category comes "La Maison d'Astrée," a mythical evocation of the château de Berny that provides the starting point for much of this chapter's analysis. Tristan's poetry is known through four main printed collections, although in all probability he composed the individual poems at different times and well before publication. *Les Plaintes d'Acante* appeared in 1633 followed by *Les Amours* (1638), *La Lyre* (1641) and finally *Les Vers héroïques* (1648).[3] Each collection is of a disparate nature, with a certain amount of overlap between their contents. Individual poems are also to be found in contemporary anthologies such as the *Recueil des plus beaux vers* (Paris, 1626-[27]), edited and published by Toussainct Du Bray, and *Les Muses illustres*,[4] or in copied manuscripts, including those of the *Recueil Conrart*.

Much of Tristan's life remains on the level of myth, partly self-styled through the colourful account of youthful adventures he gives in the *Page disgracié* (1642-43). He was born in La Marche (Limousin) of a noble but poor family and took the name of Tristan from an illustrious supposed ancestor. The poet spent much time in the service of Gaston, Duc d'Orléans and probably travelled widely throughout Europe. He was also to serve the Duchesse de Chaulnes and Henri de Guise, in whose *hôtel* he died. Tristan had been elected to the Académie Française in 1649.

Modern Tristan scholarship owes much to the pioneering *thèse* of N.-M. Bernadin, whose *l'homme et l'œuvre* style can still provide a largely reliable introduction to material forgotten in previous centuries, indeed Bernadin's numerous appendices reproduce 'lost' or little-known pieces by Tristan. Amédée Carriat has been at the heart of a resurgence of Tristan studies, his *Choix de pages*[5] providing a well-annotated anthology of the author's works. Carriat's *Tristan ou l'éloge d'un poète*[6] and Catherine Grisé's doctoral thesis, *The Poetry of Tristan L'Hermite*,[7] give an analytic overview of the poetic output. Tristan's work in general is explored by Claude Abraham's Twayne Master Series volume,[8] an indication in itself of the mainstream status Tristan has now achieved. Above all, for all aspects of modern Tristan scholarship, one should consult the yearly volumes of the *Cahiers Tristan L'Hermite* that Rougerie has published since 1979.

As with Descartes, but perhaps more surprisingly, little critical attention has been paid to the subject of Tristan and emblematics, although an important exception, Leonard Johnson's "*Amorum emblemata*: Tristan L'Hermite and the Emblematic Tradition"[9] will provide a starting point for some of this chapter's analysis. There is much to suggest that the critical neglect of Tristan's associations with emblematics is unfortunate. For example, Marin Le Roy de Gomberville's *Doctrine des mœurs*, to a large extent an adaptation of Van Veen's *Emblemata horatiana*, received Tristan's attention. The following dedicatory verse bears his name:

> Superbe galerie, où de grave stoïque
> Les austères leçons touchent si bien le sens,
> Tu n'as point de tableaux qui ne soient ravissants,
> Tu n'as point d'ornement qui ne soit magnifique.
>
> L'âme qui se promène en ta belle fabrique
> Cède sans résistance à tes attraits puissants,
> Où la philosophie en des dons si pressants
> Nous forme des vertus un concert harmonique.
>
> Mais encore qu'Horace ait illustré son nom,
> En relevant ici l'ouvrage de Zénon,
> Que le soldat barbare avait mis en poussière,
>
> Notre monarque à peine y verrait rien de beau,
> N'était que Gomberville avec tant de lumière
> A jeté de l'éclat dessus chaque tableau.

The tone has much in common with the following dedicatory verse to Jean Valdor's *Triomphes de Louis le Iuste*,[10] also by Tristan:

> Superbe Monumens d'un des plus grands Monarques
> Qui jamais triompha sur la Terre & sur l'Eau
> Chefs-d'œuvres d'un Burin qui du Temps & des Parques
> Depite noblement le Faux & le Cyseau.

> Merveilleux Mausolée où l'Art & la Nature
> En faveur de l'Histoire ont voulu s'assembler;
> Grands Tableaux ou l'Europe admire la Peinture
> Des celebres efforts qui la firent trembler.
>
> Le Temps, le Feu, le Fer, ont pû reduire en cendre,
> Et le nom de Lysipe & celuy d'Alexandre,
> Que dessus le Porphire on vit en lettre d'or.
>
> Mais en cette Sculpture à nulle autre seconde,
> Le nom du Grand LOVIS & celuy de Valdor,
> Ne craindront que le feu qui perdra tout le Monde.

Valdor's work is in the style of the biographical collections such as that of Vulson, to which we referred in chapter II. Various events of Louis XIII's reign are described—examples include "La Reddition de Caen," "Le Siege de La Rochelle" and "La Prise de Nancy"—with an accompanying engraving and a six-line verse. The volume also includes a long series of "Devises des Roys, Princes et Generaux d'Armées" by Henri Estienne, each series of three accompanied by explanatory text and portrait of the subject. Another main figure from the world of emblematics, the Père Le Moyne, provided a preliminary forty-four line poem, "A Louis le Iuste: Toujours Grand, Toujours Auguste, Toujours Victorieux." Returning to Tristan's verses, particularly interesting is the fact that in both this and the Gomberville case, the opening address—"Superbe galerie," "Superbes Monumens"—suggests that the poet views an emblem book (or similar publication) as a whole that supersedes its component parts.

In Tristan's *Amours* we find a six-line poem bearing the title "Pour mettre devant un livre d'Emblesmes d'amour":

> Pour Dieu ne lisez point icy;
> Clorinde l'unique soucy
> Des plus nobles cœurs de la terre:
> On ne void aux feillets suivans
> Que des preceptes d'une guerre
> Où vos yeux sont assez sçavants. (94)

The "livre d'Emblesmes" in question could feasibly be the work of Van Veen or Gomberville. In his *Vers héroïques* Tristan's "Sujet de la comédie des fleurs" tells of the wars and adventures of "le Lys," "la Rose" and "le Chardon," a clear play on the device-like symbols of France, England and Scotland.

Similarly, in the dedication "A Monseigneur le Duc d'Orleans" which precedes *La Mariane*,[11] Tristan states,

> L'Ange qui veille pour le salut de la France, & qui travaille si glo-
> rieusement pour sa prosperité, ne l'a pas encore conduite iusqu'à
> la grandeur où elle doit arriver. Si la IUSTICE & la PIETE, ac-
> compagnées de la VALEUR, ne promettent aux nobles projets du
> Roy, que des succez favorables, les limites de cet Estat
> s'estendront...

The emphasis upon "Iustice," "Piete" and "Valeur" coupled with the mention of an angel watching over France provide the mixture of motto and image akin to a possible device for the "nobles projets du Roy." Indeed it is even likely that Tristan is referring directly to a known device of the time.

The frontispiece to the 1645 edition of another play, *La Folie du sage*[12] (see figure 8) is also clearly emblematic: the *imago* shows corresponding attributes of the wise man and the fool, while the *motto*, "Non Procul," suggests the two are not dissimilar. The overall shape of the picture is reminiscent of the compasses used in Plantin's printer's device.

As well as citing emblem books or devices, many of Tristan's compositions play upon the general text/image interaction that was central to emblematics. In *La Carte du Royaume d'Amour*,[13] for example, the traveller encounters such places as "la grande Plaine d'Indiference," a "Hostellerie" called "Doux-Regard," and towns the likes of "Visite," "Soûpirs" and "feu declaré." Tristan provides in prose a similar creation to the schematisé "Carte de Tendre" of Madeleine de Scudéry's *Clélie*.[14] In both cases abstract emotions are personified thereby lending a pictorial quality to invisible phenomena.

More specifically, Tristan's *Plaintes d'Acante* open with a verse to be placed "Au dessus du Portrait de Sylvie," thereby requiring a mixture of image/*corps* and text/*âme* in order for the complete portrait to be achieved. Similar interaction between poetry and the plastic arts is at the base of such poems as "Sur une Statue de Didon" (*Les Amours*), "Pour un Petit Enfant de Marbre, qui tient un livre de musique devant un bain" and "Sur un Portrait" (both *Les Vers héroïques*).[15]

Jacques Thuillier in "Poètes et peintres au XVIIe siècle: L'Exemple de Tristan"[16] has pointed to the area of overlap that exists between visual and written arts with respect to Tristan's work. Thuillier examines the close ties the poet had with Laurent de La Hyre, Claude Mellan and Jacques Stella, all of whom composed frontispieces for his works. He refers to Tristan's compositions whose subject is painting and quotes his reference to *La Mariane* as a "peinture parlante" (13). Daniela Dalla Valle in "A Propos de *La Maison d'Astrée*"[17] analyses the overlap between the architecture of the château de Berny and the poetry of Tristan, but unfortunately she does not refer to Johnson's article and the Van Veen connection.

Whereas the previous chapter was broad in that it considered the wide subject of Descartes's education before analysing his works as a whole (but with emphasis on the *Discours*), this chapter has a single specific document—Glasgow University Library's SMAdd.392—as its starting point. Nonetheless the analysis of this one artifact will not only relate to the art of Tristan L'Hermite, but it will also lead to conclu-

Figure 8.   Frontispiece from Tristan L'Hermite, *La Folie du sage* (Paris: Toussaint Quinet, 1645).

sions concerning methods of reading in the seventeenth century and the influence thereupon of the emblematic mentality.

IV A
Glasgow University Library SMAdd.392

The volume now known as Glasgow University Library SMAdd.392 is an Otto Van Veen *Amorum emblemata* (Antwerp: Verdussen, 1608) onto which have been transcribed seventeenth-century manuscript additions, the majority of these being the work of Tristan L'Hermite. SMAdd.392 has been interleaved and it is these additional pages that bear most of the manuscripts. The book measures 20 by 16 cm and has 247 original numbered pages for 124 emblems with texts in Latin, Italian and French.[18] Watermarks indicate that the interleaved pages could have been added any time after 1625. As some of the interleaves are cropped it is clear that the book and its additional sheets had already been bound together prior to the present vellum binding, which probably dates from the mid to late seventeenth or eighteenth century.[19] There are manuscript additions on fifty-three pages and in at least two discernible hands. Although there are some prose additions, the majority are in verse and are somehow linked (generally thematically) to the love emblem nearest their transcription.

Little is known of the volume's provenance. It was acquired in the summer of 1997 from Maggs Bros. Ltd. of London with support from the National Museums of Scotland's National Fund for Acquisitions. Maggs in turn had purchased it from an English bookseller in whose possession the volume had been for many years, but little else is known.[20] Work by John Ashman, Glasgow University Library's conservator, in raising the initial pages that had been glued to the binding, revealed no further indication of provenance.

The main interest of SMAdd.392 lies in its manuscript additions and, specifically, their attribution in the majority of cases to Tristan L'Hermite. The first clue to Tristan's authorship is the signatures—"Tris," "Trist," "Tristan," "De Berny/Par Trist," "Trist$/En Berni," "Tris. en Bern," "De Bern. p. Tris," "Tristan dans les plaintes d'Acante"—that appear at various points.[21] The "De Berny/Par Trist" signatures point to the "Maison d'Astrée," a 410-line poem composed in celebration of the marquis de Puisieux's newly enlarged château at Berny, to the south of Paris. The poem first appeared in the *Vers héroïques* of 1648 (Paris: Loyson), but the note that follows the poem suggests the date of composition to be much earlier:

> Ce palais des Amours, qui est un des premiers ouvrages de l'autheur, n'est pas icy dans l'estat qu'il souhaiteroit, en ayant égaré quelques vers dans les voyages qu'il a faits hors du royaume. S'il peut un jour les recouvrer, vous aurez cette superbe maison mieux achevée. (187)

François Mansard enlarged the château in the 1620s, so we could tentatively attribute the poem to this period. Leonard Johnson in "*Amorum emblemata*: Tristan L'Hermite and the Emblematic Tradition" had suggested that certain verses of the "Maison d'Astrée" are descriptions of Van Veen's emblems. As these are the verses we find transcribed opposite the emblems in question in the SMAdd.392 copy, the discovery of the Glasgow manuscripts reconfirms Johnson's theories.

Of the other SMAdd.392 manuscripts in the same hand, nineteen are poems by Tristan that are also known in printed versions, namely the *Plaintes d'Acante* (1633), the *Amours* (1638) or both. In many cases there are interesting and previously unknown variants.[22] The remaining thirteen poems in this hand are hitherto unrecorded,[23] but their style and vocabulary would strongly suggest them to be the work of Tristan L'Hermite.

Given that analysis of the variants suggests the SMAdd.392 poems predate their printed versions, one hypothesis is that some of the verses were copied from a now-lost early manuscript or manuscripts.[24] It would seem logical to add the relevant sections of the "Maison d'Astrée" to the love emblems they describe; the fact that all of the transcribed poems link in some way to the juxtaposing emblem would point to a conscious continuation of this process. In certain cases the nature of the variants, the corrections or lacunae in the manuscript and the emblem-specific subject matter are such as to suggest we are witnessing the process of composition. A scribe could have been used, but it could equally be the handwriting of Tristan himself.

It is difficult to draw conclusions based on paleographic analysis as there are few pieces known to be in Tristan's hand and, furthermore, the SMAdd.392 autograph is typical of the early to mid seventeenth century. Apart from a few notorial signatures, the only known Tristan manuscript is a 1640 "Reçu" now in the Bibliothèque nationale de France (see figure 9).[25] On the basis of a comparison of this manuscript and photographs of SMAdd.392, Mme. Bléchet of the BnF's Département des Manuscrits felt that the two hands were quite possibly the same. Her colleague, M. Janin, was less sure. He however questioned the authenticity of the Paris manuscript: it belongs to a collection with little documented provenance and which includes many known forgeries. In addition the fact that a receipt be written on parchment is unusual. One possible scenario suggested is that the BnF piece would be a forgery based upon SMAdd.392, but this is of course highly speculative. Our conclusion must be that the predominant hand of SMAdd.392 could well be that of Tristan himself, but this cannot be proven through paleographic evidence.

The manuscripts of SMAdd.392 that are not in the 'Tristan hand' number two prose pieces and six poetic compositions, including three rondeaux. The latter have been identified as works of Vincent Voiture and Claude de Malleville that appear in the *Recueil de divers rondeaux*[26] of 1639. The non-Tristan poems (and the prose pieces) are not the object of this study and so would be a worthy subject for future research, but initial investigation points to a continued process of adaptation of text to emblem. The same is true of the prose piece facing page 102 ("Pour un plaisir mille douleurs") that does appear to be in the 'Tristan hand.' One piece, the misogynist invective of the preliminary pages—also in the 'Tristan hand'—defies classification!

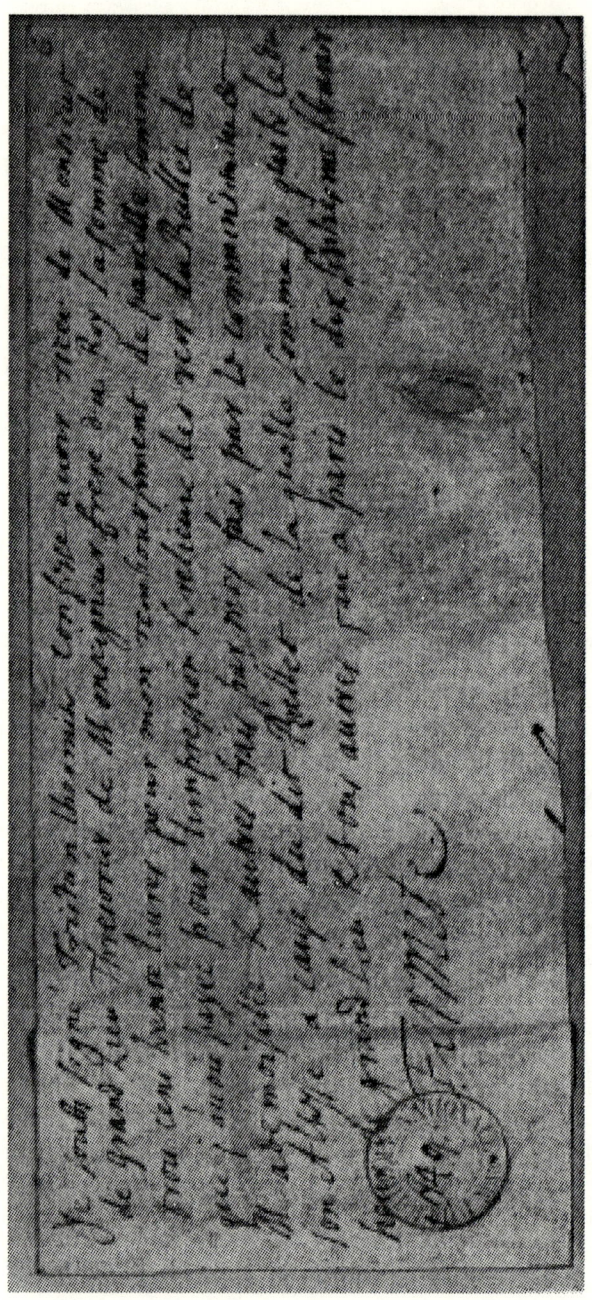

Figure 9. "Reçu" (thought to be in the hand of Tristan L'Hermite), Bibliothèque nationale de France (Département de Manuscrits, Cabinet des Titres), Pièces Originales 1711.

In the next section of this chapter I examine the possible circumstances of SMAdd.392's composition and place the work in the wider context of the emblematic reading practices of the Early Modern period. The study is by no means exhaustive, but is intended to raise questions central to an 'emblem-conscious' methodology of criticism, whilst providing an introduction to what could be one of the most important discoveries in the field of Tristan studies this century.

IV B

TRISTAN AND EMBLEMATIC READING PRACTICES

Alison Adams in her analysis of the 'Tristan hand' manuscripts[27] identifies four sets of poems: those that also appear as part of the "Maison d'Astrée," those of the *Plaintes d'Acante* of 1633, some of which were also to appear in the *Amours* (1638), those to be found in the *Amours* but not the *Plaintes*, and finally those thus far unidentified. By comparing the manuscript text with the printed versions Adams has demonstrated a process of refinement from the manuscript to the *Plaintes* and then to the *Amours*.

It is a process of refinement which, as Adams has mentioned, includes the adaptation of poems to context. In the case of the printed "Maison d'Astrée," for example, the winged cupids are the fantastic builders of the house in question, the château de Berny. They are introduced as follows:

> Ces admirables artisans,
> Dans le soin d'obeir à leur belle princesse,
> En tous mestiers se treuverent sçavans,
> Et de tous les costez travaillerent sans cesse.
> Lors on les veid se ralier
> Au plus magnifique atelier,
> D'où sortit jamais edifice,
> Apres s'estre obligez d'un serment solennel
> Chacun en son petit office
> De faire en un moment un ouvrage eternel. (174-75)

The poem goes on to tell of their work in the construction of the parterre, the entrance, the gardens and the canals. One of the cupids, "De qui Timante mesme eut apris la peinture" (line 162) decorates the house with his own image: "Cet Amour s'est dépeint en cent actes divers" (line 168). He paints himself and others of his ilk tending the flowers, sailing on the canal or hunting the stag. In these cases—to cite three of six possible examples—we recognise verses that refer to the emblems of Van Veen and have been added to the SMAdd.392 copy.

It is effectively through a process of editing that Tristan's poetry takes its defining stance. In the "Maison d'Astrée" Tristan has set the context for a hymn in praise of

Berny and to that end has created a complicated system of self-referentiality. The three levels—Van Veen's emblems, the paintings of the emblems that decorate the castle, and the cupid characters of the emblems that build the castle and in so doing produce the paintings of the emblems—have become entangled in a mythical circle of creation. With the exclusion of the lines cited above ("Ces admirables artisans...") and that of certain other passages, and the physical inclusion of the emblems, the poems sport a different, but equally valid, meaning. It is the selection and the bringing together of the parts that create the whole, just as an individual text and image are superseded by the emblem that results from their junction.

A closer study of the way in which the poems of SMAdd.392 are adapted to context can supply clues—or at least suggest possibilities—as to the method of the manuscripts' composition. In the case of those poems that also appear as part of the "Maison d'Astrée," the references to Van Veen, as Johnson had suggested, are direct and deliberate. For example, in the stanza that faces page 79, Van Veen's illustration (figure 10) of Cupid watering the plants is unmistakably described:

> Et la bas arosant des fleurs
> Afin que leurs viues couleurs
> S'augmentent par ce bon office;
> Il jnstruit mon Olinde auec cette action
> A me traiter sans artifice
> Montrant que la faueur acroist la passion.

Furthermore the content of Tristan's verse—love that grows as does a flower—is entirely in keeping with the theme of Van Veen's emblem, whose French text appears as follows:

> Arrousé i'augmente.
>
> l'On arrouse souuent de l'eau l'herbette tendre,
> A fin quelle s'aduance à croistre nuit, & jour:
> Par les douces faueurs s'accroist aussi l'Amour
> Qui le fruit à la fin de jouissance engendre.

Tristan has added an element of poetic personalisation in his reference to Olinde, but this changes little apart from giving a specific context to the general value of the emblem. Indeed the specific context effectively turns the emblem into a device, as Tristan will state explicitly in his poem facing page 71 of SMAdd.392.[28]

As stated, the textual evidence strongly suggests that Tristan had Van Veen's cupids in mind when composing his description of the château de Berny. One possibility would be that Tristan wrote the verses with the *Amorum emblemata* in mind and then later adapted them to the need for a description of the château de Berny. It seems more likely that the château would have been decorated with reproductions of the emblem book's engravings. We know that a frieze of the exploits of Henri IV deco-

Figure 10. "Arrousé i'augmente," from Otto Van Veen, *Amorum emblemata* (Antwerp: Verdussen, 1608).

rated the *grande gallerie* and that this provided the basis for stanzas 30-38 of the "Maison d'Astrée."[29] In the absence of further evidence we might conjecture that the lost interior decor included references to Van Veen. This hypothesis is supported by lines 165-68 of Tristan's text:

> Dedans le vuide des quarrez
> Qui sont en ces lambris dorez,
> Dont les chambres sont étofées,
> Cet Amour s'est dépeint en cent actes divers…. (179)

Whatever the circumstances of composition, once placed in the context of the château the cupids were to become those of the *planche* illustrating the "Maison d'Astrée" as it appeared in Tristan's 1662 *Poésies galantes et héroïques*[30] (see figure 11[31]). As Dalla Valle has pointed out, in this context the cupids are building "une espèce d'éden amoureux" so as to sing the praises of Charlotte d'Etampes-Valençay, wife of the castle's owner, the marquis de Puisieux. As such the poem fits a trend:

> C'était une mode littéraire étroitement liée à la construction, de plus en plus fréquente, de villas extra-urbaines de la part des seigneurs (de Florence, de Ferrare, de Mantoue...); mais l'exaltation se faisait en termes de transfiguration mythique et d'idéalisation, unissant—comme nous l'avons vu chez Tristan—la référence précise à la réalité avec le renvoi à un répertoire riche et varié de *topoi* suggestifs. (Dalla Valle, 34-35)

In the case of the manuscript poems that also appear in *Les Plaintes* and/or *Les Amours*, the process of composition and integration appears somewhat different. This is best illustrated through a specific example, the poem facing page 72 of SMAdd.392:

> Vous que l'ambition dispose a des effors
> Que n'oseroit tanter un courage vulguere,
> Et qui vous conduiriéz iusqu'au sejour des mortz
> Afin d'y rencontrer dequoy vous satisfaire.
>
> Vouléz vous butiner de plus riches tresors
> Que n'en ont tous les lieux que le soleil esclaire;
> Sans courir l'Ocean, n'y rauager ses bords,
> Venéz voir ma Maitresse & taschéz de luy plaire.
>
> Vous pourriéz asseruir s'il plaisoit au Destin
> Les climatz du couchant, les terres du matin,
> Et l'jsle dont la Rose est la Reyne de l'onde:

Figure 11. "Planche," from Tristan L'Hermite, *Poésies galantes et héroïques* (Paris: Loyson, 1662).

> Vous pourriéz conquerir l'Estat des fleurs de lys,
> Vous pourriéz imposer des loix a tout le monde,
> Mais tout cela vaut moins qu'un baiser de Philis.

The poem is addressed to a person of ambition who, according to Tristan, could conquer entire lands (e.g. England, line 11, France, line 12) but would still find Philis's disdain hard to overcome. The poem originally appeared in printed form in the *Plaintes d'Acante*, but was also to be included in *Les Amours*. In both cases the context is indicated by the title, "Aux Conquerants Ambitieux."

On one level the poem can be read in terms of the poet's self-glorification as he, unlike other potential suitors, has managed to please Philis, who is his "Maitresse." This viewpoint stresses the priceless nature of Philis's love by underlining the contrast between worldly and amorous conquests.[32] Alternatively, if we read "Maitresse" in the wider sense of 'loved one' (without guarantee that the love is reciprocated), the emphasis is on the antithesis between the greatness of worldly conquests and the lady's disdain, for which they are no match. In the printed versions one cannot even hope for a kiss: "Mais tout cela vaut moins qu'un regard de Philis."

Van Veen's emblem has the same subject matter but with a different angle of emphasis:

> Le ioug pour la franchise
>
> Cupidon le chappeau de liberté supprime,
> Et dresse en pied le joug, pour ses serfs assommer:
> Celuy qui sert l'Amour, libre on ne peut nommer,
> Ores que bien heureux bien souvent il s'estime.

The poet does not point to the stubbornness of one particular lady, but to the all-conquering nature of love in general. The central theme is that of love and conquest, but here love is the conqueror. In Tristan's poem the conqueror is conquered by love. The two pieces—Tristan's poem and Van Veen's emblem—complement each other through their sphere of overlap whilst nonetheless displaying different angles of approach. In the case of this version of Tristan's poem, the lack of title and the difference in the last line make the piece particularly suitable for the manuscript context of SMAdd.392.

A similar process is in evidence throughout the poems that we also know in printed versions. The poem facing page 47, like the emblem, discusses love about which the lover does not speak. However the emblem, "Plustot montrer que dire," emphasises true love as seen through reaction rather than discourse. The engraving 'enacts' the title with the cupid showing ("montrer") a picture of love (figure 12). The printed version of Tristan's poem bears the title "Respect tyrannique" and tells of the suffering of the suitor who tries to conceal his love. In the case of the emblem on pages 68-69, "Dont le cœur est plein la bouche parle," the common notion of 'love that hurts' links the distinct themes. Van Veen uses the image of a hand touching a

Figure 12.   "Plustot montrer que dire," from Otto Van Veen, *Amorum emblemata* (Antwerp: Verdussen, 1608).

wound as the mouth must tell of love. Again, the image 'enacts' the literal meaning. Tristan's version, with the printed title of "Plainte à l'amour," addresses Love directly so as to complain of the "eternel suplice" that the lady's disdain inflicts.[33]

In other cases the link clearly results from a process of adaptation, as in the manuscript facing pages 232-33. The emblem is entitled "Iusques à la fin" and states the commonplace that true love never dies. The manuscript bears the signature "Tristan dans les plaintes d'Acante" and indeed gives stanzas 69, 70 and 72 of "Les Plaintes d'Acante." The theme, in keeping with the emblem's, is that of the poet's eternal love for Cloris. Stanza 71 has not been transcribed:

> Il ne m'est plus permis d'en faire moins de cas
> Quoy que de cet exces mon esprit aprehende;
> Et i'ay les sentimens tellement delicas
> Pour les soins qu'il faut qu'on luy rende,
> Que ie tiens qu'icy bas la gloire la plus grande
> Seroit celle de la servir
> Aussi parfaitement qu'elle m'a sçeu ravir. (115)

Its discussion of servitude strays from that of eternal love and so it does not fit Van Veen's context.

The engraving on page 87 gives a literal view of the emblem's "en jouant" theme: Cupid captures his prey when one least expects it (figure 13). The manuscript poem is the first four of fourteen stanzas from "Resolution d'aymer," which appeared in printed form in *Les Plaintes d'Acante* (pages 69-71 of Madeleine's edition) and in *Les Amours* (pages 37-39 of Camo's edition).[34] The first stanza does indeed fit the engraving, where we see a cupid resisting capture with his hands whilst his foot is already trapped:

> Puisqu'Amour en ses yeux ne peut eviter
> Je ne scaurois plus resister
> Car ie ne treuue pas de gloire a me deffendre
> Ny de honte a me rendre.

Yet after the evocation of the struggle between captivity and freedom, the extract refers to the specific case of the poet and Philis. If we assume that all of "Resolution d'aimer" had already been composed, it is not surprising that only four stanzas were transcribed to their alternate context.

A pictorial link joins the engraving on page 105 ("Resister à l'aborder") and the manuscript, whose title, when the poem appears in the *Plaintes* and the *Amours*, is "Inquietudes." We see a cupid pushed from a doorway as he brandishes a torch. The final stanza of the manuscript addresses "O Raison, celeste flambeau." In the case of page 149's poem, line 5, "Pres de moy la Discorde & l'infidelité," is out of place: neither allegorical figure is present in the emblem. Yet the opening line of the poem

Figure 13. "En jouant," from Otto Van Veen, *Amorum emblemata* (Antwerp: Verdussen, 1608).

fits the engraving (figure 14) appropriately: "Cette nuit en dormant d'un somme inquieté."

The pattern for the manuscript poems in cases where we know of a printed version other than the "Maison d'Astrée" is consistent: the poem invariably has a link with the emblem with which it is associated, although the link is often limited or tenuous. Examples include a shared general theme (e.g. love as everlasting) or a specific line or aspect of the poem (e.g. the light of reason). Examination of the stanzas chosen—as opposed to those left aside—in the case of longer printed works, and in many cases of variants between the manuscript and printed versions, would suggest a careful process of editing and adaptation. This process nonetheless has its limits: the manuscript poem is relevant to the emblem, but often it is contradictory or tangential. Furthermore the manuscript poem can refer to the emblem's picture, its text, or to the emblem as a whole, but no attempt has been made towards construction of an alternative emblem.

The poems in the 'Tristan hand' that we have not been able to locate in printed form are more problematic but perhaps more significant to the modern reader. In the following cases the style is akin to that of those poems for which we also have printed versions:[35]

> Facing p. 60: "O trop aueugle erreur! ô tourment indicible!..."
>
> Facing p. 61: "Philis vous avéz tort de rompre ainsy ma cheine..."
>
> Facing p. 73: "Amour scait fort bien reprimer..."
>
> Facing p. 103: "Que la grace d'Olinde a de trais rauissans!..."
>
> Facing p. 121: "Pour moy ie tiens a perfidie..."
>
> Facing p. 129: "Olimpe auecque ce poulet..."

In the above poems, as in almost all of the non-"Maison d'Astrée" poems that do appear in printed versions, the use of a specific addressee or the insistance on the first person presents a context other than that of the emblem and its conveyance of general truth. There is a link between the manuscript and the emblem, but on the whole it does not surpass that of a shared general theme.

In the case of "Olimpe auecque ce poulet..." the vocabulary is the same as that of certain verses, bearing Tristan's name, that first appeared in the *Recueil des plus beaux vers* (1626 [-27?]) published by Toussainct Du Bray. The SMAdd.392 poem facing page 129 reads as follows:

> *Olimpe avecque ce poulet*
> *Puisque vostre Esprit est auare*
> *Je vous enuoye un bracelet*

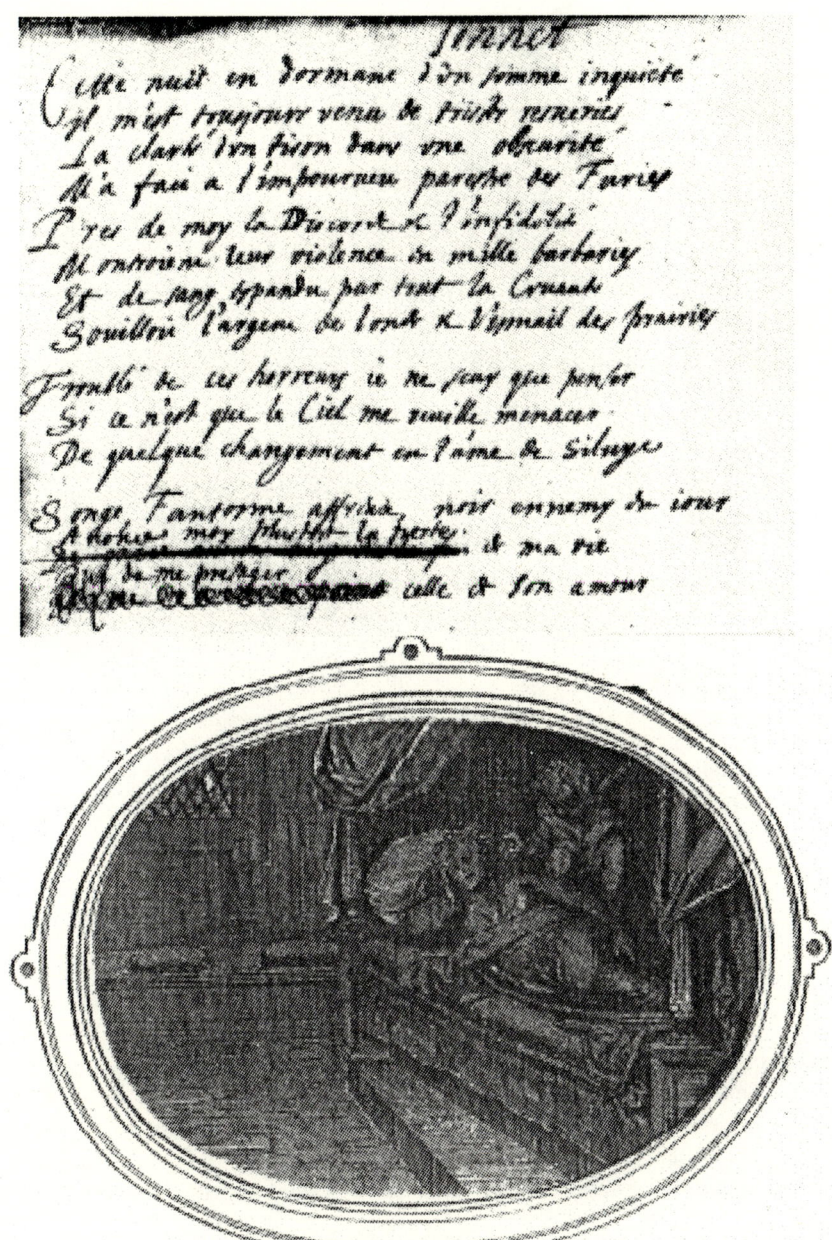

Figure 14.   "Cette nuit en dormant," from Glasgow University Library SMAdd.392 copy of Otto Van Veen, *Amorum emblemata* (Antwerp: Verdussen, 1608), with manuscript additions of verse by Tristan L'Hermite.

D'une Girassole asséz rare.
Je jure qu selon mon bien
Je ne vous refuseray rien
De ce que vous pourréz pretendre.
Dites ce que vous demandéz,
Mais ne me faite plus attendre
Les choses que vous me vandéz.

Jean-Pierre Chauveau gives the following reedition of the first two of Toussainct Du Bray's seven stanzas:[36]

Enfin guery de la folie
Qui me troubloit le sentiment,
Je me moque du changement,
Et des atraits de Pamphilie.
Enfin j'ay repris ma santé,
Mon esprit n'est plus enchanté,
J'ay brisé pour jamais ma chaisne:
Et ce perfide object qui juroit d'estre à moy
Me mettroit maintenant en peine,
S'il rentroit en humeur de me tenir sa foy.

Je m'en vais mettre dans la flamme,
Toutes les marques de mes vœux:
Tous ces nœuds, et tous ces cheveux,
Dont elle emprisonnoit mon ame.
Avec ces traistres bracelets,
La Masse de tous ces poulets,
Sera maintenant allumée;
Car c'est bien la raison, que pour ma liberté
J'en offre encore la fumée
A ce fresle Demon de la Legereté. (44)

The sections in italics (my own) point to the area of vocabulary overlap. Contextual evidence would therefore suggest that the two sets of verses might form part of a longer piece.

The following unpublished poems tell of general truths:

Facing p. 13: "Deux coeurs s'aymans parfaitement..."

Facing p. 29: "De mesme que le Cerf, blessé mortellement..."

Facing p. 33: "Celuy dont la vertu merita tant de Festes..."

These poems are entirely self-contained and they fit the context of the emblem, nonetheless we cannot assume that they were composed with the Van Veen emblem in mind. Many of Tristan's published poems were largely self-sufficient. One such example is "Les Perles ayment cherement" published in *Les Amours* with the title "Le Naturel d'amour." Its theme of love living on tears nonetheless works well in the context of Van Veen's "Amour sans pitié" (pages 162-63) opposite which it has been transcribed. In the case of the Hercules poem facing page 33,[37] the final reference to "un Enfant tout nu" directs the reader to the engravings of the *Amorum emblemata*. However a similar reference is also made by Tristan in the following verses published in *La Lyre*:

HERCULE FILANT

O Secret des Destins qui m'estoit incognu!
O puissance d'Amour fatale à ma memoire!
Ay-je en tant de combas remporté tant de gloire
Pour me voir desarmer par un Enfant tout nu?
Apres avoir estreint des Serpens effroyables,
Apres avoir dompté des Geants indomtables,
Ravagé les Enfers, & soustenu les Cieux;
Lors qu'il n'est point d'orgueil que ma valeur ne brave,
Je ne puis resister aux trais de deux beaux yeux;
Et je deviens en fin l'Esclave d'une Esclave. (193)

Two cases merit closer attention as the references to the emblem are however specific enough to suggest that composition could have taken place with the *Amorum emblemata* in mind. Firstly, let us consider the poem facing page 3, Van Veen's "Une Seule" emblem:

Quelqu'autre d'une humour commune,
Cherist tout ce qu'il void de beau,
Pour moy ie n'en veux aymer qu'une
Et L'adorer jusqu'au tombeau.
$
L'Eau qui se separe en sa source
Par deuers lits se conduisant;
Ne fait pas une longue cource,
Et se perd en se diuisant.
$
Ainsy la flame separée,
N'est jamais de longue durée;
Nous en voyons bien tost le bout:
Et pour dire ce qu'il m'en semble;

Aymer en diuers lieux ensemble,
C'est presque n'aymer rien du tout.

The poem requires or suggests no further context, and its guiding theme, that only one love exists, is that of the corresponding emblem (see figure 15). The engraving was well-known and frequently imitated, one such example being Jan Vermeer's *Lady Standing at the Virginals* (1670).[38] The reference to "L'Eau qui se separe en sa source" also brings to mind the stream that is clearly visible in the engraving.

In the case of the poem facing page 71, the emblem's title—"Loyal & secret"—appears to be the starting point for the manuscript addition:

Leale & secreto

Beauté la plus angelique
Qu'une Ame puisse adorer,
Vostre deuise me pique
Et m'oblige a soupirer.
O dieux! ie suis bien fidelle!
Je meurs pour une Cruelle
Et nul ne scait ma langueur.
De la Fidelité mesme,
Vostre deuise & mon coeur,
Pourroient bien faire un Emblesme.

Although the poem has the external context of the 'je' persona, the last two lines clarify the play between the poem's specific situation and the emblem's general import. Devoid of the Van Veen context this particular poem would lose a layer of meaning, the interplay between general truth and the specific cause of the poet's suffering. Given the added evidence of the title, which corresponds exactly to Van Veen's printed Italian title—perhaps a reference to the device's Italian-based beginnings—, it would seem that this poem was composed with Van Veen's emblem in mind.

Finally, in the case of the "Amours de Canante" (facing page 112) the gap in line 11, the various corrections and the sideways position of the last stanza due to lack of space would suggest that the poem is being composed on to the SMAdd.392 volume.[39] The fact that the concluding line—"D'un baiser qui soit humide"—fits the emblem's engraving perfectly (see figure 16) supports this hypothesis. It would also appear that the poem beginning "Philis pardonnéz moy si ie ne puis celer..." (facing page 145) is in this category. The title "Sonnet" would lead us to expect a fourteen-line verse, yet the poet has advanced no further than lines one to four (see figure 17).

Strong contextual evidence suggests therefore that the unidentified poems of SMAdd.392 that are in the 'Tristan hand' are indeed the work of Tristan L'Hermite. The style is that of Tristan, and in one case, "Olimpe auecque ce poulet...," so is the vocabulary. SMAdd.392's "Trist," "Trist en Berny" and "Tristan dans les plaintes d'Acante" 'signatures' are correct in cases of poems that are also known in printed

Figure 15. "Quelqu'autre d'une humour commyne," from Glasgow University Library SMAdd.392 copy of Otto Van Veen, *Amorum emblemata* (Antwerp: Verdussen, 1608), with manuscript additions of verse by Tristan L'Hermite.

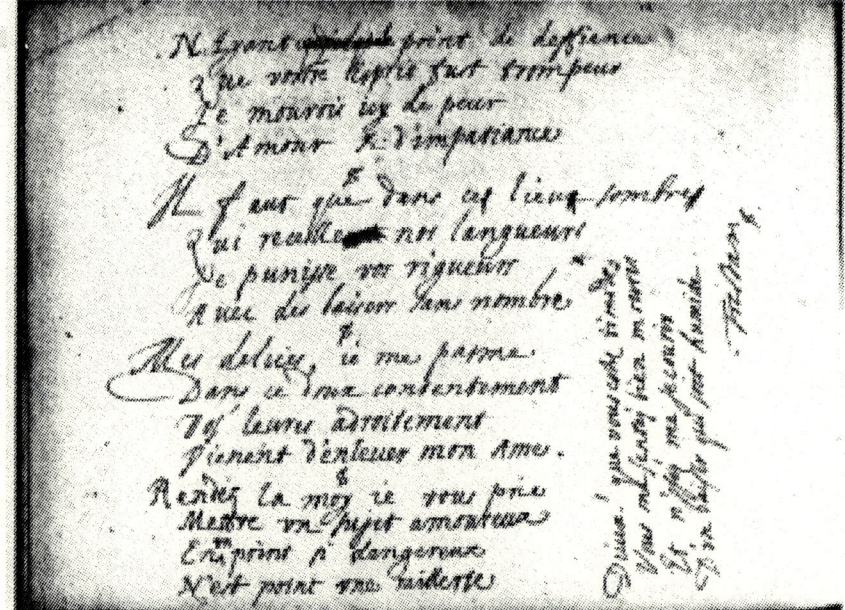

Figure 16. "Amours de Canante," from Glasgow University Library SMAdd.392 copy of Otto Van Veen, *Amorum emblemata* (Antwerp: Verdussen, 1608), with manuscript additions of verse by Tristan L'Hermite.

Figure 17. "Sonnet," from Glasgow University Library SMAdd.392 copy of Otto Van Veen, *Amorum emblemata* (Antwerp: Verdussen, 1608), with manuscript additions of verse by Tristan L'Hermite.

form, so we have no reason to believe them to be erroneous in other cases.

The origin of the unidentified poems must ultimately remain a question for conjecture, but again strong circumstantial evidence can provide the skeleton to a likely scenario. The poem beginning "Olimpe auecque ce poulet…" would appear to be part of a longer poem of which further verses are those edited by Jean-Pierre Chauveau (see above). The printed note at the end of the "Maison d'Astrée"[40] indicates the existence of a now lost text. The note explains that the "Maison d'Astrée" was one of Tristan's earlier works and indeed the date of construction of the château de Berny would place it in the 1620s-1630s. This would be in keeping with the description Tristan gives in the "Advertissement à qui lit" that preceeds the *Vers héroïques*: "ce sont quelques restes des feux volages de ma jeunesse" (35). Similarly the "Avertissement" to *Les Amours* explains that the collection's poems are of early composition: "Voicy des premieres productions de mon esprit, & des effets de ma jeunesse" (5).

Alison Adams's comparison of the printed and manuscript Tristan texts has suggested an evolution which would place the poems of the manuscript, the earliest of the versions, in the first third of the seventeenth century. It seems, therefore, that we have lost an early version (or versions) of certain Tristan texts, some of which could well be the previously unrecorded poems of SMAdd.392. One might conjecture—but it is purely conjecture—that the missing texts existed in the form of a manuscript, perhaps a *cahier*, composed during Tristan's early travels. Alternatively, they could be the "feuilles volantes" to which we are referred in the "Avertissement" to the *Vers héroïques*:

> Ce recueil de vers fait foy tout ensemble et du genie et de la negligence de l'autheur qui laissoit ensevelir dans la poudre de son cabinet beaucoup de productions d'esprit qui n'avoient point encore veu le jour, ou qui s'estoient seulement promenées chez ses amis particuliers en feuilles volantes. (34)

Analysis of SMAdd.392's watermarks permits the assertion that it was interleaved during or around the 1630s.[41] Such interleaving was not uncommon, especially with the aim of creating an *album amicorum*-style work. A parallel example exists in Oxford's Bodleian library: Douce V163 is a presentation copy, with additional drawings, of the 1608 *Amorum emblemata* which the engraver Cornelis Boel dedicated to Catharine Franqué.[42] A different example—but one that is nonetheless indicative of the general phenomenon—exists in the case of Van Veen's own *album amicorum*. The Brussels manuscript[43] consists of a number of poems, prose texts, paintings and emblems by and about Van Veen's friends and family. Van Veen's friends had written their own pieces and quoted relevant works from the Ancients in such a way as loosely to link the various paintings and writings to the theme of friendship, an obvious choice for an *album amicorum*.

SMAdd.392 is not an *album amicorum*, but it seems that an analogous process is at work. It would appear logical for the interleaved *Amorum emblemata* to bear the verses of the "Maison d'Astrée" that had been composed with Van Veen's work in mind. We can guess that the writers of the manuscript—quite possibly including Tristan himself—then continued the exercise by adding other poems, presumably taken from the conjectural lost manuscript(s), with the choice of text being directed in each instance by its appropriateness to the chosen Van Veen emblem. As we have seen, some pairings are more tenuous than others, but there is always some link. In cases where the manuscript is particularly appropriate, such as "Leale & secreto," it is possible that the poem had been composed specifically for the *Amorum emblemata*, or, if the hand is indeed Tristan's, for the SMAdd.392 copy. The same is true in the cases of poems that appear to be in the process of composition.

The existence of the non-Tristan hand(s) would suggest a continuation of the *album amicorum* process. Again, all of the texts, including the three rondeaux that can be identified as the work of Vincent Voiture and Claude de Malleville,[44] have links with the emblems to which they have been added. Significantly all three rondeaux appeared in the *Recueil de divers rondeaux* of 1639, suggesting that the writer, perhaps the new owner of what is now SMAdd.392, was using this volume as source material.

Evidently much of this analysis must remain as hypothesis. We cannot know for sure which of the hands was the first, nor, in the absence of further evidence, can the process of composition I have outlined be entirely proven. Nonetheless, beyond the questions of authorship and chronology of composition, the texts as they stand tell us much about Early Modern reading practices and norms of reception. In the case of all of the poems that exist in printed versions (and in the possible cases of hitherto unidentified poems whose original version has been lost) the change of context provided by the emblems significantly alters the way we see the poems. Stanzas that form part of a longer work, as in the "Plaintes d'Acante," become pieces in their own right when transferred to the SMAdd.392 context. In the case of the "Maison d'Astrée," texts that form part of a fantastic description and praise Berny's construction become mimetic and analytic when placed opposite the engravings to which they refer.

The adaptation of literature to context in this way is not a twentieth-century habit. Indeed academics are taken to task for quoting out of context: the 'cult of the author'—a notion rarely questioned until recently and still wholly prevalent in many quarters—requires that his or her original intentions be respected and the amalgamation of one person's writings into that of another is generally seen as plagiarism. Anthologies such as *Lagarde et Michard* carefully explain the original context of chosen extracts, and in any case such anthologies are often seen as an outdated injustice to the authors in question. In short, for many the original context of creation is an integral and almost inseparable part of a modern writer's *œuvre*.

Such has not always been the case. Medieval anthologies would adopt quotations to suitable contexts with little regard for original usage. Daniel Russell, in "Emblème et mentalité symbolique," has referred to the "redécouverte de la citation" (15) with regard to the Renaissance and it seems that such 'adaptation' existed throughout the Early Modern period. As late as 1739 Tristan's editor was 'correcting' his texts, as Jean-Pierre Chauveau has pointed out:[45]

Dans la *Préface* d'un *Choix de Poësies Morales et Chrétiennes* qu'il avait publié en 1739, Le Fort de La Morinière avait clairement exposé sa philosophie de l'édition: «Les vers, écrit-il, ne doivent point sentir le travail; et cependant ils ne sauroient être trop travaillés. En conséquence, on a cru devoir en retoucher plusieurs, qui, quoique assez beaux pour le sens, n'auroient pû passer faute d'être soutenus par l'expression. Cette liberté regarde, surtout, nos anciens Poëtes... Il est tel Poëme purement profane dans son origine, que l'on a rendu moral à la faveur de quelques pensées refonduës, et d'un petit nombre d'expressions dépaïsées...». (38)

The manuscript poems of SMAdd.392 are a clear instance of adaptation to the requirements of context playing as important a rôle as the original composition in the process of artistic creation.

Such adaptation to context was very much in keeping with the workings of the emblematic process of creation. By its very definition an emblem is the bringing together of disparate parts in the knowledge that the process of amalgamation will create a finished product that surpasses the sum of the individual elements. Even once created emblems would only gain their full sense in their application. As we have seen in the previous chapter, Jesuit emblems that were used in 1610 in mourning for Henri IV were, seventy-seven years later, adapted by Gabriel-François Le Jay in praise of Louis XIV's revocation of the edict of Nantes. The next chapter will include discussion of manuscript versions of the "Urit adorantem" sun device in the Bibliothèque de l'Arsenal's collections that could, depending on context, work in praise of Richelieu[46] or, alternatively, appear as part of pro-Fouquet propaganda.[47]

Although SMAdd.392 is not a political case, the evidence we have indicates that the poetry of Tristan L'Hermite functioned in much the same fashion: a poem could be equally valid as part of a poetic dedication to Cloris (on behalf of the Duc de Bouillon) in the "Plaintes d'Acante" or as a reinforcement of an emblem on the everlasting nature of love, one of a collection of emblems that include the subject of love as fickle.[48] Consistency as we might see it is not the main concern. What matters is not what the poet says, but how he says it. Furthermore, how he says what he says is very much dependent on the context in which his work is placed.

***

Although little work has been done on the subject, there is much to suggest that Tristan L'Hermite was a poet working within and through the emblematic tradition. Books of emblems and devices such as Gomberville's *Doctrine des mœurs* or Valdor's *Triomphes de Louis le Iuste* contain dedicatory verses by Tristan. He had also specifically composed a poem "Pour mettre devant un livre d'Emblesmes d'amour." Many of Tristan's poems, such as his "Au dessus du Portrait de Sylvie," play upon the interaction between the written word and the visual arts that is also central to emblematics. In the case of one poem, the "Maison d'Astrée," Tristan's verses describe the emblems of Otto Van Veen's *Amorum emblemata*.

Glasgow University Library's SMAdd.392 is a 1608 edition of the *Amorum emblemata* onto which have been transcribed manuscript poems, including certain verses of the "Maison d'Astrée." The same hand has also transcribed other known poems by Tristan, often followed by a signature. In all cases, however, the transcribed poem is linked, generally thematically, to the emblem it now juxtaposes. In some cases the variants between the manuscript and the known printed versions suggest a process of conscious adaptation to the emblems of Van Veen. SMAdd.392 bears a further thirteen previously unknown poems in the Tristan hand. The discovery of these *inédits* represents an important find per se, but the volume as a whole confirms the place of Tristan's poetry within the cultural context of emblematics.

Above all, SMAdd.392 tells us much about the literary reading habits of the Emblematic Age. The manuscript poems have been adapted to the emblem book context, thereby giving a very different impression to that gleaned from the reading of a printed version: a poem that in printed form may represent an address to a specific lady, might, for example, be seen as a comment on the general nature of love when placed against an emblem on that subject. Final meaning is not given by the authority of the author, but by that of the context. The poems of SMAdd.392 form a whole with the printed verses and engravings of Van Veen's emblems, just as the coming together of *motto*, *imago* and *subscriptio* supersedes the individual status of the emblem's component parts.

In this case, the analysis of one specific document confirms the author's place within the culture of emblematics whilst allowing us to draw wider conclusions concerning the often intrinsically emblematic nature of literary production in the Early Modern period. By comparison, in the next chapter a wide range of artifacts—printed, manuscript, painted and architectural—representing leading social, political and artistic figures of the age, will allow us to draw conclusions relative to the emblematic nature of the work of one leading author.

Notes

[1] Much of my work on Tristan L'Hermite—the basis for this chapter—first appeared in *Emblems and the Manuscript Tradition* (Glasgow: Glasgow Emblem Studies, 1997), ed. Laurence Grove.

[2] N.-M. Bernadin, *Un Précurseur de Racine: Tristan L'Hermite, sieur du Solier (1601-1655): Sa Famille, sa vie, ses œuvres* (Paris: Picard, 1895).

[3] We have consulted the following modern editions, all of which have useful introductions and annotations: *Les Plaintes d'Acante et autres œuvres*, ed. Jacques Madeleine (Paris: Cornélie, 1909); *Les Amours et autres poésies choisies*, ed. Pierre Camo (Paris: Garnier, 1925); *La Lyre*, ed. Jean-Pierre Chauveau (Geneva: Droz, 1977); *Les Vers héroïques*, ed. Catherine Grisé (Geneva: Droz, 1967). Champion of Paris is to publish a multivolume edition of Tristan's *Œuvres complètes*, in which his poetry will be edited by Jean-Pierre Chauveau.

[4] Ed. François Colletet (Paris: Louis Chamhoudry, 1658).

[5] *Tristan L'Hermite: Choix de pages* (Limoges: Rougerie, 1960).
[6] (Limoges: Rougerie, 1955).
[7] (U. of Toronto, 1964).
[8] *Tristan L'Hermite* (Boston: Twayne, 1980).
[9] *Renaissance Quarterly* 21 (1968), 429-41.
[10] *Triomphes de Louis le Iuste, XIII du nom, avec des vers de MM. Beys et de Corneille* (Paris: Antoine Estienne, 1649).
[11] The edition consulted is that of 1645 (Paris: Augustin Courbé), but the dedication exists from the first edition of 1636. The text in question has no page numbers.
[12] (Paris: Toussaint Quinet).
[13] Bernadin, on page 621 of *Un Précurseur de Racine...*, attributes this work to Tristan. It first appeared in volume I of the four volume *Recueil de pièces en prose* (Paris: Charles de Sercy, 1658). The edition I have consulted is that of 1660 (Paris: Charles de Sercy) in which *La Carte du Royaume d'Amour* is to be found on pages 324-31.
[14] The "Carte de Tendre" will be discussed briefly in chapter VII.
[15] For a study of Tristan's imagery in "Sur un Portrait," see John Pedersen's "«Les Yeux de la pensée»: A Propos d'une métaphore," *Cahiers Tristan L'Hermite* 5 (1983), 25-29.
[16] *Cahiers Tristan L'Hermite* 6 (1984), 5-23.
[17] *Cahiers Tristan L'Hermite* 6 (1984), 31-37.
[18] For full bibliographical analysis, see Stephen Rawles, "The Bibliographical Context of Glasgow University Library SMAdd.392: A Preliminary Analysis" on pages 105-17 of *Emblems and the Manuscript Tradition*.
[19] I am grateful to Stephen Rawles for this information.
[20] I am grateful to David Weston, keeper of Glasgow University Library Special Collections, for this information, as well as for his help in general with the project.
[21] For their full context, see Alison Adams's complete transcription of the manuscripts (Appendix A).
[22] The relationship between the SMAdd.392 manuscripts and printed versions of the Tristan poems is analysed by Alison Adams in "Glasgow University Library SMAdd.392 and the Printed Versions of Tristan L'Hermite's Poetry" on pages 141-57 of *Emblems and the Manuscript Tradition*.
[23] Neither Amédée Carriat nor Jean-Pierre Chauveau had previously seen any of the poems in question. I am grateful to them both for their help and cooperation.
[24] Alison Adams and I expand upon this hypothesis in our articles in *Emblems and the Manuscript Tradition*. See also section B of this chapter.
[25] BnF Département des Manuscrits, Cabinet des Titres, Pièces Originales 1711. For an account of all known Tristan manuscripts, see Catherine Grisé's "Towards a New Biography of Tristan L'Hermite," *Revue de l'Université d'Ottawa* 36 (1966), 295-316. I am most grateful to Claude Abraham and to Jean-Pierre Chauveau for their help with the question of Tristan manuscripts.
[26] (Paris: Courbé).
[27] See Adams's article on the subject in *Emblems and the Manuscript Tradition*.
[28] This will be further discussed below.
[29] For further information on this subject, see Jacques Wilhelm's "Un Décor disparu: Les Peintures de la gallerie du château de Berny illustrant la vie d'Henri IV et la première année du règne de Louis XIII," *Bulletin de la Société de l'Histoire de l'Art Français* (1983), 29-45.
[30] (Paris: Loyson).
[31] The signature "F.C. fecit" indicates François Chauveau as the engraver. The *planche* ap-

pears to be an accurate representation of Berny's architecture as described by Jacques Wilhelm in "Un Décor disparu…"

[32] I am grateful to David Graham for having suggested this reading to me.

[33] The variants between the printed and manuscript versions would again suggest a certain amount of adaptation to context. For further analysis of these variants, see Alison Adams's work on the subject in *Emblems and the Manuscript Tradition*.

[34] In *Les Amours* the title is "Resolutions d'aymer."

[35] Alison Adams's full transcription of these poems is given in Appendix A.

[36] "Les Débuts poétiques de Tristan," *Cahiers Tristan L'Hermite* 5 (1983), 40-46. Chauveau also points out that Bernadin had published a version of the verses taken from a later (1638) volume.

[37] The full text appears as follows:

Celuy dont la vertu merita tant de Festes
Par des exploits si beaux et & si Labourieux
Qui fit mourir Anthée & fut victorieux
Du Geant a trois corps & de L'Hydre aux sept teste [*sic*]

Celuy de qui le bras a fait tant de conquestes
Et mis tant de Lauriers sur son front glorieux
Qui purgea l'uniuers de Monstres furieux
De Tirans inhumains & de cruelles Bestes

Celuy qui surmonta tant d'obstacles offers
Qui suporta le Ciel & forcea les Enfers
Tirant cerbere au iour en despit de sa rage

Lors qu'a ce point dhonneur il estoit paruenu
Et que tous les mortels admiroient son courage
Se laissa surmonter par un Enfant tout nu.

[38] (London, National Gallery). The painting on the wall behind the sitter is a clear reproduction of the cupid from Van Veen's emblem.

[39] This has been suggested by Alison Adams in her article in *Emblems and the Manuscript Tradition*.

[40] The note appeared with the poem in the *Vers héroïques* of 1648. See the preceding section of this chapter for its full text.

[41] I am grateful to Stephen Rawles for this information. See also his article in *Emblems and the Manuscript Tradition*.

[42] I am grateful to Karl-Josef Höltgen and to Ramona Fotiade for this information.

[43] The original is in the Bibliothèque Royale de Belgique, II 874. A facsimile edition also exists edited by J. Van den Gheyn (Brussels: Société des Bibliophiles, 1911).

[44] "Vous l'entendéz mieux que Je ne pensois…" (facing page 128) is by Voiture, "Pleurer et gesmir aysement…" (facing page 162) and "Tel q'un rocher dans lhumide element…" (facing page 226) are by Malleville. Full transcriptions are given in Appendix A.

[45] "L'Ode à Olympe: Est-elle de Tristan," *Cahiers Tristan L'Hermite* 1 (1979), 36-46.

[46] In the *Symblorum selectorum centuria*, Arsenal manuscript 1172.

[47] "Urit adorantem" is one of the "Devises galantes" of Piece number 102 of *Recueil Conrart* manuscript 5131.

[48] See, for example, pages 126-27, "Loing des yeux, loing du cœur."

V
EMBLEMATIC STRUCTURES IN THE WORK OF LA FONTAINE

Jean de La Fontaine (1621-1695) is best known for his *Fables* whose publication from 1667 onwards met with immediate success. The talent for reworking Æsop's animal tales befitted his rustic upbringing in the countryside of Château-Thierry, where his father was *Maître des eaux et forêts*. It was not until the 1640s that La Fontaine started to frequent the Parisian salon circles, especially that of Valentin Conrart, in the company of such friends as François de Maucroix, Paul Pellisson and François Charpentier. From the 1650s he was in contact with Nicolas Fouquet, Louis XIV's *Surintendant des finances*, and came to live under Fouquet's protection in his château at Vaux-le-Vicomte. It was during this period, naturally enough, that La Fontaine composed many of his pieces in favour of his protector, including the *Songe de Vaux*. After Fouquet's arrest in 1661, La Fontaine hoped and campaigned for his release. One such plea for clemency was his "Elégie pour M.F.," otherwise known as the "Elégie aux Nymphes de Vaux."

It was not until 1665 that La Fontaine's first major work, his *Contes et nouvelles en vers*, was published by Claude Barbin of Paris. In 1667 Barbin published the *Fables choisies mises en vers*; these correspond to books I to VI of modern editions. They were followed a year later by *Les Amours de Psyché*, although a manuscript version of the novel had previously been offered to Fouquet. The 1678-79 edition of the *Fables choisies mises en vers par M. de la Fontaine* added the fables classed as books VII to XI of modern editions. The majority of the remaining fables appeared separately, some read by La Fontaine to the Académie Française to which he had been elected in 1683, many appearing in the *Mercure galant*. The 1693 edition of the *Fables* contained a collection of these later pieces corresponding to the modern book XII. La Fontaine died in 1695 following an illness during which he was taken by religious fervour and disowned the *Contes*.[1]

Although La Fontaine frequented the society of such leading composers of devices as Charpentier and Perrault, he himself was not directly involved in the work of the *Petite académie*. Nonetheless, direct references to "devises" in the sense of 'mottoes,' are to be found throughout his work. Of these the best known is the conclusion to *Fable* I, XVI, "La Mort et le bucheron": "Plûtot souffrir que mourir, / C'est la devise des hommes" (50). Here La Fontaine points directly to a phenomenon—the moral of a fable serving as a device-style motto—that in practice exists throughout the *Fables*. A reference to a motto of a more optimistic nature comes in the *Conte* entitled "Paté d'Anguille." This story of a bon vivant is interlaced with the repeated phrase "Diversité, c'est ma devise." The opening four lines are a good example of its employ:

> Même beauté, tant soit exquise,
> Rassasie et soûle à la fin.
> Il me faut d'un et d'autre pain;
> Diversité, c'est ma devise. (310)

Other direct references to devices are to be found in the *Contes*. In "Le Faucon," for example, La Fontaine describes the trappings of Fédéric's entourage:

> Tant il [Fédéric's money] dura, le bal, la comédie
> Ne manqua point à cet heureux objet [Clitie]:
> De maints tournois elle fut le sujet;
> Faiseurs d'habits, et faiseurs de devises,
> Musiciens, gens du sacré vallon:
> Fédéric eut à sa table Apollon. (186)

La Fontaine is aware that as the rich suitor of Clitie, it is normal for Fédéric to employ "faiseurs de devises" as one might employ "faiseurs d'habits." One of the *Nouveaux contes*, "Janot et Catin," is presented by La Fontaine as being "en vieil style, à la manière du blason des fausses amours" (319). Although the poem does not include the lengthy physical description that characterised the sixteenth-century *blasons du corps*, the style and influence of this emblematic form are undoubtedly apparent.

Three poems intended to accompany portraits require the presence of the image for the text to be fully understood and vice versa. These poems are entitled "Pour le portrait de M. Bertin," "Pour M. Vandebruge" and "Pour le Portrait de Mezzetin." The latter reads as follows:

> Ici de Mezzetin, rare et nouveau Protée,
> La figure est représentée:
> La nature l'ayant pourvu
> Des dons de la métamorphose,
> Qui ne le voit pas n'a rien vu;
> Qui le voit a vu toute chose. (749)

Pierre Clarac points out that this verse is to be found beneath Corneille Vermaulen d'Anvers's engraving of Mezzetin's portrait (1066). Similarly La Fontaine's verses on M. Vandebruge accompany his portrait in a work entitled *Recueil des meilleurs dessins de Raymond La Fage, gravé par cinq des plus habiles graveurs*. As with Montaigne's "emblematisé" portrait and that of Descartes that features in Baillet's biography, the composition requires the presence of both text and image for its full sense to be grasped.

These direct references to devices or to text/image interaction confirm the assumption that La Fontaine, like any literary man of his time, was aware of the mentality behind the fashion for emblematics. La Fontaine's direct references to emblematics do not, however, need to be underlined as those of Descartes or Tristan perhaps do; whereas critics have, up to now, been largely unconcerned by the question of the influence of emblematics upon these authors, the same is not true in the case of La Fontaine.

A general overview of criticism on La Fontaine's *Fables* until 1991 has been provided by David Lee Rubin in the introduction to *A Pact with Silence* (xi-xvi). Rubin organises his survey thematically, quoting useful sources in the fields of historical approaches, stylistics, reader response and thematics. Many of these works on the *Fables*, and others on the wider corpus of La Fontaine's writings, explore questions relevant to the student of emblematics.

Richard Danner,[2] Jean-Pierre Collinet[3] and David Lee Rubin[4] explore the composition and arrangement of the *recueils* of fables, a subject also applicable to emblem books. Another common topic is that of illustration: in "The 1668 Edition of the *Fables*: An Iconographic Interpretation" Raymond LePage raises questions of text/image interaction with respect to François Chauveau's engravings. Questions of embedded allusion and influences are at the centre of discussions by Rubin[5] and Grimm.[6] Often, as shall be seen, the grasping of the allusion to an emblem book can provide the key to a deeper understanding of La Fontaine's works. Finally, for an invaluable historical analysis contextualising the broad base of the poet's work, Collinet's *Le Monde littéraire de La Fontaine* should be consulted.

Beyond such emblem-related themes, some critics have considered the specific question of La Fontaine and emblematics. In the 1950s Georges Couton dedicated the first half of his *La Poétique de La Fontaine*[7] to the subject of emblems as related to the *Fables*. He refers to Menestrier's definition and explanation of La Fontaine's work as corresponding to the genre of the emblem: Menestrier classes La Fontaine's *Fables* as emblems in the 1684 edition of his *Art des emblèmes* (27-29). Citing the example of "Les deux mulets" Menestrier explains that,

> Pour faire de cet Apologue un emblème régulier, il ne faut que peindre ces deux mulets, l'un couché par terre et blessé, après que les voleurs lui aient enlevé sa charge, et l'autre chargé de son sac d'avoine, et d'ajouter ce Vers à la peinture
> Il n'est pas toujours bon d'avoir un haut Emploi. (28)

Menestrier continues with the example of *Fable* II, XIII, "L'Astrologue qui se laisse tomber dans un puits." Referring to the first four lines of the poem, he states,

> Les deux premiers font la peinture:
> Un astrologue un jour se laissa cheoir
> Au fond d'un puits. On lui dit, pauvre bête
> et les deux autres le mot et l'application des figures à la morale, qui

nous apprend de ne pas négliger ce qui est nécessaire pour notre conduite pour nous attacher à des choses qui sont au-dessus de nous. (29)

Couton, like LePage, also points out the importance of illustrations in the sixteenth- and seventeenth-century editions of the *Fables*. Couton also compares elements of certain of La Fontaine's fables to the "Discours moral" of an emblem. The majority of his twenty-page piece, however, is dedicated to establishing that a good number of the *Fables* share exactly the same theme as emblems by Alciato, Corrozet, Guéroult and Baudoin. In the notes to his 1962 edition of the *Fables*, Couton takes the bold step of suggesting that the emblems of these authors are possible sources for fables that had previously been attributed to the Ancients or to La Fontaine's invention.

Couton's *Écritures codées* includes a five-page section entitled "L'Emblème dans les fables de La Fontaine" (131-36), which, as he admits, is largely a summary of the 1956 piece. Couton does however draw a tentative conclusion at which he previously had only hinted:

Ces auteurs [of emblem books] nous apportent plus [than just identified sources to certain fables]: ils rendent compte de la structure de beaucoup de fables. [. . .] D'autre part, les descriptions de personnages, les croquis de paysages sont comme une illustration non gravée, mais écrite, insérée dans le texte, une illustration d'un admirable relief dans sa simplicité poétique. (135)

This notion, which Couton takes no further, will be explored in the second section of this chapter, with reference to works other than the *Fables*.

Margaret McGowan, in her "Moral Intention in the Fables of La Fontaine," is less concerned in identifying emblem-book sources of the *Fables*, but lends her attention rather to formal similarities to be found between the two. Her stated overall aim is a better understanding of the fables in context: "The Fables of La Fontaine can only be appreciated in their proper light, I feel, if we make some attempt to place them firmly in the tradition of rhetoric and poetics to which they belong" (265). As her title suggests, the central theme is that of moral intention in La Fontaine's writing as being linked to the important element of moral intention in the emblems upon which certain *Fables* are based.

Both literary forms, she points out, play upon the importance of the dual need to instruct and to please. This can, in part, account for the very layout of the early editions of the *Fables* and, specifically, for the fact that they were illustrated: "By the time La Fontaine came to publish his first book, through the influence of emblem and device books, the picture had acquired an automatic place in printed works of moral import" (271). McGowan goes on to outline the physical similarities between the emblem and the fable of La Fontaine: "So similar do the two forms appear that if one were simply to judge from the disposition of emblems and fables on the page of a printed work, it would be difficult to distinguish them" (268). Themes are also shared, and in both forms the moral is often presented in such a way that the reader must reach it by deduction.

McGowan's work complements and extends Couton's, allowing us to appreciate the truly significant influence of emblems upon La Fontaine's *Fables*. She stops short, however, of exploring exactly how the modern reader can better understand La Fontaine's texts in the light of the emblematic mentality. The same is true of Alain-Marie Bassy in his *Les Fables de La Fontaine: Quatre siècles d'illustration*:[8] he notes the links between the emblem forms and the *Fables*, specifically with reference to the question of the illustration in the case of the latter. He does not, however, analyse the reader of the emblematic age's approach to the *Fables* in the light of their need for illustration, nor does he question the motives behind the evolution of the fables' illustration (see section V B below).

More recently, Patrick Dandrey's "De l'Art des devises à la poétique de l'apologue: La Préface des *Fables* de La Fontaine (1668) à la lumière du traité des *Devises* du P. Le Moyne (1666)" explores certain elements of La Fontaine's 'manifesto' with reference to one of France's leading emblem theoreticians. The study does not imply that Le Moyne influenced La Fontaine directly, but it does place the fabulist in the same intellectual context as that of Le Moyne's treatise. In terms of structural composition, Dandrey emphasises the debt to emblem theory to be found in the preface's reference to the "corps" as the fable with the "âme" as the "moralité." The article goes on to tackle the problem of the contradiction between the need for brevity and La Fontaine's ornamental details. In similar fashion to McGowan, Dandrey concludes that the solution comes with the fables' "gaité," their mixture of light amidst the serious—with the *apologue* as a picturesque image—, a reference that also echoes Le Moyne's work. As the title suggests, Dandrey limits himself to the 1668 preface, with analysis of the fables themselves, or of any other of La Fontaine's works, clearly not being within his scope.

On the whole, however, the findings of these previous studies have done much to increase our awareness of the important links between emblematics and La Fontaine's *Fables*. As such they are useful and indeed convincing. The present study aims to suggest and demonstrate that further research still remains to be done. Our first section, based on precise examples taken from the *Fables* and from the emblems of Guillaume Guéroult, will suggest the extent to which Couton's work can be taken further. The *Premier livre des emblemes* provides not only the principal source for a few fables, but, moreover, single-line references throughout the *recueil* can only be seized by the reader armed with a knowledge of Guéroult's work.

The second section will consider broader questions: an understanding of the very nature of the emblematic mentality that pervades the *Fables* (a notion at which McGowan and Dandrey hint) could enable the modern reader to avoid falling into the trap of anachronistic readings. Furthermore, the type of analysis that can open up the *Fables* can also be applied to improve our understanding of other texts by La Fontaine. Critics have up to now ignored this last notion.

Our final section will also break entirely new ground by demonstrating that the emblematic mentality is present not only in La Fontaine's best-known texts, but that it also played a vital part in the communication of the society of which he was a part. Perhaps it is only when we grasp the wide scale of the emblematic influence that we can truly appreciate the fact that La Fontaine's works inevitably bear the hallmarks of a way of thinking that is largely lost to us today.

V. A.
LA FONTAINE AND GUÉROULT
FABLES OF INJUSTICE;
AN ANALYSIS OF THE DEPTH OF EMBLEMATIC INFLUENCE[9]

In the preface to the *second recueil* of the *Fables* (books 7-11 in modern editions) La Fontaine acknowledges his debt to Æsop and Pilpay before adding that "Quelques autres m'ont fourni des sujets assez heureux" (175). There is no shortage of critics—Georges Couton, Margaret McGowan, Alain-Marie Bassy and Jürgen Grimm are but four—ready to identify the "Quelques autres" as including Giovanni Mario Verdizotti, Gilles Corrozet, Andrea Alciato and Guillaume Guéroult. However in dealing with these sixteenth-century authors the critic will often limit his comments to the identification of a fable's modern source when it is not otherwise attributable to the ancients.

Our belief is that these "Quelques autres" play a much more complex rôle than has generally been acknowledged. Whereas Æsop and Pilpay are, in most cases, the ultimate central sources, Verdizotti, Haudent, Guéroult, and even Horapollo, are the less easily detected immediate sources; that is to say, the direct sources reflected in certain phrasings, often repeatedly when a fable's theme reoccurs within the collection, as opposed to entire narrated stories.

Certain themes that reoccur in a number of the fables also preoccupied authors of emblem books. This can best be shown through an analysis of one specific cycle of fables sharing such common links. Similarly, our comparison will largely be limited to examples taken from a single emblem writer. Our study will not therefore be exhaustive, but rather indicative of a general phenomenon.

The first question we should ask is why La Fontaine should refer to "quelques autres" rather than naming them directly. A normative judgement would suggest that such authors as Haudent and Guéroult are secondary writers not worth crediting. Moreover, as such they are authors who will not reflect well upon the poet who cites them and who should therefore be swept under the carpet with a quick "Quelques autres." Plagiarism was of less concern in the seventeenth century than it is now, but it was by no means acceptable. Antoine Furetière in his *Dictionnaire universel*[10] defines "plegiare" as applying to "Auteurs qui prennent effrontément les ouvrages d'autruy pour se les appliquer." He adds that Molière uses the term "en parlant de ces larrons de pensées et de livres." It does seem strange that La Fontaine should, if intending to deceive, risk passing for a "larron" when he willingly acknowledges the vast majority of his sources.

It is possible that the influence was of an unconscious nature, especially in cases where the model provides only a detail of phrasing or description; that is to say, cases in which La Fontaine takes only the moral, theme or select elements from an emblem, as opposed to the complete story itself. La Fontaine and his circles probably viewed authors such as Horapollo and Guéroult as being of secondary importance, if indeed they had not been forgotten. Horapollo, for example, was certainly treated with a lot less awe than had been the case a century earlier. His *Hieroglyphics* would, by La Fontaine's time, no longer have formed a direct part of the bank of elite intellectual culture, although, as Liselotte Dieckmann has pointed out in *Hieroglyphics: The History of a Literary Symbol*,[11] the work of intermediaries such as Caesare Ripa and Valeriano had become known. Similarly Guéroult's simple-to-read often amusing stories were out of fashion and little known. It seems most likely that it would have been considered unreasonable for the fabulist to seek out and acknowledge all references pertaining to an author as insignificant as Guéroult. In short, La Fontaine mentioned only his ancient models because those were the ones he was reworking. The rest was everyday material.[12]

Nonetheless La Fontaine's debt to Guéroult cannot be denied. Indeed he will be the author for our study. Other examples are of course possible (we shall refer on occasion to authors such as Verdizotti or Corrozet), and much research remains to be done on the subject, but Guéroult does appear to be a particularly good example of an emblem writer who exercised a considerable influence on the making of the *Fables*. Indeed, Couton, in the notes to his edition of the work, indicates four fables whose main source is Guéroult's *Premier livre des emblemes*. One clear-cut example, "Les Animaux malades de la peste" (*Fable* VII, I), is enough to confirm the debt beyond reasonable doubt, as we shall show later in the present section.[13]

It is not altogether surprising that La Fontaine should be familiar with Guéroult's work. A quick examination of the emblems of Guéroult as compared, for example, with the fables of Verdizotti, will show how close the two forms had become, even by the middle of the sixteenth century. Indeed the works of emblem writers were often included in the same volume as collections of fables. Even if we disregard the general popularity of emblems in their own right, La Fontaine's erudition in respect to fables and related fields would have brought him into contact with them. Furthermore, in the case of Guéroult there is another link; his *Description des animaux*[14] and *Second livre de la description des animaux, contenant le blason des oyseaux*[15] made him a major source for animal lore, one that La Fontaine would have been likely to consult.

Much of Guéroult's life remains a mystery to twentieth-century scholars, but we do know that he was involved in the important quarrel between Michel Servet and Calvin. He was an important figure in the printing trade, as were his uncle Guillaume de Bose and his brother-in-law Balthazar Arnoullet. According to De Vaux de Lancy,[16] Guéroult published prolifically, on subjects ranging from the *Histoire des plantes* (1550) to a translation of *Narrations fabuleuses* (1558) and various religious works (for example *Chansons spirituelles* of 1548, *Psaulms de David traduits par Marot et*

Bèze of 1555, *Figures de la Bible* of 1564), the latter all reflecting his Protestant faith.

Guillaume Guéroult is a representative example of an emblem writer who influenced La Fontaine. The study of a representative cycle of the *Fables*, those concerned with the injustices of society, allows us to examine the specific nature of this influence. Our general method follows that of David Lee Rubin who has noted that,

> Whenever for thematic purposes the poet models the action or characterization of the apologues on the motifs of another work—literary or nor—the reader must recognize the source, make a mental inventory of the similarities and differences between earlier and later versions, and then infer the significance of these parallels and divergences. (*A Pact with Silence*, 34)

When dealing with the various injustices of society, La Fontaine's fables take one of two approaches: some offer a statement which generally presents the world, and specifically the court, as a corrupt place in which power and force hold sway over justice and reason. The tone of such a presentation ranges from cynicism to understanding to detached acceptance of the order of things. Alternatively, some of the fables offer a possible response for the reader faced with the injustices of society. La Fontaine generally advises us to be aware of the situation and to look after our own individual interests by whatever means. Our analysis will be limited to the former group of fables, La Fontaine's statement of the problem rather than his response to it.

Fable VII, I, "Les Animaux malades de la peste," represents one of the clearest cases of the influence of Guéroult's emblems upon La Fontaine. La Fontaine's main source is Guéroult's emblem 15 (see figure 18), which consists of a title ("Les Riches sont supportés & les povres oppressés") followed by a woodcut illustration and then a four-line poem summarising the emblem's theme:

> Du riche le forfait
> N'est point reputé vice,
> Si le povre mal fait:
> Mené est au supplice.

These elements are followed by a second title ("Fable moralle du Lyon du Loup & de L'asne") and then the main text which forms the basis for La Fontaine's fable. An illustration would often accompany La Fontaine's fable,[17] but the initial four-line poem is unique to Guéroult.

The two fables—"Les Animaux malades de la peste" and the "Fable moralle du Lyon du Loup & de L'asne"—tell basically the same story, although Guéroult's version is substantially longer (96 lines as opposed to La Fontaine's 64). Guéroult's rhymes are arranged in regular groups of four, whereas La Fontaine's rhyme scheme varies throughout the poem, changing to reflect the pace and tone of events described.

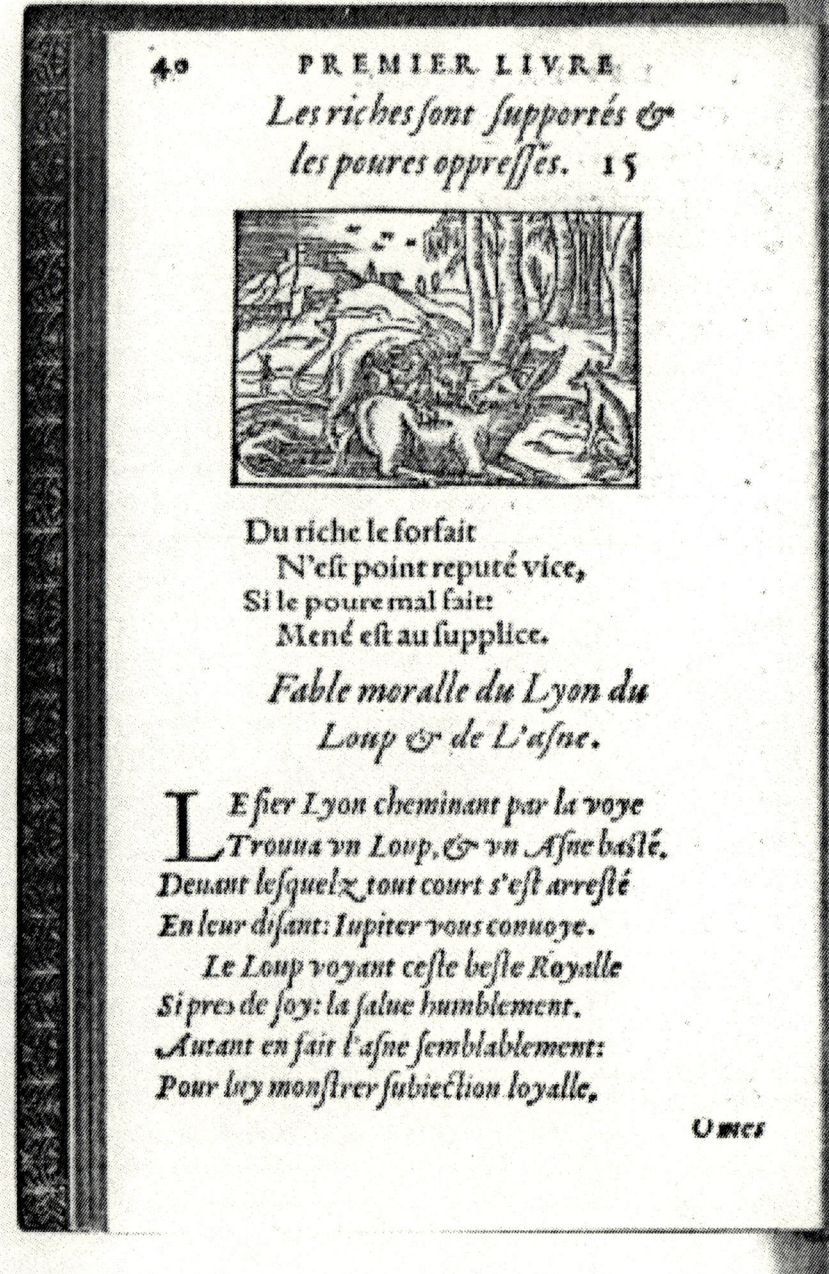

Figure 18. "Les Riches sont supportés & les povres oppressés," from Guillaume Guéroult, *Premier livre des emblemes* (Lyons: Balthazar Arnoullet, 1550).

The contents of the two poems can be summarised as follows:

La Fontaine lines		Guéroult lines
1-24	introduction and confession of sins suggested by lion	1-20
25-43	confession of lion absolved by wolf (Guér.) or fox (La F.)	21-36
44-48	confession of wolf absolved by lion (Guér.), confession of animals in general absolved by all (La F.)	37-52
49-54	confession of donkey	53-76
55-60	condemnation of donkey	77-88
61-62	killing of donkey	89-92
63-64	moral	93-96

The main differences between the two versions of the story are first the replacement of Guéroult's wolf by a fox and other animals in La Fontaine's version, and second the nature of the donkey's crime: eating grass in La Fontaine's text, eating the straw in his master's shoes according to Guéroult. La Fontaine also adds a brief element of religious satire by mentioning that a biblical-style plague provides the motive for the confession of sins.

Nonetheless, an examination of other fables shows that La Fontaine is closer to Guéroult's model than to any other. Æsop's story of the lion and the wild ass hunting together (*Fable* 21), Phaedrus's version entitled "Vacca, capella, ovis et leo" ["The cow, the goat, the sheep and the lion"] and Æsop's story of the partnership between the lion, the donkey and the fox (*Fable* 13) all revolve around the dividing up of prey. These tales correspond to La Fontaine's *Fable* I, VI, "La Génisse, la chèvre et la brebis, en société avec le lion." "Les Animaux malades de la peste," however, is a fable for which no direct source can be found in the writings of the ancients.

Verdizotti's "Il Leon, l'Asino, & la Volpe" ["The Lion, the Donkey and the Fox"] from his *Cento favole* of 1661[18] (147) has much in common with La Fontaine's "Les Animaux malades de la peste." The accompanying picture showing a donkey being devoured by a lion with a third animal (probably a wolf, but it could be taken for a fox) looking on, could, like the picture for Guéroult's emblem, easily be used to illustrate La Fontaine's fable. Often Verdizotti's verses and those of La Fontaine strike the same tone and use similar stylistic effects. Just as Verdizotti's unfortunate donkey is ironically accused "D'iniquata, d'inganno et di malitia" ["Of iniquity, of deception and of malice"] (line 13), so La Fontaine's is labelled "ce pelé, ce galeux, d'où venait tout leur mal" (line 58). Both authors heighten the irony of the situation's injustice by laying emphasis on the doing of justice! Verdizotti's lion states: "De l'Asino lo statio, e'l tristo fine / Dato m'ha de le leggi la dottrina" ["The doctrine of the law has given me the right to decide the Donkey's lot and his sorry fate"] (lines 31-32). Similarly La Fontaine's lion cries: "Car on doit souhaiter selon toute justice / Que le plus coupable périsse" (lines 32-33). Nonetheless Verdizotti's fable, like those of Æsop, centres essentially on the sharing of prey.

In fact, to the best of our knowledge, apart from Guéroult only Guillaume Haudent in *Les Apologues d'Esope*[19] gives us a story in which the donkey is condemned after a general confession of sins. The text in question is the 150-line "De la confession de l'asne du regnard & du loup" (number 40 of the "second livre"). In this version the wolf confesses at length to having eaten a family of pigs and is absolved by the fox for one pater noster. The fox, who ate the noisy cock and its hens, has to pay the penitence of three days without meat. The donkey, much abused by his master, admits to having eaten "deux ou trois brins d'estrain" from the latter's shoes. The wolf and the fox, shocked by the fact that the master could have died from cold feet, devour the donkey. Haudent concludes,

> Par la fable on voit qu'en leurs vices
> Souvent les grandz s'entre supportent
> Ou les petis souffrent & portent
> De leurs maulx peinnes & supplices. (lines 147-50)

The content of Haudent's fable may match La Fontaine's later version, but stylistically speaking the two authors are very different. Haudent lacks the concision La Fontaine, and to a lesser extent even Guéroult, will bring to the story. Furthermore Haudent's version is heavily marked by religious terminology—penitences and pater nosters—, an important element absent from Guéroult's and La Fontaine's versions.

This brief analysis of the various possible sources of La Fontaine's "Les Animaux malades de la peste" leaves us with two conclusions: first it becomes clear that the main source is, beyond any reasonable doubt, Guéroult's "Fable moralle du Lyon, du Loup & de L'asne." La Fontaine's final verses, "Selon que vous serez puissant ou misérable / Les jugements de cour vous rendront blanc ou noir" express the same notion, albeit a commonplace, as does the title of Guéroult's emblem: "Les riches sont supportés & les povres oppressés." Both versions revolve around a mock show of justice before the devouring of the donkey. Both involve the eating of shepherd and sheep by the lion, only for the sins to be excused because a king can do as he pleases. Guéroult's is the only version, ancient or modern, that contains all these elements later used by La Fontaine.

Secondly, our brief analysis has pointed to other authors very much in the same tradition as Guéroult: Verdizotti and Haudent, to whom we have referred, and Corrozet as well, all authored illustrated versions of Æsop's tales. Theirs was a tradition for which the boundary between an emblem, as in Guéroult's *Premier livre des emblemes*, and a fable, as in Corrozet's 1542 *Fables du très ancien Esope,*[20] was decidedly unclear. Rubin, in reference to La Fontaine and the fable, refers to "his systematic problematizing of the genre" (*A Pact with Silence*, 19). I would suggest that La Fontaine was only too aware of the problematisation he had already inherited through his choice of the medium of the fable. Barbara Tiemann has analysed the "Renaissance-Fabel" and the "Renaissance Moralistik," including such forms as hieroglyphs and epigrams, in her *Fabel und Emblem: Gilles Corrozet und die französische Renaissance-Fabel*.[21] Referring to Gilles Corrozet, she concludes that the fable and emblem "sind bei ihm eine Symbiose eingegangen" ["have through him fused into one"] (9). Corrozet is undoubtedly an important, but nonetheless not unique, example of an emblem writer in the tradition of the Renaissance fable.

Although critics have indeed acknowledged that La Fontaine did, on occasions, draw directly from this tradition, as in the case of "Les Animaux malades de la peste," modern scholars have not explored the possibility of a less direct but wider influence by writers such as Guéroult upon the collected *Fables* of La Fontaine; an influence in the way that any author is influenced by his cultural baggage. We often forget or overlook the fact that La Fontaine was as much indebted to the literary traditions of the Renaissance as to that of seventeenth-century Classicism, although he is invariably assigned to the latter. This question will be discussed further in the conclusion to the present chapter.

Let us return with this in mind to Guéroult's emblem 15, and its "Fable moralle du Lyon du Loup & de L'asne." The reader is immediately struck by the title that is juxtaposed with the image: "Les riches sont supportés & les povres oppressés." This concise phrase, with the striking opposition of the two rhyming words, "supportés" and "oppressés," enters easily into the reader's memory.[22] The wording of the title may not be very subtle, but, coupled with the picture, it ensures that the reader who has read the tale will have something by which to remember it.

In *Fable* I, X, "Le Loup et l'agneau," La Fontaine uses the same method with the same theme, but with a much more delicate turn of phrase. He opens his version of a well-known story with one of the most memorable verses of French literature, "La raison du plus fort est toujours la meilleure." La Fontaine's alexandrine is making the same point as Guéroult's title, but La Fontaine does it better. Guéroult uses an abstraction—"Les riches sont supportés & les povres oppressés"—which only takes on its full significance in the light of the example that will be given. La Fontaine gives us a paradox—after all "raison" and "plus fort" are often conflicting attributes—which only really becomes understandable when the story reveals the ironic use of "raison." Whatever the different stylistic approaches, we can note that in both cases the fable/emblem is headed by a short striking summary of the moral the tale will present.

La Fontaine could well have been attracted to Guéroult's work—and that of others in the same tradition—precisely because his titles created the sort of memorable impression that was such an essential part of the *Fables*. None of the direct sources from the ancients for "Le Loup et l'agneau" include a motto-like summary. Æsop (*Fable* 28) concludes with the cumbersome, "When a man is determined to get his knife into someone, he will turn a deaf ear to any plea, however just" (30). Phaedrus gives no moral.

Among the moderns, Haudent gives a four-line moral in the style of Æsop. Verdizotti concludes with a motto-like summary, "L'huomo possente, e rio, ragion non sente" ["The guilty man who is powerful does not listen to reason"] (183). This has the ironic notion of reason but does not underline the idea of the application of this "reason" by force upon the weak. Corrozet, however, gives his second fable a title which, like Guéroult's, summarises the tale succinctly and memorably: "Le mauvais cherche occasion de faire mal à l'innocent." However unlike Guéroult and La Fontaine's, Corrozet's comment is levelled at the individual, as opposed to forming an indictment upon society in general.

Such observations lead us to conclude, therefore, that La Fontaine's addition to Æsop's tale of a clever one-line summary, "la raison du plus fort est toujours la meilleure," represents an example of a technique used by writers in the emblem tradition—Verdizotti, Corrozet, and above all Guéroult. Viewing matters in this way, we can begin to see how emblem literature not only provided the subject matter for certain *Fables*, but more importantly, exercised a certain influence on La Fontaine's style.

"La raison du plus fort est toujours la meilleure" may be an outstanding example of La Fontaine's "motto-technique," but it is far from being unique. *Fable* X, X, "Les Poissons et le berger qui joue de la flute," tells the story of how Tircis is unable to entice the fish with his sweet song, but captures them easily with a net. La Fontaine compares the situation to a king trying to win the multitude over with reason. The final line of the poem, an alexandrine, summarises the moral of the story: "Servez vous de vos rets, la puissance fait tout."

Fable X, V, "Le Loup et les bergers," employs a variation on the same technique. Here the wolf, tired of being unpopular, tries to win favour with his traditional enemies by becoming a vegetarian. He changes his mind when he sees shepherds eating lamb. La Fontaine concludes with three memorable verses independent of the rest of the poem: "Bergers, bergers, le loup n'a tort / Que quand il n'est pas le plus fort: / Voulez-vous qu'il vive en hermite?" (lines 39-41). These lines evoke once again the theme of the poem that follows the picture of Guéroult's emblem 15: "Du riche le forfait / N'est point reputé vice." Moreover, La Fontaine's lines 39-40 are a direct reference to "Le Loup et l'agneau" where the wolf is "le plus fort" and in the right because "La raison du plus fort est toujours la meilleure."

Here it is interesting to note La Fontaine's technique of self-reference, his *clin d'œil* to the attentive reader. The poet creates the same playful effect in *Fable* II, XVI, "Le Corbeau voulant imiter l'aigle," when the crow tries to carry off a sheep, but is unsuccessful as, "La Moutonnière créature / Pesait plus qu'un fromage..." (lines 14-15). The reference is of course to *Fable* I, II, "Le Corbeau et le renard." Such echoes do not however imply the underlining of a previous message or moral stance. Quite the contrary. *Fable* I, X, "Le Loup et l'agneau," is marked by a tone of bitter cynicism summed up by the ironic statement that "La raison du plus fort est toujours la meilleure." In *Fable* X, V, we are induced to understand the wolf's point of view: "Voulez-vous qu'il vive en hermite?" Grimm analyses a similar process but with reference to different parts of the same fable:

> Un autre procédé, qui fait également partie des stratégies de désorientation, pourrait être qualifié par la notion de 'disproportion' entre 'le corps' et 'l'âme' de la fable, entre son récit et la moralité. La stratégie de La Fontaine, dans ce cas, consiste à orienter dans sa

> moralité finale l'attention du lecteur dans un sens tout autre que
> celui préparé ou provoqué par le récit. (185)

One of the fables he cites as examples is "Les Animaux malades de la peste."

Such contradictions are part of La Fontaine's complex view of the world. They indicate once again that in many ways La Fontaine's vision lacked the classical unity founded upon consistently followed method that critics have often labelled as the hallmark of the seventeenth century. Such consistency is lacking in the *recueils* of the *Fables*, as well as in Tristan's poetry within the context of the *Amorum emblemata*. Indeed, contradicting pieces within a single collection, be it of *contes*, chapters of Rabelais's 'novels' or of emblems, were very much a phenomenon of Renaissance literature.

The reader of the *Premier livre des emblemes* finds that the various emblems of the collection can refer to one another, especially through a common woodcut. Emblems 22 and 28, for example, have exactly the same engraving. Emblem 22, "Trop enquerre n'est pas bon," tells the story of an over-quizzical "enquesteur" whose investigations reveal his wife's unfaithfulness. Emblem 28, "En putain n'ha point de foy," presents a whore in a patrimony suit. The judge concludes by asking her to walk upon a bed of roses before telling her to "Monstre nous icy / L'aguillon seul qui t'a piquée ainsi"! The two stories alert us to the different angles of approach to the rather misogynous theme that questions should not be asked as far as women's love lives are concerned. The picture, showing an enthroned older man flanked to his left by a young woman and to his right by two young men, fits both stories equally well. In effect, the picture is like a commonplace around which different variations can be grouped. The repeated use of a single woodcut for more than one emblem may well have been a printer's expedient, but the end result was still the same.

Emblems 8, "Le Prince inique & le mauvais officier," and 20, "Le Tyrant & l'l'yvronge sont de semblable complection," also share the same engraving. Numbers 13 and 17 complement each other by their theme; thirteen, showing ants growing into elephants, has the title "Par concorde choses petites croissent." Seventeen, with its elephants becoming ants, tells us that "Discorde desole les royaumes & amoindrist les choses grandes."[23] Often the emblems of the collection are interlinked through common themes; those of hard work and God's will, for example, dominate emblems 4, 16, 23, 24 and 29. In the introduction Guéroult even claims that his unifying aim is to "enseigner la vertu." Nonetheless, one of the most noticeable characteristics of the *Premier livre des emblemes* is the fact that despite such interconnections, Guéroult makes no attempt to give his work thematic unity through a consistently upheld definition of "vertu" or of the path that leads to it.

We can see this if we briefly consider emblems 23/24 and 16. Emblem 23, based on the theme of a man digging for treasure, bears the title "Bien se doit acquerir par labeur." It tells how hard work bears the fruit of success. Emblem 24 is "Sur ce mesme propos." Surely the reader will not have forgotten the message of number 16, namely that "fortune favorise sans labeur." In a similar vein emblem 26 warns princes to avoid flatterers whereas numbers 21 and 11 are about tact and the need to flatter princes from time to time. The final emblem, number 29, tells at length the story of a "larron" who is saved by a divine vision from being crushed to death by a falling wall. The contradictory conclusion, that crime does not pay, is produced hastily and unconvincingly by the remark that God had evidently reserved for him "une mort plus cruelle." In this case Grimm's analysis of La Fontaine's work could apply just as well to that of Guéroult:

> dans bien des cas, la moralité est, pour La Fontaine, non pas tant un moyen de conclure que de détourner l'attention de la véritable substance de la fable sans pour autant en infirmer la validité. (187)

We can therefore conclude that even a work with a stated philosophical or moral aim (here, "enseigner la vertu") did not need to adhere to the presentation of a systematic doctrine. Such is a modern concern; Descartes's treatises on meteors, optics and geometry were all intended to demonstrate the method he had presented in the *Discours*; Camus's *Carnets* and short stories all support his philosophy of the Absurd; modern scholars, philosophers or politicians are taken to task if they openly contradict themselves. Such was not necessarily the case for writers of the Renaissance, particularly those of emblem books. No matter how uniformly moralising they might have appeared at first glance, emblem books were often a mosaic of all colours.[24] In short, the presentation of a coherent credo comes decidedly second to the desire for a collection of individual pieces (even if they are tenaciously linked) each presenting its own message in its own way.

This is surely the tradition with which we should associate La Fontaine. When we appreciate that La Fontaine was a conservative, a man of the pre-Cartesian world, we can understand why modern scholars have generally been unsuccessful in their quest to pinpoint a systematic doctrine within the *Fables*; the only conclusions we can safely draw in this respect tend to be vastly general; La Fontaine's love of humanity, his observation of the follies of mankind, and so on. The notion of the *Fables* being a "mosaic" in the fashion of the early emblem books is further supported by the manner of their publication; the various *recueils* have no real thematic order or logic to their presentation.[25] The same is true of the *Contes*. Attempts to prove the contrary are generally limited in scope or merely unconvincing. This is not surprising given that such endeavours amount to applying modern attitudes and norms regarding the coherence required of a published work, to a collection that is rooted in a far different tradition.

Nonetheless much has been published on the question, as the extensiveness of Richard Danner's useful bibliographic overview indicates.[26] Particularly noteworthy are the theories of Collinet, Danner himself, and Rubin. Collinet points to a number of "fables doubles"[27] and goes on to conclude that

> les correspondances secondaires se multiplient entre les différentes parties de cet ensemble [La Fontaine's work as a whole] et lui donnent sa cohésion. (413)

However, he by no means suggests any overall thematic unity to the *recueils*. Danner is convincing in his Labyrinth Hypothesis for the composition of book X,[28] but he still concludes by noting,

> how far we are and will necessarily remain from discovering a totally accurate blueprint to the intricate architecture of these marvelous poems. (98)

Rubin puts forward a persuasive argument for a cohesive pattern to the *Fables*, but it is based on formal rather than thematic considerations. He demonstrates this through particular analysis of books VII[29] and XI.[30]

We can clearly see the contradictions in La Fontaine's stance if we return to the example of the treatment of injustices of society. In "Les Animaux malades de la peste" and "Le Loup et l'agneau" his attitude is one of bitter cynicism. However "Le Loup et les bergers" and "Les Poissons et le berger qui joue de la flute" both promote an attitude of understanding as concerns the use of force. This attitude is taken one step further in *Fable* X, VI, "L'Araignée et l'hirondelle." Here, as we shall see, the poet merely accepts the order of things.

"L'Araignée et l'hirondelle" deserves closer attention as it is another fable on the theme of injustice which directly takes much from Guéroult's example. La Fontaine's fable opens (lines 1-10) with the spider's woeful plea due to the fact that the swallow has been stealing the flies from her web. Lines 11-20 abandon direct speech (although we do not realise that lines 1-10 are in direct speech until we are told so in lines 11-12) in order to recount events from the swallow's point of view—she had been taking the flies in order to feed "ses enfants gloutons, du bec toujours ouvert" (line 18). The action of the fable consists of a single split-second event that takes only five lines to tell (lines 21-25): the spider is carried away as the swallow bursts through the web. La Fontaine concludes with resignation:

> Jupin pour chaque état mit deux tables au monde.
> L'adroit, le vigilant, et le fort sont assis
> A la première; et les petits
> Mangent leur reste à la seconde. (lines 26-29)

The generally accepted source for this story is Abstemius's fable 4. I know of no critic who cites any alternative. Abstemius's brief tale does indeed relate how the swallow breaks through the web the spider had put in her habitual path. However, his spider, unlike La Fontaine's, then admits to her overambition. Abstemius concludes, "Par cette fable nous sommes avertis de ne pas tenter d'entreprise au-dessus de nos forces" (quoted in *Fables*, ed. Couton, 52). This conclusion, comprising as it does advice on an individual level, is of course a far cry from La Fontaine's casual acceptance of a social system of haves and have-nots.

The missing link is to be found with Guillaume Guéroult. His emblem 9 includes the fable "De l'araigne, de la guespe, & de la mousche." It seems likely that this emblem too was largely based upon Abstemius. Guéroult's story is in two halves; first the spider's web is ruined by a passing wasp; in the second half a fly is trapped in the web. Guéroult differs from Abstemius in that the poem is liberally sprinkled with reflections upon society's hierarchy. The spider concludes in reference to the wasp that "de pecher les gros ont liberté" (line 14). Seven lines later the fly's sad predicament provokes the comment that "Le plus petit est tousjours plus foullé." Guéroult's final stanza gives the following conclusion,

> Ainsi est il des edits de ce monde:
> Le sage en fait la demonstration.
> Car le puissant en qui richesse abonde,
> Les enfraindra sans reprehension.
> Le povre aura griefve punition
> S'il contrevient au moindre poinct qui soit:
> Voyla comment la faveur nous deçoit. (lines 22-28)

As such the conclusion echoes the title of the emblem—"Les riches s'exemptent des loix, mais les povres y demeurent"—and the poem that follows the picture:

> La loy est enfraincte
> Par l'homme opulent,
> L'homme foible & lent:
> Ha d'icelle crainte.

To sum up therefore, the subject of La Fontaine's poem comes from Abstemius; it is he who provides the story of the breaking of the web that is followed by both Guéroult and La Fontaine. La Fontaine's version keeps the original protagonists, the spider and the swallow, while Guéroult replaces the latter with a wasp and a fly. The tone of La Fontaine's poem is unique to the poet himself; whereas the models keep to a serious vein, La Fontaine introduces touches of humour and irony; Pallas's birth is "un secret d'accouchement nouveau" (line 2), the spider, in reference to Arachne, is called "autrefois tapissière" (line 12)! Finally, the theme of the fable comes from Guéroult; it is his version that manipulates the tale so as to demonstrate the notion that there is one rule for the rich and another for the poor. La Fontaine adopts Guéroult's stance when he concludes with the "deux tables au monde" idea.

One final point should be made concerning the influence of Guéroult's emblem 9, "De l'araigne, de la guespe, & de la mousche"; it also provides the conclusion for *Fable* II, XVI, "Le Corbeau voulant imiter l'aigle," whose last line reads "Où la guêpe a passé, le Moucheron demeure" (line 27). The fable tells the story of a crow who tries to imitate an eagle and carry off a sheep. He of course fails, is captured and ends up as a plaything for the shepherd's children. La Fontaine uses the example to show how one should not get ambitions beyond one's station,

> Mal prend aux Volereaux de faire les Voleurs.
> L'exemple est un dangereux leurre:
> Tous les mangeurs de gens ne sont pas grands Seigneurs
> Où la guêpe a passé, le Moucheron demeure. (lines 24-27)

This is the same sort of conclusion that Abstemius draws from his fable 4 and that Æsop draws from his story of the eagle, the jackdaw and the shepherd (*Fable* 69) upon which La Fontaine's *Fable* II, XVI is based. Line 26 alludes to the notion of social class, but once again it is through the reference to Guéroult (line 27) that La Fontaine truly adds the social aspect to the fable.

La Fontaine's conclusion to the fable—"Où la guêpe a passé, le Moucheron demeure"—forms a perfect one-line summary of Guéroult's "De l'araigne, de la guespe, & de la mousche," whose first part tells of the wasp breaking the web, while the second part gives us the capture of the "mousche petite."[31] La Fontaine does not mention the spider as there is no need. The line is sufficiently clear to serve as a memory-trigger to alert readers with the same cultural baggage. In one concise line La Fontaine evokes the story of the wasp, the spider and the fly, with its basic notion that "Les riches s'exemptent des loix, mais les povres y demeurent." He thereby adds an extra social (and maybe dangerously political) dimension to the fable. Furthermore, by serving as a memory-trigger in this way, line 27 of "Le Corbeau voulant imiter l'aigle" functions in a similar manner to that of the motto of an emblem.

This process is effectively the one Rubin labels "Embedded Allusion" in his discussion of *Fable* X, II, "La Tortue et les deux canards."[32] His conclusions are particularly valid, namely that "the sense of a given fable by La Fontaine is never to be taken for granted" and that we should take into account, "what that divergence [i.e. from the source] implies, after analysis, for the interpretation of the fable, the individual book, the *recueil*, or the entire œuvre" (50). La Fontaine's discreet use of Guéroult is surely an example of the sort of method to which Rubin points at the end of the second chapter of *A Pact with Silence*:

> So it is that La Fontaine replaced the folk wisdom of Aesopic and
> Indic fable-writing with his personal adaptation of philosophical
> principles derived from a literary model. (77)

Guéroult's "De l'araigne, de la guespe, & de la mousche" gives us an example of how emblematics could constitute a partial source and point of reference for some of the *Fables*. It shows us how individual verses and passing references can rely upon the reader's knowledge of emblematics in order for him to understand the fables in question fully. This is hardly a surprising phenomenon when we consider La Fontaine's multifarious cultural baggage. Nonetheless it is an aspect of the *Fables* that critics have virtually ignored. This too is not surprising given the volume of work involved; editors have had enough problems identifying the main source of many of the fables without worrying about passing allusions taken from La Fontaine's sixteenth-century cultural references. Nonetheless the example of *Fable* II, XVI does demonstrate that seizing the reference can allow us to understand a whole new important dimension of the fable—here, the fact that the fable is concerned with the injustices of society, not just individual folly as might at first glance appear to be the case. A thorough knowledge of emblematics could well provide the key to open other similar references throughout the *Fables*.

Cross-references such as these indicate an intertextuality whereby close stylistic links and readily grasped references enable the two forms—the emblem and La Fontaine's *Fables*—to play upon one another. Such dynamics are also very much in keeping with the intertextuality of the emblem form (and certain other Renaissance works) whose nature required borrowings from different written sources as well as from compatible plastic arts.

The in-depth analysis of a single *Fable*—"Les Animaux malades de la peste"— whose source is Guéroult's *Premier livre des emblemes*, has suggested that Couton's discoveries regarding emblematics and La Fontaine are only the tip of the iceberg and that the influence goes beyond general inspiration for a few individual fables. Much work, it would seem, remains to be done in this field.

V. B.
VISUAL INTERACTION WITH LA FONTAINE'S TEXTS
HIS WORKS IN GENERAL:
AN ANALYSIS OF THE BREADTH OF EMBLEMATIC INFLUENCE[33]

The analysis of Poussin's *Et in Arcadia ego* with which we concluded chapter II suggested that an emblematic mentality contributed to French culture of the *Ancien régime* in a manner surpassing even that evident in the publication of hundreds of collections of emblems and devices. Emblem books flourished because of a mentality that encouraged the interaction of text with image whereby each depended on the other for full comprehension of the whole. The images could be engravings in a book, but they could also be architectural surroundings or elements of décor to which a text might refer. La Fontaine's texts were inevitably structured in accordance with the mentality of his time.

Nonetheless, when critics of La Fontaine have referred directly to emblematics, it has generally been to consider the influence of specific emblems rather than that of the emblematic mentality. Furthermore, no work on La Fontaine and emblematics has addressed writings other than the *Fables*. If works such as *Les Amours de Psyché*, the *Contes* or the *Songe de Vaux* have remained lesser-known, it is conceivably because the modern non-emblematic mind has been unable to appreciate them as the reader/ viewer of La Fontaine's time would have been.

Perhaps it is easiest for the time-distanced reader to grasp the visual manner of La Fontaine's texts by understanding how they lend themselves to illustration.[34] Indeed, whether it was La Fontaine's intention or not, from the very first edition of the *Fables* the work appeared illustrated. The 1668 edition, containing books I to VI of modern versions, included the work of one of the master engravers of the time, François Chauveau.[35] Significantly enough, he had also been responsible for engravings to accompany salon discussion pieces such as *Le Grand Cyrus* and *La Célie*, as well as works by leading emblem theorists such as Pierre Le Moyne.[36]

Chauveau's style is marked by the simplicity that is also characteristic of many of the engravings of the early emblem books. The woodcut is dominated by a pictorial representation of the main "event" of the fable whereas the background offers simple details (trees, hills, etc.), but nothing to distract the reader's attention from the main characters in the foreground. Chauveau's woodcuts do not attempt to portray the allegorical sense of the fables, either by emotional personification, or by allegorical background action. A typical example is the illustration for *Fable* VI, IX, "Le Cerf se voyant dans l'eau": Chauveau gives us the image of lines 1 to 10 of the fable in which La Fontaine describes the stag and its reaction to the reflexion it sees. In this case, as throughout, Chauveau's illustration is placed directly above the fable's title.

After Chauveau's death the remaining fables were illustrated by various artists of his school. One such pupil was Nicolas Guérard, but the others, on the whole, have remained anonymous. In the eighteenth century, illustrations were provided by Jean-Baptiste Oudry and Charles-Nicolas Cochin. These were far more embellished than Chauveau's versions, with intricate backgrounds and sumptuously decorated decors very much in keeping with the taste of the time.[37] Nonetheless these continued to portray the protagonists and action of the fables, giving a direct visual representation of the descriptive verses of La Fontaine's texts. As with Chauveau, Oudry made no attempt to represent the allegorical meaning of the fables.

It was not until the late eighteenth century that allegorical illustrations of the *Fables* appeared, starting with the works of Charles Monnet (1765 Fessard edition) and Meyer (1773 Fessard edition). In the case of the former, elements were added to the illustration in order to illustrate visually certain non-visual elements of the fables: the unsharing ant of *Fable* I, I, for example, is portrayed next to a mirror and a snake, symbols of narcissism and evil. The numerous illustrated editions of the nineteenth and twentieth centuries (Hippolyte Le Compte, Gustave Moreau, Gustave Doré, Marc Chagall and others) invariably give more than just a representation of the directly visual elements of the fables. Protagonists might be portrayed in the guise of politicians of the day, the action of the fable portrayed through a comic-book style series of illustrations, or the allegorical meaning of the fable made clear by the emotion on the characters' faces. Above all, the illustration could portray the moral directly, as for example in a picture of a family suffering the cold of an unprepared snowy winter in the case of *Fable* I, I.

Others (Bassy, Collinet) have catalogued the style of the fables' illustration, but none have commented on the relevance of the differences in terms of the tastes of the emblematic age.[38] On the contrary, modern critics have been prone to explain La Fontaine's fables in the light of illustrations that were not of his time. Bassy seems unaware that an emblem functions through the interaction of component parts. Accordingly he states, "L'art de La Fontaine apparaît comme une constante suggestion d'images. En cela il fait le contraire de ce qu'a fait l'emblème: sa rhétorique ne va pas de l'image à l'idée mais de l'idée à l'image" (60). He justifies his conclusions by the evidence of illustrators working at least two centuries after La Fontaine: "Des illustrations comme celles de Chadel et surtout celles de Maurice Boutet de Monvel suffisent à le prouver: ceux-ci font en effet de chaque fable une succession d'images" (60). On the other hand, Bassy dismisses Menestrier's associations of the *Fables* with the emblem as the work of an "esprit confus" (60).

Given such anachronistic assumptions, it is normal for Bassy to be concerned by the lack of "une image unique et prégnante, contenant en elle toutes les données de la fable et les rassemblant jusqu'à en devenir le symbole." He expresses surprise that "Même chez Chauveau, qui ne consacre pourtant qu'une seule vignette à chaque fable, les représentations sont incompréhensibles sans le secours de la fable et du texte" (55). Bassy does not point out that this is, in effect, how an emblem works, nor that Chauveau presents, in engraved form, certain static images created within parts of La Fontaine's fables. LePage, however, is aware of this process:

> His [Chauveau's] method consists in selecting the most visually arresting moments in a fable—those moments which inevitably highlight anxiety, aggression, defiance, or some form of terror. He sets them down in such a way that he is able to capture the mainspring of each fable's action while still conveying the primitive sense of the animal stories. (68)

It seems to me that Chauveau's images interact with the non-static part of the texts, rather than the text coming to the "secours" of the inadequate illustration, as Bassy suggests.

The evidence of the fashion for emblems would suggest that until the latter half of the eighteenth century illustrations accompanying texts generally were considered sufficient if they provided a good global image enabling the reader to grasp easily and retain mentally certain central visual elements of the piece in question. The interaction of text and image would form the whole, with the text providing the moral element (the "âme") necessary to complete the static visual scene (the "corps").

With the end of the emblematic age this interaction was no longer in accordance with the general reading habits of the time. The reader could no longer be expected to retain a global image in his mind against which he would juxtapose the text in question. On the contrary, given that a picture and a text, even a picture accompanying a text, came to be viewed (and generally still are) as complete entities in their own right, a picture that did not illustrate all of the aspects of the text could justifiably be seen as lacking in some way. Since the allegorical or moral aspect of a fable was often regarded as its 'important' part, it would have seemed natural that an illustration that could not cover all aspects should concentrate on these. However hypothetical the analysis of mentalities, it is a demonstrable fact that the general switch to allegorising illustrations of La Fontaine's *Fables* occurred in union with the waning of the fashion for emblems, devices and the mode of thinking that allowed them to flourish. It seems plausible to link the former to the latter.

Although the *Fables* are the best documented of La Fontaine's works with regard to illustration, they were by no means his only illustrated publication. The 1685 Amsterdam edition of the *Contes* by Debordes, for example, was the first of many to include engravings by Rommyn de Hooch. Indeed these were reproduced in editions until the end of the first half of the eighteenth century (Collinet, "La Fontaine et ses illustrateurs," cxxviii). As with the engravings by Chauveau, these tend to give the principal characters from the story in the stance of a specific, often central, scene. The engraving is positioned directly above the title of the *Conte*. Again it is only with such later illustrators as Nicolas Lancret, Jean-Honoré Fragonard, Charles Eisen or Jean-Michel Moreau that the illustrations take on a life entirely independent of the text's physical descriptions, portraying the emotion of a denouement or concentrating on the libertine interest of the stories. These changes in fashion regarding the illustrations have been noted by Collinet in "La Fontaine et ses illustrateurs" (cxxviii-cxlvii), but, to the best of my knowledge, no critic has attempted to analyse La Fontaine's texts themselves in the light of such evidence of a change in taste and mentality.

Other works by La Fontaine are illustrated by a method that for convenience's sake we shall label "virtual illustration." By this we mean that certain of La Fontaine's texts refer to paintings, tapestries, buildings or scenes that were well enough known to evoke immediately a visual image without an accompanying description of detail being necessary. In such cases the text would be simultaneously illustrated by the reader's memorised image of the palace or work of art in question. The image would be "virtual" as it would be engraved in the reader's mind as part of his everyday cultural baggage rather than being printed on the paper in front of him.

This principle is best illustrated by a specific example. In the first book of *Les Amours de Psyché*, Psyché is taken by Venus to "un Palais superbe" (77), this being the palace of Cupid. La Fontaine, in the guise of his narrator named Poliphile, then evokes the delights that Psyché finds before her. The Nymphes lead her into a vestibule,

> d'ou l'on pouvoit découvrir, d'un costé les cours, et de l'autre costé les jardins. Psiché le trouva proportionné à la richesse de l'édifice. De ce vestibule on la fit passer en des salles que la magnificence, elle mesme, avoit pris la peine d'orner, et dont la dernière enchérissoit toûjours sur la précédente. (78)

Psyché goes on to explore the multitude of "chambres" and "cabinets" and admires "les merveilles de ce Palais":

> On fit ses murs d'un marbre aussi blanc que l'albastre
> Les dedans sont ornez d'un Porphire luisant.
> Ces ordres dont les Grecs nous ont fait un présent,
> Le Dorique sans fard, l'élégant Ionique,
> Et le Corintien superbe et magnifique,

> L'un sur l'autre placez élèvent jusqu'aux Cieux
> Ce pompeux édifice où tout charme les yeux.
> Pour servir d'ornement à ses divers estages,
> L'Architecte y posa les vivantes images
> De ces objets divins, Cléopâtres, Phrinez,
> Par qui sont les Héros en triomphe menez. (81-82)

The text then reverts to prose,

> Les endroits où la Belle s'arresta le plus ce furent les galeries. Là les raretez, les tableaux, les bustes, non de la main des Apelles et des Phidias, mais de la main mesme des Fées, qui ont été les maistresses de ces grands hommes, composoient un amas d'objets qui ébloüissoit la veuë. . . . (82)

Psyché considers, "les richesses, les précieux meubles, les tapisseries de toutes les sortes, et d'autres ouvrages conduits par la fille de Jupiter," and we are told that "sur tout on voyoit une grande variété dans ces choses, et dans l'ordonnance de chaque chambre . . ." (83). The heroine stops before a tapestry which is described in some detail. She also finds that her own image abounds: "Il sembloit que ce Palais fust un temple, et Psiché la Déesse à qui il estoit consacré" (85).

La Fontaine/Poliphile also refers to the gardens and the exterior:

> sur le soir elle s'alla promener dans les cours et dans les jardins, d'où elle considéra quelque temps les diverses faces de l'édifice; sa majesté, ses enrichissemens et ses grâces; la proportion, le bel ordre, et la correspondance de ses parties. Je vous en ferois la description, si j'estois plus sçavant dans l'Architecture que je ne suis. (86)

This main section of the tour of the palace ends with a thirty-nine line poem which opens as follows:

> Assemblez sans aller si loin
> Et nos jardins et leurs nayades,
> Y joignant en cas de besoin
> Et des canaux et des cascades.
> Cela fait, de tous les costez
> Placez en ces lieux enchantez
> Force jets affrontans la nuë,
> Des canaux à perte de veuë.
> Bordez les d'Orangers, de Myrtes, de Jasmins,
> Qui soient aussi géants que les nostres sont nains. (86-87)

In emblematic terms, by use of ekphrasis, La Fontaine creates a verbal *imago*, an evocation of the palace that allows it to be retained in the reader's mind in the same way that he might retain the memory of an engraving or a woodblock. However, in creating this verbal *imago* La Fontaine draws on references far beyond those of a direct description. Indeed, the section in which we visit Cupid's palace contains little authentic description as such, but rather it presents a list of qualities or virtues of the building.[39]

The process is analogous to one present in early emblem books. Jacques de Maulevant, for example, in his dedicatory verse to Guillaume de La Perrière,[40] refers to the images of *La Morosophie* as being described:

> En tes escritz sont sentences subtiles,
> Et d'abondant cest œuvre as composé
> Tout par quatrains, et si bien disposé
> Qu'aux premiers vers descrite est la peincture
> Le sens moral aux derniers est posé
> Pour que grand sens fust en peu d'escriture. (verses 5-10)

These however are not proper descriptions either. Rather, La Perrière presents a series of 'tags' which require the reader to engage in interaction with the image. David Graham has analysed this process in "'Voiez icy en ceste histoire...': Cross-Reference, Self-Reference and Frame-Breaking in some French Emblems": he refers to a system of "anaphoric deixis directed to visual sense perception" (5) whereby certain terms in the emblematic text serve as pointers ("anaphoric deixis") that are understandable by reference to the image. Similarly, Irene Bergal[41] points to La Perrière's use of a 'persona' who encourages the reader to discover the link between pictures and verbal messages, and by extension teaches him to do likewise in his own environment.

The 'descriptions' in La Fontaine's *Psyché* function in much the same way: they are 'place-holders' for works of art or structures which could be assumed to be resident in the reader's memory. Their lack of descriptive content enables them to function as tagging devices in the manner of the 'tags' Graham describes. Indeed in the previous section of this chapter we discussed a similar notion of emblematic 'memory triggers' in the context of specific lines and aspects of the *Fables*. In the case of *Psyché,* the word-image in question functions primarily because La Fontaine's description triggers images with which the reader is already wholly familiar, namely images of the Palace of Versailles.

To the reader of the late 1660s the "cours" were surely the *Cour de marbre* and the *Cour royale*, the endless suites of rooms, the *Grands appartements* and *Petits appartements* of the king and queen, the "tableaux," "bustes," "meubles" and "tapisseries" those by Charles Le Brun, Gian Lorenzo Bernini (Bernin), Jean Warin, Nicolas Poussin (and others) with which Louis XIV's palace was overflowing. The "Dorique sans fard, l'elegant Ionique / Et le Corintien superbe et magnifique" bring immediately to mind the columns of Versailles's east façade; "la proportion, le bel ordre, et la correspondance" is surely a reference to the outstanding example of Classicism that was the Palace of Versailles. As for the "cascades," the "force jets affrontans la nuë," the "canaux à perte de veuë" and the "Orangers," one is inevitably reminded of the Palace's landscaped gardens.[42]

The image is already a virtual one as it is evoked rather than drawn and the text only supplies elements of a picture of Versailles. However the 'tags' are clear enough for the reader's cultural associations to remind him immediately of the Palace. Such an image could conceivably be similar to the well-known engravings that artists such as Israël Silvestre were producing at this time; alternatively, the image could be a truly global impression encompassing architecture, furnishings and gardens—or variations thereupon according to individual personal memories—, as only lived experience could provide.[43]

Virtual images such as this alter the significance of La Fontaine's text. However, the nuances of meaning can only be fully grasped when one is aware of the approach that formed part of the emblematic mentality. The triggering of the associations with Versailles creates, in emblematic terms, the virtual *imago*; this *imago* is a global one, installed in the reader's mind as he reads. It is also a purely physical one, a picture of an architectural reality the reader knows well. As such La Fontaine has created the *corps* of an emblem. The *âme* is provided by the description of Psyché and her reactions in the Palace of Cupid. In emblematic terms, the text is therefore the *subscriptio*. It is the interaction of the component parts that creates the complete sense of La Fontaine's work.

The reader with the emblematic image of Versailles in his mind will naturally assimilate this to the developing story of Psyché's predicament. Her initial reaction is one of wonderment as she marvels at the beauties of the palace. However it soon becomes clear that the novelty of the palace's wonders is wearing thin and there are elements of apprehension. Effectively Psyché is no more than a prisoner within the demi-god's power. She has no personal freedom: "En ce moment Là son mary la voyoit peut-estre de quelque endroit d'où il ne pouvoit estre veu; et outre le plaisir de la voir il avoit celuy d'apprendre ses plus secrètes pensées . . ." (85-86). The interaction of the virtual *imago* with the text allows La Fontaine to present a reserved judgement on the wonders of Louis XIV's absolutism as enacted at Versailles. It is a reservation that is generally lost to the twentieth-century reader as the two elements of the whole—Psyché's adventure and the Palace of Versailles—need to be conceived simultaneously, as in the text/image interaction of an emblem, in order for the full significance to be grasped. The *imago* serves a different purpose from modern illustration.

One further example shows the same process in action. After exploring the palace, Psyché wanders in the garden and comes across a stream. This in turn leads her to a grotto:

> C'estoit une Grote assez spacieuse, où dans un bassin taillé par les seules mains de la nature couloit le long d'un rocher une eau argentée, et qui par son bruit invitoit à un doux sommeil. Psiché ne

se pût tenir d'entrer dans la Grotte. Comme elle en visitoit les recoins, la clarté qui alloit toûjours en diminuant luy faillit enfin tout à coup. Il y avoit certainement dequoy avoir peur. . . . (88)

In the context of the Versailles of the 1660s, "une Grote assez spacieuse" flowing with "une eau argentée" could only be the underwater décor and fountains of the *Grotte de Thétis*. Built between 1664 and 1665 on the site where the chapel now stands, this was one of the most important attractions of Versailles. It would have been well-known to La Fontaine's readers either by personal experience or, from the 1670s onwards, through the engravings added to André Félibien's *Description de la Grotte de Versailles*[44] (see figure 19). As with Cupid's palace, it is reasonable to assume that here too La Fontaine is creating a virtual *imago*, in this instance in reference to the *Grotte de Thétis*.

Emblematic association has a further rôle to play given the context of Louis XIV's personification through his sun device. It was Thétis, goddess of the sea, who welcomed the sun at night after his journey through the sky. Indeed the grotto, like the night, invites sleep ("invitoit à un doux sommeil"). The sun's resting place beckons Psyché ("Psiché ne se pût tenir d'entrer dans la Grotte"), but as she enters, the security offered by the sun's light leaves her ("la clarté qui alloit toûjours en diminuant luy faillit enfin tout à coup"). Once again, La Fontaine's reader finds that the glorification of Louis XIV is in fact being subverted through the interaction of the emblematic *imago* (here the *Grotte de Thétis*) with the narrative of the text. The sun-king's lair becomes a place of fear: "Il y avoit certainement dequoy avoir peur."

To those aware of the historical context, such emblematic subversion does not seem out of place.[45] Eight years before the publication of *Les Amours de Psyché*, Nicolas Fouquet, La Fontaine's close friend and protector, had been arrested upon orders of the king. As Louis XIV's *Surintendant des finances*, Fouquet had risen to heights of glory through adept financial management. He had taken La Fontaine under his wing (the "Chambre de La Fontaine" can still be seen at Vaux-le-Vicomte) and commissioned several pieces, including the *Songe de Vaux*, that told of the beauties of Vaux's castle and gardens. The height of Fouquet's success was marked by a fête given on 17 August 1661, attended by the court and by the king himself. It included the first performance of Molière's *Les Facheux*, an elaborate display of the gardens' fountains, and a sumptuous fireworks display. A few weeks later, on 5 September, Fouquet was arrested by D'Artagnon upon Louis XIV's orders. Accused of financial irregularities, with the case for the prosecution mainly instigated by Tellier and Colbert, Fouquet was sent to prison after three years of trial.[46]

La Fontaine had never stopped fighting for the release of his patron. In the meantime Louis XIV had employed Louis Le Vau, the architect of Fouquet's castle at Vaux-le-Vicomte, André Le Nôtre, the architect of Fouquet's gardens and Charles Le Brun, Fouquet's master-painter, for the creation of the expanded palace at Versailles. In the light of such events, it is not surprising that La Fontaine's celebration of the glories of Versailles should bear a touch of suspicion. Nor is it surprising that the expression of such bitterness should be prudently veiled behind the emblematic mode

Figure 19. "La Grotte de Thétis," from André Félibien, *Description de la Grotte de Versailles* (Paris: Imprimerie Royale, 1676).

of expression to which La Fontaine's readers were accustomed.

Other textual references in *Les Amours de Psyché* support such conclusions. As Jeanneret points out, the original description of the gardens of Cupid's palace reads,

> Asemblez sans aller si loin
> Vaux, Liencourt, et leurs Nayades;
> Y joignant en cas de besoin
> Ruël avecque ses cascades. (86)

A prudent La Fontaine removed such open praise of Versailles's forerunner by replacing the reference to Vaux with "Et nos jardins et leurs nyades."

Less open is the praise that La Fontaine gives of Vaux through frequent reference to the orange trees of Versailles. Any friend of Fouquet knew that these had been grafted directly from trees at Vaux-le-Vicomte. Armed with this knowledge and with the knowledge that any mention of the sun could be seen as a reference to Louis XIV's device, the following lines, taken from the section on Versailles that precedes Poliphile's narration of the Psyché story, take on new significance:

> Comme nos gens avoit encor de loisir, ils firent un tour à l'Orangerie. La beauté et le nombre des orangers et des autres plantes qu'on y conserve, ne se sçauroient exprimer. Il y a tel de ces arbres qui a résisté aux attaques de cent hyvers. (61)[47]

The orange trees might have survived a hundred winters, but ironically enough, they were uprooted by the "sun." The lines of poetry that follow are even more telling; addressing directly the orange trees, the verses conclude,

> Vous estes nains; mais tel arbre géant,
> Qui déclare au soleil la guerre,
> Ne vous vaut pas;
> Bien qu'il couvre un arpent de terre
> Avec ses bras. (62)

Fouquet may not have been able to resist Louis XIV, but he had La Fontaine's admiration. The pun ("Ne vous vaut pas") was surely intentional.

Although on the surface *Les Amours de Psyché* expresses admiration for the achievements of the sun-king, other emblematic references also throw the praise into question. When Venus is carried to Cythère, she is served by her Tritons: "L'un luy tient un miroir fait de cristal de roche; / Aux rayons du soleil l'autre en défend l'approche. / Palémon qui la guide, évite les rochers . . ." (70). The goddess must be protected from the sun as the chariot from the rocks. Further on in the text Psyché, left on the mountain to meet with her fate, begs the sun for help ("Implore le Soleil"). Her pleas, however, are to no avail:

> Le Soleil las de voir ce spectacle barbare
> Précipite sa course, et passant sous les eaux
> Va porter la clarté chez des peuples nouveaux.
> L'horreur de ces déserts s'accroist par son absence:
> La nuit vient sur un char conduit par le silence:
> Il ameine avec luy la crainte en l'Univers. (77)

In the iconography of Versailles, Apollo, the Sun God and therefore by implication Louis XIV, brings his light to the world. La Fontaine subtly points out that the sun was also capable of abandoning his subjects and leaving them to the terror of the night.

The frequent references to the sun are a feature of La Fontaine's invention not to be found in Apuleius's original text. The same is also true of the Versailles-evoking description of Cupid's palace. The whole grotto episode is unique to La Fontaine's version. It seems clear, therefore, that a knowledge of emblematics and of the emblematic mode of reading associated with such passages—be it through the signalling of virtual *imagines* or by references to Louis XIV's sun device—could do much to enhance the modern-day reader's appreciation of *Les Amours de Psyché*.

Indeed the work's narrative structure as a whole bears the mark of a certain emblematic mentality, as well as being, in Joan DeJean's words, "The Reflecting Pool of Classicism."[48] La Fontaine, the author, presents a narrator, Poliphile, who tells his three friends, Gélaste, Ariste and Acante, the story of Psyché's discovery of Cupidon. Poliphile, by unfolding the tale with pauses at strategic moments, keeps his three friends—and indeed the reader—in suspense. Similarly, Cupidon, by not revealing his identity, maintains Psyché's uncertainty. The mirroring effect is repeated in the story's framework: Psyché visits Cupidon's palace; the four friends visit Cupidon's palace—through the narrative—whilst visiting Versailles; the reader visits Cupidon's palace and Versailles through the two levels of the text and, in all probability, through his or her own experience of Versailles.

In short, in *Les Amours de Psyché* we are presented with a narrative that operates on increasingly distant levels. The final levels, as DeJean points out, are the reflections of Louis XIV's régime and of Classicism in general:

> In their efforts to control a situation by means of seduction, La Fontaine and Cupidon borrow the tactics developed by the master artist whose presence is in filigree throughout the work, Louis XIV. Versailles' 'author' built a pleasure palace remarkable for its dazzling interplay of surfaces, an interplay whose brilliance could, like that of the king's would-be namesake, blind the subjects who dared look at it directly. (107-08)

Psyché can be described as a *mise en abyme* of the functioning and goals of Classicism. The dazzling surfaces of Classicism constitute a brilliant machine for controlling all readers, for keeping them in the dark, for discouraging them from asking questions about the identity of the master artist who surrounds them with 'dorures' and who caresses them when the lights are out. (109)

The *mise en abyme* style was well-known to those familiar with emblem books, although here the comparison is not with the early productions of the Renaissance, but rather with those of the seventeenth century, when the genre had evolved. The Jesuits in particular believed such emblematics to be a fit pathway towards the mysteries of the divine, perhaps due to the mystical associations attached to some early forms.[49] As we have stated in the context of our study of Descartes, Jesuit emblematic expression was often based on the clarification of abstract notions through recourse to the senses, and in particular through visual phenomena giving access to the invisible and divine. In chapters II and III we have cited the particular, but not atypical, example of the "Speculum creaturarum," emblem 8 of Jean David's *Duodecim specula* (see figure 3). As stated above, here the process in operation is twofold. The emblem book's earthly theme, through which the work's spiritual message is presented, is that of the mirror. Furthermore the emblem in question describes the very process in action: a man and a woman look into a mirror in which are represented earthly phenomena; the sea, the sky, land, ships (thus the wind) and so on. These earthly phenomena allow the couple to see the work of God, the angels and the heavens in general. The divine is to be seen and understood in the form of God's creations on earth, these creations being a mirror through which the viewers can see God himself. At the same time the couple represents the reader and the mirror represents the emblem book, the *Duodecim specula*, that he is in the act of reading. To make things clear the image is glossed with the letters 'A,' 'B' and 'C' and summed up by the words 'Invisibilium per visibilia contemplatio.'

The multiple mirrored layers of David's emblem function in much the same way as those of La Fontaine's palatial visits. As DeJean has indicated:

> Psyché's visit to Cupidon's palace proves that a naïve or innocent spectator may be disarmed by the seductive charms of a powerful artistic creation. The fact that Polyphile gives an account of her itinerary to his friends shortly after the description of their own visit to a similarly magnificent palace invites a comparison between these two examples of 'touristic' curiosity. (101)

Poliphile and Psyché both visit the exterior of the palaces, then the interior, before finishing with the seclusion of a water grotto. Psyché is ill at ease there (see above), while the four friends try and avoid getting wet:

> Les quatre amis ne voulurent point estre moüillez. Ils prièrent celuy qui leur faisoit voir la Grote de réserver ce plaisir pour le Bourgeois ou pour l'Allemand; et de les placer en quelque coin où ils fussent à couvert de l'eau. (67)

Presumably La Fontaine's reader could follow the same itinerary. However, whereas David uses this *mise en abyme* method to demystify the divine goodness that we cannot know directly, La Fontaine appears to 'play with mirrors' so as to veil his portrayal of the threatening might of Louis XIV's absolutism.

A narrative structure in keeping with the emblematic mentality is hardly surprising in the context of a work that is narrated by Poliphile, whose name is surely a reference to Francesco Colonna's *Hypnerotomachia Poliphili*.[50] Editions of the *Hypnerotomachia Poliphili* had appeared in Italy from 1499. The work tells of Poliphile's quest for Polia, a journey taking him through a series of decorated triumphal arches. The text is interspersed with illustrations that form part of the story's development. These can be inscriptions, illustrations of a procession, or a rebus-style pictorial message.[51] A French translation of the *Hypnerotomachia Poliphili* appeared in at least three editions from 1546, under the title of *Songe de Poliphile*.[52] The work's essential interaction of image and text make it one of the main forerunners to the emblem form. By chosing Poliphile as his narrator, La Fontaine clearly places *Les Amours de Psyché* within the same tradition.

On a more precise level, the name of "Poliphile" means "he who likes many things." La Fontaine suggests as much, telling us that "on peut dire que celuy-cy [Poliphile] amoit toutes choses" (60). Here it is interesting to apply Jean Rousset's[53] decoding of the allegorical meaning of the four friends whose conversation forms the frame to the story of Psyché and Cupidon that Poliphile will narrate; he sees,

> en Gélaste la plaisanterie galante ou la Comédie, en Ariste la pitié sensible ou la Tragédie, en Acante, ami des jardins, des fleurs des beaux ciels, l'Idylle ou la Pastorale; et Poliphile, qui aime "toutes choses" et qui est l'auteur, aura pour tâche de tenter la synthèse et la fusion des genres, de combiner en une neuve harmonie ces dispositions composites. (118)

By attempting "la synthèse et la fusion des genres" in the work that he presents, Poliphile gives us a text to be read in the same way as the emblematic *Songe*. Rousset's emphasis on "fusion" is appropriate: the pieces of prose narration and description, dialogue, poetry and direct reference to the visual arts of painting, tapestry and architecture of which La Fontaine's work is comprised, only form the complete *Amours de Psyché* through an act of fusion on the part of the reader.

The *Songe de Poliphile* directly influenced another of La Fontaine's works, the *Songe de Vaux*. Probably composed around 1659 and upon Fouquet's order, four of the work's fragments were published in the *Contes et Nouvelles en vers* (1665) and the *Fables nouvelles* (1671) during La Fontaine's lifetime, the five other fragments did not appear until the posthumous *Œuvres diverses* of 1729 (Clarac, 78). The link with the *Songe de Poliphile* goes beyond that of the title. In the "Avertissement" of 1671, La Fontaine refers to fragments of the *Songe de Vaux* as "des échantillons" (78) of different styles. He then goes on to cite the *Songe de Poliphile* as a guiding example:

> Ce n'est pas qu'un songe soit si suivi, ni même si long que le mien sera; mais il est permis de passer le cours ordinaire dans ces rencontres; et j'avais pour me défendre, outre le *Roman de la Rose*, le *Songe de Poliphile*, et celui même *de Scipion*. (79)

La Fontaine closes the "Avertissement" by telling of the discovery of an "ecrin de pierreries" on which,

> se lisait en lettres d'or cette devise, que l'on n'avait pu entendre je suis constant, quoique j'en aime deux. (79)

The box's cover bore the portrait of the king, and on its underside was to be found a riddle referring to Vaux and to the meaning of the "devise." Of the "savantes fées" who came to try and win the king's portrait and thus the "ecrin," La Fontaine names four: "l'Architecture, la Peinture, l'Intendante du jardinage, et la Poésie: je les appelle Palatiane, Apellanire, Hortésie et Calliopée" (80).[54] Their speeches, according to La Fontaine, make up the second fragment of the *Songe de Vaux*. Again, the reader acquainted with emblematics is reminded of the episode in the *Hypnerotomachia Poliphili* in which Poliphile discovers a tomb-like treasure chest ("veterrima sepultura") surmounted by a statue of a queen and carrying an inscription:

> QVISQVIS ES, QVANTVN
> CVNQVE LIBVERIT HV
> IUSQUE THESAVRISVME AT
> MONEO. AVFER CAPUT.
> CORPVS NE TANGITO.[55] (sig. b-viii-r and v)

In Colonna's work an illustration depicts the treasure chest.

La Fontaine's introduction places the fragments to come firmly in an emblematic context. The interaction of genres and of the visual with the textual is suggested by the reference to the *Songe de Poliphile*. The fact that the second fragment will consist of recitals by the visual and textual arts of Architecture, Painting, Landscape-Gardening and Poetry further supports this idea. Most importantly, La Fontaine's aspirations as a whole are presented through an emblematic riddle. The "ecrin de pierreries," the box of riches, is closed by Orante's careless handling. Orante, in the salon language of the time, was Fouquet's pseudonym. The box would thus represent the glories amassed and lost by La Fontaine's protector. Also present is the portrait of the king. Between the two is the "devise": "Je suis constant, quoique j'en aime deux." The "Avertissement" appeared in 1671, ten years after Fouquet's arrest. La Fontaine was still hoping for his return to grace (the reopening of the "ecrin"), nonetheless open support for Fouquet and criticism of the king, as would certainly be understood by the ensuing description of the glories of Vaux, was risky business. Given the situation, the "devise" appears to be La Fontaine's justification of his stand. Caught between loyalty to the former glories of Fouquet and to the king himself, the poet makes a prudent statement: he remains true to Fouquet but is also loyal to Louis XIV ("je suis constant, quoique j'en aime deux"). The statement operates through the interaction of the visual—the diamonds and the king's portrait—with the textual—the "devise."

Many of the fragments of the *Songe de Vaux* create a virtual image of the castle at Vaux-le-Vicomte in the same way that the references to Cupid's palace installs images of Versailles in the reader's mind. Fragments I and II (81-96), for example, comprise the verses on the architecture, gardens and paintings of the palace as promised in the "Avertissement." Fragment V (104-06) praises Le Brun's painting of the Muses on the ceiling of the main hall as still can be seen today. Fragment IX (115-19), "Les Amours de Mars et de Vénus," is the poetic evocation of an eight-panel tapestry that hung in the *Chambre des Muses*. In all of these cases the reader would have been familiar, in all likelihood, with the places or works of art in question. For the reader who had never been to Vaux, the engravings by Israël Silvestre were well-known. La Fontaine refers to these in fragment I when he mentions "cette maison magnifique avec ses accompagnements et ses jardins lesquels Silvestre m'avait montrés" (82).

Static images of this kind—the castle, engravings of the castle, the tapestry or the paintings by Le Brun—were brought to mind and processed by the habits of emblematic reading. The virtual image, such as the painting by Le Brun or the tapestry, could then be completed by interaction with La Fontaine's text, and vice versa. Such interaction of the various arts epitomised Fouquet's creation at Vaux-le-Vicomte. The classical columns of Le Vau's architecture were matched by the symmetry of Le Nôtre's gardens or Le Brun's paintings. Vaux-le-Vicomte was not just a castle, but a melting pot of architecture, landscape-gardening, interior décor, statues and commissioned works of literature. *Le Songe de Vaux,* with its texts that refer to paintings and tapestries, is a microcosm of the wider process that Fouquet had sponsored.

Nonetheless, for the interaction to be truly emblematic, the visual and textual elements must provide different parts of the newly completed whole. A catalogue description of the *imago* in question would therefore not suffice. In the case of the *Songe de Vaux* it is the text/*subscriptio* that provides the animation bringing the static *imago* to life. Fragment V, for example, bears the title, "Acante, au sortir de l'apothéose d'Hercule, / est mené dans une chambre / où les Muses lui apparaissent" (104). Acante describes his reaction upon entering the room and seeing the Muses who were "si bien peintes que je crus voir ces déesses en propre personne." He questions the Muses, in verse, asking them the reason for their "robes eclatantes" (104). Ariste describes the Muses' activity, explaining that "Melpomène médite" and "Thalie en est jalouse," giving their desire to please Orante as the motive for their behaviour. Acante tells us that the painting,

> me remplissait l'âme d'une douceur que je ne saurais exprimer. Elle était telle que celle que j'ai quelques fois ressentie, me voyant au milieu de ces déesses, sous le bel ombrage de Hélicon, favorisé comme à l'envi de toute la troupe. (105)

Emblematic Structures in the Work of La Fontaine

The fragment interprets the ceiling at Vaux-le-Vicomte at the level of emotional reaction and mythological fantasy, but La Fontaine's references are largely lost to the reader who does not have the painting in mind.

The emblematic *imagines* that La Fontaine evokes are often accompanied by a *motto*. In the case of the *Fables* such a procedure is easy to isolate; the motto can be identified with the moral of the fable, as expressed by such memorable lines as "Plutôt souffrir que mourir, / C'est la devise des hommes" (50), "Il ne se faut jamais moquer des misérables: / Car qui peut s'assurer d'être toujours heureux?" (146) or "Rien ne sert de courir; il faut partir à point" (161). The emblematic influence is nonetheless widespread, and the creation of such mottoes is not limited to the *Fables*.[56]

The *Contes* provide many good examples of this phenomenon. "Le Faiseur d'Oreilles et le Raccommodeur de Moules," a *conte-en-vers* on the age-old theme of jealousy and cuckoldry, concludes, "Je dis à moins; car mieux vaut, tout prisé / Cornes gagner que perdre ses oreilles" (62). Similarly "La Fiancée du roi de Garbe" contains many emblematic motto-style dictums: "On ne vit ni d'air ni d'amour. / Les amants ont beau dire et faire, / Il en faut revenir toujours au nécessaire" (123-24); "Jeunes coeurs sont bien empêchés / A tenir leurs desirs cachés" (125); "Mais qu'est-ce qu'un amour sans crainte et sans désire?" (126); "Sage en amour? Hélas, il n'en est point" (129); "Il est bon de garder sa fleur; / Mais, pour l'avoir perdue, il ne se faut pas pendre" (138). In all of these cases the dictum forms a natural part of or conclusion to the *Conte* in question. The fact that the dictums do not operate in isolation differentiates them from proverbs or maxims.

Similarly, in *Les Amours de Psyché* La Fontaine often draws a motto-like conclusion after an event or description. For example, having betrayed Cupid, Psyché decides to kill herself. After a description of the events and reactions, La Fontaine states: "Nous supportons le malheur, et ne sçaurions supporter la honte" (139). Such mottoes in the style of the emblem are to be found throughout the work of La Fontaine.

In short, it is fair to talk of an emblematic structure at the base of much of La Fontaine's work. By this we are referring to texts which in themselves follow the tripartite structure of the emblem; descriptive sections or clear references to specific plastic arts evoke a verbal or virtual *imago*. The bulk of the text, acting as *subscriptio*, interacts with the *imago* to give a fuller sense often not immediately obvious to the twentieth-century reader. The whole may be summarised by a sententious *motto* in the form of the moral. This emblematic structure responds to the method of reading that was in fashion in La Fontaine's time. To demonstrate the importance of this point we shall return to the example of *Fable* VI, IX, "Le Cerf se voyant dans l'eau":

> Dans le cristal d'une fontaine
> Un Cerf se mirant autrefois
> Louait la beauté de son bois,
> Et ne pouvait qu'avecque peine
> Souffrir ses jambes de fuseaux,
> Dont il voyait l'objet se perdre dans les eaux.
> Quelle proportion de mes pieds à la tête!

> Disait-il en voyant leur ombre avec douleur:
> Des taillis les plus haut mon front atteint le faîte;
> Mes pieds ne me font point d'honneur.
> Tout en parlant de la sorte,
> Un limier le fait partir;
> Il tâche à se garantir;
> Dans les forêts il s'emporte.
> Son bois, dommageable ornement,
> L'arrêtant à chaque moment,
> Nuit à l'office que lui rendent
> Ses pieds, de qui ses jours dépendent.
> Il se dédit alors, et maudit les présents
> Que le Ciel lui fait tous les ans.
>
> Nous faisons cas du beau, nous méprisons l'utile;
> Et le beau souvent nous détruit.
> Ce Cerf blâme ses pieds qui le rendent agile;
> Il estime un bois qui lui nuit. (160-61)

Based on Phaedrus's *Fabula* I, XII, "Cervus ad fontem," *Fable* VI, IX presents us with the stag admiring the beauty of his antlers while despising his feet's ugliness. The stag is then chased through the forest by a hound; his feet speed him away, but his antlers slow him down by getting caught in the branches of the trees. As a result, the stag gives up. La Fontaine's moral tells us that what is beautiful is not always useful. Particularly interesting, as far as we are concerned, is the fact that the poem divides very neatly into three sections: lines 1-10 describe the stag before the water; lines 11-20 give the action of the fable, namely the chase through the woods; lines 21-24 then present the fable's moral.

The lengthy description of the stag by the waterside is not to be found in Phaedrus's version, and so can be assumed to be of La Fontaine's creation. Through the first ten lines of the fable there is no action as such. The image created is a static one, that of the stag admiring himself in the water. La Fontaine insists upon the reflection in the water as well as upon the juxtaposition of the beautiful antlers with the skinny legs. The latter point is reinforced by alliteration: the "b"s of "beauté" and "bois" in reference to the antlers are in contrast to the hissing 's's—"souffrir," "ses," "fuseaux"—used to describe the legs. The use of alexandrines for verses 6-10 makes the reading of these lines all the slower. In short, La Fontaine has created a verbal image, one which can easily be visualised within a static framework. Indeed pictures of stags, often by the water, were commonplace in the emblem literature of the period.[57] After lines 1-10 of the fable, therefore, the reader of the emblematic age would have formulated a global image—the narcissistic stag by the waterside—that would stay with him as he reads the rest of the poem.

Lines 11-20 are, accordingly, very different. The short lines and the abundance of mono- or bi-syllabic words require a very much quickened reading. La Fontaine does not dwell upon details as the principal action of the story is swiftly unveiled: the hound's appearance, followed by the passage through the forest, the encumbering trees and the stag's defeat. Here the poet is creating a *subscriptio*, that fits the picture into a narrative leading to the moral. The juxtaposition formed by the *imago*—the beauty of the stag's antlers against the ugliness of his feet—must constantly be borne in mind as the récit questions the value of championing such purely aestetic criteria.

The final lines sum up with the moral. This is short and to the point compared with the ten lines given to the *imago* and to the action. Furthermore the carefully weighted oppositions of line 21 ("Nous faisons cas du beau, nous méprisons l'utile") and the striking monosyllabic internal rhymes of line 24 ("bois qui lui nuit") form a lapidary style that the reader can easily remember. This is the same process that operates ideally in the case of an emblem or device's *motto*.

Analysed in this way, *Fable* VI, IX is shown to consist, in true emblematic style, of a global image that interacts with the specifics of the *subscriptio* so as to create the overall effect. Accordingly the writing skills used by La Fontaine in lines 1-10 are very different from those of lines 11-20 or 21-24. We have pointed out some of these skills; to appreciate their different usage is to appreciate the genius of La Fontaine. This is not a poem to be read in uniform fashion from beginning to end as might be the tendency today.

One more point: lines 19 and 20 of the fable—"Il se dédit alors, et maudit les présents / Que le Ciel lui fait tous les ans"—seem out of place and unnecessary in a concise récit that is marked by the elimination of all superfluous details. The lines are of La Fontaine's invention (i.e. they do not feature in Phaedrus's version), yet add nothing to the story. The explanation is linked to the global image that La Fontaine has created in lines 1-10. Of the various emblematic stag images familiar to La Fontaine's reader, one was that of Horapollo's *Hieroglyphics*. As Liselotte Dieckmann points out in her *Hieroglyphics: The History of a Literary Symbol*, French theorists of the seventeenth century, specifically Caussinus, Estienne and Menestrier, had analysed Horapollo's work (55-61).[58] This work was, among other things, an attempt to decode the significance of various mysterious symbols to be found in nature, thereby giving the initiated access to certain higher truths. Although taken seriously in the Renaissance, the work's promise of the key to the mysteries previously known by the Egyptians was viewed with less awe in La Fontaine's time: "Not long after Menestrier's vain attempts to revive a dying art form, it received its death blow from authors who had been thoroughly imbued with the rational spirit of the Cartesian age" (61).

The 1543 Kerver edition of the *Hieroglyphics*[59] represents a stag in similar fashion to the global image the reader would retain as he progresses through *Fable* VI, IX (figure 20). The accompanying text explains how the antlers represent long life:

> Comment ilz signifioient long temps
> ou vivre longuement.
> Ilz paignoient le cerf a qui tous les ans les cornes repullulent &
> renouvellent. (18)

Figure 20. "Le Cerf," from Horapollo, *De la signification des notes hiéroglyphiques* (Paris: Kerver, 1543).

The theme of the renewal of the stag's antlers is also that of La Fontaine's lines 19 and 20. La Fontaine, by concluding with the expression "tous les ans," echoes the "tous les ans" of Horapollo.[60] The process at work is again that of "Embedded Allusion," as illustrated by Rubin through the example of "La Tortue et les deux canards" (*A Pact with Silence*, 34-35). Here the relevance of La Fontaine's statement can only be seized by the reader who, armed mentally with the global image of the stag, is reminded of the *Hieroglyphics*. In the context, La Fontaine is providing a wry smile at the expense of those who claimed to fathom the mysteries of the Ancients with the aid of Horapollo's work: the stag's antlers, supposedly the symbol of long life, are the very reason for his early demise!

Taking the specific example of Guillaume Guéroult and certain *Fables*, our previous section suggested ways in which a knowledge of emblematics could better our understanding of La Fontaine's writings. This could be on the level of certain textual references or indeed regarding the nature of the composition of the *recueil*. In this section I have suggested that the same sort of conclusions could be relevant to the broad mass of La Fontaine's writings—not only the *Fables*, but also the *Contes*, *Les Amours de Psyché* and other works. More importantly, we should be aware of a method of writing that involves the creation of images—verbal or virtual by direct reference to the plastic arts—to be interacted with other parts of the text in the fashion of an emblem. In short, La Fontaine's texts are structured differently from modern texts; they still bear the marks of an age whose reading mentality made emblems a fashion.

V. C.
LA FONTAINE AND FOUQUET
HIS SOCIAL MILIEU:
AN ANALYSIS OF THE GENERAL NATURE OF EMBLEMATIC INFLUENCE

Arsenal manuscript 3135 of the *Recueil Conrart* contains a piece (number 32) addressed to M. Fouquet declaring that "Nous sommes à ceste heure dans le vaste Royaume des allégories, ou rien ne se dit ni se fait sans mystère." The text goes on to give details of the kingdom's component parts, these being regions such as "hyperbole," or "Anacronisme." "Mystère" in this context is not an inexplicable phenomenon but rather the hiding of meaning until it can be deciphered by those enlightened enough to do so.[61] Emblematics—that is to say emblems, devices and related forms such as rebuses and Renaissance hieroglyphs—undoubtedly played a leading rôle in the communication through "mystery" in this "vaste Royaume des allégories." The object of this section of our study is to explore some examples of such a phenomenon. More importantly, we shall place our research in the context of the society of the addressee, Fouquet, that is to say in the very circles that La Fontaine would have frequented.[62]

The Arsenal's *Recueil Conrart* gives us a privileged view of this society. Valentin Conrart (1603-1675),[63] man of letters, *saloniste* and first secretary of the Académie

Française, made the *Recueil* his life's work. It consists of manuscripts from such literary friends and acquaintances as Mme. de Sévigné, Vincent Voiture and La Fontaine himself, transcriptions ordered by Conrart of other pieces composed by leading society figures and various documents in Conrart's own hand. Often it is impossible to be exactly sure of the pieces' authorship; this is much more a concern of the twentieth century than of the seventeenth century. Very little recent critical analysis[64] has been applied to the holdings of the *Recueil Conrart*, yet it is obvious that Conrart's collection gives us a first-hand chronicle of the society of which he was a central figure, the literary society of seventeenth-century France. This was precisely the milieu that dominated much of La Fontaine's life from 1645 until his death in 1695.

Although manuscripts can obviously present an early stage of the process of literary creation, we should not fall into the trap of regarding those of the seventeenth-century purely and exclusively as rough drafts, a view of manuscripts that is often held today. Two important social phenomena should be taken into account: first, the printed text in the seventeenth century was still a comparatively rare and expensive pleasure. Second, literary activity was largely limited to the members of the close-knit salon circles. It is not surprising therefore that the need to publish was felt much less strongly then than it is today. Indeed Conrart's transcriptions can often represent the final stage of literary output as far as the salon exchanges were concerned. Another consequence is that on occasions lavish manuscripts could surpass the printed text, particularly when the audience targeted was limited, maybe even to a single person (e.g. the king).

Item 7 of *Recueil Conrart* manuscript 4171 can give us a good example of the use of devices in literary society of the time. As the piece refers to Fouquet's arrest, it was probably composed between 1661 and 1665. It is approximately four pages long and bears the title "Devises tirées de l'Ecriture, en faveur de Fouquet." It consists of a list of thirty-six persons or institutions involved in Fouquet's arrest and trial. Each is followed by a Latin motto taken from a biblical context. The devices bear no illustration. The seven following examples are typical:

> Le Parlement : Regnum meum non est de hoc mundo[65]
> ....
> M^r. le Prince : Mitte gladius [sic] in vagina[66]
> ....
> Le Roy : Quem osculatus ficero,
>   ipse tenere eum[67]
> ....
> M. Fouquet : Parce eis, nescuit quid facuit[68]
> ....
> M. Le Tellier : Voluit se Regem facere[69]
> ....
> M. de Colbert : Peccavi tradens sanguine justum[70]
> ....
> Acquereurs de Domaine : Reddite Caesari quae sunt Caesaris[71]....

In the case of M. Fouquet, for example, the motto "Parce eis, nescuit quid facuit" immediately brings to mind an image of the gentle Christ forgiving his accusers. The device's picture is therefore a virtual one provided by an outside context, that of the motto's Biblical allusion. To the reader who picks up the allusion (that is to say anyone in literary circles of the time) the device works as an allegory, with Fouquet being represented as the stoic saviour. This allegory is thus triggered by a single concise phrase.

Let us compare this process with the one by which the message of La Fontaine's *Fables* is conveyed. In *Fable* I, XVI, "La Mort et le bucheron," the bulk of the text describes the woodcutter's struggle with his load. The fable works as an extended allegory of man's struggle to exist, a commonplace in the tradition of the "Dances of Death." La Fontaine's allegory is summarised by the final two verses: "Plutot souffrir que mourir / C'est la devise des hommes." In "Le Renard et l'ecureuil" the tale of the high-climbing squirrel and the troubles he faces is an obvious allegory for Fouquet's situation. Here the summarising motto/moral is given at the beginning: "Il ne se faut jamais moquer des misérables / Car qui peut s'assurer d'être toujours heureux?"

When comparing the style of such fables with the Fouquet devices of manuscript 4171, immediate differences spring to mind; the devices' field of reference is biblical whereas La Fontaine's is secular; similarly the devices use humans where La Fontaine tends to use animals. Nonetheless the common ground is the use of a short sententious motto alongside a more or less extended allegory. However whereas it is the biblical motto that immediately suggests the allegory of Christ, La Fontaine's mottoes, in these examples and throughout the *Fables*, tend to serve as a way of summarising the allegory and allowing us to remember it once it has been given in the fable.

A quick glance at the other devices reveals that they tend to fit this pattern. Indeed the allegory of Fouquet as Christ is more or less continued throughout. Ironically it is "Le Roy" who plays the rôle of Judas, betraying Fouquet with a kiss ("Quem osculatus ficero, / ipse tenere eum"). Colbert is Pilate who sins with the blood of the just ("Peccavi tradens sanguine justum") and Le Tellier, again ironically, is guilty of the crime of which Fouquet/Christ is accused: "Voluit se Regem facere." Finally the message to the "Acquereurs de Domaine" is clear enough, although Fouquet now plays the rôle of Caesar rather than Christ: "Reditte Caesari quae sunt Caesaris."

It is important to note that these devices "en faveur de Fouquet" provide another example[72] of what Russell calls the "redécouverte de la citation" ("Emblème et mentalité," 15). Biblical passages had been commonly used in this way since the late Middle Ages; however, whereas medieval works would use phrases taken from commonplace sources with no regard to their original context, here it is precisely the quotation's context that provides the literary image, the basis for the allegory. In similar fashion, La Fontaine's motto-like morals are most effective in the context of the fable's accompanying pictorial allegory. In both cases, it is the fact that the mottoes function in the specific context the fable/biblical reference has given that differentiates them from maxims or dictums. The link may well be much stronger than that of two concurrent literary trends; indeed it is not out of the question that La Fontaine or members of his close social circles could have had a hand in the composition of the "Devises tirées de l'Ecriture, en faveur de Fouquet." The devices are understandably anonymous given their rebellious nature; however La Fontaine was one of Fouquet's strongest defenders after his arrest (as the "Elégie aux nymphes de Vaux" shows), as well as being a main contributor to the *Recueil Conrart* and a leading figure in the Academician's circle.

Piece number 102 of *Recueil Conrart* manuscript 5131 consists of a series of twenty "devises heroiques" followed by forty "devises galantes." Each is composed of a title, followed by a brief description of an *imago*, the *motto* in Latin and its French translation. In the case of the "devises heroiques" the title is occasionally replaced by a dedication. The following examples are typical:

>Devises heroiques:
>
>........................
>Pour le Pape Urbain 8
>Un essaim d'abeilles
>Sponte Favos Aegre Spicula
>De Gre le Miel L'Aiguillon a regret
>
>........................
>Pour M^{ons}. Fouquet Prisonnier
>Un ver a soye filant dans sa logue
>Inclusum labor illustrat
>Et sa prison le rend par son travail illustre
>
>........................
>Retraite du monde
>Un ver a soye dans sa logue
>Donec veniat immutatia mea
>Jusqu'au temps de mon changement
>
>........................
>Majorité du Roy
>Le soleil se tenant au milieu et dissipant les nuages
>Quos extulit ortu
>Qu'il avoit esleve au Temps de sa naissance
>
>........................
>Devises galantes:
>
>........................
>Beauté renevée [sic]
>Le soleil allumant de ses rayons le busher que s'est fait le Phoenix
>Vrit adorantem
>il brule qui l'adore
>
>........................
>Tristesse d'une Absence
>Un arbre depouillé de ses feuilles
>Fin che il sol ritorni[73]

....
Perdre compte d'un amant
Une levrette qui abondonne un lievre qu'elle a pris
Despicior Captus
Elle m'a pris et me mesprise. . . .

The device "Pour M^{ons}. Fouquet Prisonnier" conveys its message in much the same way as do all the devices of the collection: Unlike the devices in manuscript 4171, the picture does not come from the motto's context, but rather it is clearly defined as "Un ver a soye filant dans sa logue." The image is described but it could just as well be drawn. The viewer/reader is therefore presented with the metaphor of "M^{ons}. Fouquet Prisonnier" as a silkworm in its cell. The possible associations at this stage are multiple; our attention could be drawn by the prison aspect, the production of silk, even the lowly insect. In short, the comparison per se presents a global picture that remains imprecise with respect to the message being conveyed. Precision comes with the motto—"Inclusum labor illustrat"—which allows us to understand that Fouquet may be enclosed like the lowly insect, but his resulting product (silk) will bring him glory.

The device's communication process has much in common with that of La Fontaine's *Fables*. La Fontaine will often present us with a global but imprecise image—the presentation of a scene or characters accompanied by the retelling of a series of events—from which the precise message can be drawn by the application of the fable's moral. Rubin, briefly speaking, refers to the retelling of events as the "apologue" and the moral as the "exposition." He points out that there are two types of fable, the inductive and the reductive, depending on whether the "apologue" is presented first with the "exposition" then drawing a conclusion—inductive—, or vice versa (*A Pact with Silence*, 8-10). The difference between this process and that of the device is that whereas the device's image is purely static, the "apologue" of the fable includes dramatic elements; nonetheless the basic process of communication is similar.[74]

The close links between the device and the fable become even clearer in the light of an anonymous piece that forms part of the *Recueil Conrart* manuscript 5420. The poem in question is entitled "Fable des vers a soie et du Moucheron":

> Les vers à soie, en leur bobine,
> Travaillaient tous à qui mieux mieux.
> Avançons, disaient-ils, ce travail précieux
> En quoi notre espoir raffine
> Fuyons l'oisiveté, évitons la paresse
> Du moucheron qui vole autour de nous.
> — Si je suis paresseux, dit-il, vous êtes fous
> Avec votre art et votre adresse
> Vous faites, je l'avoue, un ouvrage fort beau;
> Mais il vous enferme au tombeau.

> Pour moi, j'aime mieux ne rien faire,
> Et je trouve à ce prix que la gloire est trop chère.
> — Mais en ne faisant rien que bruire dans les airs,
> Se rend-on immortel, dirent-alors les vers?
> — Immortel? nullement, je mourrai comme un autre.
> — Et tu trouves ton sort plus heureux que le nôtre?
> Ha, puisqu'également nous devons tous mourir,
> Il nous faut du moins acquérir,
> Par une illustre vie, une fin glorieuse,
> Et c'est où doit butter une âme généreuse.

The subject of the fable, like that of the device, is a "ver a soye filant dans sa logue." Both apply an "ars longa vita brevis"-style moral to the silkworm image; the device by its motto—"Et sa prison le rend par son travail illustre"—, the fable by its concluding moral:

> Ha, puisqu'également nous devons tous mourir,
> Il nous faut du moins acquérir,
> Par une illustre vie, une fin glorieuse,
> Et c'est où doit butter une âme généreuse. (lines 17-20)

The main difference is the obvious concision of the device, compared to the fable with its secondary details such as the Moucheron and the conversation. The device also names Fouquet, making the allusion obvious, whereas the fable remains more general. Nonetheless it does suggest the reference to Fouquet by lines such as, "Vous faites, je l'avoue, un ouvrage fort beau; / Mais il vous enferme au tombeau" (lines 9-10).

For our purposes it is particularly interesting that a salon allegory—Fouquet as the silkworm—could find its expression equally well in a device or in a fable. Indeed the similarities between our two silkworm pieces clearly demonstrate the close links between the two forms of expression. Examples such as this one underline the notion that by La Fontaine's time emblems, devices and fables were still very much interchangeable forms. The implication is that if we can understand how a device works, we will be able to understand better the workings of La Fontaine's masterpiece.[75]

The "Pour M[ons]. Fouquet Prisonnier" is therefore of particular interest stylistically speaking when compared to the manuscript "Fable des vers a soie et du Moucheron." However we might also consider the devices of Arsenal manuscript 5131 in respect to their content. It is possible to see certain elements of the collection in terms of pro-Fouquet propaganda worthy of La Fontaine in the *Songe de Vaux*.

In some cases the pro-Fouquet propaganda is obvious. The two silkworm devices, "Inclusum labor illustrat" and "Donec veniat immutatia mea" clearly praise Fouquet's endeavours and express hope for a change in his fortune. Others can be seen as criticising the king; "Quos extulit ortu," with the sunrise dispelling clouds, would appear flattering; however we should remember that *ortu* can also mean "new beginning"; in the context of the events of 1661 the device now takes a sinister turn; Fouquet is summarily dispelled ("quos extulit") with the coming of the new regime ("ortu").

Similarly the "devises galantes" can be taken in a context other than that of love. "Vrit adorantem" can be applied to the king's attitude towards Fouquet; attitudes towards Fouquet's imprisonment could be summarised as "Tristesse d'une Absence" thereby rendering the "arbre depouillé de ses feuilles" picture and the "Fin che il sol ritorni" motto most appropriate. Another interesting example is that of the "levrette qui abandonne un lievre qu'elle a pris"; the French translation, "Elle m'a pris et me mesprise," indicates that the device is clearly about love, however it is not entirely accurate; the use of the passive verb in the Latin motto, "dispicior captus" means the phrase could appropriately be applied to Fouquet's plight in the light of his fall from grace. Indeed the general themes of the "devises galantes" are those of unrequited love, inconstancy, "passion d'un souverain," "fidelité invincible," "Rien ne plait en absence," "beauté dangereuse" and so on.

In short, an overwhelmingly high percentage of the Arsenal manuscript 5131 devices—especially the "devises galantes"—can be read on the level of pro-Fouquet propaganda. This could be seen as pure coincidence or the product of a fertile imagination, were it not for the fact that the reader/viewer is unambiguously directed to the Fouquet affair by the silkworm devices, one of which is dedicated "Pour M^{ons}. Fouquet Prisonnier." Furthermore the devices are to be found in a *Recueil* that includes a letter from Fouquet's mother to the king pleading for clemency (piece 60) as well as La Fontaine's famous account of his journey into exile (piece 104). In this context the various devices on ingratitude, abandon and absence can reasonably evoke Fouquet's fall from grace. It is highly possible that the collection of "devises heroiques" and "devises galantes" could have been put together by one or more of Fouquet's loyal protegés.

Our analysis thus far has dealt with manuscripts that would, presumably, have been intended for salon consumption. Nonetheless we should not dismiss the devices in question as mere frivolities to which little importance and value were attached. This becomes clear when we consider some of the luxury manuscript productions. One such case is Arsenal manuscript 1172, entitled *Symbolorum selectorum centuria*. The work consists of one hundred devices each taking up two facing pages. On the left the picture is carefully painted in bright colours, accompanied by a bandereau bearing the motto. The facing page is intended for the device's number and accompanying verse of six lines. Unfortunately the verse has been completed in only three of the cases, the remaining facing pages bearing an empty space. Although the piece is by no means of the same outstanding quality that *Les Devises pour les tapisseries du roy* undoubtedly is, it is nonetheless a painstakingly produced work of art.

Only the central devices, numbers 50 and 51, stray from the work's uniform pattern. These two face one another, each bearing half of the central motto: "Dum terra Herculem habet [number 51] / Properet malum quodcumque [number 50]" ["While the earth has Hercules / Let whatever evil come forward"]. Device 50 shows the various beasts slain by Hercules whereas 51 bears a portrait of Richelieu in cardinal's garb. The allusion to Richelieu as Hercules may well be in reference to the supression of the Huguenot cause in France and/or to the defeat of Austria. This would allow us to date the manuscript to some time in the early 1640s.

Of the *Symbolorum selectorum centuria*'s one hundred devices twelve figure among the "devises heroiques" and "devises galantes" of manuscript 5131. In general the description of the image given in manuscript 5131 (e.g. "le soleil allumant de ses rayons le busher que s'est fait le Phoenix") corresponds exactly to the painting of manuscript 1172. The latter's bandereau gives the motto ("Vrit adorantem") word for word but without the translation. All three elements however—description, motto and translation—are to be found in the "table" at the end of the volume. On a few occasions manuscript 5131's devices follow virtually but not quite exactly those of manuscript 1172.

Immediate conclusions can be drawn. First, the painstaking quality of manuscript 1172 underlines the fact that the art of the device was taken very seriously and valued highly. Secondly, it reminds us that a certain corpus of devices had come into existence, a corpus that would have formed part of a literary man's cultural baggage. In chapter III we cited the case of the devices at La Flèche (figure 6) that Le Jay was to use several years later. To come back to the example of "Vrit adorantem," not only does it feature in manuscripts 1172 and 5131, but the device also appears in the Département des Estampes *Pièce Te 120* and is discussed by M. Clément in his *Regles pour la connoissance des devises*. In the context of manuscript 1172 the "Vrit adorantem" device serves as a gentle warning against cruelty on the part of the wise and powerful,[76] or indeed as nothing more than an example of a good device. To see it as a serious criticism of the powers-that-be makes little sense in the context of a collection whose centrepiece exalts Richelieu by comparing him to the beast-slaying Hercules.

In the context of manuscript 5131, however, the device appears completely different. When juxtaposed with a device "Pour M^{ons}. Fouquet Prisonnier," "Vrit adorantem" will inevitably bring to mind Louis XIV's treatment of his *Surintendant des finances* (at least when seen from the point of view of the pro-Fouquet camp). The collection as a whole is by no means a criticism of the king—such would be folly—as it includes ample praise of his "générosité" and "justice," but the reader is left with the distinct impression that as concerns his treatment of Fouquet, Louis has strayed from his normal wisdom.

The implication is, therefore, that the *Recueil* of manuscript 5131 consists effectively of a selection of devices that would for the most part have already been known to salon society. At least twelve, for example, had already appeared in manuscript 1172. The process is similar to that of Tristan's poetry in the context of SMAdd.392: it is the new arrangement and implied application of the various devices that give the *Recueil* its specific interest. Originality of selection wins the day over originality of composition.

It is not hard to see the link between this method and that of La Fontaine's *Fables*. *Fable* II, II, for example, "Conseil tenu par les rats" is taken directly from Abstemius's *Fable* 196, but it is La Fontaine's newly-chosen context that allows us to apply it to *La Cour en Conseillers* of the reign of Louis XIV. The fable tells of the council of rats that agrees to attach a bell to the cat's neck, unfortunately no-one is prepared to do the deed. La Fontaine's conclusion is explicit:

> Ne faut-il que délibérer,
> La cour en conseillers foisonne;
> Est-il besoin d'exécuter,
> L'on ne rencontre plus personne. (lines 29-32)

Similarly *Fable* II, V, "La Chauve-souris et les deux belettes," an Æsopic piece like so many of La Fontaine's fables, is adapted to the theme of turncoats of the time. The story is that of the bat who classes herself as a bird or as a mouse according to the needs of the situation. La Fontaine makes the contemporary allusion clear with the final two lines: "Le Sage dit, selon les gens: / Vive le Roi, vive la Ligue." La Fontaine's genius is to be found therefore not in originality of content but in the way that he chooses well-known pieces to fit the context of his time. This style has of course been noted by many a critic;[77] less documented, however, is the fact that the collections of devices of the period could function in much the same way, as the example of manuscripts 1172 and 5131 demonstrates.[78] We see, therefore, that this was a common way of working rather than a technique peculiar to La Fontaine.

To sum up, seventeenth-century society had come to possess a set stock of devices (one might even say a canon) that was generally taken very seriously, as the lavishness of productions such as manuscript 1172 indicates. Well-known devices could be applied to different contexts in the same way that intertextual references are exploited in other genres. In such cases—an example of which is to be found in manuscript 5131—the originality of the creation is decidedly less important than the originality of the application. La Fontaine therefore applied a process to his *Fables* (and indeed his other works) that members of his social milieu were applying to devices. This should not, however, be seen as a unique case, but rather an important instance of a general phenomenon. Forms of literary expression were, as Russell has pointed out, discovering the notion of the quotation in context ("Emblème et mentalité"). Devices and fables were, at the time, parallel forms following similar directions of evolution.

One final series of manuscripts provides another example of luxury production, the *Devises pour les tapisseries du roy*. Figure 4 shows the "Praestant interna coronae" device from the Bibliothèque nationale de France's painted version of this collection (ms. fr. 7819). According to the British Library catalogue, the Harley manuscript 4377 version was designed to be presented to Louis XIV ("The book appears to have been bound and blazened [sic] for the King of France"). The manuscripts were probably completed in the late 1660s or early 1670s. The devices themselves were conceived to illustrate the orders of the Gobelins tapestries which, according to Perrault in his *Discours sur l'art des devises*,[79] "furent faites immédiatement après la conclusion de la paix générale, en l'année 1662" (fol. 13v). Our two manuscripts, and a further copy in Vienna, are not identical, but the differences are basically of little importance.[80]

The Bibliothèque de l'Arsenal has two rudimentary manuscript versions of the *Devises pour les tapisseries du roy*, of which one, to be found in sections of Perrault's *Discours sur l'art des devises* (ms. 3328), is discussed at some length in the next chapter. The other, piece 46 of *Recueil Conrart* manuscript 5418 is also Perrault's work—it is attributed to "M. Perraut" [sic]—and consists of six of the "quatre saisons de l'année" devices.[81] The picture is replaced by a one-line description (e.g. "Un faucon fondant sur sa proye") but the motto, explanation, and madrigal are as per the presentation copies. It seems likely that this document represents a discussion piece, a sample for Conrart's close circles. It is interesting to note that the piece is to be found in a volume that includes several of La Fontaine's *Contes* and some of his *Nouvelles* as well as pieces in favour of Fouquet.

Links between the *Devises pour les tapisseries du roy* and La Fontaine's work go beyond those of Conrart's literary circles as indicated by the fact that both are to be found in manuscript 5418. Indeed Marc Fumaroli, in "Un Art royal,"[82] points out that the devices and madrigals appeared in the 1671 *Recueil de poésies chretiennes et diverses* bearing La Fontaine's name (7). More importantly, as Fumaroli goes on to demonstrate, there are considerable stylistic similarities between the *Devises pour les tapisseries du roy* and the *Fables*. In his opinion, Perrault, La Fontaine's friend, and Bailly, "ont eu à l'esprit les fables (qui circulèrent dans le monde bien avant leur publication) tandis que l'un composait ses madrigaux et l'autre ses miniatures" (10). Rather than Perrault and Bailly "copying" La Fontaine, it seems more likely that the similarities in style are due to the influence of a prevailing mentality, one that encouraged the interaction of verbal and visual elements, one that would have left its mark on exponents of the two genres at the time. Fumaroli hints at this when he later states,

> Une aussi intime parenté à laquelle il faut laisser son mystère, est due d'abord à vue humaine, à ce qui rapproche deux genres «mineurs», la fable ésopique et la devise morale, et au fonds commun narratif où puisent ensemble fabulistes, auteurs et graveurs de devises. (11)

More important than the question of the "fonds commun," although not stressed by Fumaroli, is the notion of a common emblematic mentality, as described in the previous section of this chapter.

A particularly interesting case, cited by Fumaroli, is that of the "Praestant interna coronae" device, whose picture, a partially opened pomegranate, is ostensibly marked by the presence of a seated squirrel (see figure 4). We are inevitably reminded of Fouquet and his squirrel device. Fumaroli interprets the reference as follows: "L'animal symbolique de Fouquet, oubliant son ancien maître, a choisi la ronde joyeuse qui fait cercle autour de l'irrésistible prince charmant" (17). Such an unflattering stance towards Fouquet—namely that his friends would abandon him after his loss of favour with Louis XIV, the "prince charmant"—strikes us as surprising coming from a work signed by Charles Perrault who, whilst being under the protection of Jean-Baptiste Colbert, Fouquet's prosecutor, was nonetheless a close friend of La Fontaine.

Indeed Fumaroli's interpretation does not take into account Perrault's explanation of the device's motto, "Pour dire que comme la courronne de la Grenade n'est pas comparable aux fruits qu'elle cache au dedans puisqu'elle n'en est que l'ecorce & le dehors. Il en est de mesme de sa Majesté...." The *Devises pour les tapisseries du roy* date from a time when Fouquet's future was unsure and there was still hope that he would escape imprisonment or even be forgiven and allowed to return to power. The specific reference in Perrault's device to the pomegranate's "fruits qu'elle cache au dedans," that is to say Louis's soft and magnanimous heart as opposed to his hard and powerful external appearance, is surely a discreet plea attempting to win clemency through flattery.

Another *Recueil Conrart* piece (ms. 5420) from around the same period conveys the same message of hope. The fable in question is entitled "Le Renard et l'ecureuil." The fable has been identified as being the work of La Fontaine.[83] In line 13—"Tu cherchais les lieux hauts et voisins de la foudre"—La Fontaine refers directly to Fouquet's "quo non ascendet?" device. Surely La Fontaine's is the same squirrel that surmounts Perrault/Bailly's pomegranate device. La Fontaine's message of hope comes in line 19, "Lorsque l'ire du Ciel à l'écureuil pardonne."[84]

The same theme dominates another piece from this volume of the *Recueil Conrart*, number 57, "Sur la devise de M. Fouquet." The sonnet in question, addressed to Colbert, concludes with a prophesy of Fouquet's return to grace: "Mais, en fin sa vertu l'élève dans un point / Qui fait dire par tout, malgré ton entreprise, / Où ce rare Fouquet ne montera-t-il point?" (lines 12-14).[85] In short, we see once again that a similar theme can be expressed equally well through a sonnet, a device in a luxury manuscript destined for the king, or indeed a fable by La Fontaine.

The conclusions that can be drawn from this particular analysis are in keeping with those to be drawn from the manuscript study as a whole:

First, the study of manuscripts gives us access (as far as is humanly possible given a distance of three centuries) to La Fontaine's milieu in the period 1645-1695. This is particularly true of the *Recueil Conrart* whose volumes place pieces by La Fontaine alongside those of other leading literary figures of the time—Mme. de Scudéry, Boileau, Perrault and Conrart himself—as well as alongside a vast number of anonymous or unidentifiable pieces. The very nature of the collection means that it represents, in all probability, an agenda of salon discussion for the period in question. It is particularly interesting as far as we are concerned, therefore, to note that collections of devices held sway within the same circles to which the *Fables* and *Contes* of La Fontaine were introduced.

Second, the subject matter of certain of the collections of devices indicates a historical connection with La Fontaine. Collections from the post-1660s would often deal with the Fouquet affaire, either in their entirety (e.g. manuscript 4171's "Devises tirées de l'Ecriture en faveur de Fouquet") or at least in part (e.g. manuscript 5131's "devises heroiques"/"devises galantes"). Given La Fontaine's close associations with both the *Surintendant des finances* and the society producing these *recueils de devises*, there is a possibility that the fabulist or his close associates could have had a hand in their composition.

Third, our study of the various manuscripts suggests the existence of a canon of courtly devices towards the end of the seventeenth century.[86] To take the example of "Vrit adorantem," the variety of the device's applications is suggested by the fact that not only is it to be found among the informal scribblings of the *Recueil Conrart* (ms. 5131), it is discussed in a tract by M. Clément (ms. 5420) and features in a luxury production intended to exalt Richelieu (ms. 1172). Similar diversification can be noted in the case of the *Devises pour les tapisseries du roy*. The resulting effect is that the context of the application plays an important rôle in the articulation of meaning, a meaning that does not depend uniquely upon the original composition in question. In concrete terms, the same device can—depending on the context—either serve as an example of how to excel in the art of emblematics (ms. 3328) or as a pure glorification of the king (Harley ms. 4377).

This notion of the application of a context can also be seen within the literary functioning of the devices themselves; the "Devises tirées de l'Ecriture en faveur de Fouquet" operate through the transfer of the biblical context, an allegory that is only effective to the reader who catches the original reference. We see therefore that our canon of devices conforms, alongside other literary forms, to the phenomenon of the discovery of the quotation; the meaning of "Vrit adorantem" (or in the case of manuscript 4171, the words of Christ) can be read on the primary universal level (man's tendency to "burn" those who devote themselves to him) or the second, closer level, that of the application of a universal truth to a specific situation (e.g. Louis XIV's attitude towards Fouquet). Needless to say, the fable is an example of a set body of texts, a canon based here upon the work of the ancients, that was applied in the seventeenth century according to much the same process.

Finally, similarities in the subject matter and contents of certain devices and fables suggest that the two forms were operating within the same field of reference. The comparison of Fouquet to a silkworm, for example, whose imprisonment would lead to greater riches, could be expressed through a device or through a fable, the main difference being the latter's use of narrative and embellishment of detail. In the case of Tristan we have seen similar overlap and interplay between his poetry and the emblems of Van Veen. The same is also true of certain *Recueil Conrart* sonnets that are based upon devices. It is an overlapping that seems not to occur between other literary forms and which, furthermore, is now lost to us, as our approach to modern devices (logos, advertising panels, etc.) is a far cry from our way of reading a modern fable/moral short story.

***

One of the most frequently and fervently discussed questions amongst critics of La Fontaine has been that of the arrangement of the various *recueils* of fables. It is a question which, by extension, leads us to consider the very nature of La Fontaine's fable genre and the tradition within and from which he was writing.

Jean-Pierre Collinet in *Le Monde littéraire de La Fontaine* had noted the existence of a series of "fables doubles" which make for a "jeu des parallélismes ou des oppositions" (163, see also pages 164-226). He points to the cohesion of La Fontaine's work as a whole: "car les correspondances secondaires se multiplient entre les différentes parties de cet ensemble et lui donnent sa cohésion" (413). It is surely no coincidence that Leo Spitzer[87] uses the same terms in reference to what he calls La Fontaine's "technique de la transition":

> Et cette technique devient finalement l'expression d'un regard sur le monde, qui découvre partout des passerelles, des convergences et des correspondances. (192)

Parallelisms and echoes through fables which refer to one another suggest that La Fontaine's work is carefully constructed, but this is a far cry from it having a rigid structure.

Rubin in *A Pact with Silence* provides a convincing explanation for such an arrangement:

> La Fontaine did not arrange fables at random, or purely by theme, in his twelve books. As my third chapter suggests, he followed the baroque precedent of avoiding causal or logical principles to achieve *recueil* arrangement, but at the same time he sought and found another technique far removed from conventional, paratactic, or associative *dispositio*. Book 11 is typical of the *Fables* in that it establishes, deviates from, and finally returns to a complex formal, technical, and stylistic, as well as thematic, norm. (104-05)

He concludes by suggesting that,

> La Fontaine was to the baroque poets what he had been to Lucretius: a *discipulus*, in the full sense of the Latin term—not only a follower and a continuator, but above all a successor, who modified, adapted, and at times broke with, his predecessors' examples. (105)

Rubin is of course correct in pointing to the tradition from which La Fontaine took his influence as being of primary importance if we are to understand the very nature of these *Fables*. Even more importantly, Rubin underlines the fact that the tradition in question is not that of classicism, that of Corneille and of Descartes, but rather an earlier one. Pointing directly to the poets of the early seventeenth century, he also draws our attention to a certain critical void:

> A crucial problem of La Fontaine studies, and, more broadly, of the historiography of early modern French literature, is the seeming disconnectedness, even isolation, of the *Fables* from the general trend of seventeenth-century lyricism. (97)

Rubin's conclusion that "La Fontaine shared with the baroque poets a fascination with the undoing of rigorous sequence in the lyric" (107) could fruitfully be taken beyond the 'mainstream' baroque poets. The case for the influence of writers such as Boileau is indeed convincing, but I would suggest an extension of Rubin's methods: La Fontaine manipulated not only the poets we know as canonical, but also the minor authors and exponents of trends of the time. Of these, writers in the emblem book tradition were among the foremost.

In the 1668 "Préface" to the *Fables*, La Fontaine states that "Le Corps est la fable; l'Ame, la Moralité" (10). These are exactly the same terms of reference used by Menestrier in his general analysis of the emblem, and, more specifically, in his justification of his definition of La Fontaine's *Fables* as emblems (*L'Art des emblèmes, où s'enseigne la morale*, 27-29). La Fontaine's *Fables*, indeed his works as a whole, are a product of an age that expressed itself naturally through emblematics. The notion of a "Corps," to a mind of the emblematic age, implied a mixture of text and, significantly, image, whose interaction formed the "Ame." To the modern reader, however, a fable is a short narrative with an appended moral. A picture is neither required nor expected.

A shift in attitudes of this kind inevitably creates changes in our approach to the texts of a bygone age. Concrete evidence of these changes is to be found in the classification system of one of America's larger, but not atypical, libraries, the Carnegie Library of Pittsburgh. Of the Carnegie's twenty or so editions of the *Fables*, some are classed as literature, some as children's books. In some cases the large print and colourful drawings clearly indicate a young target audience, whereas the opposite is true of certain scholarly editions. In the majority of cases, however, the classification appears somewhat arbitrary. Nonetheless a closer look reveals a clear criterion for distinction: without exception, all the fully-illustrated editions are classed as children's literature. A selection of one hundred fables dating from 1900,[88] for instance, clearly bears the stamp "Central Boys and Girls Division" (figure 21). This is in spite of the fact that the boys and girls of Pittsburgh could not really be expected to understand the reference to François de La Rochefoucauld's "Maxim Book" in "The Man and his Image."

Classification of illustrated works as fit for children shows how modern understanding of textual/visual interaction is far different from notions prevalent in La Fontaine's time. His works are therefore often read without a full contextual understanding. A knowledge of emblematics—as we have shown in this chapter—can, on the other hand, afford us a deeper appreciation on several levels.

Firstly, our study has revealed and explained some textual references which until now have remained hidden. One such case is the reference to the stag's antlers (" . . . les presents / Que le Ciel lui fait tous les ans") which can be explained in the light of Horapollo's *Hieroglyphics*. As well as being a major proto-emblematic work, the *Hieroglyphics* were also an important source of animal lore. Furthermore, the work's first edition (1505) was published in the same volume as a version of Æsop's *Fables*. It seems more than likely that La Fontaine knew the *Hieroglyphics* well and, moreover, that *Fable* VI, IX is not the only piece to refer to them. In the case of

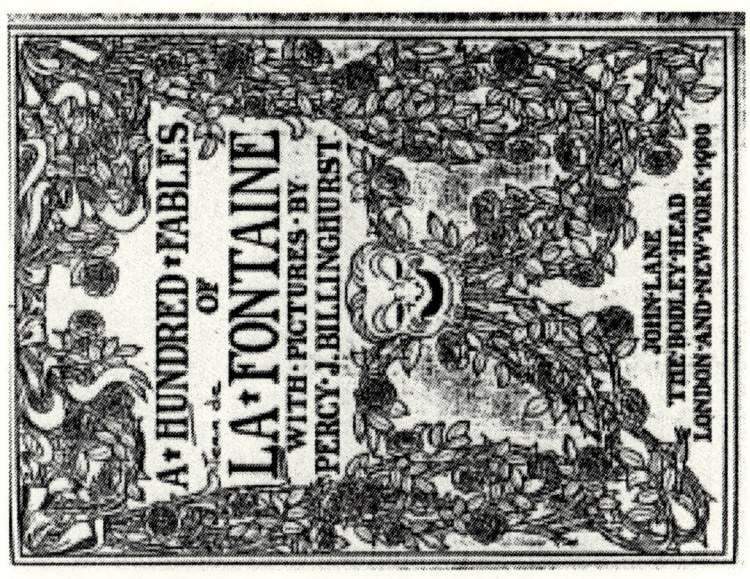

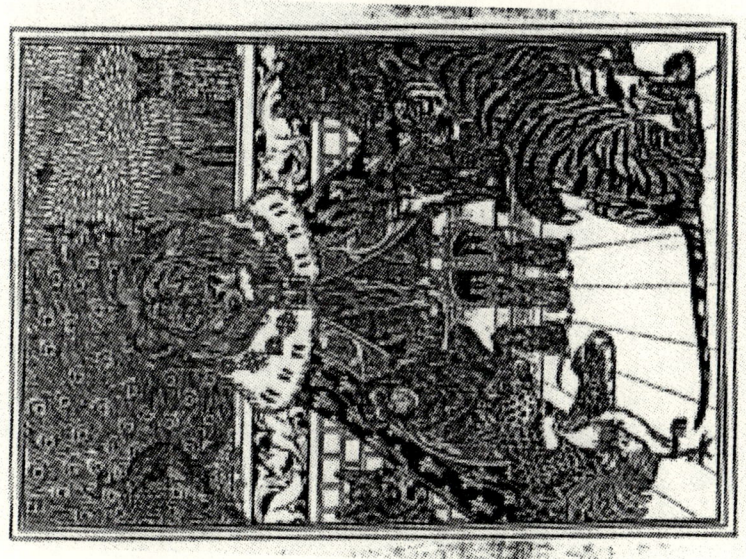

Figure 21. Frontispiece from Jean de La Fontaine, *A Hundred Fables of La Fontaine with Pictures by Percy J. Billinghurst* (London: John Lane, 1900). Carnegie Library of Pittsburgh copy.

Guillaume Guéroult, critics have already pointed to his *Premier livre des emblemes* as being the inspiration for several *Fables*. None, however, has explained references to Guéroult in seemingly unconnected fables, as is the case of the final verse of "L'Araignée et l'hirondelle." Such examples indicate that the extent of the influence of emblematics upon La Fontaine has been vastly underestimated or indeed ignored.

Such underestimation becomes clearly perceivable when we accept that the emblematic influence is not just limited to direct textual references, but that it dominates a whole mentality of reading. Our analysis of certain manuscripts of the *Recueil Conrart* has suggested that within La Fontaine's social circles emblematics provided the vehicle of communication even on the most everyday level. It is natural that the constructs of such communication—the creation of static global images whose full value is obtained by interaction with an analytic and interpretive text—should comprise an essential part of the structure of La Fontaine's works.

To the reader aware of such a process La Fontaine's texts become considerably more enlightening. On a general level we can start to appreciate elements of textual composition, such as lengthy static descriptions or a mixture of poetry and prose, that might otherwise appear disconcerting. An ability to spot and read "textual emblems" as La Fontaine's reader might have done can turn the key to subtleties of meaning (pro-Fouquet propaganda, reticence before the splendours of Versailles . . .) that the modern reader could easily overlook. Such awareness throws not only the *Fables*, but even La Fontaine's entire *œuvre* into a new light.

The evolution in the fashion in the illustrations of La Fontaine's texts, can, in the context of emblematics, tell us something about the way approaches to reading have changed. Conversely, an understanding of reading approaches can explain fashions in illustration. Post eighteenth-century allegorical illustrations of the *Fables*, for instance, may charm the modern reader or critic, but in asking why such portrayals are purely post eighteenth-century we are effectively asking why and how our attitudes have changed. The factor we propose to explain this shift is the decline of the emblematic age. If Chauveau's simple representations sufficed in La Fontaine's time, it was because the mechanics of reading, the interaction of textual image with textual récit, provide a dynamics of production with regard to the moral that can no longer be expected of the modern reader. To consider such questions is to consider La Fontaine's texts in context, in a way that his readers would automatically have done. This in turn heightens our awareness of their true complexity and richness.

NOTES

[1] The sources for this outline biography are Georges Couton's introductions to his editions of the *Fables* (Paris: Garnier, 1990) and of the *Contes et nouvelles en vers* (Paris: Garnier, 1985), and Pierre Clarac's introduction to his edition of the *Œuvres diverses* (Paris: Gallimard, 1991). For an excellent overview of La Fontaine's work in a biographical and historical context (including the Fouquet affair), see Marc Fumaroli, *Le Poète et le roi: Jean de La Fontaine en son siècle* (Paris: Falloir, 1997).

[2] See "La Fontaine's *Fables*, Book X: The Labyrinth Hypothesis," *L'Esprit Créateur* 21.4 (1981), 90-98. This and the following references will be further discussed at relevant points in this chapter.

[3] In *Le Monde littéraire de La Fontaine*.

[4] In *A Pact with Silence*.

[5] In *A Pact with Silence*.

[6] In "Stratégies de désorientation dans les 'Fables' de La Fontaine."

[7] *La Poétique de La Fontaine: Deux études: La Fontaine et l'art des emblèmes: Du Pensum aux Fables* (Paris: Presses Universitaires de France, 1957).

[8] (Paris: Promodis, 1986).

[9] A version of parts of this section has appeared under the title "Les *Fables* et les emblèmes: L'Influence de Guillaume Guéroult" in *Fabuleux La Fontaine*, eds. Kees Meerhoff and Paul J. Smith (Amsterdam: Rodopi, 1996), 64-71.

[10] 3 vols. (The Hague and Rotterdam: A. and R. Leers, 1690).

[11] (Saint Louis: Washington UP, 1970).

[12] For a discussion of the way in which La Fontaine combined sources in a particular *Fable* (I, III), see H. Gaston Hall's "*Contaminatio* in a Fable by La Fontaine (1,3)." It is a process which Grimm, in his "Stratégies de désorientation dans les 'Fables' de La Fontaine," labels "le jeu de cache-cache avec l'autorité d'Esope, de Phèdre, de Pilpay et d'autres" (182).

[13] Both McGowan and Couton (*Fables*) have stated La Fontaine's debt to Guéroult in the case of *Fable* VII, I, but neither have provided demonstrative analysis of the example.

[14] (Lyons: Balthazar Arnoullet, 1549).

[15] (Lyons: Balthazar Arnoullet, 1550).

[16] The source for our biographical information on Guéroult is De Vaux de Lancey's introduction to his edition of the *Premier livre des emblèmes* (Rouen: Lainé, 1937).

[17] All of the early editions of La Fontaine's *Fables*, and many editions from the eighteenth century onwards, included illustrations. The question of illustration will be discussed at greater length in the next section of this chapter.

[18] *Cento favole bellissime dei più illustri antichi, e moderni autori Greci, e Latini* (Venice: Giovanni Pietro Brigonei).

[19] *Trois centz soixãnte & six apologues d'Esope* (Rouen: Iehan Leprest, 1547). A reprint edition edited by Charles Lormier (Rouen: Société des Bibliophiles Normands, 1877) also exists.

[20] (Paris: D. Janot).

[21] (Munich: Fink, 1974).

[22] It should be noted that such a technique fell within the rhetorical tradition of the time; Thomas Sébillet's *Art poétique françoys* includes a section on the effectiveness of epigrams and Le Moyne's *Art des devises* comments on the use of internal rhymes as a rhetorical tool.

[23] This is a theme that goes back to Francesco Colonna's *Hypnerotomachia Poliphili*.

[24] Indeed in the preface to his *Emblematum liber* Alciato had referred to his emblems as being akin to mosaics. Nonetheless a mosaic does present a general and completely unified picture.

[25] Although this was a characteristic of sixteenth-century emblem books, it is interesting to note that by the seventeenth century many emblem books did boast thematic unity.

[26] Pages 132-38 and 170-76 of his *Patterns of Irony in the Fables of La Fontaine* (Athens: Ohio UP, 1985).

[27] See in particular I, III chapter 3, pages 163-226—"Le Cas particulier des fables doubles"— of *Le Monde littéraire de La Fontaine*.

[28] "La Fontaine's *Fables*, Book X: The Labyrinth Hypothesis."

[29] "Triple Calculus: Notes Towards a Poetic and Rhetoric of La Fontaine's *Fables*, Book 7," in

The Ladder of High Designs: Structure and Interpretation of French Lyric Sequence, eds. Doranne Fenoaltea and David Lee Rubin (Charlottesville VA: UP of Virginia, 1991), 91-109.

[30] Pages 78-95 (i.e. chapter 3) of *A Pact with Silence*.

[31] Couton (*Fables* 425) points to a similar reference by Rabelais (V, 12). However whereas Guéroult, like La Fontaine, uses the example of a "guespe," Rabelais tells of the "gros taons."

[32] *A Pact with Silence*, pages 34-35 and 46-50. We have already cited an important passage from this section: "Whenever for thematic purposes the poet models the action or characterization of the apologues on the motifs of another work—literary or not—the reader must recognize the source, make a mental inventory of the similarities and differences between earlier and later versions, and then infer the significance of these parallels and divergences" (34).

[33] Parts of this section have appeared as "La Fontaine, Emblematics and the Plastic Arts: *Les Amours de Psyché* and *Le Songe de Vaux*," in *Emblems and Art History*, eds. Alison Adams and Laurence Grove (Glasgow: Glasgow Emblem Studies, 1996), 23-39.

[34] Much work has been done on the question of the illustration of La Fontaine's *Fables*. Alain-Marie Bassy's *Les Fables de La Fontaine: Quatre siècles d'illustration* in particular gives a well-documented historical overview of the subject, going from the earliest editions to the twentieth century. For a discussion that includes the illustration of works other than the *Fables* (specifically the *Contes*), see Jean-Pierre Collinet's "La Fontaine et ses illustrateurs" in *Œuvres complètes: I: Fables: Contes et nouvelles* (Paris: Gallimard, 1986), lxiii-cxlviii.

[35] For a full introduction (including bibliographic information) to the engravings of Chauveau with specific reference to his work for the early editions of the *Fables*, see Raymond LePage's "The 1668 Edition of the *Fables*: An Iconographic Interpretation." LePage does briefly compare Chauveau's work with Jean Baudoin's 1631 edition of Æsop's fables (note 6, page 68). Indeed, throughout the article LePage could often be describing the way in which an emblem functions although his subject in hand is actually the relationship between La Fontaine's text and Chauveau's images.

[36] See, for example, the *Saint Louys ou la sainte couronne reconquise: Poeme heroique* (Paris: Augustin Courbé, 1668). The opening page of each "livre" is headed by a device and juxtaposed against a full-page engraving, both the work of Chauveau.

[37] For fuller details on these and on the other illustrators of the *Fables*, see Bassy.

[38] I.e. the age that made emblems a fashion. This is generally seen as coming to an end towards the final years of the eighteenth century.

[39] E.g. "sa majesté, ses enrichissemens et ses grâces; la proportion, le bel ordre, et la correspondance de ses parties" (86). I am grateful to David Graham for suggesting the ideas expanded in this and the following paragraphs.

[40] Immediately preceeding the first emblem of the 1553 *Morosophie*.

[41] In "Discursive Stategies in Early French Emblem Books."

[42] It is important nonetheless to differentiate such references from the various descriptions of the Palace and gardens that served as visitors' guides. Boris Donné underlines this caveat in *La Fontaine et la poétique du songe*, especially on pages 23-27, 185-88 and 251-54.

[43] For an analysis and examples of the impression that could be created through the interaction of architecture and its décor, see Judi Loach's "Architecture and Emblems: Issues in Interpretation," in *Emblems and Art History*, eds. Alison Adams and Laurence Grove (Glasgow: Glasgow Emblem Studies, 1996), 1-21. Loach also addresses the important differences that one should bear in mind when considering architectural *imagines* as opposed to printed ones.

[44] (Paris: Imprimerie Royale).

[45] For a general but thorough analysis of the way in which La Fontaine subverts by appealing

to different readerships, some more 'alert' than others, see Anne L. Birberick, *Reading Undercover: Audience and Authority in Jean de La Fontaine* (Lewisburg: Bucknell UP, 1998).

[46] For a full description of the fête, see George Bordonove's *Fouquet: Coupable ou victime?* (Paris: Pygmalion, 1976), 197-207. For an account of the Fouquet affair in general, see Paul Morand, *Fouquet, ou le soleil offusqué* (Paris: Gallimard, 1961; Paris: Le Grand Livre du Mois, 1996). See also chapter IV (pages 203-37), "Nicolas Fouquet, ou comment on ne devient pas le favori de Louis XIV," of Marc Fumaroli's *Le Poète et le roi*. Jürgen Grimm ("Stratégies de désorientation," 175) has outlined criticism relating the Fouquet trial to the *Fables*, a subject to which we shall return in the next section of this chapter.

[47] For an alternative analysis of this passage, see Donné, especially pages 27-37.

[48] See Joan DeJean's "La Fontaine's *Psyché*: The Reflecting Pool of Classicism." I am indebted to this article for much of my analysis of the structure of *Les Amours de Psyché*.

[49] E.g. Renaissance hieroglyphics.

[50] For a full discussion of the influence of Colonna upon La Fontaine, see Françoise Charpentier's "De Colonna à La Fontaine: Le Nom de Poliphile," *L'Intelligence du passé: Les faits, l'écriture et les sens: Mélanges offerts à Jean Lafond*, eds. Pierre Aquilon, Jacques Chupeau and others (Tours: Université François Rabelais, 1988), 369-78. Boris Donné, on pages 162-80 of *La Poétique du songe*, devotes an important section to the influence of Colonna. Finally, see also Collinet, *Le Monde littéraire de La Fontaine,* 95-106 and 435-38. These latter pages comprise Collinet's "Appendice IV," "La Fontaine et le Songe de Poliphile." Here Collinet outlines the direct influence through borrowings of the *Songe* upon *Les Amours de Psyché* and *Les Filles de Menée*.

[51] For an analysis of the workings of Colonna's text, see Giovanni Pozzi's "Les Hiéroglyphes de l'*Hypnerotomachia Poliphili*" in *L'Emblème à la Renaissance*, ed. Yves Giraud (Paris: Société d'Education et d'Enseignement Supérieur, 1982), 15-27 and 139-41.

[52] For a general study of the *Songe de Poliphile*, see Lazare Sainéan's "Le Songe de Poliphile," *Problèmes littéraires du seizième siècle* (Paris: Boccard, 1927), 251-60.

[53] *L'Intérieur et l'extérieur: Essais sur la poésie et sur le théâtre au XVIIe siècle* (Paris: Corti, 1968).

[54] On the individual rôles and interaction of the four Allegories in the *Songe de Vaux*, see Robert N. Nicolich's "The Triumph of Language: The Sister Arts and Creative Activity in La Fontaine's *Songe de Vaux*."

[55] "Whoever you are, take this treasure as you wish. I warn you, take the head, do not touch the body."

[56] For a fuller discussion of La Fontaine's 'motto-technique' in the context of the *Fables*, see the previous section of this chapter.

[57] For specific examples, see Michael Bath, "Weeping Stags and Melancholy Lovers: The Iconography of *As You Like It*, II, i," *Emblematica* 1.1 (1986), 13-52, and *The Image of the Stag: Iconographic Themes in Western Art* (Baden-Baden: Verlag Valentin Koerner, 1992). See also David Graham, "De la haine de l'autre à l'horreur de soi: Conception et représentation du corps dans les *Devises et emblesmes d'amour moralisez* d'Albert Flamen," *Biblio 17: Le Corps au XVIIe siècle*, ed. Ronald W. Tobin (Paris: Biblio 17, 1995), 161-76. Using the example of two mid seventeenth-century stag emblems by Flamen, Graham pays particular attention to the antler motif and its implications of cuckoldry. Horapollo's stag hieroglyph is given in figure 20 and discussed below.

[58] Dieckmann should be consulted for a general, but thorough, introduction to the question of Renaissance hieroglyphs and emblematics. See in particular chapter 2, "Emblematic and Mystic Hieroglyphics" (48-99).

[59] *De la signification des notes hiéroglyphiques des Ægyptiens, c'est à dire des figures par les quelles ilz escripvoient leurs mystères secretz et les choses sainctes et devines.*

[60] In Latin editions of the *Hieroglyphics* the term used is "quotannis," the exact equivalent of "tous les ans." The text of the 1551 Kerver edition, for example, reads "Quo modo longæuum ac diuturnum. Cervis quotannis cornua renascuntur. Hic depictus longissimam vitam significat" ["How to depict long and lasting duration. The antlers of the stag are reborn each year. When depicted it signifies very long life"].

[61] Furetière defines "mystère" as a "chose cachée, secrete ou difficile à comprendre" before later pointing out that "Les Prestres Egyptiens cacheoient leurs mystères au peuple sous des caractères hyeroglyphiques." Such a definition therefore implicitly connects "mystère" to emblematics.

[62] For an introduction to the Fouquet case, see the previous section of this chapter.

[63] For further information on the life and works of Valentin Conrart, see Auguste Bourgoin's *Un Bourgeois de Paris lettré au XVIIe siècle: Valentin Conrart, premier secrétaire perpetuel de l'Académie Française et son temps, sa vie, ses écrits, son rôle dans l'histoire littéraire de la première partie du XVIIe siècle* (Paris, 1883; Geneva: Slatkine, 1971) and André Mabille de Poncheville's *Valentin Conrart, le père de l'Académie Française* (Paris: Mercure de France, 1935).

[64] Critical anaysis, as opposed to acknowledgement of the collection's holdings in respect of editions of its authors' works.

[65] "My kingdom is not of this world."

[66] "Put the sword in the sheath."

[67] "He betrayed him with a kiss."

[68] "Forgive them, they know not what they do."

[69] "He wanted to make himself king."

[70] "I have sinned through the blood of the innocent."

[71] "Give back to Caesar what is Caesar's."

[72] See also our discussion of Tristan, section IV B above.

[73] "Bare until the sun's return."

[74] Again, for a general comparison of the fable and emblem forms with specific reference to the example of Gilles Corrozet, see Barbara Tiemann's *Fabel und Emblem: Gilles Corrozet und die französische Renaissance-Fabel.*

[75] The silkworm example is not a unique case; the same sort of analysis can be made of the "De Gre le Miel L'Aguillon a regret" device and certain "bee" fables (e.g. piece 19 of ms. 5131) in the *Recueil Conrart*.

[76] This device is one of three whose texts have been completed. It bears the following six-line verse:

>Cet astre pur & glorieux
>Est la felicité des yeux
>Le jour s'en peint l'air s'en colore
>Mais en un point sa cruauté
>Fait déshonneur à sa Beauté
>Il brule celui qui l'adore.

[77] See, for example, Fernande Bassan's "La Fontaine héritier d'Esope et de Pilpay," *Comparative Literature Studies* 7 (1970), 161-78; Anne Birberick's *Reading Undercover: Audience and Authority in Jean de La Fontaine*; Jules Brody's "La Fontaine, Les Vautours et les pigeons (VII, 8): An Intertextual Reading" in *Convergences: Rhetoric and Poetic in Seveenteenth-Century France*, eds. David L. Rubin and Mary B. McKinley (Colombus: Ohio State UP,

1989), 143-60; Michael Vincent's *Figures of the Text: Reading and Writing (in) La Fontaine* (Amsterdam: John Benjamins, 1991).

[78] This is not a unique example. Manuscript 5417, for example, includes anti-Richelieu propaganda based upon an adaption of the Cardinal's devices at Bois-le-Vicomte.

[79] See Appendix B for the full text of the *Discours*.

[80] The work turned out to be popular enough to merit several printed editions later; full details on this and other aspects of the *Devises pour les tapisseries du roy* are given by Marc Fumaroli and Marianne Grivel in their edition of the Bibliothèque nationale manuscript (Paris: Herscher, 1988). See our next chapter for a fuller discussion of the work in the context of Perrault's *Discours*.

[81] Two of the devices are in fact by Charpentier and Cassagnes.

[82] In *Devises pour les tapisseries du roi* (Paris: Herscher, 1988), 7-17.

[83] According to Couton's notes to his edition of the *Fables*, the identification was first made by P. Lacroix in his *Œuvres inédites de La Fontaine* (Paris, 1863). The fable appears on pages 399-400 of Couton's edition.

[84] Jürgen Grimm also points to "Le Lièvre et la perdrix" (*Fable* V, XVII), whose four opening lines are the same as those of "Le Renard et l'ecureuil," as referring to the Fouquet case. However, as Grimm points out, "cette dernière fable ["Le Lièvre et la perdrix"], dont les protagonistes trouvent la mort, est assez probablement écrite après la condamnation définitive du surintendant" (183).

[85] The piece explains that in Brittany a squirrel is called a Fouquet. The entire sonnet appears as follows:

>   Colbert, tu croiois voir Fouquet hors de défence,
> & ta rage aveuglée en prenant ses Ecrits,
> te disoit sourdement tous ses moyens sont pris,
> mais il avoit encor sa force & sa prudence.
>   Tes coups n'ont point atteint jusqu'à son innocence,
> & ses nobles travaux doivent t'avoir appris
> Qu'un Fouquet dont l'essor surpasse tant d'esprits
> Pouvoit bien sur une Aigle avoir la préséance.
>   Dans ton lâche dessein tu t'es long-temps flatté,
> D'abbatre ce Fouquet plus qu'il n'estoit monté
> & de faire changer le sens de sa Devise.
>   Mais, en fin, sa vertu l'élève dans un point
> Qui fait dire par tout, malgré ton entreprise,
> Où ce rare Fouquet ne montera-t-il point?

[86] Such a notion is entirely in keeping with the nature of the printed collections often attached to the work of emblem theorists such as Le Moyne and Menestrier.

[87] *Etudes de style* (Paris: Gallimard, 1970).

[88] *A Hundred Fables of La Fontaine with Pictures by Percy J. Billinghurst* (London: John Lane).

VI
Perrault's Debt To The Device

Charles Perrault (1628-1703) is best known to the twentieth-century reader for his *Contes* (1697),[1] which include such well-known tales as "La Belle au bois dormant," "Le Petit Chaperon rouge," "Cendrillon" and "Peau d'âne." These, like the *Mémoires de ma vie* (1702),[2] were presented as being intended for the education of his two sons. Most of Perrault's career was, however, spent in a very different environment, that of the court and literary circles of the reign of Louis XIV.

Perrault was born in Paris, the son of an *avocat au Parlement de Paris*, and the youngest of seven children. Of his brothers, Claude (1613-1688) published diversely on natural sciences, physics and architecture and is generally credited with the design of the Colonnade du Louvre. Nicolas Perrault (1611-1611) was a *docteur en théologie* excluded from the Sorbonne for his support of Arnauld's Jansenist doctrines. Charles was educated at the Collège de Beauvais in the Latin Quarter in Paris and at the University of Orléans, where he studied law.

In 1654 Charles became *Receveur général des finances* and aide to his brother Pierre. It is at this time that he started to write poetry and joined the society of writers that included François Charpentier and Philippe Quinault, as well as Nicolas Fouquet. In 1663 Colbert named Perrault as *Contrûleur général de la surintendance des bâtiments du roy* and created the *Petite académie* with him as secretary. Consisting of only four members—initially Jean Chapelain, l'Abbé de Bourséis, François Charpentier and Jacques Cassagnes, but Perrault replaced Cassagnes as a full member in 1679— the *Petite académie* was essentially concerned with the creation of devices for royal occasions. It was later to become the *Académie des inscriptions et belles lettres*.[3]

At the age of forty in 1668 Perrault published *La Peinture*, a 656-line poem in praise of Charles Le Brun. This was followed two years later by the *Courses de testes et de bagues*, an elaborate account of the 1662 Carousel with engravings by François Chauveau and Israël Silvestre. The period also saw the creation of the *Devises pour les tapisseries du roy*,[4] the devices on the themes of the seasons and the elements initially designed for the borders of Gobelins tapestries. In 1671 Charles Perrault was elected to the Académie Française.

Charles-Senvel and Charles, Perrault's sons, were born in 1675 and 1676 respectively, three and four years after his marriage to nineteen-year old Marie Guichon. His third son Pierre, to whom he was to dedicate the *Contes*, was born in 1678, the year of Marie's death. The following years saw the publication of Perrault's *Le Ban-*

quet des Dieux pour la naissance de Mgr le Duc de Bourgogne, an allegorical work that mixes prose with verse. The 1680s also saw Perrault's fall from grace, due largely to the death of Colbert in 1683 and to Louvois's subsequent succession to the post of *Surintendant des bâtiments*. Louvois replaced Perrault with André Félibien in the *Petite académie*, thereby leaving Perrault without official post.

The main literary debate of Perrault's later years was the *Querelle des anciens et des modernes*, concerning the relative values of the literary achievements of the seventeenth century as compared to those of the past. The *Querelle* was sparked off by the reading of Perrault's *Siècle de Louis le Grand* (1687) before the Académie, much to Boileau's indignation. As a result Perrault instigated the *Parallèles des anciens et des modernes* which appeared on various subjects—arts and sciences, war, philosophy, poetry—from 1688-96. He also published his *Cabinet des beaux arts* (1690), a series of commented engravings on iconographic representations of the Arts, and *Les Hommes illustres* (1696), similar in format to emblematic biographies such as the *Abregé de l'histoire des Roys de France* or Marc de Vulson's *Les Portraits des hommes illustres*.[5]

The first edition of the *Histoires ou Contes du temps passé* appeared in 1697, although several of the stories, including "Les Souhaits ridicules" and "Peau d'âne" had been published elsewhere previously. Around this time Perrault was working on the manuscript *Discours sur l'art des devises* (the subject of section A of this chapter) and his *Mémoires de ma vie* (also discussed in section A and in the conclusion to this chapter), which provides the basis for much of our knowledge of Perrault's life and times. Charles Perrault died aged seventy-five in 1703.

Despite the clear link between emblematics and much of Perrault's courtly life and work, it is a subject which has attracted little specific critical attention. Jeanne Morgan Zarucchi's "Charles Perrault et l'éloquence de la devise"[6] analyses the style of the *Devises pour les tapisseries du roy* and Marianne Grivel's "Genèse d'un manuscrit"[7] contextualises them historically. To the best of my knowledge, however, little is available on the potentially emblematic nature of *Le Banquet des dieux* or *Le Cabinet des beaux arts*. Concerning *La Peinture*, Jean-Luc Gautier-Gentès's edition of the text[8] includes a full introduction and ample explanatory notes. With respect to the *Contes*, the title of Louis Marin's "Préface-Image: le Frontispice des contes de Perrault"[9] might suggest analysis of text/image interaction, but the article concentrates rather on the way in which the frontispiece marks the tone and potential audience of the tales.

More general studies of Perrault's work are not hard to find, although the *Contes* inevitably play a central rôle. They are the subject of chapters IV and V of Jacques Barchilon and Peter Flinders's *Charles Perrault*.[10] The work opens with a biographical overview, including an important section on his official function within seventeenth-century society. Perrault's rôle in the *Querelle* and his latter works are the subjects of chapters III and VI respectively. Marc Soriano's approach in *Le Dossier Perrault*[11] is quite different. It has a biographical base drawing much of its material from the *Mémoires*, but avoids a purely chronological approach. Soriano stresses the importance of a pluridisciplinary approach, using historical, psychological and literary analysis. Finally, for an overview of Perrault's rôle in and attitude towards seventeenth-century literary society, Jeanne Morgan Zarucchi's *Perrault's Morals for Moderns*,[12] a study that also takes the *Mémoires* as a central source, should be consulted.[13]

A work to which Perrault refers directly in his *Mémoires*, the *Discours sur l'art des devises*, will provide the main subject matter for section A of this chapter. As with our study of Tristan L'Hermite, we will concentrate on the presentation and analysis of a specific manuscript document, thereby establishing a clear link between Perrault and emblematics. This example, however, is intended to examine the importance of a different aspect of emblematics and seventeenth-century French culture, the theory of the device. As with Tristan, a specific case study will lead to broader conclusions—section B of this chapter—concerning the writings of Charles Perrault and the art of the device, with an indication of areas worthy of further exploration.

VI A

Bibliothèque de l'Arsenal ms. 3328[14]

The original of the *Discours sur l'art des devises* that is reproduced in Appendix B comprises piece 1 (fol. 1-46) of Arsenal ms. 3328. Henri Martin's *Catalogue des manuscrits* of 1887 merely labels the piece by its title, giving no further information. Manuscript 3328 as a whole bears the simple title of *Recueil* and is comprised of 13 pieces (295 sheets) with little common link (e.g. piece 2 "Memoire touchant la manière de faire de l'indigo," piece 7 "Discours contre les spectacles"). The *Recueil* comes from the library of the Marquis de Paulmy, founder of the Bibliothèque de l'Arsenal, and contains manuscript pieces from the seventeenth and eighteenth centuries. The green leather binding was commissioned for the Bibliothèque de l'Arsenal. Its spine bears the inscription, "Portefeuille du Mis. de Paulmy - Mélanges."

The *Discours* consists of four booklets of twenty pages, each comprising five folded sheets of paper, followed by a final booklet of twelve pages comprising three folded sheets. The final three and a half pages of the last booklet remain blank. Each page measures 19 cm by 26.5 cm and bears a watermark of vertical lines and an encircled bird somewhat crudely drawn. Raymond Gaudriault's *Filigranes et autres caractéristiques des papiers fabriqués en France aux XVIIe et XVIIIe siècles*[15] identifies this as a phoenix and gives the date of 1669. The text itself is in black ink and occupies the central part of each page. The left margin measures 3 cm, the right margin 4.5 cm, the lower margin 6 cm and the upper margin 2.5 cm. Ample space has been left between the lines of text, thereby giving eighteen lines per page. Various additions and corrections have been made in red ink, as well as three marginal notes (fols. 2, 12 and 16v) and a few corrections in the original black ink. This would indicate that the work was thoroughly reviewed by the copyist and by the author himself.[16] The style of the handwriting can be seen in figures 22a and 22b and may be contrasted with the style of the autograph *Mémoires de ma vie* reproduced in figure 23.

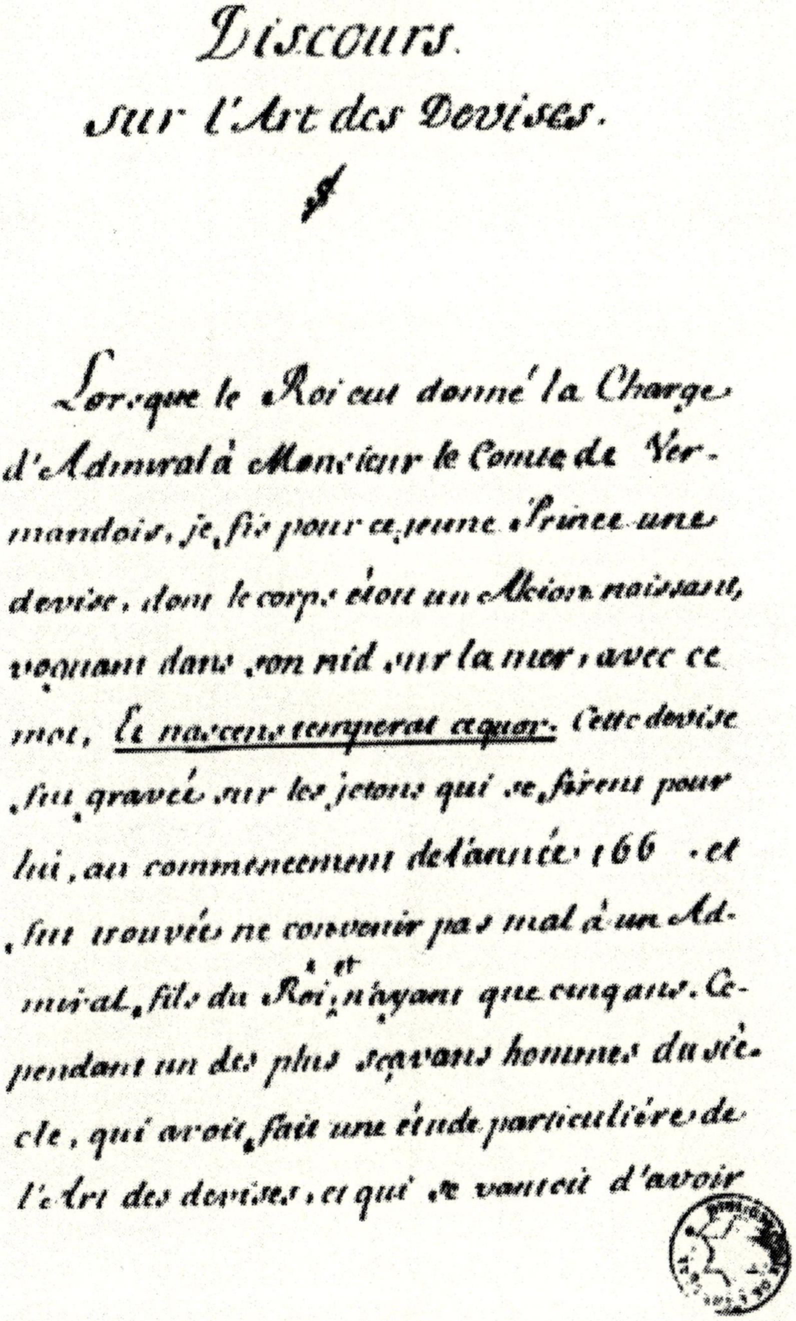

Discours

sur l'Art des Devises.

Lorsque le Roi eut donné la Charge d'Admiral à Monsieur le Comte de Vermandois, je fis pour ce jeune Prince une devise, dont le corps étoit un Alcion naissant, voguant dans son nid sur la mer, avec ce mot, *Et nascens temperat æquor*. Cette devise fut gravée sur les jetons qui se firent pour lui, au commencement de l'année 166 . et fut trouvée ne convenir pas mal à un Admiral, fils du Roi, n'ayant que cinq ans. Cependant un des plus sçavans hommes du siècle, qui avoit fait une étude particulière de l'Art des devises, et qui se vantoit d'avoir

Figure 22a. Opening page from Charles Perrault, *Discours sur l'art des devises*, ms. 3328 pièce 1, Bibliothèque de l'Arsenal.

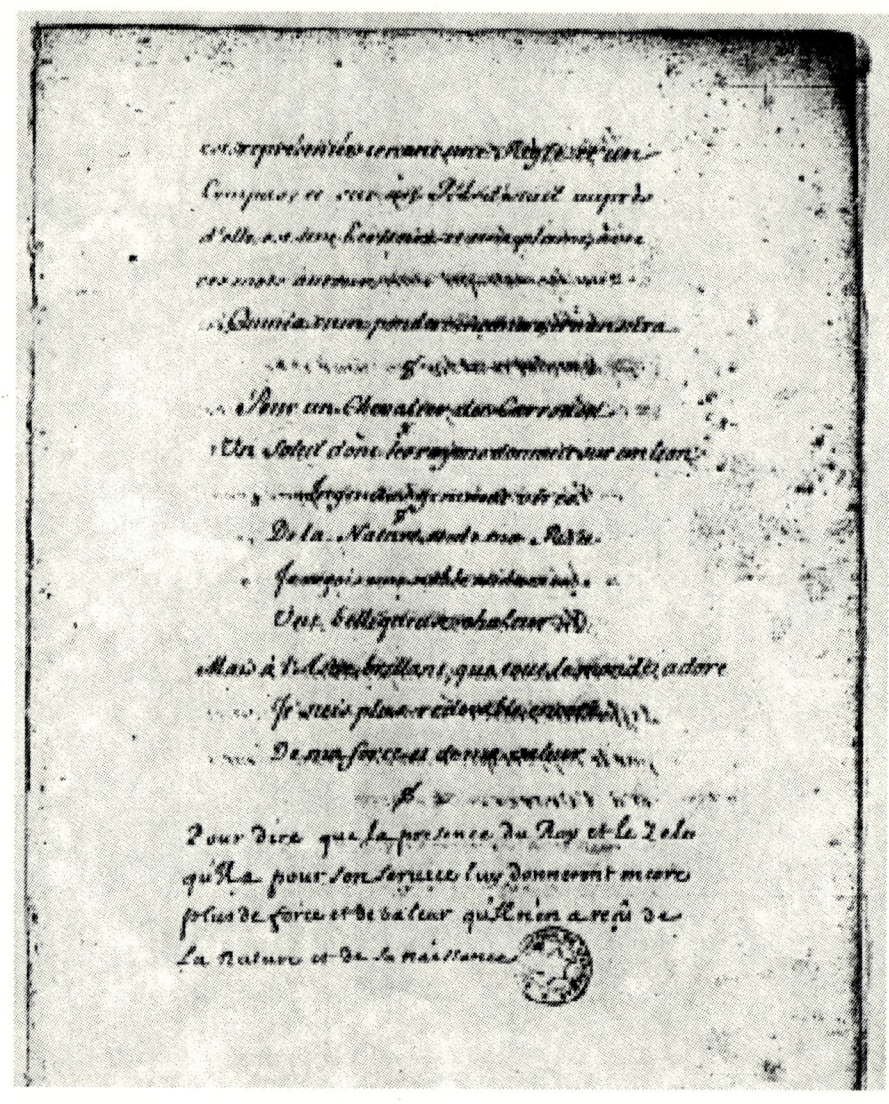

Figure 22b.   Folio 41 (including four additional autograph lines) from Charles Perrault, *Discours sur l'art des devises*, ms 3328 pièce 1, Bibliothèque de l'Arsenal.

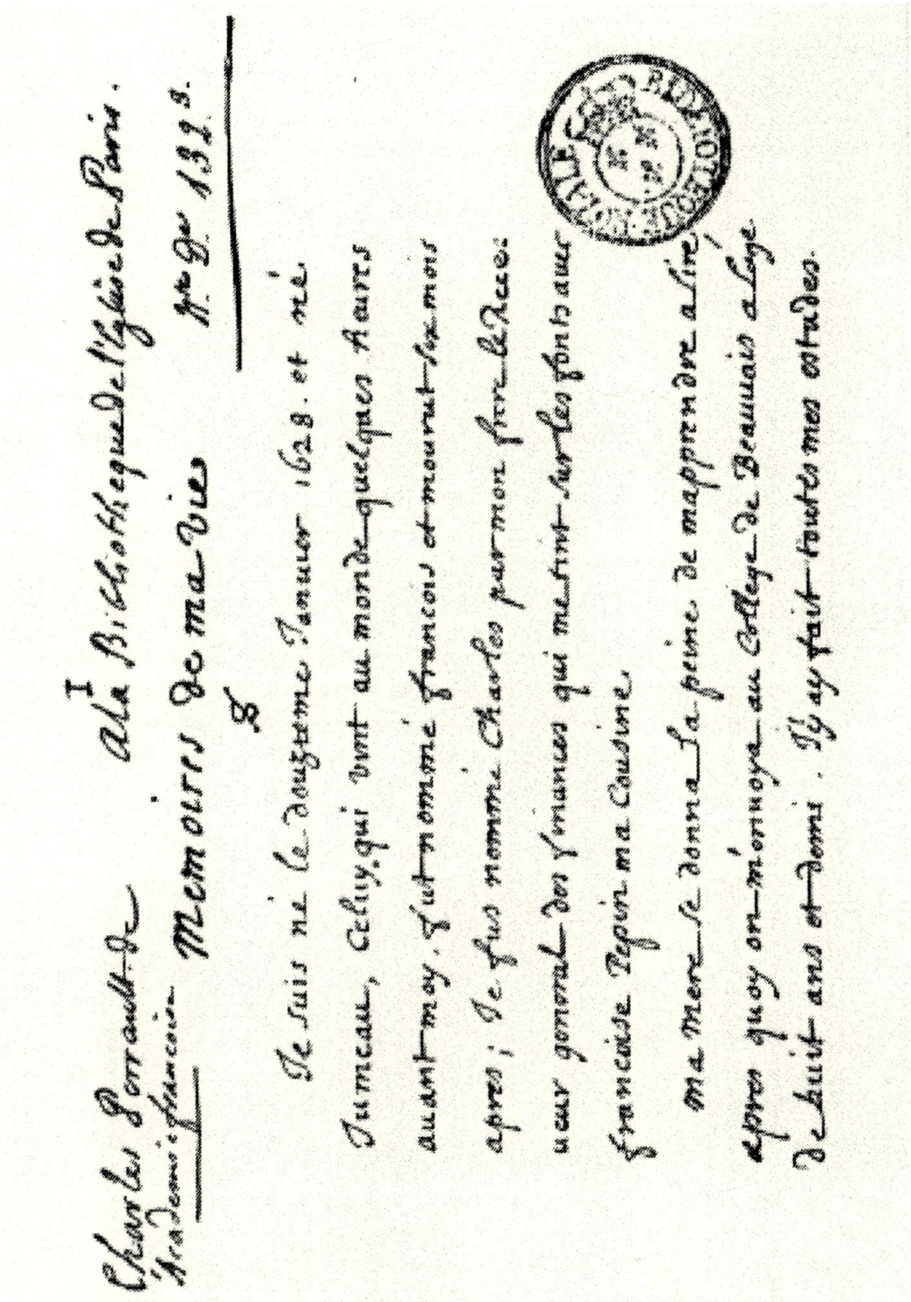

Figure 23. Opening page from Charles Perrault, *Mémoires de ma vie* (autograph manuscript), ms. fr. 23 991, Bibliothèque nationale de France.

The work is anonymous but it can beyond any reasonable doubt be attributed to Charles Perrault. This attribution is supported mainly by two texts:

(i) *Devises pour les tapisseries du roy*. This work has been discussed briefly above and will be discussed further in the next section of this chapter. It is enough for us to know that the texts for the *Devises* were composed by Charles Perrault, François Charpentier and Jean Chapelain around 1662. On folio 21v of our *Discours*, in reference to the "Tapisseries, ou les quatre saisons étoient représentées" our author states,

> Il y a quelques unes de ces devises, qui ne sont pas de moi, mais j'ai crû les devoir mettre ici toutes, avec le nom de leurs auteurs, lorsqu'elles ne sont pas de ma façon pour ne pas démembrer cet ouvrage.

Those devices in our piece which bear no name are precisely those which elsewhere are identified as being the work of Charles Perrault.

(ii) *Mémoires de ma vie*. This text of 1702, ms. 23991 of the Fonds français of the Bibliothèque nationale de France, has been reproduced in a 1909 edition by Paul Bonnefon.[17] This in turn has been reprinted in Antoine Picon's edition of the *Mémoires de ma vie*.[18] In the section entitled "Tapisseries des Quatre Saisons"[19] (Bonnefon, 40), Perrault states,

> La verité est que j'ai eu du talent pour faire des devises et je crois en avoir fait moi seul pendant quinze ou seize années, autant que tous les autres ensemble. Il y en a un recueil que l'on trouvera parmi mes papiers en suite d'un discours sur les devises.

Bonnefon's edition, generally highly annotated, has nothing to say about this remark. Although the evidence is circumstantial, it does seem more than probable that Perrault is here referring to a text whose only known copy is now piece 1 of Arsenal ms. 3328.

The majority of the manuscript is not in Perrault's hand, but in that of a copyist, as is indicated by the abundant use of accents (Perrault's 1702 manuscript *Mémoires* is marked by its scarce use of accents)[20]. However, the corrections are in Perrault's own hand, as can be seen from the four-line addition at the bottom of folio 41 (see figure 22b). The copy was probably prepared in the late seventeenth or early eighteenth century. This theory is supported by the fact that the dates on folio 41v have been corrected to 1670, 1671 and 1672 from 1690, 1691 and 1692. This is the type of slip that could have easily occurred if the document had been written in the 1690s.

It seems likely that Perrault's original manuscript would have been composed over a period of years. Its abrupt ending suggests it may have been unfinished. The earliest possible date would be 1669, the date of the watermark and the year when the Comte de Vermandois was named admiral (fol. 1). The "Devises pour les Jetons de l'Ordre du Saint-Esprit," given on folio 41v, stop at 1672. The last date to which the text refers (fol. 44v), regarding a monument to the birth of the Duc de Bourgogne, is

1682. Finally, the composition of the *Recueil* could have gone on to an even later time, one much closer to 1702. The basis for this suggestion is the fact that the collection's final device (fol. 45), "pour un Auteur qui ne pille pas les autres," reflects the concern that dominates the *Mémoires*: here Perrault goes to some length to make it clear that his brother was not guilty of plagiarism. In short, our *Discours* and *Recueil* were probably composed over the thirty years between 1669 and the end of the century.

The *Discours* itself only takes up approximately eleven of the manuscript's forty-five sheets. The rest of the work consists of examples of various devices, sometimes with commentaries, sometimes not, thereby effectively forming Perrault's *Recueil*. Folios 13v-29 contain the *Devises pour les tapisseries du roy*, folios 29-45 give us *Diverses devises*.

The *Discours* is based around a supposedly autobiographical anecdote regarding the reception of a device Perrault had composed—a halcyon with "Et nascens temperat æquor"—to celebrate the infant Comte de Vermandois's accession to the rank of admiral in 1669. One of the most "sçavans hommes du siècle" (perhaps Menestrier or Bourséis) found the device lacking and made a speech to the Académie Française to explain his case (fols. 1-2), namely that that the body of a device (here 'æquor') should not be named. Perrault uses the rest of the *Discours* to justify his case, and in so doing explains his view of the workings of the device, aided by intermittent examples.

It is in this respect, given the furious climate of intellectual debate centred around emblematics at the time, that we find the immediate interest of the *Discours*. Perrault is giving his opinion regarding the discussion hitherto animated by characters such as Menestrier and Bourséis, Mr Clément, "Conseiller en la Cour des Aides" (see fol. 11) and the "Pere Le Moine" (fol. 11). Indeed his introductory technique is in keeping with the tradition: Menestrier, for example, in his *Devise du roy, justifiée* of 1679, had also used the justification of a particular device, here Louis XIV's 'nec pluribus impar,' as the starting point for a general treatise on the subject. Indeed on the fifth page of the unnumbered preface, Menestrier states, "Ce n'est pas une chose nouvelle de voir un livre entier pour l'explication, ou la justification, d'une Devise." He refers to several Italian authors of such books, before giving a list of French writers whose devices he will cite. Fourth on the list is "M Perrault de l'Academie françoise."

The first main section of Menestrier's text proper, pages 1-114, covers a variety of topics relating to the 'nec pluribus impar' device and, by extension, often to devices in general: the history of 'nec pluribus impar,' essential rules concerning its composition and the various categories of devices.[21] This part above all provides descriptions of other devices which fit the various categories. Menestrier also discusses examples of 'nec pluribus impar' on public display. From page 115 onwards the theoretical discussion is replaced by a collection of devices generally bearing an association with the sun and organised thematically, as suggested by the title:

> Le Monde entier consacré à la gloire du roy,
> Recueil de Devises faites pour le Roy, dont tous les corps
> sont rangez selon l'ordre naturel des choses.

Menestrier cites some of Perrault's "devises des elements."[22] The general format—theoretical discussion followed by a *recueil*—is shared by Perrault, although the latter's *Discours*, perhaps as an inevitable result of the manuscript format, does not boast the length or structure of the *Devise du roy, justifiée*.

A good part of Menestrier's work is given to stating and explaining the precepts to be followed for the ideal device, which he also simplifies into twelve rules (36-37). The same approach is followed in his *Art des emblemes*,[23] which has chapters on the origins of emblems, their various types (e.g. "moraux," "politiques," "doctrinaux," etc.), the different parts that form the emblem, how emblems might be used, and so on. Once again, the theoretical aspects are amply illustrated by examples of specific emblems. This general pattern is also followed by Pierre Le Moyne in his *De l'Art des devises* of 1666: five "livres" comprising some 230 pages give the history of the device, definitions of the various types, rules concerning the "figure" and the "mot" and a comparison with the emblem. Then follows a recueil consisting of 271 pages of devices organised under such titles as "Cabinet de devises," "Jardin de devises," "Devises royales" and "Devises adoptées."

Many of these devices are taken from the work of M. Clément,[24] whose treatise on devices, the "Regles pour la connoissance des devises, par M..., Conseiller en la Cour des Aydes," like Perrault's, has been left to us in the form of an Arsenal manuscript. As the title would suggest, the emphasis is on the explanation, with examples, of a series of rules concerning the composition of a device. These include the relationship between text and image, the nature of the image, the use of colours, the relative clarity (or not) of the message, their subject matter and their language. Such subjects also form the core of a similar work, M. Gardien's "Discours sur les devises, emblesmes, et revers de medailles," which appeared on pages 214-68 of the 1678 *Mercure Galant, extraordinaire d'octobre*.[25] Again, Gardien gives an outline of the form's history (as he sees it), and he considers the relationship between "paroles" and "figures," the subject matter—including the common topic of whether human figures should be portrayed—the length of the "mot," the grammar of the "mot" (e.g. it should not be indicative and third person!), the device's clarity (or not) and the language used.

If theoreticians of emblematics of the mid to late seventeenth century are therefore largely concerned with elaborating a system that sets out the conditions for an ideal device, Perrault's *Discours* seems to conform. He broaches such questions as the definition of device, the nature of a 'perfect' device (e.g. it should consist of "corps simples" and "corps naturels" and not human figures, apart from those taken from "fables" etc.) and the rôle and nature of the accompanying verse ("ces vers ne sont autre chose que l'explication et la paraphrase du mot de la devise" fol. 10v). In the context of this latter subject, Perrault gives us to understand that he was evidently at home with the leading theoreticians in the field: "Je m'en expliquai un jour avec M^r.

Clement Conseiller en la Cour des Aides, et avec le Pere Le Moine Jesuite, tous deux excellens en cette matière" (fol. 11). Indeed his definition of a device—"Une devise n'est en soi qu'une comparaison de deux choses, dont l'une est représentée, et l'autre sous entenduë; avec un petit discours qui convient également à toutes les deux" (fol. 3)—might be compared with the opening sentence of Clément's treatise: "La Devise n'est autre chose qu'un composé de figures & de paroles, qui explique une [sic] dessein, ou une pensée, par comparaison" (85).

However, upon closer examination Perrault's stance appears quite different from that of his peers. Before giving the above definition of the device, Perrault presents a caveat:

> Pour bien connoître si ce que je dis est vrai, il faut commencer par laisser là toutes les règles, qui d'elles-mêmes sont aussi propres, en quelque art, et en quelque science que ce soit, à induire en erreur, qu'à conduire dans la voie, et {et il faut} pénétrer dans l'esprit, dans l'intention, et dans l'essence de la devise, seul moyen de ne se tromper jamais. (fol. 3)

He goes on to conclude,

> Quiconque aura une fois bien compris cette definition, n'a plus que faire des regles, parce qu'elles y sont toutes renfermées, ainsi que j'espère le faire voir. (fol. 3)

A few pages later, at the end of the anecdote of the debate with the "sçavant Abbé," Perrault restates his point:

> Il n'est pas seulement vrai, que la seule connoissance des règles de la devise {,} ne sert le plus souvent qu'à faire tomber dans l'erreur, comme le prouve assez la petite histoire que je viens de rapporter. (fol. 7)

Given that the leading treatises of the time would typically formulate and defend a series of rules for the creation of devices, Perrault's insistence on the potentially damaging effect of set rules suggests him to be going against the norms of the genre—the "discours sur l'art des devises"—in which he is working. Further subversion comes in the form of a back-handed compliment to the Abbé who, despite his undoubted erudition, is painfully long-winded:

> Le sçavant Abbé à qui j'adressois la parole, répondit mille choses très-belles et très-curieuses, dont le récit me meneroit trop loin. Nos Juges témoignèrent être contents de mes réponses, mais non pas autant qu'ils l'étoient, pour épargner à mon adversaire le cha-

> grin de s'être mépris dans sa dissertation, qui étoit d'une heure et
> demie de lecture. (fol. 7)

Perrault contrasts this with the succinct effectiveness of his own style, which requires no more than a short tale to make the point ("comme le prouve assez la petite histoire que je viens de rapporter," fol. 7).

It is indeed the anecdotal style, worthy of the author of the *Contes*, that distinguishes it from other contemporary treatises on the device. The long-winded Abbé provides a stock figure, almost a buffoon-like villain, that encourages us to read on. The anecdote is short and clear, but ironically allows Perrault to state his own 'rules' for the device, whilst emphasising the importance of free-spirit, the *moralité* at the base of this *conte*.

In other ways Perrault's *Discours* strikes us as being more literary than the pure theory of Menestrier, Le Moyne and Clément. One of the direct results of the notion that set rules can lead to error just as much as to progress, is the stressing of a less tangible "esprit" or "génie":

> la connoissance seule de l'esprit et de l'essence de la devise suffit
> pour n'en point faire de mauvaises. Car pour les bonnes et les ex-
> cellentes, c'est le genie seul qui les produit. (7-7v.)

Perrault sums up this notion through heavy insistance on the quotation from St. Paul that "la lettre tuë, et l'esprit vivifie" (fol. 1v.).

The quote is taken from the second "Epistre de S. Paul aux Corinthiens"[26] in which the contrast is made between the Spirit of the living God written in the hearts of man and ink that is merely on "tables de pierre." Verse 6 of chapter III reads,

> Qui [i.e. the strength God has given us] nous a aussi rendus capa-
> bles d'être ministres du nouveau Testament; non pour de lettre,
> mais d'Esprit: car la lettre tue, mais l'Esprit vivifie.

The idea that Perrault should put M. L'Abbé in his place by using a well-known quotation from the Bible lends an extra hint of irony in keeping with Perrault's style.

Furthermore, by using this particular quotation, Perrault is placing himself within the context of a rich literary tradition. A central point of Erasmus's *Enchiridion militis christiani* is the importance of the Pauline distinction between spirit and body. This is specifically the subject of Erasmus's section entitled "De Homine interiore et exteriore, & de duabus partibus hominis ex literis sacris"[27] ["On the inward and outward man, and on the two parts of man as discussed in Holy Scripture"] (35v.-39v.). Erasmus underlines Paul's distinction in terms of the words of philosophers:

> Iam vero philosophorum levis sit authoritas, nisi eadem omnia,
> tametsi verbis non iisdem, sacriis in literis præcipiuntur. Quod
> philosophi rationem, id Paulus modo spiritum, modo interiorem

hominem, modo legem mentis vocat. Quod illi affectum, hic interim
carnem, interim corpus, interim exteriorem hominem, interim legem
membrorum appellat.[28] (36)

For Erasmus, the actual words used can indeed be different, but this is of little importance as it is the deeper sense that really matters.

Blaise Pascal in his *Pensées*[29] (number 299, page 278) also quotes Corinthians:

> Figures.
> La lettre tue
> Tout arrivait en figures.
> *Il fallait que le Christ souffrît.*
> Un Dieu humilié. Voilà le chiffre que saint Paul nous donne.

Pascal places the quotation in the context of a section on "Figures" which broaches the use of figurative expression and possible readings of the scriptures. The different approaches are summed up in his warning against extremes (number 284, page 271):

> Deux erreurs: 1. Prendre tout littéralement. 2. Prendre tout spirituellement.

Perrault is also writing in the context of figurative expression, that of the device, but is arguing against a strictly governed theorization of the "figures" that would impose literal interpretation with little scope for "esprit."

Whereas Pascal's *Pensées* supply a strong Jansenist message, Georgette de Montenay's *Emblemes, ou devises chrestiennes* were to promote her Protestant faith. Nonetheless, emblem 87, "Scientia Inflat" ["Knowledge Inflates"] (see figure 24) puts the Pauline quotation to use in this context. Its *subscriptio*'s first lines are as follows:

> Pour avoir leu longuement l'escriture,
> L'homme souvent en vain se glorifie.
> Car science enfle: & qui n'a que lecture,
> N'a pour cela l'esprit qui vivifie.

Once again, Montenay stresses the importance of understanding ("Ouvre le sens," line 5) as opposed to lengthy reading devoid of circumstantial application.

In short, the emphasis that Perrault gives to his reply to M. l'Abbé—"la lettre tuë, et l'esprit vivifie"—places his *Discours* in the context of practical and persuasive emblematics—the work of Georgette de Montenay—as well as within that of some of the most subtle literature of his time. Like Erasmus,[30] Perrault makes his point through sophisticated irony: he uses a quote from the Bible, one to be reused in emblem books,

Figure 24. "Scientia Inflat," from Georgette de Montenay, *Emblesmes, ou devises chrestiennes* (Lyons: Jean Marcorelle, 1571).

as ammunition against a man of the church for the defence of his own work on emblematics. Perrault's style is indeed a far cry from M. l'Abbé's fastidious rules.

The re-use of a quote from the Bible but in the context of Perrault's time raises a wider question of literary debate, that of the *Querelle des anciens et des modernes*, in which Perrault played a leading rôle. On an immediate level, the very purpose of the *Recueil*'s devices is the glorification of the men of the time, in a manner akin to that of *Le Siècle de Louis le Grand*. This in turn is in keeping with the style of emblematic bibliographies such as Marc de Vulson's *Les Portraits des hommes illustres*.[31] One of Perrault's protagonists, François Charpentier, to whom our author refers as one of "nos amis communs" (fol. 2) was a leading supporter of the *modernes* in the *Querelle*. It is in his "Lettre à Monsieur Charpentier"[32] that Perrault discusses his *Critique de l'Opéra*—one of the *Querelle*'s main texts, the subject of which was Philippe Quenault's *Alceste*—and Jean Racine's reaction to it.

More specifically, Perrault seeks further to advance his cause by his latent praise of the French language: he states that for the motto all languages are good, especially French; some claim that Latin is better, but Perrault points out that "ils se trompent" (fol. 10). The "sçavans" to whom he is referring would include Le Moyne who entitles chapter XIII of the fourth book of *De l'Art des devises*,

> En qu'elle [*sic*] langue se doit faire le Mot des Devises: Si les modernes et les vulgaires y peuvent entrer: Les avantages du Latin sur toutes les autres Langues. (187)

Le Moyne's stance on the use of Latin is very much that of the *anciens*:

> Je prefererois pourtant le Latin à toutes les autres Langues. Il est plus majestueux, & la source d'où il nous est venu est plus noble. Les plus grands Hommes du Monde, les Maistres du Monde ont parlé Latin. Le Latin d'ailleurs se tourne plus rondement, & en moins de mots: Il a plus de dignité & plus de force: il est plus capable de l'harmonie qui se fait de nombres & des mesures. Et puis, outre qu'il est entendu de plus de Gens, il est susceptible de certains traits & de certaines couleurs, qui peuvent donner plus de beauté à la Devise, qu'en n'en peut recevoir d'aucune autre Langue. (189)

Le Moyne cites the widespread usage of Latin—"il est entendu de plus de Gens"—as an advantage, but M. Clément is more précise as to the types of "Gens" concerned:

> Mais par la raison que les galanteries, comme il a esté dit, ne sont pas faites pour les ignorans, on a de coutume d'y employer un autre langage que le vulgaire. Parmy-nous, le Latin, l'Italien, &l'Es-

pagnol, sont plus en usage que les autres, y ayant peu d'honnestes-gens qui ne les sachent, au moins, qui ne les entendent. (91)

One of the main arguments of the *modernes* was that Latin could indeed be used to obscure rather than enlighten.

Perrault, by contrast, does not give lengthy explanations for his preference, in line with the *modernes*, for French. He simply states that for those who believe Latin to be better, "ils se trompent" (fol. 10), explaining their error to be a question of habit brain-washed into them. Similarly, as concerns the need to cite the *anciens* in the motto, Perrault simply comments, "je fais peu de cas de cette dernière beauté" (fol. 9v).

Perrault's *Discours*, therefore, while clearly in the tradition of the treatises of Menestrier, Le Moyne and Clément, is nonetheless a very different kind of work. His anecdotal style lacks the pedantry of his predecessors and, furthermore, his emphasis on a certain disregard for 'rules' almost undermines the *raison d'être* of his peers' work. Yet such a cavalier attitude towards 'rules' is particularly interesting coming from a pillar of the century of classicism. We may be dealing with the period that gave us the Académie Française, Malherbes's strict poetic criteria and the three unities in theatre, but Perrault's emphasis on "esprit" reminds us that there are always counter-currents. That said, when Perrault recommends "le bon sens tout seul," we cannot but help being reminded of Descartes.

VI B

CHARLES PERRAULT AND THE ART OF THE DEVICE

Although the *Discours sur l'art des devises* can now be read as Perrault's final *credo* on the subject, the emblem-related work for which he is best known to the modern reader is the *Devises pour les tapisseries du roy*. The tapestries in question, praising the king for securing peace, were executed in the 1660s by the Gobelins manufactory. Perrault had created the majority of the sixteen *Devises des elements* and the sixteen *Devises des quatre saisons* which decorated the tapestries' borders.[33] These appeared in unillustrated manuscripts as well as in various printed editions and in luxury manuscript form (with engravings by Bailly) for presentation to the king.

The unillustrated manuscript versions are found in *Recueil Conrart* ms. 5418 as well as in folios 13v-29 of the *Discours sur l'art des devises*. Of the several printed versions, many were without text. Examples include the *Devises pour les tapisseries du roy*[34] of 1668 with engravings by Sébastien Le Clerc but no text, and the *Tapisseries du roy, où sont representez les quatre elemens et les quatre saisons: Avec les devises qui les accompagnent, et leur explication*.[35] Three full versions are known to exist in luxury manuscript form: Vienna National Library Series-nova 24204, British Library Harley Manuscript 4377 and Paris BnF ms. fr. 7819.[36] In addition, Sandra Sider and Barbara Obrist[37] cite leaves from a *Tapisseries du roy* manuscript that belong to Harvard University Library (ms. Typ 619), the Pierpont Morgan Library (M 1076.1-2) and the Getty Museum (mss. 11 and 11a). They also note a similar manuscript at the Musée Condé in Chantilly (ms. 951-1573).

The importance that Perrault placed on the *Devises pour les tapisseries du roy* is clear from the lengthy section dedicated to the subject in the *Mémoires de ma vie*.[38] Indeed the section could have been longer, but as Perrault states,

> Comme ces tapisseries se voient tous les jours et qu'elles sont en estampes qui avec le discours qui les accompagnent forment un très-beau volume, je n'en dirai pas davantage. (132)

The commissioning of the tapestries was part of the work of the *Petite académie*, of which Perrault was a founder member. At first the *Académie*'s domain, basically the glorification of Louis XIV, covered all spheres of learning and the arts. This was narrowed down to the composition of devices, inscriptions and medals. Louvois, the new *Surintendant des bâtiments* after Colbert's death (1683), moved the *Académie*'s twice-weekly meetings to the Académie Française's chamber in the Louvre. In 1701 the body officially took the name of *Académie royale des inscriptions et médailles*, with its rôle being defined as largely historiographic. Much expanded, in 1716 it became the *Académie des inscriptions et belles lettres*. Notable members throughout the years included Jean Racine, Nicolas Boileau-Despréaux and André Félibien.

The importance with which Perrault viewed his rôle in the *Petite académie* is clear once again from his comments in the *Mémoires*. In this instance, Perrault lets Louis XIV himself make the point:

> Après que M. Colbert nous eut présentés au Roy, il nous dit ces paroles: «Vous pouvez, Messieurs, juger de l'estime que je fais de vous, puisque je vous confie la chose du monde qui m'est la plus précieuse, qui est ma gloire. Je suis sûr que vous ferez des merveilles; je tâcherai de ma part de vous fournir de la matière qui mérite d'être mise en œuvre par des gens aussi habiles que vous êtes.» (134)

The *Devises pour les tapisseries du roy* were not the only emblematic composition to reflect Perrault's official functions. His *Hommes illustres*[39] is, as the title would suggest, in the same vein as Vulson's *Les Portraits des hommes illustres* to which we referred in chapter II. *Les Hommes illustres* consists of one hundred portraits of famous men of Perrault's century divided into various categories: the church, the military, the judiciary, men of letters and artists. In each case the engraving of the "homme illustre" takes up one page with the initial page of a description—never longer than two pages in total—of the person's life and deeds opposite. In the introduction to the work Perrault's description of the composition uses the type of terms dear to emblem theoreticians: referring to the "illustre Curieux" supposedly responsible for the collection, Perrault states,

> Sa passion ne s'en est moins tenuë là, il a souhaité que ces Portraits fussent accompagnéz d'Eloges historiques, qui en joignant l'image de leur esprit à celle de leur visage, les fissent connoistre tout entiers.

The essential emblematic principle of text and image uniting to create the whole is clearly present.

Charles Perrault was also responsible for the *Courses de testes et de bagues* which we have mentioned in chapter II in the context of the 1662 Carrousel that the work describes. The opening sentence of the preface explains that those "qui ont entrepris d'écrire l'Histoire des Grands-Hommes" should not limit themselves to describing battles, but should also consider "leurs plaisirs & leurs divertissemens" (1). In this printed account of the courtly parades, Perrault intersperses the illustrations of the troupes or processions with sections devoted to the devices of those involved. For example, page 27 gives five devices, first and foremost of which is that of the king, the sun with the motto "Ut Vidi Vici" ["As I Saw I Conquered"]. On the facing page (28), we find a brief explanation to accompany each device. Perrault gives us the name of the bearer, a summary of the image ("Un Soleil"), the motto with its French translation and a few lines of explanation. In the case of the "Ut Vidi Vici" device, Perrault points out that,

> comme le Soleil n'a qu'à se faire voir pour dissiper les tenebres, ainsi ce Grand Monarque n'a besoin que de la presence pour vaincre ses ennemis. (28)

In all there are fifty-five devices over a total of twenty pages.

Charles Perrault's talent and passion for the composition of devices was therefore an important asset for a career within the ranks of French society's officialdom. It is hard to imagine that Perrault would have been able to cut himself off from this world when composing what is now his best known work, the *Contes*, even if their manner of publication appears far flung from the workings of Louis XIV's institutions. Nonetheless it seems clear that La Belle aux Bois Dormant's palace with its "grande avant-cour" (101), "grande cour pavée de marbre" (102), "Salon de miroirs" (103), "Chapelle du Château" (103) and "cours et basses-cours du Château" (106) is not without similarities to Versailles. Likewise, the ball to which Cendrillon goes can, with some justification, be compared to the context of court festivities. It would also seem reasonable, therefore, to consider the *Contes* within the context of emblematics.

As with La Fontaine's *Fables*, the early editions of Charles Perrault's *Contes* were all illustrated. To take a specific example, in the case of the first edition of "Cendrillon,"[40] the opening page (see figure 25) is dominated by an engraving of the ball scene at the moment when Cendrillon flees leaving her slipper behind. Beneath the engraving comes the title, "Cendrillon ou la petite pantoufle de verre: Conte." The third element of this first page is the beginning of the story, which will, as we know, eventually clarify the significance of the illustration and of the fable. The story conti-

CENDRILLON

OU LA PETITE PANTOUFLE DE VERRE

CONTE.

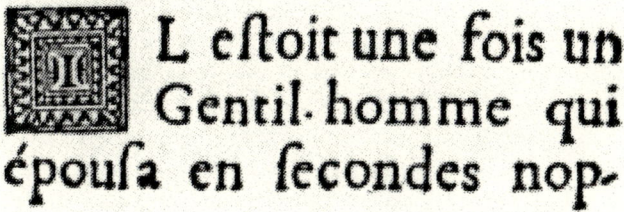L eſtoit une fois un Gentil-homme qui épouſa en ſecondes nop-

Figure 25.   "Cendrillon," from Charles Perrault, *Histoires ou contes de temps passé* (Paris: Claude Barbin, 1697).

nues for thirty pages, ending with Cendrillon marrying off her sisters to "deux grands Seigneurs de la Cour" (146). Then follow a "Moralité" of twelve lines of verse and an "Autre Moralité" of nine lines.

This tale, like all those of the *Histoires ou Contes du temps passé*,[41] follows the general structure of the emblem. The title serves as *motto* giving the reader a shorthand reference for the *conte* and the engraving creates a global image that encapsulates a precise and telling moment of the story. The tale itself gives the full 'explanation' in prose, whereas the "moralité," like those of the fables of La Fontaine[42] can be seen as providing one or more additional mottoes.

Once again we find that forms such as the fable, *conte* and emblem, which are quite distinct to the modern mind, are not clearly distinguishable in Early Modern productions. As previously stated, Barbara Tiemann has analysed admirably the overlap between fable and emblem with precise reference to Gilles Corrozet. In the same vein we might consider the emblems of Guillaume Guéroult as compared with the tales of Charles Perrault. The long narrative element provides the central core for both, with the engraving, the title and the summarising verses as supporting factors, although the exact relationship between the various parts remains somewhat ambiguous. The collections' various emblems or tales broach a variety of seemingly unrelated subjects in an often humourous manner, although contemporary social comment or satire is often quite apparent.

The potentially emblematic status of collections of fables brings us to another of Perrault's literary endeavours, his translation of Gabriel Faene's *Cent Fables*. In the "Avertissement" to the first edition of Perrault's translation,[43] we learn that Faene was "Le second Phedre,"[44] but that his works were only discovered by M. Pithou at the beginning of the seventeenth century "dans la poussière d'une ancienne Bibliothèque." The answer to de Thou's claim that Faene had copied Phaedrus suggests the "Avertissement" to be in keeping with Perrault's stance in the *Querelle*: de Thou's opinions were based on,

> la forte persuasion où sont tous les Amateurs outrez de l'Antiquité,
> qu'un Auteur moderne ne peut pas faire rien d'excellent, s'il n'a
> un Auteur ancien pour modelle.

This does, however, seem to contradict the stance of the Preface, in which, by means of an explanation of initial reticence to translate, Perrault praises the qualities of "brieveté" and "clarté," which, as we have seen,[45] were dear to emblem writers:

> Je connus que la chose [i.e. translation] n'estoit point possible;
> parce que la brieveté & la clarté, qui chez les Grecs & les Romains
> faisoient toute la beauté d'une narration ne suffisent pas pour charmer les Français d'aujourd'hui. (ii v.)

Facing the title page of this first edition is an engraving placed above a *subscriptio* of four verses. Nonetheless the fables are not illustrated until the editions post-dating

Perrault's death. By this time, however, the editors had clearly decided to produce a work in the tradition of the emblem-book style layout of La Fontaine's fables (see figure 26 for an example taken from the 1743 edition[46]). In the preface to the original edition Perrault claims he does not dare compare himself with La Fontaine, but the opening lines of his rendition of the crow and the cheese story—"Sur le haut d'un chêne, un Corbeau / Tenoit dans son bec un fromage" (50)—would suggest that further comparison could prove interesting.

The *Labyrinthe de Versailles* is another emblematically-styled publication that links La Fontaine and Perrault. The *labyrinthe* itself was constructed in the gardens of Versailles in the 1660s, with the ground plan finished in 1667. The entrance was flanked by statues of Æsop and l'Amour and at strategic points in the maze were mechanical fountains displaying key scenes from Æsop's fables. Next to each fountain was a plaque with four verses by Charles Perrault which summarised the fable in question. In the case of "Le Coc et le Renard," for example, the statue showing the fable's protagonists (see figure 27 for an illustration from the printed version) was accompanied by the following verses:

> Le Renard dit au Coc, une paix éternelle
> Est concluë entre nous, descends: oûï, deux Levriers
> Viennent, répond le Coc, m'en dire la nouvelle:
> Le Renard n'osa pas attendre les Couriers.

The printed version, the *Labyrinthe de Versailles*,[47] is attributed to Perrault and could serve as a guidebook to the maze. It opens with a "Description du Labyrinthe de Versailles" (3) that suggests the statues as appearing in the thick of the action they portray and that "l'eau qu'ils jettent imite en quelque sorte la parole que la fable leur a donnée" (14). Initially the book gives a precise description of each fountain, a summary of the fable and an indication of its comparative whereabouts. The main section of *Le Labyrinthe* then consists of an engraving of each of the forty statues accompanied by the fable's title and the four summarising verses (see figure 27 for an example). In the BnF copy of the work—the one reproduced by Michael Conan's facsimile—the final index is followed by a manuscript "Renvois aux fables de La Fontaine."

It should be clear from figure 27 that the layout of the printed *Labyrinthe de Versailles* places it within the emblematic tradition of *imago*—the engraving—, *motto*—the fable's title—and *subscriptio*—the verse. Indeed the maze itself can be seen as a product indicative of the age that made emblems a fashion: for full appreciation of the attraction visitors would have had to amalgamate the visual pleasures of the fountains and the global image they provide with the textually-based four-line verses on the plaques. The process might be compared with that by which the reader of La Fontaine's *Psyche* would bring together his understanding of the text and his personal experience of the Grotte, a process described in greater detail in chapter V B above. Finally, it is interesting to note that despite the *labyrinthe*'s seventeenth-century success, as the eighteenth century progressed it gradually fell into disrepair until the Conte

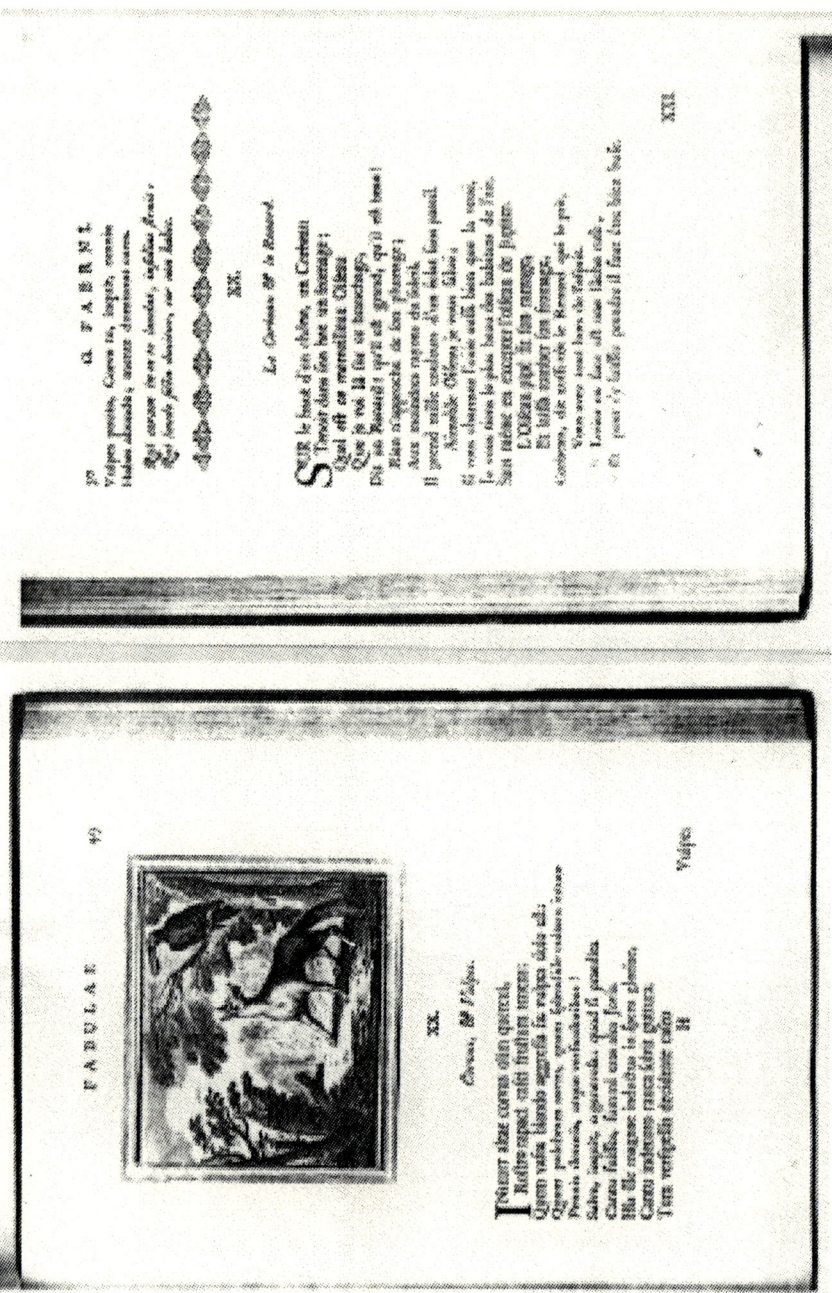

Figure 26. "Le Corbeau et le Renard," from Gabriel Faene, trans. Charles Perrault, *Cent Fables* (London: Darres et Du Bosc, 1743).

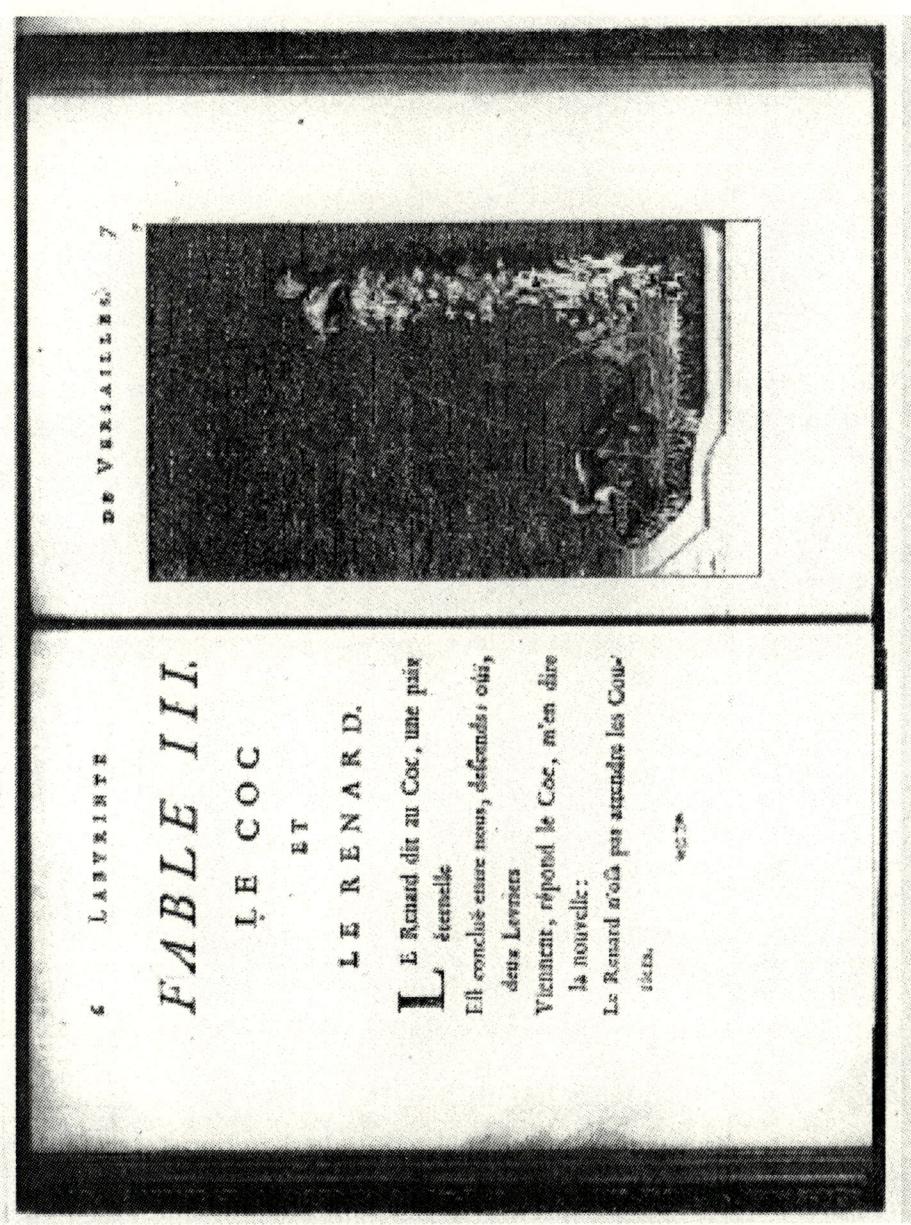

Figure 27.   "Le Coc et le Renard," from Charles Perrault, *Le Labyrinthe de Versailles* (Paris: Imprimerie Royale, 1677).

d'Angiviller took the decision to have it dismantled in 1774. The end of the *labyrinthe* coincides, therefore, with the time generally seen as heralding the end of the *aetas emblematica*.

Other minor emblematic pieces are to be found throughout the work of Charles Perrault. *La Peinture*, for example, a 1667 poem[48] in praise of Charles Le Brun, has, as its title suggests, the art of painting as subject. Nonetheless the piece is far from being a theoretical treatise or even a work of instruction on the subject, but rather, as Gautier-Gentès suggests,

> [*La Peinture*] est en elle-même une peinture ou une succession de peintures. Une «galerie», un «cabinet» constitué de mots. (56)

The creation of a painting made up of words is in keeping with the text/image interaction central to emblematic productions such as the biographical portrait "galeries" or "cabinets" to which we have alluded above.

The early lines of the poem place it within the *picta poesis* tradition of the time:

> A peine eut de Chaos la discorde bannie,
> Et le vaste pourpris de l'Empire des Cieux
> A peine estoit encor peuplé de tous ses dieux,
> Qu'ensemble on vit sortir du sein de la Nature
> L'aimable Poësie, & l'aimable Peinture,
> Deux sœurs dont les appas égaux, mais differens,
> Furent le doux plaisir de l'esprit & des sens:
> L'aisnée eut en naissant la parole en partage,
> La plus jeune n'en eut le moindre usage,
> Mais ses traits & son teint ravirent tous les Dieux; (lines 14-23, page 85)

Indeed by suggesting that poetry and painting are equal but different, but that together they charm "l'esprit" and the "sens," Perrault is using the very terms of emblematic theory.

This turns to practice later in the poem (lines 472-85) when Perrault describes the way in which painters would use Time as an emblem:

> Puis qu'on sçait que le Temps, Peintre judicieux,
> Qui des Maistres communs les tableaux décolore,
> Rendra les tiens plus beaux, & plus charmans encore,
> Lors que de son pinceau secondant ton dessein
> Il aura sur leurs traits mis la derniere main.
> Ce fut ce qu'autrefois un sage & sçavant Maistre
> Aux Peintres de son temps sceut bien faire connaître,
> Il sceut par son adresse en convaincre leurs yeux,
> Et leur en fit ainsi l'emblême ingenieux.

> Il peignit un vieillard, dont la barbe chenuë
> Tomboit à flots épais sur sa poitrine nuë,
> D'un sable diligent son front estoit chargé,
> Et d'aisles de Vautour tout son dos ombragé,
> Prés de luy se voyoit une Faux argentée… (124-25)

Perrault goes on to describe how the "vieillard" would touch certain paintings rendering them immortal, whereas in other cases he would pass his sponge across and remove all trace of the works.

Perrault's use of the term "emblême" appears fairly wide as no textual component is mentioned. Nonetheless he does provide interesting interplay between the written description of a visual Father Time figure and his effect upon paintings, again the visual subject of the written verse. Furthermore, the description that Perrault gives of the "vieillard" is so precise in its detail that one could easily imagine Perrault having a specific emblem-book image in mind.[49]

This section of *La Peinture* was to be reproduced in isolation under the title "Emblème ingenieux d'un peintre" on pages 268-69 of the first volume of the *Passe-Temps poetiques, historiques et critiques* of 1757.[50] The same volume, on pages 270-71, also attributed the short "Devise: Un Lys sur sa tige" to Perrault. These are examples of specific compositions that place Perrault clearly within the flourishing world of emblematics and indeed, as we hope to have demonstrated, much of his life and works was associated with this *milieu*. Viewed in this light, it seems fitting that one of his last endeavours should have been the *Discours sur l'art des devises*. When other works, such as the *Contes*, are approached and analysed within this context, it would appear that the subject of Perrault and emblematics could well sustain a book-length study in itself.

***

Reference in Charles Perrault's *Mémoires de ma vie* to the "talent que j'ai eu pour les devises" indicates the esteem in which he held emblematics. The culminating point of this esteem can be seen as his own *credo* on the subject, his *Discours sur l'art des devises*, composed and personally corrected at the end of his life and also mentioned in the *Mémoires*. In this work not only does Perrault describe some of the major devices of his composition, including the *Devises pour les tapisseries du roy*, he also, by means of an anecdotal account of a discussion with a certain M. l'Abbé, enters the theoretical debate spearheaded by such figures as Claude-François Menestrier, M. Clément and Henri Estienne.

Nonetheless Perrault's contribution is different. Whereas predecessors would run often to hundreds of pages, systematically dividing their text by subject matter—the history of the device, the *imago*, the use of Latin or French in the motto and so on—Perrault limits his work to a few pages in which the 'story' is given through protagonists—almost 'goodies' and 'baddies'—and, to a certain extent, summed up by a 'catch phrase'—"la lettre tuë, et l'esprit vivifie"—that is heavy with nuance.

On one level Perrault's approach can be seen as indicative of a new style of emblem theory, a method encapsulated in what was to become one of the most popular works of the eighteenth century, Dominique Bouhours's *Les Entretiens d'Ariste et d'Eugene*. First published in 1671,[51] this work went to several editions, including at least four from 1700 onwards. The *Entretiens* is divided into six chapters on a variety of subjects, of which the last discusses the device. The reader is not, however, given bare theory. Ideas are presented through the mouths of the work's main characters, Eugene and Aristide. In the case of the chapter on devices, the discussion is sparked off by the arrival of a ship decorated in several places by the "nec pluribus impar" sun device.

The anecdotal style is also a hallmark of Perrault's best-known work, his *Contes*. The *Discours sur l'art des devises* is worthy of attention not only for its contribution to seventeenth-century emblem theory, but also as a piece that allows us to set Perrault's work in a truer context. If, upon closer inspection, the *Contes* bear many of the stylistic traits of the emblem-related forms of the time, it is precisely because such forms played an important rôle in Charles Perrault's cultural make-up. The author of the *Contes* was also the author of the *Devises pour les tapisseries du roy*, of the *Hommes illustres*, of the *Courses de testes et de bagues,* of the *Labyrinthe de Versailles* and of *La Peinture*, all of which, as I hope to have demonstrated, can only be fully understood in the context of emblematics.

To understand such connections is also to re-evaluate the way in which we, as twentieth-century readers, view the works of seventeenth-century France. If the *Discours sur l'art des devises* was 'lost' for nearly three centuries, it is surely not because it was 'hidden'—the Arsenal is one of France's main and best catalogued libraries—but because no one was looking for it. We have tended to view the *Contes* in isolation, rather than as a logical product of a man who for much of his life was a pillar of seventeenth-century French officialdom. The art of the device was Charles Perrault's career and also his passion. It is by taking this into account, by considering and analysing his innovations and preoccupations in this field, that we can see his *œuvre* as a whole in its wider and more accurate context.

NOTES

[1] The edition of the *Contes* we have consulted is that of Classiques Garnier (Paris: Bordas: 1991) edited by Georges Rouger. Our introductory biography is based largely on Rouger's notes to this edition.

[2] This work will be discussed further, with full bibliographic references, below.

[3] For further information concerning the *Petite académie* and the *Académie des inscriptions et belles lettres*, see the introduction to volume I of Josèphe Jacquiot's, *Medailles et jetons de Louis XIV d'après le manuscrit de Londres, Add. 31908* (4 vols., Paris: Klincksieck, 1968).

[4] This work will be discussed further below.

[5] For further discussion of these works, see chapter II above.

[6] *Merveilles et Contes* 5.2 (1991), 167-78.

[7] On pages 107-19 of *Devises pour les tapisseries du roi*, eds. Marc Fumaroli and Marianne

Grivel (Paris: Herscher, 1988).

[8] (Geneva: Droz, 1992).

[9] *Europe* 68.739-40 (1990), 114-22.

[10] (Boston: Twayne, 1981).

[11] (Paris: Hachette, 1972).

[12] (New York: Peter Lang, 1985).

[13] These works all provide general but scholarly introductions to Perrault's life and the wide span of his works. For more specific studies, see Claire-Lise Malarté's *Perrault à travers la critique depuis 1960: Bibliographie annotée* (Paris: PFSCL Biblio 17, 1989). Malarté provides full references and clear annotations for over 160 entries, as well as indications of further bibliographical sources.

[14] This piece was brought to my attention by Professor Daniel Russell. It was he who first suggested that the *Discours sur l'art des devises* might be the work of Charles Perrault. Much of the following section is taken from the introduction to my edition of the text as it appeared in *Emblematica* 7.1 (1993), 99-144.

[15] (Paris: CNRS, 1995), planche 95, no. 859.

[16] In my transcribed version I have used curved brackets—'{ }'—to indicate the red ink additions and corrections. It should be noted that the additional underlinings are in red ink and that the added '§' indicated at the end of a line is placed centrally between the two lines of text in the original.

[17] (Paris: H. Laurens).

[18] (Paris: Macula, 1993). Antoine Picon's's introduction, "Un Moderne paradoxal," provides useful background information to Perrault's life and times, as well as to the *Mémoires*. Jeanne Morgan Zarucchi has also edited a translation, *Memoirs of my life* (Columbia: U of Missouri P, 1989), supplemented by a useful introduction and copious notes.

[19] For the sake of convenience we have followed Bonnefon/Picon's edition, which is generally accurate. It should be noted however that the spelling, punctuation and paragraphing do at times differ from the original manuscript.

[20] For this information I am grateful to M. Bernard Barbiche of the Ecole des Chartes.

[21] I.e. "propres & personnelles," "d'occasion" and "attribuées."

[22] See pages 152, 155-57, 162-63 and 173-74. In the case of the devices on pages 155-57 and 173-74 Menestrier does not acknowledge Perrault's authorship.

[23] We have followed the 1684 edition which, as Judi Loach points out "is not an entirely new work but rather an elaboration of the first" ("Menestrier's Emblem Theory," 317).

[24] See page 80 of Russell's introduction to Clément's text.

[25] See page 92 of Russell's introduction to Gardien's text.

[26] I am grateful to David Graham for this information. The edition I have used is *La Sainte Bible* (Amsterdam: P. and J. Blaeu, 1687).

[27] The edition consulted is [Strasbourg]: Apud Felicem Argentinam, [1522].

[28] "Let the authority of the philosophers be of little weight, except with regard to that which is taught in the Holy Scriptures, even if the words used are different. What the philosophers call reason *ratio* Paul sometimes calls spirit, sometimes inner man, sometimes the law of the mind. What they label passion *affectus*, he sometimes labels flesh, sometimes body, sometimes outward man, sometimes the law of the limbs."

[29] The edition consulted is that of Philippe Sellier (Paris: Bordas, 1991).

[30] Cf. for example *Laus stultitiae*.

[31] See chapter II above.

[32] See pages 113-22 of William Brooks, Buford Norman and Jeanne Morgan Zarucchi's edi-

tion of Philippe Queneau's *Alceste, suivi de La Querelle d'Alceste* (Geneva: Droz, 1994). The text followed by the editors is that of the *Recueil de divers ouvrages en prose et en vers* (n.p.: n.d.), which they date to 1680-85.

[33] For an illustration of the "Praestant Interna Coronae" devise, see figure 4.

[34] (Paris: C. Blageart).

[35] (Paris: Sebastien Mabre-Cramoisy, 1679).

[36] The Paris manuscript has been published in facsimile edition with notes and introductions by Marc Fumaroli and Marianne Grivel.

[37] See pages 31-32 of their *Bibliography of Emblematic Manuscripts* (Montreal: Queens-McGill UP, 1997).

[38] See pages 132-33 of Picon's edition of the *Mémoires*.

[39] *Les Hommes illustres qui ont paru en France pendant ce siècle, avec leurs portraits au naturel*, 2 vols (Paris: Antoine Dezaillier, 1696-1700). For a general discussion of the work and a consideration of its rôle in promoting the cause of the *modernes*, see David Culpin, "Perrault as Moralist: *Les Hommes illustres*," *French Studies* 52.2 (1998), 142-51.

[40] (Paris: Claude Barbin, 1697). Jacques Barchilon's edition of the *Contes de Perrault* (Geneva: Slatkine, 1980) includes a facsimile of the 1697 Barbin volume.

[41] The following stories also appeared in the early editions: "Le Petit Chaperon Rouge," "La Barbe Bleue," "Le Maitre Chat," "Les Fées," "Cendrillon," "Riquet a la Hoppe" and "Le Petit Poucet."

[42] See, for example, our discussion of "Le Cerf se voyant dans l'eau" in section V C above.

[43] (Paris: J.-B. Coignard, 1699).

[44] The "Avertissement" is unnumbered.

[45] See, for example, section III B above.

[46] (London: Darres et Du Bosc).

[47] (Paris: Imprimerie Royale, 1677). For a modern reprint with a comprehensive Postface, see Michael Conan's 1982 edition published by Du Moniteur of Paris.

[48] This date of composition is suggested by Jean-Luc Gautier-Gentès on page 14 of the introduction to his edition of *La Peinture*. This is the edition we have followed.

[49] For possible examples, see Erwin Panofsky's chapter on "Father Time," pages 69-93 of *Studies in Iconology* (New York: Oxford UP, 1939). See also Michael Bath, "The Iconography of Time" in *The Telling Image: Explorations in the Emblem*, eds. Ayers Bagley, Edward Griffin and Austin McLean (New York: AMS, 1996), 29-68.

[50] (2 vols., Paris: Duchesne).

[51] (Paris: Sebastien Mabre-Cramoisy).

VII
Conclusion:
Further Possibilities

The case studies that make up the previous chapters include elements relating purely and specifically to the authors in question. Our brief analysis of Descartes's use of language in the context of Jesuit emblematics, for example, should shed new light on the *Discours de la méthode*. Certain textual references, such as those to the love poetry of Tristan, to La Fontaine's "L'Araignée et l'hirondelle" or to Perrault's *Discours* are highly specific. On this level our study remains pertinent purely to scholars of our four chosen authors.

Nonetheless, even the most specific analysis has its foundation in wider fields of research. Grasping the possible emblematic implications of Descartes's ivy imagery requires prior knowledge of the Jesuit emblems and devices that formed part of his cultural education. Evidence indicating that the device was a popular means of expression among members of La Fontaine's salon society goes far in explaining the existence of emblem-like structures in La Fontaine's texts.

We have suggested that the seventeenth-century reader may have had an approach to reading text/image interactions that was often closer to the mentality of the Renaissance than to that of modern times. The phenomenon of global (as opposed to linear) readings following the creation of certain textual *imagines* could be of interest far beyond the single example of La Fontaine. The fact that the significance of Tristan's poetry should change according to its adaptation to different visual contexts is in keeping with a general phenomenon that can seem alien to modern readers. In the case of Descartes, it goes without saying that he was not the only seventeenth-century author to make different use of images that the Jesuits had appropriated for pedagogical purposes.

Beyond specific examples, this study should therefore be of greatest interest as an example of method. The work of Charles Perrault is indicative of how emblematics constituted a major cultural phenomenon in the life of seventeenth-century France. The insight into the mentality of an age provided by a knowledge of a major cultural phenomenon allows us to understand literary productions of the time in their true historical context. We have taken the examples of a limited number of writers, but the implication is that the same method of research and analysis can usefully be applied to many authors of the Grand Siècle: not just poets or authors of philosophical prose, but playwrights,[1] novelists, composers of sermons, indeed writers involved in literary production of all types.

To the reader acquainted with seventeenth-century French literature, the examples examined in the previous chapters would already have brought to mind possible parallels. The reader acquainted with emblematics may have been reminded of the studies, although limited in number, that have already been carried out in this field. The aim of this conclusion, as its title implies, is to suggest and explore briefly certain further possibilities.

The method of research we have followed regarding the influence of Jesuit emblematics upon Descartes could conceivably be applied in the case of the emblematic imagery of Port Royal. Although the Jesuits and the Jansenists were bitter religious rivals, the dissemination of their respective messages often called upon similar means of expression. An example in case is the Jansenist Le Sieur de Royaumont's *L'Histoire du Vieux et du Nouveau Testament représentée avec des figures et des explications édifiantes tirées des Saints Pères pour régler les moeurs dans toutes sortes de conditions*.[2] Otherwise known as the *Figures de la Bible* or *Figures de Royaumont*, this work contains approximately 250 half-page engravings, each illustrating the textual account of an episode of the Bible and each with a historical and allegorical commentary.

The book's purpose is outlined in the dedicatory preface to the Dauphin:

> Ce livre, MONSEIGNEUR, vous pourra donner une entrée facile dans ces Histoires sacrées d'une maniere tres-agréable, en vous les representant dépeintes dans les figures, & en faisant passer ainsi de vos yeux dans vôtre esprit des instructions tres-importantes. (sig. a-ii-v)

The "Avertissement" gives a justification, in true emblematic style, of the motto-like titles that appear beneath each engraving:

> On avoit pensé d'abord à mettre les propres paroles des Saints imprimées en autre lettre. Mais souvent leurs passages estoient trop longs pour tenir dans le petit espace qui restoit aprés la representation de chaque histoire, & ils n'auroient plus eu cette breveté vive & animée qui paroist si necessaire à des reflexions qu'on veut joindre à un discours historique. On a donc esté obligé de les abreger. (sig. e-i-r)

Nicolas Fontaine's *Dictionnaire chretien* of 1691[3] is another Port Royal publication to which little attention has been paid, but which gives a clear indication of the emblematic mentality of the Jansenists. This is clear from the full title itself: *Dictionnaire chretien où sur differens tableaux de la nature, l'on apprend par l'ecriture et les Saints Peres a voir Dieu peint dans tous ses ouvrages et a passer des choses visibles aux invisibles*. The opening words of the "Avertissement" repeat the notion that God's creation paints the picture of his invisible greatness:

> Il n'y a point de Chretien qui ne sçache que Dieu a donné ses Creatures à l'homme comme un tableau visible, où, selon que saint Paul l'assure, il a peint ses grandeurs invisibles. Sa bonté & sa sagesse ont voulu se servir de ce moyen comme d'un degré pour nous faire monter à luy. Notre foiblesse avoit besoin de ce secours [. . .] & on doit déplorer le malheur de ceux qui ouvrant l'oreille à tant de choses indignes de leur application, ne sont presque sourds qu'à cette parole muette qui leur crie à tout moment. (sig. a-ii-r)

It is the dictionary that provides the text to accompany the "tableau visible" thereby forming an emblematic key to God's mysteries. The explanation of the use of "lierre," for example, is very much in keeping with the ivy of the emblem tradition:

> Le lierre qui se tient fermement attaché à la muraille, ou à l'arbre qu'il environne, est la figure de la fidelité des amis qui se tiennent attachez à leurs amis lors mesme qu'ils sont malheureux, & qu'ils sont décheus de leur estat dans le monde, comme le lierre se tient toujours attaché à l'arbre mesme aprés qu'il est tombé: *Hæretque cadenti*. (sig. Y-y-iii)

In this instance, the inclusion of the phrase "Hæretque cadenti," a summary of the notion that the ivy clings even to the falling tree, forms the *motto* for which the ivy itself provides the *imago*.

The *Figures de Royaumont* and the *Dictionnaire chretien* are just two of the many emblematic Bibles that Port Royal produced. A full understanding of the mentality behind such Jansenist productions, as well as an in-depth analysis of the images (often emblematic ones) used, would open the way for a much clearer understanding of the mentality behind the works of Blaise Pascal and others who, like him, came under the influence of Port Royal. The study of Jansenist emblematics could lead to deeper understanding of the works of Antoine Arnauld, Jean Racine and François de La Rochefoucauld.

Jean Racine is a particularly good example. His upbringing at Port Royal would have exposed him to the general mentality that formed part of any Jansenist's cultural baggage. Racine's social and literary circles—the Hôtel de Bourgogne, the Hôtel de Nevers, the court of Louis XIV—as well as his post as *Historiographe du roi* (from 1677 onwards) would have put him into direct contact with the genre of courtly emblematics as outlined in chapter II. A major part of the function of the *Historiographe du roi*, for example, was the composition of devices in celebration of the king to be used in royal entries and fêtes. In short, there is little doubt that emblematics formed part of Racine's cultural baggage.

In *Écritures codées* Couton has pointed out, but only in passing, Racine's debt to the iconographical representations of certain of the Port Royal Bibles. Indeed the inventory made of Racine's books after his death includes several iconographical Jansenist works. These include Louis-Isaac Le Maitre de Sacy's translations of the Bible and the *Iconae Biblicae* published in Strasbourg in 1630. Referring to the *Figures de Royaumont*, Couton concludes,

> Il me paraît hors de doute cependant que Racine non seulement les connaissait mais les pratiquait assidûment: à chaque page, qu'il s'agisse des décors, des costumes, des rites, de l'histoire du peuple juif, des événements mis en scène dans *Esther* et plus encore dans *Athalie*, le souvenir des *Figures* s'impose. L'étude de cette source de Racine est encore, croyons-nous, à faire. (60)

It is precisely the stark nature of Racine's classicism, the power of the passions expressed in very few words, that make the pictorial images that he does offer all the more interesting. The *récit de Théramène*, the famous account of Hippolyte's death in *Phèdre*, includes several highly pictorial images which are framed by the limits of the speech. Leo Spitzer has given us a thorough stylistic analysis of the *récit*[4] in which he emphasises the important question of visualisation, nonetheless he makes no reference to contemporary prints or paintings of the subject. This question is, however, discussed by Françoise Siguret[5] who pays specific attention to Charles Le Brun's frontispiece to *Phèdre* in which he portrays the scene of Hippolytus's death. Amy Wygant, in a forthcoming work, considers the *récit* in the light of Rubens's art and, interestingly, both she and Siguret independently point to an iconography of Hippolytus as Christ figure. Wygant convincingly supports the assertion by reference to a shell emblem—Rubens's painting of Hippolytus's death includes sea shells—in which Camerarius's theme is the afterlife.

In general terms, we are, once again, in the presence of a word emblem as defined by Peter Daly. The *récit* opens with a static description of Hippolyte:[6]

> Il était sur son char; ses gardes affligés
> Imitaient son silence, autour de lui rangés;
> Il suivait tout pensif le chemin de Mycènes;
> Sa main sur ses chevaux laissait flotter les rênes.
> Ses superbes coursiers, qu'on voyait autrefois
> Pleins d'une ardeur si noble obéir à sa voix,
> L'œil morne maintenant et la tête baissée,
> Semblaient se conformer à sa triste pensée. (lines 1499-1506)

Although the hero is represented on his chariot, Racine conveys no idea of movement. Indeed the verb tense is the imperfect, the tense for description. The lines that then follow, however, starting with "Un effroyable cri," describe the violence of the monster's apparition. The monster itself is the subject of a verbal image:

Conclusions: Further Possibilities

> Son front large est armé de cornes menaçantes;
> Tout son corps est couvert d'écailles jaunissantes;
> Indomptable taureau, dragon impétueux,
> Sa croupe se recourbe en replis tortueux. (lines 1517-20)

This baroque sea monster seems out of place in the context of the restrained classicism of Racine's play. It would fit much more naturally into the context of the baroque emblem book engravings in which sea monsters or giant fish often featured.

One such giant fish is the "daulphin" of emblem 96 of La Perrière's *Le Théâtre des bons engins*. This has nothing in common with the modern notion of a dolphin, but is rather a sharp-toothed scaly sea monster as large as the armoured man with which it struggles. Racine's reference to an "Indomptable taureau, dragon impétueux" triggers further associations with emblem book monsters: Alciato, Camerarius, Nicolaus Taurellus and Sebastián de Covarrubias all composed emblems showing fearsome dragons (Henkel and Schöne, columns 623-26). Number 54 of Covarrubias's *Emblemas morales*[7] of 1610, for example, shows a horned sea dragon attacking Perseus's reflection in the water.

Four lines suffice for Racine to create such associations. He could be sure that an accumulation of certain key references, such as "cornes menaçantes," "corps [. . .] couvert d'écailles," "Indomptable taureau" or "dragon impétueux," would function as 'memory tags'[8] and thereby allow his audience to visualise already familiar emblem engravings far more monstrous than a page of description. Indeed the fact that such associations allow Racine to by-pass wordy description heightens further the impact and immediacy of the récit.

Further emblematic echoes give Racine's text a layer of complexity not obvious to the modern reader. The *dizain* that forms part of La Perrière's sea-monster emblem opens as follows:

> Plus tost pourras arrester le daulphin,
> Que refrener femme de cueur volaige.
> Combien que soit l'homme subtil & fin,
> Esprit de femme est ruse d'avantaige.

Phèdre could certainly be considered a "femme de cueur volaige," one "ruse d'avantaige." Similar associations are suggested by Hernando de Soto's Hippolytus emblem on page 60b of his *Emblemas moralizades*[9] (see figure 28). The woodcut engraving shows Hippolytus's chariot and horses while the hero is being thrown to the ground. Nonetheless the horses we see are static, they are indeed "superbes coursiers" with "L'œil morne même maintenant et la tête baissée." The emblem's motto, "Consilium pravæ mulieris" ["the advice of a depraved woman"], is expanded by the *subscriptio*: trusting his evil wife Phaedra, Theseus had caused Hippolytus's death; "Que siempre consejos tales / Da una perversa muger" ["an evil woman always gives such advice"] (lines 7-8). Phaedra does not feature in the engraving, but she is the main subject of the emblem. Racine did not need to know this emblem to

Figure 28. "Consilium pravæ mulieris," from Hernando de Soto *Emblemas moralizades* (Madrid: Por los Herederos de Iuan Iniguez de Lequerica, 1599).

Conclusions: Further Possibilities

write the scene, but it does give an idea of the climate of opinion in which it would be received: any mention of Hippolytus's death could be synonymous with his stepmother's, even woman's, perfidy.

Such knowledge can throw a different light on Racine's text in much the same way that understanding emblematics might alter our reading of Descartes's use of language. Firstly, after the description of the sea monster, the text of *Phèdre* returns to recounting the action as Hippolyte's horses bolt and he is dragged to his death. Racine has therefore presented the reader/viewer with static images, those of the proud Hippolyte and of the fiery monster, that only take on their full pathos and horror through interaction with the movement of the description of the hero's death. His demise is all the more shocking to the reader of the time who, familiar with sea monster emblems, has already fully visualised the horrific details to which Racine alludes. Furthermore, the static image he has of Hippolyte's proud stance (lines 1499-1507) constantly contrasts the evolving description of his body being dragged through the dust. These emblematic associations add to Racine's rhetorical force by allowing the text to keep its pace, while nonetheless retaining the depth of pictorial detail.

Secondly, the iconographical associations of Hippolyte's death with woman's perfidy throw an interesting interpretation upon this culminating violent scene of *Phèdre*. Throughout the play it is Thésée and Hippolyte who stand as heroic men of action. Nonetheless, it is the women, Phèdre and Œnone, who throw the wheels of fate into motion. The modern reader might overlook the contrast during the *récit de Théramène*; events that concern Hippolyte are recounted by Théramène to Thésée, neither Phèdre nor Œnone are physically present. The women's absence from this, the play's climax, might lead the modern reader to underestimate their importance. For the audience of Racine's time, however, emblematic associations with Hippolyte's death served to underline Phèdre's instigating rôle in the play's denouement.

Phèdre's epithet, "La fille de Minos et de Pasiphaé" (line 36), has certain similarities with a courtly device to the extent that both are periphrastic references to their subject. Hippolyte applies the label after Théramène has pointed to his master's ill-ease:

> Hé! depuis quand, Seigneur, craignez-vous la présence
> De ces paisibles lieux, si chers à votre enfance,
> Et dont je vous ai vu préférer le séjour
> Au tumulte pompeux d'Athène et de la cour? (lines 29-32)

For the audience of Racine's time, the association of "tumulte pompeux" with courtly life would not bring to mind the court of a Greek city state, but rather the pomp and ceremony of Versailles. Part of this pomp was the likening of Louis XIV to Apollo in reference to his sun device. The definition of Phèdre as "La fille de Minos et de Pasiphaé" may function in much the same way.

We have examined references to Apollo and Louis XIV's sun device in La Fontaine's *Les Amours de Psyché*. The same sort of analysis can be applied to the case of Phèdre's ancestry. Minos, God of the shadows and judge of the underworld, is in contrast to Pasiphaé, daughter of Helios, the sun. Throughout the play Racine uses associated imagery of the shadows and of the light, a theme explored by Robert J. Nelson in his "Night Unto Day Unto Night: Racinian Tragedy."[10] Phèdre's guilt is represented by the shadows of the palace in which she dwells, the opposite of the pureness that the light represents:

> Les ombres par trois fois ont obscurci les cieux
> Depuis que le sommeil n'est entré dans vos yeux [Phèdre's eyes],
> Et le jour a trois fois chassé la nuit obscure
> Depuis que votre corps languit sans nourriture. (lines 191-94)

Phèdre dwells on her guilt: "Je me cachais au jour, je fuyais la lumière" (line 1242). Only death can resolve the conflict: "Je voulais en mourant prendre soin de ma gloire, / Et dérober au jour une flamme si noire" (lines 309-10). Indeed Phèdre's death brings the pureness of daylight:

> Déjà je ne vois plus qu'à travers un nuage
> Et le ciel et l'époux que ma présence outrage;
> Et la mort, à mes yeux dérobant la clarté,
> Rend au jour, qu'ils souillaient, toute sa pureté. (lines 1641-44)

By expressing Phèdre's conflict through the imagery of shadows and light, Racine plays upon associations with her "fille de Minos et de Pasiphaé" epithet; in similar fashion, writers of the seventeenth century might have referred to someone by allusion to the themes of their device. We have already cited the example of La Fontaine's reference to Apollo's descent into the "Grotte" in *Les Amours de Psyché*; as Louis XIV, through his sun device, gave himself the guise of Apollo the Sun God, La Fontaine could play upon references to the sun in order to comment on the character of the king. Louis XIV's device and Phèdre's epithet both provide the basis for a continued series of metonymic references.

The influence of Port Royal is even stronger in the case of Blaise Pascal. Georges Couton, again in his *Écritures codées*, has already analysed certain figurative aspects of the *Pensées*. He sums up as follows:

> Tout un jeu d'oppositions entre le «littéral» et le «spirituel», qui attesterait, s'il en était besoin encore, l'importance de l'explication par les figures bibliques dans sa vision du monde et de l'histoire. Au centre des *Pensées* il y a un grand encouragement ou une pressante injonction à décrypter l'Écriture. (67)

Couton explores the notion that Pascal presents Christ's life as a model for imitation in the manner of the *faut mourirs*, or *artes moriendi*, the guides consoling the Christian in the face of his mortality by comparison of his situation with that of the Saviour. As an example of this form Couton cites *La Manière de se bien préparer à la mort par des considérations sur la Cène, la Passion et la Mort de Jésus-Christ avec de très belles estampes emblématiques expliquées par Mr. de Chertablon 1700.*[11] Chertablon's "estampes emblématiques" give an episode from the Christian's life, with a framed representation of the equivalent passage in Christ's existence. In the case of the Christian on his death-bed, for example, a member of the entourage is shown holding up an engraving of Christ on the cross. Couton's argument, in brief, is that Pascal presents Christ's life as an emblem book for the guidance of that of man (67-68).

Certain of Pascal's *Pensées* fit naturally into the background of emblematic expression. One such example is *Pensée* 481 (Sellier edition, page 378):

> L'éloquence est une peinture de la pensée. Et ainsi ceux qui, après avoir peint, ajoutent encore, font un tableau au lieu d'un portrait.

The idea of a "peinture de la pensée," a seventeenth-century commonplace frequently attributed to Plutarch, also reminds us of the "peinture parlante" and "poésie muette" of the introduction to Aneau's *Picta poesis*. Another influential and emblematic source is Blaise de Vigenère's 1615 version of Philostratus's work, *Les Images ou tableaux de platte peinture*.[12] On the sixth page of the unnumbered preface to the latter Vigenère states,

> Plutarque au traicté *de la lecture des Poëtes*, dit que *la Poësie est une imitation, & une science correspondante à l'art de la peinture: tellement que la Poësie est une peinture parlante, & la peinture une Poësie muette*. [Vigenère's italics]

Pascal also mentions that nature has engraved its image: "la nature ayant gravé son image et celle de son auteur dans toutes choses" (*Pensée* 230, page 249). The implication, therefore, is that God, "son auteur," allows man to see him through his image in the form of nature. Pascal, although Jansenist, is not far from the Jesuit Ioannes David's rhetorical notion of the world as man's mirror to God, the "Speculum creaturarum" (see figure 3), with its contemplation of the invisible through the visible ("Invisibilium per visibilia contemplatio").

Other *Pensées* point to Pascal as playing upon visual images that were well-known in the emblem tradition: "Eloquence qui persuade par douceur, non par empire, en tyran, non en roi" (number 485, page 379); "Quand tout se remue également, rien ne se remue en apparence, comme en un vaisseau" (number 577, page 410); "L'homme n'est qu'un roseau, le plus faible de la nature, mais c'est un roseau pensant" (number 231, page 255). In all of these cases, and others like them, Pascal evokes the image by use of a motto-like epigram. In the case of number 15, the *Pensée* is supplemented by the reader's visual image of a king. La Perrière had followed much the same procedure in emblem 21 of his *Morosophie*. The engraving shows a kindly king addressing a disorderly mob. The accompanying text explains that "Appaiser faut d'un peuple la fureur, / Non par menace, ains par parolle affable."

In the case of *Pensées* 577 and 231 the use of visual concepts already pregnant with meaning adds further nuance to Pascal's message. We have discussed some of the emblematic boat images in reference to Descartes. In the case of *Pensée* 577, the image of the boat as the public cause, or indeed as man's salvation in Christ, adds the entirely appropriate nuance of the need for mankind to work in unison for common good. Fontaine's *Dictionnaire chretien* is even more specific, stating that "Le Vaisseau c'est l'Eglise toute entière." Fontaine's work postdates Pascal, but the undercurrents of his imagery were surely felt in Pascal's time. Whereas Descartes appears to be using the nuances of the emblematic ship's meanings to underline the difference in his philosophy, in Pascal's case his text is reinforced by the implications of the emblematic imagery.

Images of the reed were also common in the emblem tradition. Hadrianus Junius in emblem 43 of his *Emblemata*[13] and Georgette de Montenay in her *Emblemes, ou devises chrestiennes* both attest to the reed's apparent weakness being compensated by its resilience against the storm. Montenay's emblem 63 compares the reed to the mighty tree that gives in the storm:

> Cest arbre grand & puissant est rompu
> Au souffle seul du vent plus que luy fort:
> Mais l'arbrisseau ainsi briser n'a peu,
> Qui s'est ployé sous un si grand effort. (lines 1-4)

This is also the theme of La Fontaine's *Fable* I, XII, "Le Chêne et le roseau." The story is a reworking of Æsop's fable, but the addition of visual details create an *imago* in the manner of an emblem. The reader of *Pensée* 347 approaches the reed image with emblematic notions of the strength of the meek through perseverance. Pascal's usage conforms to expectations in that man, like the reed, is weak compared to the might of the "ample sein de la nature" (number 230, page 247). Pascal differs from the tradition in giving the reed its strength through reason, just as man differs by the fact that he is indeed "un roseau pensant." In this instance Pascal, like Descartes, gives force to the image by differing from the expectations of the iconographic traditions upon which it is built.

Another epigrammatic work in good emblematic practice was the *Maximes* of François de La Rochefoucauld, and the *Caractères* of Jean de La Bruyère also employ short maxim-like pieces as the vehicle for social and moral commentaries. Both these works are products of the court society of which emblems and devices were a major form of expression. It would have been natural enough for the authors in question to use the very form of expression best understood by the pillars of court society, as a means of undermining certain values represented by that milieu. Scholars have not yet attempted, however, to identify or catalogue references to courtly devices that might feature as a *clin d'œil* to those reading the moralists' scathing portraits of court society.

On the other hand, Christoph Strosetzki in "Hieroglyphentradition und Devisenkunst als Hintergrund der Maximen von La Rochefoucauld"[14] has shown beyond doubt that there is scope for research into the influence of emblematics upon La Rochefoucauld. Strosetzki makes much of the similarities between the stylistics of Jesuit emblematics and those of La Rochefoucauld, especially in respect to motifs such as the sun, or the expression of court happenings through devices. He concludes by suggesting that La Rochefoucauld must have been aware of Jesuit emblematics and influenced accordingly. His argument is convincing even if La Rochefoucauld by no means had the historical links with the Jesuits that Descartes did. Indeed the austerity of certain aspects of the *Maximes* would perhaps guide us to the classicism of Port Royal as an influencing factor. Strosetzki's article stands as an example of what can be achieved on the broadest level when emblematics are applied to the study of literature. In the cases of La Rochefoucauld and La Bruyère the question would undoubtedly bear much closer scrutiny.

An example of such closer scrutiny already exists in the case of Mme. de La Fayette's *La Princesse de Clèves*. Kurt Weinberg's "The Lady and the Unicorn, or M. de Nemours à Coulomiers: Enigma, Device, Blazon and Emblem in *La Princesse de Clèves*" stands as an example in case of the way in which a work of the seventeenth century can appear considerably more complex in the light of emblematics. Weinberg's study explores twists in the plot of *La Princesse de Clèves* as significantly linked to the devices of the characters involved. Only the reader who is aware of the implications of such devices (as indeed Mme. de La Fayette's readers would have been) is able to enjoy to the full the subtleties of the novel's plot. As in the case of our study of Descartes's reference to ivy, the reader's initial reaction might be that such research does no more than open up interesting details hitherto lost to the twentieth-century audience. Weinberg's work demonstrates convincingly, however, that the accumulation of such details can comprise a significant element of the very structure of the work in question.

The writings of La Rochefoucauld, La Bruyère and Mme. de La Fayette give us valuable insight into the activities and values of seventeenth-century French court society. Theirs was also the society reflected in the manuscripts of the *Recueil Conrart*. Our study has analysed pieces from the *Recueil Conrart* in reference to the close social circles of Jean de La Fontaine. Other areas of literary expression fell within the same domain: the early years of the seventeenth century were marked, for example, by the success of *préciosité*. This fashion, satirised in Molière's *Les Précieuses ridicules*, grew from the polite social gatherings that had formed in the salons of the time. Manuscripts of the *Recueil Conrart* that we have already discussed in reference to La Fontaine also give us many of the written versions of the *précieux* exchanges; these include Mme. de Scudéry's account of events at "Tendre" (manuscript 5131, piece 1), letters between "Sapho," "Acante" and "Trasyle" (manuscript 5414), or a piece concerning Sapho's doves (manuscript 5418, piece 157). In the case of one such collection, the *Recueil de devises données à Marie de la Tour, duchesse de La Trémoille* (Arsenal manuscript 5217), the elegant parchment pages contain the devices of social figures and salon personalities like Charlotte-Marguerite de Montmorency, the Princesse de Condé, or Mme. de Rambouillet herself.

As we have stated, Pierre Le Moyne in his *De l'Art des devises* makes it clear that devices formed a part of salon conversation: "il se faut contenter de les dire à l'oreille, ou de les faire voir sur des Tablettes dans une Ruelle" (117). It seems more than likely that the various devices of the *Recueil Conrart* would have been put to such a use. Given strong circumstantial evidence of this kind, an in-depth study could well show that the rôle of devices in *précieux* salon activity was much more important than has thus far been realised.

Such salon discussion found its published expression in the *précieux* novels that had become so popular. The *Astrée* by Honoré d'Urfé consists of over five thousand pages; it includes certain moralising epigrams that would have been worthy of the motto of a device. For example, beneath two myrtle branches a painting of a shepherdess bears the title "C'EST LA DEESSE ASTRÉE." The emblematic portrait is completed by an accompanying verse: "Plus digne de nos voeux, que nos voeux ne sont" (142). Certain scenes also have a vivid pictorial quality, as has been described by Anne Desprechins in "Images de «L'Astrée»: Etude de la réception du texte à travers les tapisseries."[15] There she points to the fact that the pictorial nature of many of the *Astrée*'s key scenes made the work an ideal subject for tapestries. Accompanied by a motto-like statement, such pictorial scenes take on the structure of an emblem.

The "Carte de Tendre," one of the most highly celebrated components of the *Clélie* by Madeleine de Scudéry—along with the *Astrée* the *Clélie* was the most discussed novel in salon circles—was classed by Menestrier as being emblematic (*Art des emblèmes*, 45). Even if Menestrier did tend to see emblems wherever he looked, we might explore the implications of the "Carte de Tendre"'s attempt to personify and schematise the range of human feelings. As with Tristan's *La Carte du Royaume d'Amour*,[16] in the "Carte de Tendre" the various emotions and *états d'âme* are placed under classifying titles, examples including "Inclination," "Soumission," "Tendresse" or "Obéissance." The "Carte de Tendre" then renders such precise schematisation visual in the form of a map. The emotions become place names such as "Tendre sur Inclination" or "Tendre sur Reconnoissance," and they are reached by the appropriate rivers ("Inclination Fleuve," "Reconnoissance Fleuve"). The map represents the rivers as might a geographical map of the period and the place names are accompanied by drawings of towns. Although this milieu is far removed from that of the Jesuits, the rhetorical process is similar: the "Carte de Tendre" renders the invisible, namely human emotions, visible through representations of towns and rivers.

Still in the salons, one might also explore possible links between the symbolics inherent in devices and that of the pseudonyms of *précieux* communication. Vincent Voiture, one of the poets whose works have been transcribed onto SMAdd.392, addressed letters "à une lionne," or "de la carpe au brochet." The "lionne" in question is Charlotte-Marguerite de Montmorency, Princesse de Condé. We have already pointed to pieces in the *Recueil Conrart* that refer to Fouquet through his squirrel device; of these one such fable, "Le Renard et l'ecureuil," has since been identified as the work of La Fontaine. In the case of Tristan L'Hermite, "Leale & Secreto" refers directly to the construction of a device in the course of the address to the loved-one. Tristan and Voiture were surely not the only poets whose compositions played on the subject of a friend's device. The poems of Isaac de Benserade or Paul Scarron will also appear richer to the reader able to decipher the emblematic codes of expression popular in the *ruelles*.

Other poets might be approached from different angles, but still with emblematics in mind. François de Malherbe's allegorical language with its personification of abstract nouns and mythological references, his use of common emblematic themes such as the sun or the world as a glass and, above all, his rôle as court poet serving the official entries of the royalty, are all aspects of his life and works that could link him to the fashion for emblems and devices. A completely different poet, Marc-Antoine de Girard, sieur de Saint-Amant, often based his works on visual images such as "Le Melon," "Le Fromage" and "La Pipe." The meaning of these objects in emblem books could give added innuendo to Saint-Amant's texts as they stand. It seems to me that seventeenth-century poets continued to structure their works in a way that resembles the word-emblems described by Russell in his "Emblematic Structures in Sixteenth-Century French Poetry."

In previous chapters we have mentioned and analysed the pulpit oratory of Père Philibert Quartier. Similarly, the funeral sermons of Jacques Bénigne Bossuet might profitably be compared with the emblematic rhetoric of Menestrier in his *Lettre sur l'usage d'exposer des devises dans les églises pour les décorations funèbres*[17] of 1687. Engravings from *Série Qb 1* in the Département des estampes of the Bibliothèque nationale show us, for example, that for the funeral of Henriette d'Angleterre the Basilica at Saint Denis was adorned with coats of arms and *têtes de mort*. Bearing in mind the example of Quartier's sermon illustrated by the emblems that Le Jay describes, it is not hard to imagine Bossuet pointing to the *têtes de mort* as he announced that "Je veux dans un seul malheur déplorer toutes les calamités du genre humain, et dans une seule mort faire voir la mort et le néant de toutes les grandeurs humaines"[18] (84).

In reference to Pierre Corneille's possible borrowings from Caesare Ripa's *Iconologie*, Georges Couton makes an important point concerning seventeenth-century expression:

> Il nous suffit de savoir qu'au XVIIe siècle existe et est largement
> utilisé un vocabulaire et une imagerie que nous appellerions indif-
> féremment métaphorique, symbolique, emblématique. (76)

Understanding the functioning and references of this "vocabulaire" can, as we have attempted to demonstrate, undoubtedly better our understanding of the century's literature in general.

***

A conclusion that aims to consider a subject as broad as seventeenth-century French literature will necessarily involve choices and inevitable shortcomings: Racine is discussed through detailed analysis but only of a limited number of texts, no more than passing references are made to other playwrights of the age, the overview given of the concept of *préciosité* and its manifestations is necessarily superficial. Similarly, it would have been possible to choose other authors for the main case studies, or indeed alternative approaches to the authors chosen. The broad historical contextualisation that underpins the studies of Descartes and La Fontaine is clearly different from the analysis of a specific manuscript artifact upon which the Tristan and Perrault sections are largely based. This study of the century often classified for its unity might, at first glance, appear surprisingly eclectic and disparate. Nonetheless, upon further inspection the mosaic is intended to reveal an overall picture.

Despite the variety of approaches, authors studied and texts chosen, certain key concepts repeatedly surface. Firstly, in the case of all four authors, we have mentioned or analysed works of a directly emblematic nature, and not just Perrault's *Discours sur l'art des devises* or the Tristan poems of the SMAdd.392 manuscript. Descartes refers on at least two occasions to his own "devise," Tristan composed prefatory poems for emblem books, La Fontaine's "Le Renard et l'ecureuil" plays upon Fouquet's squirrel device and Perrault's *Courses de testes et de bagues* reproduces the devices of the ceremony's participants, to cite but a few examples. If such works have largely remained unknown to the modern reader, it is not necessarily due to their poor quality, but rather as a reflection of modern values and choices. Nonetheless it is important to note that we can expect to find directly emblematic writings within the *œuvre* of any major seventeenth-century French author.

Perhaps more importantly, analysis of works that at first sight may not appear 'emblematic' has revealed a system of constructs that is not always second nature to the modern reader. Be it the example of Tristan's poetry and Van Veen's emblems or the manipulation of devices that now form part of the *Recueil Conrart*, we have found that the sense of a text in a given circumstance is not necessarily that of the author's intention (even were we truly to know what this was), but rather such meaning is dependent upon the context of its use and the reader's interaction with that context. Like the emblem itself, the meaning of our authors' text comes from the bringing together of disparate elements such as historical context, printed, manuscript and plastic sources, known literary topoi and subtle deviations from predetermined expectations.

Yet within this complex system of bringing together of often far different elements, there is a recurring catalyst, that of the global image. Such images vary in both tone and theme, be they the ivy motif or the boat and its helmsman, the putti constructing the château de Berny, the stag with its beautiful antlers or the *Grotte de Thétis*, the fastidious M. l'Abbé or Cendrillon's ball in the royal castle. Nonetheless if we were to provide a common strand, the emblematic element that we have found reappearing most often in the way in which the literature of the Grand Siècle functions, it would be the creation of the static global image that interacts with other, often narrative, elements of the text thereby rendering the invisible see-able and memorable, "Invisibilium per visibilia contemplatio."

Why this should be so is a matter for conjecture. A glance at any bibliographic survey of emblem books will confirm that the mid to late seventeenth century represented the height of the *aetas emblematica*, a period that saw the defining and, to a certain extent, standardising of the emblem book before its decline in the eighteenth

Conclusions: Further Possibilities

century. One can only guess that the hybrid form came as a result of hybrid technology, the invention and refinement of printing which revolutionised the dissemination of the written word. Yet the oral and visual cultures of the previous age (e.g. the stained-glass windows of the cathedrals) were still part of the collective psyche. Putting the two elements together created a culture for which the amalgam of text and image was second nature.

Although our own culture is undoubtedly rooted in text-based forms (e.g. the novels of the nineteenth century), technology is again changing the way we read and view the world around us. The invention of cinema and television, as well as further refinements in the art of printing, have accustomed us to a new visual culture, although the current success of hybrid forms such as advertising panels, *bandes dessinées* and the internet would again suggest the written word is far from forgotten. Perhaps an understanding of emblematics within seventeenth-century literature is most valuable as a potential key to our new Emblematic Age.

Notes

[1] Albrecht Schöne's *Emblematik und Drama im Zeitalter des Barock* (Munich: Beck, 1964) discusses the subject of emblems as related to German Baroque drama.
[2] (Paris: Pierre Le Petit, 1671).
[3] (Paris: Elie Josset).
[4] "The 'Récit de Théramène'," chapter 3 (pages 87-134) of *Linguistics and Literary History: Essays in Stylistics* (Princeton: Princeton UP, 1948).
[5] "'Le Ciel avec horreur voit ce monstre sauvage': Genèse de textes d'images," *PFSCL* 14.26 (1987), 83-102.
[6] The edition followed is that of Jean Salles (Paris: Bordas, 1967).
[7] (Madrid: Por Luis Sanchez). A reprint edited by Carmen Bravo-Villasante (Madrid: Fundación Universitaria Espagñola, 1978) is also available.
[8] The concept of 'memory tags' as explored by David Graham has been discussed in chapter V above.
[9] (Madrid: Por los Herederos de Iuan Iniguez de Lequerica, 1599).
[10] Pages 95-112 in *La Cohérence intérieure: Etudes sur la littérature française du dix-septième siècle présentées en hommage à Judd D. Hubert*, eds. Jacqueline Van Baelen and David Lee Rubin (Paris: Place, 1977). Nelson explores the theme of shadows and light as occurring throughout the works of Racine, but pages 103-06 refer specifically to *Phèdre*.
[11] Although Couton cites the 1700 edition of the *Manière de se bien préparer à la mort*, the work itself actually dates from thirty years earlier.
[12] This work is mentioned briefly in chapter II above. I am grateful to David Graham for reminding me of its direct reference to "peinture parlante."
[13] (Antwerp: Plantin, 1565).
[14] *Romanistisches Jahrbuch* 36 (1985), 104-21.
[15] *Revue de l'Histoire Littéraire de la France* 81.3 (1981), 355-66.
[16] See the introduction to chapter IV above.
[17] (Paris: R. Pepie).
[18] We have followed Abbé Velat and Yvonne Champaillet's edition of Bossuet's *Œuvres* (Paris: Gallimard, 1961).

Appendix A
Tristan L'Hermite:
The GUL SMadd.392 Manuscripts

TRANSCRIBED BY

ALISON ADAMS

    The manuscript texts are transcribed here exactly as they appear in the original, apart from the exclusion of the long 's.' Punctuation is often irregular or lacking, particularly the apostrophe, for instance for the distinction 'quelle'/'qu'elle,' and there are some obvious errors. The position of the poems within the *Amorum emblemata* is indicated according to the facing pages(s) of the printed text. Italics are used for the small number of texts in a hand which, in the editors' view, is unlikely to be that of Tristan L'Hermite. The Rondeaux (facing pages 128, 162 and 226), the poem facing page 5 and the prose passage facing pages 150-51 seem to be in one hand, and the very first poem (following the title page and on the front cover), the fragment facing page 76 and probably the prose passage facing page 2 would appear to come from three further distinct hands, though the prose passage has certain characteristics in common with the hand associated with Tristan. Some poems are signed with a form of the name Tristan, sometimes accompanied by an indication of the poem to which the manuscript text is related. Berni/Berny is the name of the property described in the "Maison d'Astrée." These signatures are reproduced here. It will be noted that sometimes the familiar $ is used for the 's' of Tristan, as well as to separate stanzas and in other normal contexts. A group of $ (often three, with a further single one below) is frequently seen where a signature might be expected, or indeed in association with a signature; this has not been reproduced (facing pages 2, 3, 13, 29, 47, 60, 61, 72, 102, 104-05, 122, 163, 166, 171). These occurrences correspond to texts attributable to Tristan L'Hermite, including the prose passage facing page 2. In four out of five cases, the 'rondeaux' hand is accompanied by a kind of signature. In two places intertwined letters (B/C and C/C) serve as signature and these are indicated in the text below (facing pages 2 and 71).

    Where a printed version of a poem by Tristan L'Hermite has been identified, page numbers are given: JM: *Les Plaintes d'Acante et autres oeuvres*, ed. Jacques Madeleine; PC: *Les Amours et autres poésies choisies*, ed. Pierre Camo; Md'A: "La Maison d'Astrée" in *Les Vers Héroïques*, ed. Catherine M. Grisé, pages 173-87.

Appendix A: Tristan L'Hermite

AFTER TITLE PAGE AND ON COVER

Auec la pointe de ses traits
Amour graua Ces beaux portraits
Et Ces aimables Caracteres.
Car Ces Images, Ces vers
Monstrent touts ses secrets mysteres
Et tous les sentimens divers.

PRELIMINARY PAGES

Il y a des gens bien extravagans, et souvent sous l'auspice d'une fausse devotion. Y-a-til rien de plus absurde que les discurs de ces gens la.

Mon estomac se souleve, et ma bile s'emeut toutes les fois que je pense a une femme, je suis faché, et jay honte de devoir ma naissance a une femme, et je crache quand j'entends parler d'une femme. Kerac, Krac. Kraaaaque.on. hem-hem-hengr.

Il y a des Misantropes si ennemis de la propagation[1] que Dieu a ordonné quils se servent d'alimens pour énerver la chair. Dans le boire et manger ils se servent d'herbes et de remedes pour chasser la force de la nature, en l'affoiblissant, et tuent leur race dans leurs propres entrailles.

Un ouvrier qui travailloit chez les Jesuites, quoiqu'on lui donna a manger et a boire, ne pouvoit neantmoins carresser sa femme, et quand il travailloit chés d'autres gens, Il faisoit tres bien son devoir nocturne, n'eut il beû que de l'eau, ceque voyant sa femme, ne voulut plus qu'il travailla[2] chez les Jesuites.

FACING P. 2 (VNE SEULE)

Si uous pouuiés uous contenter dun captif, ma liberté seroit déia entre uos mains; mais uous estes trop belle pour n'assubiettir qu'un ami et trop sensible pour n'estre touchée que dun amour; pardonnés moy donc, si ie uous dis que ie ne ueux pas donner mon coeur pour la moitie dun, ni mettre tout mon esprit a uous faire des discours de ma passion, lors que uous ny presteres que lune de uos oreilles; que sçay ie si les souspirs que uous ietteres en ma presence ne seront point pour un absent, ou pour un mort peutestre; que ses beaux mots dont uous flatteres mon martire, uous auront déia serui pour en tromper dautres; et que uous ne me ferés point de serment dont uous n'aiés déia esté pariure. Toutesfois ie ueux croire que uous m'aimerés, et qu ie seray de la trouppe de ces bien heureux a qui uous dispenseres uos faueurs, mais en uostre conqueste, ie nauray pas plus de gloire quun simple soldat en la prise s'une uille.

Sign: BC intertwined; C and backwards C intertwined

FACING P. 3 (UNE SEULE)

>   Quelqu'autre d'une humour commune,
>   Cherist tout ce qu'il void de beau,
>   Pour moy ie n'en veux aymer qu'une
>   Et L'adorer jusqu'au tombeau.
>   *
>   L'Eau qui se separe en sa source
>   Par deuers lits se conduisant;
>   Ne fait pas une longue cource,
>   Et se perd en se diuisant.
>   *
>   Ainsy la flame separée,
>   N'est jamais de longue durée;
>   Nous en voyons bien tost le bout:
>   Et pour dire ce qu'il m'en semble;
>   Aymer en diuers lieux ensemble,
>   C'est presque n'aymer rien[3] du tout.

Sign: Tris*

FACING P. 5 (DEUX COEURS S'VNISSENT)

>   *Sur des fleurs, et dessoubz des chesnes*
>   *Eudoxe escouta mon amour,*
>   *Et Je causay si bien, qu'auant la fin du Jour,*
>   *Elle eust aultant que moy de chaisnes.*
>   *Amour Industriux, pour nostre bien commun,*
>   *De deux coeurs nen fit q'un.*

Sign: go

FACING P. 13 (TOUT COMMUN)

>   Deux coeurs s'aymans parfaitement
>   Goustent ensemble toutes choses:
>   Ils partagent egalement
>   Et les Espines & les roses.

Appendix A: Tristan L'Hermite

Tousjours une mesme chaleur
Rend leur avanture commune:
Receuant des trais du malheur,
Ou des faueurs de la Fortune.

Quoy que puisse faire l'Enuie
Leurs iours n'ont rien qu'un pareil[4] sort
Car viuans d'une mesme vie
Ils meurent d'une mesme mort.

Sign: Trist.

FACING P. 29 (C'EST TROP TARD)

De mesme que le Cerf, blessé mortellement,
Apres le coup, receu fuit inutilement;
Et treuue le trespas plustost que le Dictame.
Ainsy, quand d'un regard on a senti l'effort;
On a beau s'esloigner des beaux yeux de sa Dame,
On emporte par tout sa blessure & sa mort.

FACING P. 33 (AMOUR SOURCE DE VERTU)

Sonnet

Celuy dont la vertu merita tant de Festes
Par des exploits si beaux & si Laborieux
Qui fit mourir Anthée & fut victorieux
Du Geant a trois corps & de L'Hydre aux sept teste

Celuy de qui le bras a fait tant de conquestes
Et mis tant de Lauriers sur son front glorieux
Qui purgea l'uniuers de Monstres furieux
De Tirans inhumains & de cruelles Bestes

Celuy qui surmonta tant d'obstacles offers
Qui suporta le Ciel & forcea les Enfers
Tirant cerbere au iour en despit de sa rage

Lors qu'a ce point dhonneur il estoit paruenu
Et que tous les mortels admiroient son courage
Se laissa surmonter par un Enfant tout nu.

FACING P. 47 (PLUSTOST MONSTRER QUE DIRE)

Sonnet

Il n'est point de douleur egale a mon martire
Un Objet tout diuin me force a l'adorer
Et le voulant seruir ie voy que ie desire
Des honneurs qu'un mortel ne doibt pas esperer

Qu'est ce qu'en mon tourment ie puis deliberer
Lors que traitant mon ame auec un mesme Empire
L'Amour & le respect ne peuuent endurer
Que ie cele mon mal, ny que ie l'ose dire

Dans les extresmitez de cette passion
Dont l'ardeur est egale a ma discretion
Apren moy ma raison quel conseil il faut suiure

Sans espoir de secours ie brusle nuit & iour
Et desirant mourir je suis contraint de viure
De crainte que ma mort parle de mon amour.
         (JM109, PC 21)

FACING P. 60 (AMOUR AUEUGLE)

Sonnet

O trop aueugle erreur! ô tourment indicible!
Je voy bien que Philis ayme un autre Berger,
Et son Engagement ne me peut desgager;
On me blesse dans l'ame Et j'y suis insensible.

J'adore une Beauté qui d'un desdain visible
En receuant mes voeux se plaist de m'affliger:
Et lors que mon Esprit la deuroit negliger,
Je fais pour la seruir tout ce qui mest possible.

Mon Coeur est tout remply de mescontentement,
Je ne puis endurer ce mauuais traitement,
Et ne scaurois sortir de ce cruel seruage:

Je suis honteux de voir comment ie me soumets,
Mais je croy que le bien d'estre amoureux & sage
Est un don que les Dieux n'acorderent iamais.

Appendix A: Tristan L'Hermite

FACING P. 61 (AMOUR AVEUGLE)

Sonnet

Philis vous avéz tort de rompre ainsy ma cheine;
Elle auoit trop d'apas pour ne durer qu'un iour;
Je scay que ie n'ay point merité vostre amour,
Mais ie n'ay point aussy merité vostre hayne.

Celuy que vous ayméz, vous tient dans une gesne
Qui vange asséz mon coeur d'un si perfide tour:
Il vous donne des loix & ie vous fis la Cour,
Vous estes son Esclaue & vous estiéz ma Reyne.

Quelque charme secret vous trouble la raison;
Vostre Ame, par l'effet dun magique poison
Est pour moy si superbe & pour luy si craintiue:

Si cette aueugle erreur ne vous donnoit la loy,
En reuenant a vous, ô belle fugitive,
Il vous seroit aysé de reuenir a moy.

FACING P. 68 (DONT LE COEUR EST PLEIN, LA BOUCHE PARLE)

Sonnet

Toy qui de mon erreur es l'aueugle complice
Amour dont la douceur n'est qu'une trahison
Puisque la violence a si peu de raison
Je veux dire tout haut qu'elle est ton injustice

Tu me fais adorer une belle prison
A fin de me gesner d'un éternel suplice
Et me faire aualer d'un si cruel poison
Que pour m'en deliurer je cherche un precipice

Celle dont les apas ont causé ma langueur
Traite mes passions auec tant de rigueur
Qu'elle m'outrage mesme alors quelle me flate.

Et tout ce qui l'oblige a tant de cruautéz
C'est que mes sentimens pour aymer cette jngrate
Mesprisent aujourdhuy les plus rares beautéz.

(JM104, PC14)

Facing p. 71 (Loyal & secret)

Leale & secreto

Beauté la plus angelique
Qu'une Ame puisse adorer,
Vostre deuise me pique
Et m'oblige a soupirer.
O dieux! ie suis bien fidelle!
Je meurs pour une Cruelle
Et nul ne scait ma langueur.
De la Fidelité mesme,
Vostre deuise & mon coeur,
Pourroient bien faire un Emblesme.

Sign: Tristan   B/C intertwined; less decorative than facing p. 2

Facing p. 72 (Le ioug pour la franchise)

Sonnet

Vous que l'ambition dispose a des effors
Que n'oseroit tanter un courage vulguere,
Et qui vous conduiriéz iusqu'au sejour des mortz
Afin d'y rencontrer dequoy vous satisfaire.

Vouléz vous butiner de plus riches tresors
Que n'en ont tous les lieux que le soleil esclaire;
Sans courir l'Ocean, ny rauager ses bords,
Venéz voir ma Maitresse & taschéz de luy plaire.

Vous pourriéz asseruir[5] s'il plaisoit au Destin
Les climatz[6] du couchant, les terres du matin,
Et l'jsle dont la Rose est la Reyne de l'onde:

Vous pourriéz conquerir l'Estat des fleurs de lys,
Vous pourriéz imposer des loix a tout le monde,
Mais tout cela vaut moins qu'un baiser de Philis.

(JM62, PC7)

Facing p. 73 (Le ioug pour la franchise)

Amour scait fort bien reprimer
Tous les courages les plus braues

Appendix A: Tristan L'Hermite

Si tout le monde veut aymer
On ne verra que des Esclaues
Hier Maistre & ma liberté
Je viuois a ma volonté
Exempt de peine & de tristesse
Aujourdhuy forcé d'endurer
Les cruautez d'une Maitresse
Je n'ose mesme soupirer.

Sign: Trist.

FACING P. 76 (NY ÇA, NY LÀ)

Sonnet

quuu....
qu'un amant est heureux
quand de l'objet qu'il aime
les desirs sont conforme aux siens.

FACING P. 79 (ARROUSÉ l'AUGMENTE)

    Et la bas arosant des fleurs
    Afin que leurs viues couleurs
    S'augmentent par ce bon office;
Il jnstruit mon Olinde auec cette action
    A me traiter sans artifice
Montrant que la faueur acroist la passion.

Sign: de Berny / Par Trist.

(Md'A180)

FACING P. 86 (EN IOUANT)

Stances

Puisqu'Amour en ses yeux ne se peut euiter
    Je ne scaurois plus resister
Car ie ne treuue pas de gloire a me deffendre
    Ny de honte a me rendre
  *   *   *
Qu'elle ait de la pitié, qu'elle ait de la rigueur
    Philis est Reyne de mon coeur
C'est inutilement que ma raison s'opose

>   Aux Loix qu'elle m'impose
> *   *   *
> Vouloir veincre l'ardeur qu'elle scait allumer
>   Et se diuertir de l'aymer
> Seroit vouloir en vain d'une erreur obstinée
>   Veincre sa Destinée
> *   *   *
> Seruons la donc mon ame & sans plus differer
>   Faisons nous autant admirer
> Par la fidelité de nostre obeissance
>   Qu'elle par sa puissance.

(JM69, PC37)

FACING P. 93 (AMOUR TROUUE MOYEN)

>   En ce lieu voguant sans vaisseau
> D'un bandeau sur sa trousse il a formé des voiles;
> Pour auirons de ses trais il fend l'eau
> Et tire a deux beaux yeux dont il fait ses Estoiles.
>   Ainsy, malgré les soins jalous,
>   Et tout le celeste courous
>   Qui peut s'oposer a leurs joyës;
> Auecque les clartéz qu'ils ont dedans le sein
>   Les Amans treuuent mille voyes
> Pour faire succeder un amoureux dessein.

Sign: Trist $ / En Berni

(Md'A179)

FACING P. 102 (POUR UN PLAISIR MILLE DOULEURS)

> $ Vous seriez bien marrie de respondre mieux a mes lettres qu'a ma passion, de sorte que ie puis bien dire que Je ne sers pas seulement une jnsensible, mais encore une sourde & une paralitique.[7] pleust a dieu ne vous auoir jamais veüe, ou vous auoir moins consideree! Mais quoy$ puisque cest mon destin que ma prudence ne peut euiter, qu'il faut que ie voue toute ma vie a l'jngratitude & que ie ne recoiue jamais de mes soins & de mes deuoirs, que de l'indiference, ou du mespris, il faut que ie cherche dans mes Larmes la consolation de ma douleur Et que ie me pleigne autant du malheur d'auoir esté blessé de vos veux, que si i'auois esté frapé du Tonnerre.

Appendix A: Tristan L'Hermite

FACING P. 103 (POUR UN PLAISIR MILLE DOULEURS)

Que la grace d'Olinde a de trais rauissans!
Malgré cette froideur dont mon Esprit se vante
Amour a sa faueur s'est fait Roy de mes sens,
Et la Raison chez moy n'est plus qu'une Seruante.

Cependant je me perds en ces voeux inocens
Qui ne font qu'irriter son humeur insolente
Et m'apercoy bien tard que joffre de l'encens
A qui veut tousjours voir sa victime sanglante.

O Dieux! ma passion ne se peut destourner,
Malgré mon jugement ie me laisse mener
Dans ce nouveau Dedale ou mon ame s'engage.

Et vers le precipice ou ie vais me jeter,
Je suis comme un Vaisseau que les ventz & l'orage
Poussent contre des Bancs qu'il ne peut euiter.

FACING PP. 104-05 (RESISTER À L'ABORDER)

D'où uient qu'un penser indiscret
M'entretient tousjours en secret
D'un Objet qui m'est si contraire;
Et conueincu de trahison,
Ne scauroit jamais se distraire
De me presenter du poison?
* * *
Quel doux & cruel mouuement
Veut rendre ainsy de mon tourment
Mes volontez mesmes complices
Et flatant de nouueaux desirs
Sous l'aparance des delices
Me desguise les desplaisirs
* * *
Apres tant de regretz conceus
Et tant d'ayguillons aperceus
Sous le trompeur éclat des roses:
Suis ie bien assez malheureux
Pour permettre aux plus belles choses
De me rendre encore amoureux.

Apres tant de viues douleurs
Apres tant de sang & de pleurs

Que i'ay verséz dessus ma flame
Auroy ie l'jndiscretion
De liurer encore mon ame
Au pouuoir de ma passion?
*   *   *
O prudente & forte raison
Qui m'as tiré d'une prison
Ou ie respendois tant de larmes
Subtile & secrette clarté
Veille encore prendre les armes
Pour Deffendre ma Liberte
*   *   *
J'apercoy desja mon trespas
Couuert des inocens apas
Qu'Olinde scait mettre en usage
Ce diuin Miracle des Cieux
Qui n'a de douceur qu'au visage
Ny d'amour que dans ses beaux yeux.

O Raison, celeste flambeau,
Acheue un ouurage si beau
Mes ardeurs sont tantost passees
Et desja les sages propos
Dissipent toutes ces pensées
Qui s'oposoient a mon repos.

Sign: Tristan

(JM67, PC 36)

FACING PP. 112-13 (AMOUR AIME LA NUIT)

Amours de Canante

Stances

Canante que'lle merueille
Adoucist enfin mon sort?
Au temps que le soleil dort
J'en treuue un autre qui veille.
*
Comment estes vous sortie
Sans qu'on s'en soit auisé?
Amour a fauorisé
Nostre secrette partie.

*

S'il ne vous auoit conduite
Les chiens auroient aboyé
Et vostre ... effroyé
Auroit apris vostre fuite.

Nayant point[8] de deffiance
Que vostre Esprit fust trompeur
Je mourois icy de peur
D'Amour & d'impatiance
*
Il faut que dans ce lieu sombre
Qui recelle[9] nos langueurs
Je punisse vos rigueurs
Auec des baisers sans nombre
*
Mes delices, ie me pasme
Dans ce doux consentement
Vos leures adroitement
Vienent d'enleuer mon Ame.
*
Rendez la moy ie vous prie
Mettre un[10] sujet amoureux
En un point si dangereux
N'est point une raillerie

Dieux! que vous estes timide
Vous me sentéz bien mourir
Et n'oséz me secourir
D'un baiser qui soit humide.

Sign. Tristan

FACING P. 121 (LE MAL D'AMOUR INCURABLE)

Pour moy ie tiens a perfidie
Tous les conseils de ma raison
Tant jabhorre la guerison
D'une si chere maladie.

Deus Deus meus, da mihi donum Continentiae sed non tam cito. S. Aug.[11]

FACING P. 122 (L'ABSENCE TUE)

    Quelle cruelle Destinée!
    Celle pour qui ie meurs d'amour,
    S'apreste a partir dans un iour
    Pour ne reuenir d'une année.
    O Dieux! j'ay beau me tourmenter
    Je ne la scaurois arester
    N'y treuuer moyen de la suiure.
    De sorte qu'a bien discourir,
    Je n'ay plus qu'un moment a uiure;
    Et plus de mille ans a mourir.

                                                 (JM75, PC99)

FACING P. 123 (L'ABSENCE TUE)

        Dans ces aymables promenoirs
  Qu'il imprime a regret de sa diuine piste;
  Loin d'un bel oeil, les lys luy semblent noirs,
  Le jour luy paroist sombre & la verdure triste.
            Aussy lors que ie suis priué
            De Celle qui m'a captiué
            Je ne treuue que des suplices:
  Tous les Objets de joÿe irritent mon tourment,
            Et pour moy toutes les delices
  Ne sont que des sujets de mescontentement.

Sign: Tris. en Bern.

                                                   (Md'A180)

FACING P. 125 (TOUS AMANS MISERABLES)

  Je soufre tant de maux que ma belle Inhumaine
  Ne peut s'imaginer La moitié de ma peine
  Elle reste jncredule & moy ie meurs martir.
  Amour, puisqu'il est vray que ie sers a ta gloire
  Fay luy croire le mal que tu me fay sentir
  Ou ne m'en fay sentir qu'autant qu'elle en peut croire.

                                               (JM80, PC100)

Appendix A: Tristan L'Hermite

FACING P. 128 (AMOUR FAIT MOUT, ARGENT FAIT TOUT)

Rondeau

Vous l'entendéz mieux que Je ne pensois,
Si quelque amant bien disant et mutois
Vous croit payer en vous nommant son ame,
cest du latin qui passe vostre game
Vous m'entendèz des termes si courtois
   Mais s'Il en vient qui dise a haulte voix
Qu'il veult prouuer, fut Il turc ou anglois
Par beaux effectz la grandeur de sa flame
   Vous l'entendéz.

Je donneray telle somme par mois
Oultre cela pierreries de choix
Satin, velour, a souhait a Madame,
Cet entretien vous charme et vous enflame
C'est Dire d'or, et parler bon françois.
Vous Lentendéz

Sign: go

FACING P. 129 (AMOUR FAIT MOUT, ARGENT FAIT TOUT)

Olimpe auecque ce poulet
Puisque vostre Esprit est auare
Je vous enuoye un bracelet
D'une Girassole asséz rare.
Je jure qu selon mon bien
Je ne vous refuseray rien
De ce que vous pourréz pretendre.
Dites ce que vous demandéz,
Mais ne me faite plus attendre
Les choses que vous me vandéz.

FACING P. 131 (CHASSER AUANT LA PRINSE)

Chassant un Cerf de ce costé
Qu'a force de courir il a mis hors d'haleine
Il nous fait voir comment une Beauté
Ne se peut aquerir sans deuor & sans peine.

           (Md'A180)

FACING P. 145 (L'AMOUR PAROIST)

Sonnet

Philis pardonnéz moy si ie ne puis celer
L'ardeur dont vos regars ont embrasé mon Ame
C'est en vain que j'essaye a la dissimuler
Des que i'ouure la bouche il en sort de la flame.

FACING P. 149 (NUIT, & JOUR)

Sonnet

Cette nuit en dormant d'un somme inquieté
Il m'est tousjours venu de tristes resueries
La clarté d'un tison dans une obscurité
M'a fait a l'impourueu parestre des Furies

Pres de moy la Discorde & l'infidelité
Montroient leur violence en mille barbaries
Et de sang espandu par tout la Cruauté
Souilloit l'argent de londe & l'esmail des prairies

Troublé de ces horreurs ie ne scay que penser
Si ce n'est que le Ciel me veuille menacer
De quelque changement en l'ame de Siluye

Songe Fantosme affreux, noir ennemy du iour
Anonce moy plustost la perte[12] de ma vie
Que de me presager[13] celle de son amour

(JM117, PC28)

FACING P. 150-51 (LES REGARDS DARDS)

J'aduoue que cest une gloire digne de vous, de donner des loix a celuy duquel toutte la terre en reçoit, et de fouler aux piedz L'orgueil d'un tyran qui faict lictiere de l'or et de la pourpre, mais J'ose vous dire que vous travailléz trop a la grandeur de cet ennemy, et qu'en luy gaignant tous les Jours mille batailles, et portant son pouuoir par tout ou vous aléz, vous vous rendéz vous mesme L'Jnstrument de sa gloire; n'esce pas par vos beautéz qu'il rend son regne universel? vos yeux ne luy fournissent Jls pas les feux dont Il embraze les plus froides ames, et n'esce pas de vos attraits quil faict ses plus dangereux traicts! ce temeraire qui n'usoit que de surprises, et qui n'auoit acquis le renom de puissant que par la

Appendix A: Tristan L'Hermite

foiblesse de ceux qu'il attaquoit, deuenu fort par vostre assistance, va maintenant adescouuert, et en se Jouant Jl sacquiert aultant desclaues que vous voyéz de personnes. en fin pour estre tout absolu Jl ne luy reste qu'a vous vaincre, prenéz garde qu'il ne se mescognoisse, et qu'apres auoir par vostre moyen triumphé de touttes les libertéz, Jl ne veuille faire de la vostre, comme de la plus Jllustre, le couronnement de ses trophées, le galand n'a pas espargné sa propre mere J'espere qu'il ne vous traictera pas plus fauorablement.

Sign: go

FACING P. 162 (AMOUR SANS PITIÉ)

Rondeau

Pleurer et gesmir aysement
est un Infaillible argument
du tourment qu'Amour nous enuoye
Et qui de luy deuient la proye
verse des pleurs Incessamment,
     S'Jl perd ce qui le va charmant
Son regret est si vehement
Qu'il n'est moment qu'on ne le voye
     Pleurer.
Mais si durant l'esloignement
Il pleure de ressentiment
au retour Il pleure de Joye.
Et partant Il fault que l'on croie
Qu'en tout temps on void un amant
     Pleurer.

FACING P. 163 (AMOUR SANS PITIÉ)

Les Perles ayment cherement
l'Humour dont le Ciel les arose,
Les Serpens ont pour aliment
La fraischeur dans la terre enclose.
L'air est aymé par les Oyseaux,
Les poissons cherissent les Eaux
Et la Salamandre les flames;
Les abeilles ayment les fleurs,
Mais l'Amour, ce Tiran des Ames,
Le cruel n'ayme que les pleurs.

(JM174, PC92)

FACING P. 166 (SONGER ESIOUIT)

Sonnet

Je suis prest a partir voicy mon dernier iour
Je ne voy plus Philis & le Ciel que i'jmplore
Pour comble de malheurs veut ajouter encore
La chaleur & la fieure a celle de l'Amour

Alors que le soleil prepare son retour
Et que les préz sont plains des larmes de l'Aurore
Quelque fois en dormant ie me treuue au sejour
Ou vient de s'en aler la Beauté que i'adore

Surpris d'estonnement par cette vaine horreur[14]
Moy qui n'apercoy rien que des objets d'horreur
Et dont les tristes yeux ne s'ouurent plus qu'aux larmes

Je croy que du trespas j'ay ressenti l'effort
Et que tant de beautéz, de graces & de charmes
Sont les felicitéz qu'on treuue apres la mort.
                                        (JM116, PC28)

FACING P. 167 (SONGER ESIOUIT)

Je nay plus de relasche au soucy qui me ronge
Depuis que ma Philis s'esloigne de ces lieux
Si ce n'est que la nuit il m'arriue qu'en songe
Ce bel Astre D'Amour se presente a mes yeux

Alors dans dans la douceur ou cette erreur me plonge
Je croy que des Enfers ie monte dans les Cieux
Et ie renoncerois a la gloire des Dieux
Si ma felicité n'estoit point un mensonge

Madame en un moment par un charme si dous
Se vient rendre en mes bras malgré tant de jalous
Et tant d'empeschemens qui sont si dificiles

Sommeil dont la bonté merite des Autels
Si les biens que tu fais n'estoient point si fragiles
Tu serois le plus grand de tous les Inmortels.

Sign: ?de Tristan, but largely illegible on account of severe cropping.
                                        (JM114, PC26)

Appendix A: Tristan L'Hermite

FACING P. 169 (L'Vn Amour guerist l'autre)

>Chef doeuure sans Exemple ou l'Art & la Nature
>Ont employé leur soin si liberalement,
>Toy qui par tes secrets, peux si facilement
>Conduire tes Amys loin de la sepulture.
>
>De Lorme, ie t'implore en ma triste auanture,
>Je suis dedans le sein blessé cruellement;
>Et tout ce que i'ay fait pour mon soulagement,
>N'a rien fait jusqu'icy qu'irriter ma blessure.
>
>Je sens dans mes humeurs un grand feu s'embraser,
>Trauaillé de douleurs ie ne puis reposer,
>Et n'espere plus rien qu'en ton scauoir extresme:
>
>Mais que peux tu fournir qui serue a m'a langueur?
>Las! iay le coeur attaint & tu m'as dit toy mesme
>Qu'il nest point de remede aux blessures du coeur.
>
>(JM105, PC17)

FACING P. 171 (Secours me nuit)

>Sonnet
>
>Je surpris l'autre iour La Nimphe que i'adore
>Ayant sur une jupe vn peignoir seulement
>Et la voyant ainsy L'on eust dit proprement
>Qu'il sortoit de son lit une nouuelle Aurore
>
>Ses yeux que le sommeil abandonnoit encore
>Ses cheuueux autour d'elle errans confusement
>Ne Liérent mon coeur que plus estroitement
>Ne firent qu'augmanter le feu qui me deuore
>
>Amour si mon Soleil brusle dés le matin
>Je ne puis esperer en mon crüel destin
>De voir diminuer l'ardeur qui me tourmente
>
>Dieux! qu'elle est la beauté qui cause ma langueur!
>Plus elle est negligée & plus elle est charmante,
>Plus son poil est espars, plus il presse mon coeur.
>
>(JM63, PC10)

FACING P. 173 (POUR DURER LA BRUNETTE)

Epigrame

Deux Merueilles de l'uniuers
Tienent en leurs mains ma fortune
Et leurs apas sont bien diuers
Car l'une est blanche & l'autre brune
Mais elles ont tant de beautéz
Qu'elles gagnent mes voluntéz
Auec une egale puissance
Et dans leur glorieux destin
Je ne voy que la difference
D'un beau soir & d'un beau matin.

(JM180, PC99)

FACING P. 178 (TEL REFUSE, QUI APRES MUSE)

Stances

Philis vous auéz eu tort
D'auoir rebuté si fort
Mes soins & mes sacrifices
Vous auréz des entretiens
Et receurez des seruices
Qui ne vaudront pas les miens.

(JM189, PC123)

FACING P. 188 (MES PLEURS TESMOIGNENT)

Sonnet

O cruauté barbare, ô rigueur sans seconde!
A quel malheur o Dieux, m'auéz vous destiné?
Et quel crime ay ie fait pour me voir condemné
A prier nuit & jour sans que l'on me responde?

Aux peines que ie prens ie seme dessus l'onde;
Et flatant les beaux yeux qui m'ont empoisonné,
Je ne puis esmouuoir un courage obstiné
D'une amour qui pourroit esbranler tout un monde.

Pleuray ie incessament,[15] on se rit de mes pleurs,
Montray ie mes soucys, on les prend pour des fleurs,

Appendix A: Tristan L'Hermite

Contay ie mon ardeur, on ne croit pas ma flame:

Et lors que j'ay la terre & les Cieux pour tesmoins
Qu'auec le plus d'exces on outrage mon ame,
C'est lors qu'on fait semblant qu'on y pense le moins.

(JM88, PC16)

FACING P. 182 = 192 (PENSER CONTENTE)

Sonnet

Que l'objet est diuin qui s'est fait mon veinqueur
Qu'il a de jugement qu'il a de cognoissance
Amour a tous momens ie benis ta puissance
D'auoir si bien graué son jmage en mon coeur

Bien qu'elle ait ordonné que ie meure en langueur
Auec tant de contrainte & si peu de licence
J'ose mesme auoüer que i'ayme sa rigueur
Puisque sa cruauté maintient son inocence

Madame est sans exemple & qui scait les clartéz
Dont ses rares vertus releuent ses beautéz
Ne scait comment borner lhonneur qu'on luy doit rendre

Si ie l'adore aussy pardonnéz moy grans Dieux;
En un pareil[16] sujet on se peut bien mesprendre
Il n'est rien icy bas qui vous ressemble mieux.

(JM63, PC8)

FACING P. 193 (PENSER CONTENTE)

Mon fidelle Conseil & mon doux entretien
Pensers chers confidens d'une amour si fidelle
Tenéz moy compagnie & me parléz de celle
Dont aujourdhuy la veüe est mon souuerain bien

Despeignéz moy Philis dites moy sil est rien
De rare de parfait & daymable comme elle
Et s'il peut iamais naistre une femme assez belle
Pour auoir un Empire aussy grand que le sien

Vn coeur se peut il rendre a de plus belles choses
Ses yeux sont de saphirs & sa bouche de roses
Dequi le vif esclat du're en toute saison?

Dieux! que ce resconfort flate mes resueries
De Voir comme les Cieux pour faire ma prison
Mirent les fleurs en oeuure auec les pierreries!

(JM123, PC34)

FACING P. 206 (NULLES LAIDES AMOURS)

Sonnet

FACING P. 211 (PATIENCE VAINCQT TOUT)

Icy chamaillant sans cesser
Ce chesne qu'il veut renverser
Auec de si petites armes;
Par sa perseuerance il enseigne a l'Amant
Qu'un flus continuel de larmes
Pourroit enfin cauer un coeur de Diamant.

Sign: De Bern. p. Tris.

(Md'A180)

FACING P. 226 (IAMAIS REPOS)

Rondeau

Tel q'un rocher dans lhumide element
est de cent flotz battu diuersement
Durant les ventz la tempeste et l'orage.
Tel est mon coeur dedans vostre seruage
De cent pensers assailly vainement
Mais quelque mal que Je souffre en aymant
Dans la rigueur de vostre traittement
Je me resous, et fais voir un courage
Tel q'un rocher.

Rien ne scauroit m'esbranler seulement.
Et d'un amour si fort et vehement
Je deburois bien tirer quelque aduantage,
Mais vous auéz la rigueur en partage

Appendix A: Tristan L'Hermite

Et vostre coeur est veritablement
Tel q'un Rocher.

Sign: go

FACING P. 231 (TOUSIOURS DE MESME)

Icy faisant voir par pitié
Le peu durable estat des oeilletz & des roses
Il monstre aux coeurs qui sont sans amitié
Que le temps fait ainsy passer les belles choses.

Sign: Trist. en Berni

(Md'A180)

FACING PP. 232-33 (IUSQUES À LA FIN)

Cloris, il est certain luy dis ie en soupirant
Que cette passion m'a rendu miserable
Ma peine auec le temps va tousiours enpirant
   Et Siluye est inexorable
Mais quoy? ton apareil treuue un mal incurable
   Je n'en scaurois iamais guerir
Et quand ie le pourrois, i'aymerois mieux mourir
     *
Mon ame est si portée a cherir sa prison
Qu'elle pense tousiours a la rendre plus forte
Et ne scauroit soufrir que jamais la Raison
   Luy parle d'en ouurir la porte
O prodige nouueau que i'ayme de la sorte
   Et que ce coeur de Diamant
N'ait point osté la force a des liens d'Aymant[17]

Jusqu'au dernier soupir ie veux continüer
De suporter les fers de son cruel empire
Desormais mon amour ne peut diminüer
   Pour voir augmenter mon martire
Car l'ombre seulement du bonheur ou j'aspire
   Me promet des Contentemens
Q'on ne peut obtenir auec trop de tourmens.

Sign: Tristan dans les plaintes d'Acante

(JM28, PC114)

Notes

[1] propation > propagation.
[2] deletion before travailla.
[3] point > rien.
[4] mesme > pareil.
[5] conquerir > asseruir.
[6] ?terres beneath Climatz.
[7] Paralitique in left margin, probably replaced because of severe cropping which affects the legibility of this page.
[8] quelque > point.
[9] ces lieux sombres / Qui recellent > singular.
[10] un inserted.
[11] The French and Latin texts on this page do not appear to have been written at the same point.
[12] De grace auertis moy ??? ???fin > Anonce... perte.
[13] ?Mais ne m'annonce point.
[14] ?erreur > horreur.
[15] nuit & iour > incessament.
[16] si beau > pareil.
[17] aymant > Aymant.

Appendix B
Charles Perrault's
Discours Sur l'Art des Devises

[fol. 1] Discours

sur l'Art des Devises

§

Lorsque le Roi eut donné la Charge d'Admiral à Monsieur le Comte de Vermandois,[1] je fis pour ce jeune Prince une devise, dont le corps étoit un Alcion naissant, voguant dans son nid sur la mer, avec ce mot, <u>Et nascens temperat æquor.</u> Cette devise fut gravée sur les jetons qui se firent pour lui, au commencement de l'année 166 . et fut trouvée ne convenir pas mal à un Admiral fils du Roi, {et} n'ayant que cinq ans. Cependant un des plus sçavans hommes du siècle,[2] qui avoit fait une étude particulière de l'Art des devises, et qui se vantoit d'avoir [1v] lû tous les livres qui en ont traité, y trouva fort à redire, et fit une longue dissertation pour prouver qu'elle péchoit contre les règles principales de ce bel Art. Il lut la dissertation à l'Academie Françoise à la réception d'un Académicien, où il se trouva un grand nombre de sçavans hommes, outre ceux qui la composent. La dissertation, quoique bien écrite, et pleine d'un nombre infini d'eruditions très-curieuses, ne persuada personne, et la devise fut appouvée [sic] de toute la Compagnie. La première fois que je me rencontrai avec ce sçavant homme que j'honorois extrémément, je ne pus m'empêcher de lui dire avec la liberté académique dont nous usons {usions} ensemble: M^r. l'Abbé, la lettre tuë, et l'esprit vivifie. Il entendit ce que je voulois [2] lui dire; et il me repondit, Cela est vrai; mais vous avez péché, et contre la lettre, et contre l'esprit de la devise. Si vous voulez bien m'écouter, repris-je, je me justifierai aisément de cette accusation. Deux {*, *margin note* *M. Chapelain[3] et M. Charpentier[4]} de nos amis communs qui étoient présens, l'un et l'autre très-habiles en toutes choses, et particulièrement en cette matière, et qui avoient assisté à la lecture de la dissertation, dirent qu'il étoit raisonnable de m'entendre dans ma justification. Et nous étant assis, je parlai de la sorte: M^r l'Abbé me reproche d'avoir mis le mot <u>æquor</u> dans la légende de ma devise, et prétend que j'ai eû tort; parce qu'une des principales régles, et même la plus essentielle de toutes, est de ne point nommer le corps de la devise; ajoûtant, que pour rendre la mienne régulière [2v] il falloit mettre seulement, <u>Et nascens temperat;</u> ou bien, <u>Temperat</u>

et nascens; ce qui auroit fait deux bons effets; l'un, d'éviter la plus lourde faute qu'on puisse commettre en cette matiere, qui est de nommer la chose représentée; et l'autre, de rendre la légende plus courte, et par conséquent plus vive et plus élégante, à tout cela, continuai-je en riant, je ne vous dirai autre chose pour réponse, que les paroles de mon texte; <u>La lettre tuë, et l'esprit vivifie</u>. Et pour m'expliquer, je dis qu'il est vrai qu'une des règles les plus essentielles, est de ne point nommer le corps de la devise; mais que cela se doit entendre seulement du corps principal, et nullement des corps accessoires, qu'il est autant bon de nommer, qu'il est mauvais de nommer le corps principal. [3] Pour bien connoître si ce que je dis est vrai, il faut commencer par laisser là toutes les règles, qui d'elles-mêmes sont aussi propres, en quelque art, et en quelque science que ce soit, à induire en erreur, qu'à conduire dans la voie, et {et il faut} pénétrer dans l'esprit, dans l'intention, et dans l'essence de la devise, seul moyen de ne se tromper jamais. Une devise n'est en soi qu'une comparaison de deux choses, dont l'une est représentée, et l'autre sous entenduë; avec un petit discours qui convient également à toutes les deux. Quiconque aura une fois bien compris cette definition, n'a plus que faire des regles, parce qu'elles y sont toutes renfermées, ainsi que j'espère le faire voir. Si le discours de la devise, qu'on appelle légende, et qui en est l'ame, [3v] doit convenir également au signe et à la chose signifiée; c'est-à-dire, à la chose représentée et à la chose sousentenduë, il s'ensuit nécessairement qu'il ne faut point nommer le corps principal de la devise; parce qu'alors cette légende seroit déterminée à ce corps là, et n'iroit plus également, et au signe, et à la chose signifiée. Si dans la devise dont il s'agit, j'avois nommé l'Alcion, et que j'eusse mis; Et nascens Alcion temperat æquor, cette legende seroit déterminée à l'Alcion, et n'iroit plus à M^r. l'Admiral. Si d'un autre côté j'avois nommé le Prince de Vermandois, et que j'eusse mis, Et nascens Princeps temperat æquor, j'aurois également mal fait; parce qu'alors la légende attachée au Prince, n'auroit pû aller [4] ni se joindre à l'Alcion; ce qui pourtant est nécessaire pour l'essence de la devise: Au lieu que n'ayant nommé ni l'un ni l'autre, on void d'un seul coup d'œil la ressemblance réciproque qui se trouve entre cet oiseau admirable, qui dès le moment de sa naissance, est tellement le maître de la mer, qu'elle n'ose se mouvoir, s'il faut ainsi dire, sans sa permission, avec le jeune Prince, qui revêtu de la puissance que le Roi lui communique, a un empire absolu sur la mer, quoiqu'il soit extrémement jeune, et ne fasse encore que de naître. Or les mêmes raisons qui défendent de nommer le corps principal, tant du signe, que de la chose signifiée, obligent à nommer les corps accessoires, quand on le peut; parce que l'énonciation qu'on en fait, [4v] sert à établir et à faire voir davantage la justesse de la comparaison, sans qu'il en résulte l'inconvénient qui se trouve à nommer le corps principal, parce que les corps accessoires ne peuvent se nommer, que lorsqu'ils conviennent également au signe et à la chose signifiée: ce qui fait voir qu'ils ont en cela de la ressemblance. Ainsi, bien loin qu'il faille me reprocher d'avoir mis le mot d'<u>æquor</u> dans ma devise, le soutiens que cette enonciation, quoique d'une chose représentée, la perfectionne, en marquant distinctement, que le pouvoir de l'Alcion et du Prince n'est pas seulement sur des choses qui se ressemblent, mais sur la même chose, qui est la mer: et cette identité de sujet sur lequel ils agissent l'un et l'autre, rend la compa- [5] raison meilleure que ne feroit une simple ressemblance. Si je

Appendix B: Charles Perrault's Discours Sur l'Art des Devises

n'étois persuadé que le raissonnement que je viens de faire est convainquant, je défendrois ma devise par l'exemple d'une infinité d'autres devises très excellentes où les corps accessoires sont nommés dans la légende, et les embellissent au lieu de les gâter. On a fait pour Louis treizième cette devise: Le Soleil en figure humaine parcourant le Zodiaque, où sont représentés les douze signes sous la forme de Taureau, de Sagittaire, de Scorpion &c, avec ces mots, Nec monstra morantur euntem. Suivant la règle mal entenduë, de ne point nommer le corps, le mot de <u>monstra</u> seroit vicieux, Car les monstres sont représentés dans le Zodiaque; cependant il est certain que ce mot éclaircit et embellit [5v] la devise, et que la légende est meilleure, que s'il y avoit seulement, comme M^r. l'Abbé le doit vouloir selon ses principes, Nec morantur euntem. Voici encore d'autres devises de la même nature: Un Soleil-levant, qui répand sa lumière de tous côtés, <u>Lux</u> precit ardori. Le Soleil entouré de rayons, et au milieu de quatre vents qui soufflent, Nec <u>radium</u> executient. Une étoile qui tombe du Ciel, et qui marque en tombant, une grande trace de lumière; Sequitur <u>lux magna</u> cadentem. Un orenger [sic] chargé de fleurs et de fruit, <u>Flos unà fructrusque</u> manent. Dans toutes ces devises, qui sont assurément très-bonnes, les corps accessoires, comme la lumière et les royons [sic] à l'égard du Soleil, la trace de lumière à l'égard de l'étoile, et les fleurs et les fruits à l'égard [6] de l'oranger sont nommés, et la devise n'en est que meilleure; quoiqu'on pût leur faire un reproche qu'on ne peut pas faire au mot d'<u>æquor</u> de ma devise, sçavoir, que ces mots qui conviennent au signe dans leur sens propre, ne conviennent à la chose signifiée que dans le sens figuré et métaphorique, puisque la lumiere, les rayons, et les fruits ne sont point de véritables lumières, de véritables rayons, ni de véritables fruits à l'égard des personnes pour qui les devises ont été faites: au lieu que le mot æquor convient dans le sens propre, et au signe, et à la chose signifiée, à l'Alcion, et à M^r l'Admiral; et que la mer sur laquelle ils ont un absolu pouvoir, est la même en l'un et en l'autre. Il ne me reste plus [6v] qu'à répondre a [sic] ce qu'on dit, que le mot æquor, qu'on prétend inutile, étant retranche, la légende seroit plus courte et plus élégante. Je conviens qu'elle seroit plus courte, mais non pas plus élégante. Le sens qui demeureroit indefini, s'il n'y avoit que, Et nascens temperat, ou, Temperat et nascens, seroit obscur, et on auroit trop de peine à chercher quelle est la chose sur laquelle l'Alcion et l'Admiral ont du pouvoir; cette peine est levée par l'enonciation du mot æquor. Je prétens d'ailleurs, que cette légende, Et nascens temperat æquor, qui n'est pas plus longue que celle de <u>Donec totum impleat orbem</u>, si belle et si estimée, a un sens plus élégant, plus plein, et plus agreable à l'oreille que celle qu'on y veut substituer, qui sont {est} [7] obscure et écourtée. Le sçavant Abbé à qui j'adressois la parole, répondit mille choses très-belles et très-curieuses, dont le récit me meneroit trop loin. Nos Juges témoignèrent être contents de mes réponses, mais non pas autant qu'ils l'étoient, pour épargner à mon adversaire le chagrin de s'être mépris dans sa dissertation, qui étoit d'une heure et demie de lecture.

Il n'est pas seulement vrai, que la seule connoissance des règles de la devise {,} ne sert le plus souvent qu'à faire tomber dans l'erreur, comme le prouve assez la petite histoire que je viens de rapporter; mais que la connoissance seule de l'esprit et de l'essence de la devise suffit pour n'en point faire de mauvaises. Car pour les bonnes et les excellentes, c'est le genie seul qui [7v] les produit; et sans cette fleur d'imagination, qui a seule le bon {bonheur} de les trouver, et la force de s'en saisir, la connoissance la plus parfaite de l'essence d'une devise, qui empêche, comme je viens de dire, de faire des fautes, n'en fera point, toute seule, qui touchent, qui charment, et qui enlèvent.

Il résulte trois choses de ce que je viens de dire, que la seule connoissance des règles sert autant à s'égarer, qu'à se conduire; que le seul esprit de l'art suffit sans les règles, pour s'empêcher d'en faire de mauvaises; et que c'est le génie seul de l'ouvrier qui en fait d'excellentes; étant possible pourtant, que ce beau génie y fasse des fautes; s'il n'a l'esprit de l'art dans lequel il travaille. On doit encore considérer que s'il y a des préceptes dont on ne [8] puisse pas abuser, ce sont des préceptes qui ne disent que ce qui est sçû de tout le monde; par exemple, qu'il doit y avoir de la noblesse et de la delicatesse dans le corps et dans l'ame d'une devise; qu'il faut qu'elle soit ingénieuse, qu'elle soit claire, et qu'elle frappe l'esprit agreablement. Et en effet, si l'on manque a [sic] donner ces qualités là aux devises que l'on fait, peut-on croire que ce soit faute d'en être bien averti, puisqu'il n'y a personne qui naturellement n'ait envie que ce qu'il fait soit ingénieux, spirituel, et agréable? Je ne laisse pas de demeurer d'accord qu'il est bon de se faire instruire de plusieurs choses dont les hommes sont convenus, quoique le bon sens tout seul pût suffir pour les trouver: Par exemple, que les corps simples, comme une étoille, [8v] un lion, un arbre, une fleur, sont meilleurs que les corps composés, tels que sont un soleil dont les rayons réflechis par un miroir ardent, vont brûler un arbre où un Aigle a bati son aire: Que les corps naturels, tels que je viens de nommer, sont preferables aux corps artificiels, comme sont, une épée, un canon, un cadran, un [sic] horloge, une gruë à élever des pierres, et autres semblables. Ce n'est pas qu'il ne se fasse tous les jours beaucoup de devises avec ces sortes de corps artificiels, qui valent mieux que beaucoup de celles qui ont des corps, et simples, et naturels: mais toutes choses pareilles, les corps naturels et simples l'emportent sur les autres. Il est bon de sçavoir encore, que des membres séparés du corps, comme une main ou un bras, sont desagreables, quoi- [9] qu'on les fasse sortir d'une nuée: Que des figures d'hommes ou de femmes toutes entières n'y doivent point entrer, à moins que ce ne soient [sic] des personnages de la fable; comme Hercule, Minerve, Amphion, Apollon, &c. parce que la devise n'est {n'estant} autre chose, qu'une comparaison de deux choses de différentes espèces, qui ont quelque propriété par où elles se ressemblent; cela ne se rencontre pas lorsqu'on compare un homme avec un homme.

Pour ce qui est de l'ame ou de la légende, il suffit de sçavoir que les plus courtes sont les meilleures, pourvû qur leur brièveté ne les rende pas obscures: Qu'il est à souhaiter qu'elles fassent la fin d'un vers héxamètre, si elles sont en Latin et que cette fin de vers soit d'un Poëte célèbre, comme, [9v] Virgile, Horace, Ovide, Juvenal &c. Je fais peu de cas de cette dernière beauté, et je n'aime pas moins une légende, toutes choses étant pareilles d'ailleurs, quand elle est toute neuve, que quand elle prise d'un Auteur, quelque célèbre qu'il puisse être. C'est mon goût particulier dont je me défie un peu, et que je n'ai garde de donner pour règle. Toutes les Langues bien connuës, comme l'Italienne et l'Espagnole, y sont bonnes, et la Françoise autant que pas une autre, mais la difficulté y est beaucoup plus grande. La devise d'une hirondelle, avec

Appendix B: Charles Perrault's Discours Sur l'Art des Devises

ce mot, <u>Le froid me chasse</u>, est aussi agréable et plus galante que toutes celles qui ont jamais été faites en Latin. Il est vrai que les sçavans soutiennent qu'elles sont plus belles en cette Langue; mais [10] j'ose dire qu'ils se trompent. Cette prévention vient de l'accoutumance qu'ils ont prise au Collège, de réciter le Latin avec emphase, et sur le ton de la déclamation. Les paroles de la devise qui a pour corps un serpent à plusieurs têtes, Plus grande en sera la victoire, sont aussi résonnantes, et auroient autant d'emphase que les plus belles des devises Latines, si l'on vouloit les prononcer du même ton, et avec la même véhemence. Cette question ayant été traite à fond dans la petite {', 'a petite' *has been crossed out*} academie des devises et des {Inscriptions[5]} qui est la même qui se tient encore au Louvre à l'issuë des Assemblées de l'Academie Françoise; il fut résolu que les Langues Latine et Françoise y étoient également bonnes; mais qu'il étoit pour l'ordinaire plus difficile d'y bien réüssir [10v] en François: de sorte qu'il falloit les faire en l'une ou en l'autre langue, selon que le mot qui se présentoit étoit le plus heureux, et cela a été pratiqué dans les devises qui se sont faites pendant plusieurs années.

On a accoutumé quand on fait peindre des devises, de mettre des vers au dessous, qui leur servent d'explication. Quand j'ai commencé à en faire, on y nommoit sans scruple, ou le signe, ou la chose signifiée, et quelque fois tous les deux ensemble. Personne n'ayant encore bien considéré que ces vers ne sont autre chose que l'explication et la paraphrase du mot de la devise, et qu'il faut par conséquent qu'ils soient de la même nature; c'est-à-dire, qu'ils ne doivent non plus que la légende, nommer, ni la chose qui est représentée, ni celle qui est [11] sousentenduë, parce qu'il faut que toute l'énonciation de ces vers aille également à l'un et à l'autre, pour mieux faire voir la justesse de la comparaison, en quoi consiste toute la bonté et toute l'essence de la devise. Je m'en expliquai un jour avec M[r]. Clement Conseiller en la Cour des Aides,[6] et avec le Pere Le Moine Jesuite,[7] tous deux excellens en cette matière. Comme ils ne s'étoient jamais assujettis a [sic] cette règle, ils me dirent que la chose n'étoit pas possible, et que ce seroit se donner des entraves très-fâcheuses et très-inutiles. Je leur repartis qu'il pouvoit y avoir de la difficulté, mais non pas bien grande, puisque je l'avois surmontée dans plusieurs devises que j'avois faites, et que j'étois persuadé que l'observation de cette règle étoit absolument nécessaire. Je leur [11v] en dis les raisons que je viens de déduire, qu'ils ne purent s'empêcher d'approuver, et qu'ils louèrent même autant que le pouvoit permettre le petit chagrin qu'ils avoient de ne s'en être pas encore avisés. Je vais rapporter des devises où cette règle n'est pas observée, et j'en rapporterai ensuite d'autres où l'on y a eu égard.

Devise où le signe est nommé dans les vers qui l'expliquent

Un aiglon qu'un aigle conduit, avec ces mots
Patre viam monstrate. {§}
Dans cette région où regne la tempête
Je menace de l'œil, j'affronte de la tête
Le nuage qui gronde, et la foudre qui luit,

Et gagnant le dessus, à la gloire j'appelle
Du feu de mon regard, et du bruit de mon aile,
[12] La jeunesse et l'ardeur de l'Aiglon qui me suit {*cropped margin
note* Le
P. Le Moin} {§}

L'Aiglon est le corps principal, et par conséquent ne devoit point être nommé.
Exemple où l'expression va à la chose signifiée.
Un Soleil ecclipsé avec ces mots:
Deficit et sufficit

§

En vain pour m'ôter l'assurance,
Une fatale defaillance
Porte mes jours à leur extremité:
Tout foible que je suis j'emplis la Terre et l'Onde,
Et les restes de ma clarté
Pourroient suffire à plus d'un monde.

§

Cette expression, mes jours, convient très-bien au Cardinal de Richelieu pour qui la devise a été faite, mais point du tout au [12v] Soleil ecclipsé, qui n'est jamais ecclipsé qu'une heure ou deux, et de qui l'on ne peut jamais dire que ses jours sont portés à l'extrémité, parce que les jours veulent dire là, le cours et l'étenduë de la vie, ce qui n'a point de rapport au Soleil.

Exemple où le signe et la chose signifiée sont exprimés, et le sont de maniere que ce qui est dit de l'un, ne se peut pas dire de l'autre au propre, mais seulement {au} figuré.

Une Lune au milieu de la nuit, avec ces mots:
Nec de nocte nigrescit. {§}
En vain cet habit de ténèbres
Ces ombres tristes et funèbres
Après la mort du jour ont pensé m'obscurcir,
Crêpes, voiles, bandeaux cèdent à ma lumière
Et de plus, leur plus noire matière,
Ni le deuil, ni la nuit, ne peuvent me noircir. {§}

[13] Cette devise fut faite pour la Reine-mère au deuil de la mort du Roi d'Espagne.[8] Ces mots: Après la mort du jour, ne conviennent au propre, qu'à la Lune, et point du tout à la Reine, mêmes au figuré; et ces mots, Crêpes, voiles, bandeaux, ne conviennent au sens propre qu'à la Reine, et très-peu à la Lune dans le sens figuré. Car l'obscurité de la nuit, qui ne sert qu'à rendre la Lune plus éclatante, ne peut être appelée ni un crêpe ni un voile, ni un bandeau à son égard; et c'est seulement d'un

Appendix B: Charles Perrault's Discours Sur l'Art des Devises

nuage qui la couvriroit en partie, que cela se pouroit dire. Enfin dans le dernier vers le mot de <u>deuil</u> va seulement à la Reine, et celui de <u>nuit</u> seulement à la lune, contre l'intention de la legende d'une devise, dont toutes les expressions doivent aller égalemt [sic] [13v] et au signe, et à la chose signifiée.

Les Devises qui suivent, et les vers qui les servent d'explication, sont dans les règles que j'ai marquées

Devises qui ont été employées dans les tapisseries du Roi, ou les quatre Elemens sont repréntés [sic][9]

Il faut sçavoir que ses tapisseries qui furent faites immédiatement après la conclusion de la paix generale, en l'année 1662[10] avoient pour sujet les biens et la félicité que Sa Majesté avoit causés, en donnant cette paix à l'Europe; et les quatre devises qu'on a placées aux quatre coins de chacune de ces tapisseries, louoient sa Majesté de quatre vertus principales qui éclatent en [14] son auguste Personne, et qui plus que toutes les autres avoit contribué au grand ouvrage de la paix. Ces quatre vertus sont la Piété, la Magnanimité, la Bonté, et la Valeur. La Piété, qui avoit fléchi le Ciel, et l'avoit comme contraint à donner cette paix qu'il avoit refusée à nos voeux pendant tant d'années.

La Magnanimité, qui avoit fait concevoir à Sa Majesté le noble et grand dessein de rendre ses Peuples heureux, et de préférer cette gloire à celle des conquêtes qui lui étoit assurée.

La Bonté, qui l'en avoit sollicité, et qui en avoit pressé l'exécution.

Et la Valeur enfin, qui ayant rendu sa Majesté redoutable à toute la Terre, avoit disposé ses ennemis à la recevoir à des [14v] conditions raisonnables

Il est à observer que tous les corps de ces devises sont tirées [sic] de l'Elément qu'elles accompagnent; et que ces devises étant toutes semblables pour le sujet, sont toutes différentes, et pour le corps, et pour les paroles.

Pour la Piété dans l'élement du feu.
Un encensoir avec ce mot: <u>Et sacro {carpitur igni.}</u> {<i>additional underlining</i>}
{§}
carpitur igni {<i>here</i> 'carpitur igni' <i>has been crossed out</i>} pour {Pour}
marquer le Zèle ardent de Sa Majesté pour les choses divines, et
pour tout ce qui regarde la Religion {§}
Son extrême ferveur, à nulle autre semblable
Rend le Ciel doux et favorable
Aux desirs des mortels;
Il cède avec plaisir au feu qui le consume,
Et ce feu divin ne s'allume
Que pour le culte des Autels. {§}
[15] Pour la Magnanimité dans l'element du feu.
Une fusée volante, avec ces paroles: <u>Splendet et ascendit</u>
{<i>additional underlining</i>}: pour faire entendre que la gloire de Sa</p>

Majesté est toûjours éclatante, et va toujours en s'élevant.
J'éblouïs tous les yeux de ma vive splendeur
Et rien n'est égal à l'ardeur
Qui me transporte et qui m'anime;
Quiconque observera mon cours,
Verra que noble et magnanime
Je m'elève toujours

§

Pour la Bonté dans l'element du feu.

Un Phare, avec ces paroles: <u>In publica commoda fulget</u> {*additional underlining*}: pour représenter cette bonté agissante de Sa Majesté, qui veille sans cesse pour le bien et le salut de tous les peuples.

[15v] Pendant que loin du bruit la Nature sommeille,
Seul j'agis et je veille,
Ignorant du repos les charmes les plus doux;
Et d'une ardeur infatigable,
J'épans de tous côtés ma splendeur secourable,
Pour le salut de tous.

§

Pour la Valeur, dans l'élément du feu.

Un foudre abatant un grand Arbre, et qui a pour mot: <u>Micat exitiale superbis</u> {*additional underlining*}: pour signifier que Sa Majesté pardonnant aux humbles, terasse et détruit les superbes, ainsi que le Foudre, qui épargnant les joncs et les roseaux qui lui obéissent, abat et détruit les grands arbres qui lui résistent.

Le Foible et le Soûmis, qui cèdent à mes coups,
N'ont point à craindre mon courroux;
[16] On évite, en ployant, ma plus grande vengeance:
Mais quand je fais trembler et la Terre et les Cieux
Que les traits puissans que je lance
Sont à craindre aux Audacieux !

§

Pour la Piété dans l'élement de l'air.

Un Arc-en-Ciel, ayant pour mot, <u>Terras devinxit Olympo.</u> {*additional underlining*} Comme ce Météore est une assurance à la Terre contre la colère du Ciel, on peut dire que la Piété de Sa Majesté nous a mis a [sic] couvert de cette même Colère, après nous avoir réconciliés avec lui, et en avoir attiré la Paix sur nous.

Lorsque des Cieux l'âpre courroux
S'étoit déclaré contre nous
Par une longue et triste Guerre,
Il bannit de nos coeurs la crainte pour jamais;
[16v] Et se faisant voir à la Terre
Il la vient assurer d'une éternelle Paix.

§

Appendix B: Charles Perrault's Discours Sur l'Art des Devises

Pour la Magnanimité dans l'élément de l'air.

L'Oiseau que l'on appelle de Paradis, {*margin note,* avec ce mot Semper sublimis} si l'on en croid les Naturalistes, se soutient toujours élevé en l'air, sans jamais toucher à terre: ce qui, joint avec ces paroles: Semper Sublimis, exprime assez bien la grandeur d'ame de Sa Majesté, qui est toujours occupée à de grandes choses, et qui ne se propose rien que de magnifique et de sublime.

Il n'est rien de si relevé,
Où si son vol n'est arrivé,
Il ne monte sans peine, et sans trop entreprendre
Il ne cesse d'agir, et jamais il n'est las:
Il regarde sur nous; et void, sans y descendre,
[17] Tout ce qui se passe ici bas.
§

Pour la Bonté dans l'élément de l'Air.

Le Roi des Abeilles, avec ce mot, <u>Signat Clementia Regem</u> {*additional underlining*}. Ce Roi est reconnoissable entre ses sujets, en ce qu'il n'a point d'aguillon; et de cette sorte peut être considéré comme le symbole des bons Princes; tel que Sa Majesté, dont la Clemence est le véritable caractère: {§}

Non par un mouvement de crainte,
Mais par amour, et sans contrainte,
Mon Peuple obéït à ma Loi;
Et ce n'est pas tant ma Puissance,
Que ma Douceur et ma Clémence
Qui me font connoître pour Roi.
{§}

Pour la Valeur, dans l'élément de l'Air.

[17v] Un Aigle tenant un Foudre dans ses serres, avec ce mot: <u>Meruitque timeri nil metuens</u> {*additional underlining*}. Les Poëtes ont feint que cet Oiseau portoit le Foudre de Jupiter; parce qu'il est le seul de tous les animaux qui ne craint point le Tonnere, et sur lequel il ne tombe jamais. Ainsi la Valeur de Sa Majesté fait trembler toutes les Puissances de la Terre, parce qu'il n'y en a point au dessus d'elle, et qu'elle n'a aucun Foudre à redouter. {§}

De Foudre menaçant, qui forme les Tempêtes
Au dessus de nos têtes,
Il void loin, sous ses piés la fureur éclater;
Il le porte, et son feu jusqu'a [sic] lui n'ose atteindre:
Ainsi ne voyant rien qu'il doive redouter,
Il ne void aussi rien qui ne le doive craindre.
§

Pour la Piété, dans l'élément de l'Eau.

[18] Une mer, avec ce mot: <u>Nusquam data littora transit</u> {*additional underlining*}. Quelque vaste que soit l'Ocean, il ne passe jamais les limites que le doigt de Dieu lui a marquées sur son rivage: Ainsi quelque grande que soit la puissance de Sa Majesté, elle ne va jamais audela des bornes de la Justice, qui sont lès seules que Dieu lui a

données, et que sa Piété lui rend inviolables. {§}

>Bien qu'en tout l'Univers mon Empire s'étende,
>Que le plus ferme coeur ma colère appréhende,
>Et tremble au moindre de mes coups;
>Je ne m'étens jamais au delà des limites
>Qu'à mon vaste pouvoir l'Eternel a prescrites,
>Même au plus fort de mon courroux.

{§}

Pour la Magnanimité, dans l'élément de l'Eau.

Une Fontaine jaillissante, avec ce mot: <u>Petit</u> {*additional underlining*} [18v] <u>impiger ortus</u> {*additional underlining*}. Pour signifier que comme ces sortes de Fontaines remontent aussi haut que leur source; ainsi Sa Majesté égalera Elle seule tous ses Ancêtres, et portera sa Puissance et ses Vertus à un degré aussi eminent que les saints Louis et les Charlemagnes.

>Pendant que l'on void mes semblables,
>Ou ramper sur la Terre, ou croupir miserables
>Dans une molle oisiveté;
>Par les divins ressorts d'une vertu divine,
>Je monte, et je m'éleve avec rapidité
>aussi haut que mon Origine.

§

Pour la Bonté, dans l'élément de l'eau.

Un grand Fleuve, avec mot: <u>Facit omnia læta.</u> {*additional underlining*} Les grands Fleuves portent l'abondance et la fertilité par-tout où ils [19] passent: de même les bons Princes, tels que Sa Majesté, font le bonheur et la richesse des Peuples qui leur obéïssent. {§}

>Loin de moi tout périt, tout languit de foiblesse,
>Et sèche de tristesse,
>Faute de mon secours:
>Près de moi tout fleurit, tout profite et s'avance,
>Et l'on me void porter la joie et l'abondance
>Par-tout ou je porte mon cours.

{§}

Pour la Valeur, dans l'élément de l'Eau.

Un Dauphin, avec ce mot: <u>Hunc et monstra timent</u> {*additional underlining*}. Ce poisson est le maître légitime de la mer; et bien qu'il s'en trouve de plus grands que lui, les Naturalistes assurent qu'il n'y en a point de si terribles qu'il ne combate et ne surmonte. On peut dire la même chose de Sa Majesté, et qu'il n'y [19v] a point de Puissance, quelque grande et monstrueuse qu'elle soit, qui ne le craigne. {§}

>La Mer n'a point de bords, de gouffre, ni d'abîme
>Dont il ne soit Roi légitime
>Et qui ne rende hommage à sa noble Valeur;
>Elle a des monstres effroyables;

Appendix B: Charles Perrault's Discours Sur l'Art des Devises

Mais il est pourtant vrai, que des plus redoutables,
Dans un juste combat il demeure vainqueur.
{§}
Pour la Piété, dans l'élément de la Terre.

Un Girasol, avec ce mot: <u>Cœlestes sequitur motus.</u> {*additional underlining*} Pour dire que Sa Majesté se conduit par les mouvemens du Ciel, en toutes ses actions, ainsi que le Girasol suit le mouvement du Soleil, qu'il regarde toujours.

Malgré l'élément qui m'enserre,
Et la loi du destin, qui m'attache à la Terre,
Dans le plus haut des Cieux sont mes tendres amours.
[20] Du divin auteur de ma vie
J'ai toujours la trace suivie
Et la suivrai toûjours.
{§}
Pour la Magnanimité dans l'élément de la Terre.

Un Sapin, et ce mot: <u>Rectà se tollit in altum</u> {*additional underlining*}. Sa Majesté qui se plaît dans les choses grandes et élevées, va droit à la Gloire, ainsi que le Sapin, qui se plaît sur les montagnes les plus hautes, et qui s'élève droit en haut, sans jamais se courber.

Plein d'une fierté magnanime
Jusqu'aux Cieux j'élève ma cime,
Affermi par mon propre faix:
Rien ne peut faire que je plie,
Moins encor, que je m'humilie;
Je m'élève toujours, et ne gauchis jamais.
{§}
[20v] Pour la Bonté, dans l'élément de la Terre.

Une Houlette, avec ce mot: <u>Et regit, et servat</u> {*additional underlining*}. Une houlette n'a que deux usages; l'un, de conduire le troupeau; l'autre, de le garder contre les loups: Et en cela elle est le véritable symbole d'un bon Prince, tel que Sa Majesté, qui n'a point d'autre soin, ni d'autre occupation que de bien gouverner son Peuple, et de le défendre contre ses ennemis.

Parmi la joie et l'abondance
Et loin de toute violence
Vivent ceux que je tiens à ma garde soumis:
Rien n'est plus doux que mon Empire;
Mon but n'est que de les conduire,
Et de les garantir contre leurs ennemis.
§
Pour la Valeur, dans l'élément de la Terre.

[21] Un Lion qui se repose, et ce mot: <u>Quis hunc impunè lacesset</u> {*additional underlining*}? La Valeur de Sa Majesté n'a pas seulement fait la paix, en obligeant ses ennemis à la demander: mais elle la conserve, en les empêchant de rien faire qui la

puisse rompre. Et c'est en quoi on peut bien dire que Sa Majesté ressemble à un lion, qui ne craint point qu'on trouble son repos, parce qu'on ne le peut faire impunément.

Dans ces climats heureux, si charmans, et si calmes,
Et sous l'ombre de tant de Palmes
Il peut bien prendre son repos.
Qui seroit assez temeraire,
De le troubler mal-à-propos
Et s'exposer à sa colere ?
{§}

Ensuite de la Tapisserie des élémens, se [21v] fit une autre tenture de Tapisseries, ou les quatre saisons étoient représentées. Le sujet étoit, que le Roi, qui avoit remis l'ordre dans les élémens, avoit rendu aux saisons leur premiere beauté: ce qui fit y ajouter les divertissemens qu'il donnoit à la Cour dans ces mêmes saisons. Or il y avoit aussi des devises à la louange de sa Majesté, dont il y en a deux dans chaque pièce, qui ont rapport à la saison, et deux au divertissement. Il y a quelques unes de ces devises, qui ne sont pas de moi; mais j'ai crû les devoir mettre ici toutes, avec le nom de leurs auteurs, lors qu'elles ne sont pas de ma façon, pour ne pas démembrer cet ouvrage.

Devises de la Tapisserie
des Saisons.
Pour la pièce du Printems.

[22] Des Fleurs printanières dans un parterre, qui ont pour ame ce mot, <u>Terræ amor et decus</u> {*additional underlining*}: Pour signifier que si la Terre aime les fleurs comme ses premières productions, et celles qui font son plus bel ornement, Sa Majesté n'est pas moins l'amour et l'ornement de toute la Terre.

Si lors que la Terre separe
De ce présent des Cieux, si charmant et si rare,
Elle l'aime si tendrement;
N'est-il pas juste qu'on la voye
En faire ses plaisirs, son amour, et sa joye,
Comme elle en fait son ornement.
{§}

Une Hirondelle, avec ce mot: <u>Et tempora læta reducit</u> {*additional underlining*}. Comme cet oiseau est estimé chasser l'hyver, et ramener le Printems avec lui; on peut dire de même, que le Roi [22v] a ramené le beau tems et la paix, après une longue et ennuyeuse guerre. {§}

Quand par l'ordre des Tems, une fâcheuse guerre
De biens et de plaisirs a dépouillé la Terre,
Et fait languir ses Habitans;
Je viens leur rendre l'espérance,
Je viens apporter l'abondance
Et ramène avec moi la joie et le beau Tems.
{§}

Appendix B: Charles Perrault's Discours Sur l'Art des Devises

Une lance accompagnée de ce mot: <u>Ludo, pugnæque paratur</u> {*additional underlining*}: Pour dire que le Roi n'est pas moins redoutable à la tête d'une armée, qu'il est aimable dans un divertissement tel que le Carousel: Ce qui est représenté par une lance, qui sert également et à la guerre, et aux jeux militaires. {§}

    Mon adresse par fois s'exerce en une Lice,
     Mais mon véritable exercice
[23] Est la guerre qui seule a pour moi des appas.
    Par-tout m'accompagne la Gloire;
   Et j'emporte toûjours le Prix ou la Victoire
     Dans les Jeux et dans les Combats.
      {§}

Une Rose avec ses épines, et ayant pour Ame ces paroles: <u>Juncta arma decori</u> {*additional underlining*}. Il se trouve dans la Rose de la beauté et de la fierté tout-à-la-fois; et elle est comme une image de la Paix et de la Guerre jointes ensemble. La même chose se peut dire des Courses de bagues et des Carousels, qui sont des jeux, mais des jeux militaires, où il faut beaucoup de force et d'adresse dans les Armes, avec beaucoup de bonne mine et de bonne grace, qui sont des choses qui se rencontrent souverainement en Sa Majesté.

  [23v] A mon aïr attrayant, doux, charmant, agréable
     De plaisir on se sent toucher,
Mes traits en même tems me rendent redoutable;
Sans amour et sans crainte on ne peut m'approcher:
    Aussi parmi l'horreur des Armes
    On ne vid jamais tant de charmes.
      §
    Pour la pièce de l'Été

Une Gerbe de blé, et ce mot. <u>Vitæ melioris in usum</u> {*additional underlining*}. Le blé que l'Été produit, ayant succédé au gland, dont les premiers hommes se nourrissoient, a rendu la vie plus agreable qu'elle n'étoit auparavant. On peut dire de même, que le Roi a été donné à la France, pour rendre ses habitans plus heureux qu'ils n'ont jamais été.

  [24] Quoi que la fable ait raconté
 Du Règne de Saturne, où plein de liberté
  Chacun vivoit content, au gré de son envie;
Je fais que les Mortels, bien plus heureux encor,
    Mènent une plus douce vie,
  Qu'aux premiers jours du siècle d'or.
     §

Un Lis, et ce mot, <u>Candore omnia vincit</u> {*additional underlining*}. Le Lis, qui est le symbole de la Candeur et de la Sincérité, a été choisi pour représenter le procédé noble, sincère, et genereux de Sa Majesté dans toutes ses actions. {§}
    Rejeton glorieux d'une Tige sublime,

> Je monte vers le Ciel, d'un effort magnanime,
> Et brille d'un éclat qui n'a rien d'emprunté:
> Rien de ce que je suis, aux Mortels ne se cache
> Mon front toujours ouvert, aussi bien que sans tache,
> [24v] Sert de parfait symbole à la Sincérité.
>
> Charpentier.

Un Alcion bâtissant son nid sur la mer, qui se tient calme, pour ne pas troubler un bâtiment si merveilleux, avec ce mot: <u>Miratur Natura silens</u> {*additional underlining*}: Pour exprimer la beauté des Bâtimens du Roi, qui est telle, qu'il semble que toute l'Europe ne se soit tenuë en paix, lorsque Sa Majesté a recommencé d'y faire travailler, que pour en admirer mieux la structure surprenante et incomparable. {§}

> Lorsque de l'édifice où je dois habiter,
> Et que le Tems doit respecter,
> J'entreprens la structure à nulle autre pareille,
> La Nature s'impose une profonde paix
> Pour mieux considérer l'incroyable merveille
> [25] Du Bâtiment que je me fais.

{§}

Une Équaire, ayant pour mot: Dirigit obliqua. Pour marquer le soin et l'application de Sa Majesté à réformer les abus de son Estat, et à redresser les mauvaises coutumes qui s'y étoient introduites. {§}

> Sur la droite raison s'établit ma puissance,
> Pour combatre en tous lieux l'erreur et l'ignorance,
> Que ma sincérité ne peut dissimuler:
> Je découvre l'abus quelque part qu'il se glisse;
> Et sans jamais gauchir, j'exerce une justice
> Dont nul ne sçauroit appeler.
>
> Charpentier.

Pour la pièce de l'Automne

Le Corps de la Devise est une Grenade [25v] un peu entr'ouverte, pour laisser voir les grains qu'elle renferme. Ces paroles lui servent d'ame: <u>Præstant interna Coronæ</u> {*additional underlining*}: Pour dire que comme la Couronne de la Grenade n'est pas comparable aux fruits qu'elle cache au dedans, puisqu'elle n'en est que l'écorce et le dehors; il en est de même de Sa Majesté, qui par les qualités admirables de sa Personne, s'élève encore davantage au dessus des autres hommes, que par l'éclat de son Rang et de sa Couronne. {§}

> Quelque avantage que me donne
> La Royale Couronne
> Dont mon front est paré,

Appendix B: Charles Perrault's Discours Sur l'Art des Devises

> Toutefois ce beau Diadème
> Ne sçauroit être comparé
> Aux trésors infinis que j'enferme en moi-même.

[26] Une Vigne de Virginie, qui de ses banches [sic] couvre une grande Pyramide, et s'étend encore au-delà. On lui a donné pour Ame ces paroles: <u>Crescit in immensum:</u> {*additional underlining*} Pour marquer la vaste étenduë de l'Ame et de la Puissance de Sa Majesté, qui ne trouvant point de bornes en elles-mêmes, ne sont limitées que par les sujets où elles peuvent s'étendre, et s'appliquer. {§}

> Un progrès sans pareil a suivi ma Naissance
> Par une merveilleuse et secrette puissance
> On me void élever toujours:
> Il n'est obstacle ni limites,
> Qui puissent retarder mes démarches subites,
> Ni qui puisse {puissèt} borner mon cours.
>
> Charpentier.

Un Cor de Chasse, avec ce mot: <u>Ducit</u> {*additional underlining*} [26v] <u>et excitat agmen</u> {*additional underlining*}. Le Cor assemble, conduit, et encourage la Meute, et il est comme l'Ame de toute la Chasse. Il en est de même de Sa Majesté, qui est l'Ame de tout son Royaume, et particulièrement de ses Armées, qui n'ont de mouvement, que celui qu'il leur donne. {§}

> Si tôt que je me fais entendre,
> Tous près de moi viennent se rendre,
> Et par eux aussitôt mes ordres sont suivis:
> J'allume dans leurs coeurs le desir de la Gloire;
> Et pour remporter la victoire,
> Je les anime et les conduis.

Un Faucon fondant sur sa Proie, et ce mot: <u>Et fulminis ocyor alis.</u> {*additional underlining*} Cet oiseau est le plus vîte, et le plus vigoureux de tous; en sorte qu'il représente parfaitement [27] cette diligence et cette vigeur incroyable avec laquelle Sa Majesté execute tous ses desseins. {§}

> Lorsque le combat m'est permis,
> Et qu'à perdre mes ennemis
> Leur mauvais sort m'a fait résoudre,
> Je fonds sur eux d'un mouvement
> Aussi terrible que la Foudre,
> Et plus rapide que le Vent.
>
> Charpentier.

Pour la pièce de l'Hyver.

Une fleur nommée Perce-neige, avec ce mot: <u>Nil florere vetat.</u> {*additional underlining*} Cette fleur s'épanouït au milieu de la neige, et malgré les rigueurs de l'hiver: ce qui peut se dire de la gloire de Sa Majesté, que tous les [27v] obstacles ne peuvent empêcher d'éclater, et qui fleurit au milieu des difficultés. {§}

        Ce n'est qu'aux saisons favorables
        Que l'on void mes semblables,
        Par leur brillant éclat les regards attirer:
        Pour moi qui ne vois point d'assez fort adversaire
        C'est dans le tems le plus contraire
        Que je fleuris le plus, et me fais admirer.
                                      Chapelain.

Un Foyer, avec ce mot, <u>Tempus mitescit ab illo.</u> {*additional underlining*} Comme pendant l'hyver le plus froid et le plus âpre, un Foyer plein de feu adoucit la vigueur de la saison: ainsi dans les plus mauvais effets de l'inclémence de l'Air et des Elémens, qui sont cause quelquefois de la stérilité de la Terre, le Roi adoucit et répare le malheur de ces tems [28] fâcheux; comme sa Majesté en donna un exemple mémorable durant la dernière famine où elle assista ses Peuples avec une bonté paternelle, et une magnificence Royale. {§}

        Lorsqu'un tems ennemi du bonheur de la Terre
        Lui déclare la guerre,
        Et par mille rigueurs s'oppose à son desir,
        Je viens avec ardeur secourir la Nature,
        Des cruelles saisons je répare l'injure,
        Et comble les Humains de joie et de plaisir
                                      Cassagnes[11]

Un Amphitheatre, avec ce mot, <u>Deliciæ populi</u> {*additional underlining*}. Le Peuple Romain aimoit tellement les spectacles, qu'on peut bien dire qu'il en fesoit ses plus grandes délices: comme {*'comme' crossed out*} l'on peut aussi les comparer à un [28v] bon Prince, tel que Sa Majesté qui fait les plus chères delices de son Peuple. {§}

        Le Peuple m'aime avec tendresse,
        Ne me void qu'avec allegresse,
        Et par mille applaudissemens,
        Qui de sa passion sont d'assûrés indices,
        Me fait connoître à tous momens,
        Que je suis de son coeur les plus chères delices.
                      §

Une Machine, avec ce mot: Naturam superat: Pour dire qu'une Machine par ses mouvemens surprend et charme les Spéctateurs, et surpasse les effets ordinaires de la Nature. Ainsi Sa Majesté par ses vertus et ses actions héroïques, étonne et ravit tous ceux qui en sont les témoins, et surpasse les forces naturelles, et la portée ordinaire

Appendix B: Charles Perrault's Discours Sur l'Art des Devises

des Hommes.

[29] Quel merveilleux objet, quel auguste miracle,
Par son rapide cours surmontant tout obstacle,
Ravit les yeux et les esprits ?
D'un art victorieux sa force est animée,
Et de ses mouvemens la Nature charmée,
L'admire, et lui cède le prix.

Cassagnes.

Diverses Devises pour le Tresor Royal.[1] [2]

Le Soleil qui élève des vapeurs, avec ce mot, Potiora rependit {*additional underlining*}. De même que les vapeurs que le Soleil tire de la Terre, lui sont renduës en pluyes et en rosées qui la rendent féconde: Ainsi les levées que le Roi fait sur ses peuples, leur retournent avec profit, par les [29v] dépenses utiles qu'il en fait pour la seureté et l'embellissement de son Royaume; en sorte que ce qu'il leur rend vaut mieux que ce qu'il a tiré. {§}

Dans tous les lieux où s'étend ma puissance
Je fais régner la joie et l'abondance;
Pars les benins regards que sur eux je répans;
Sur eux j'exerce un doux Empire
Et tout ce que j'en tire
Ne sçauroit égaler les biens que je leur rends.

§

En voici encore une sur le même Corps, Non sïbi, sed orbi. Elle n'a pas besoin d'explication.

§

Autre sur le même Corps des vapeurs qui s'élèvent de la Terre, mais où le Soleil n'est point représenté. Cogimur in {*additional underlining*} [30] fulmen: {*additional underlining*} Pour dire que si les vapeurs forment le [sic] Tonnerre qui se fait craindre par-tout; les Tributs que le Roi lève, lui fournissent des armes, qui ne sont pas moins terribles à ses ennemis.

§

Un Porc-épic, avec ces mots, Telorum æterna seges {*additional underlining*}. Comme le Porc-épic ayant lancé ses traits, en reproduit sans cesse de nouveaux; il en est de même du Tresor Royal, qui fournit sans cesse de nouveaux soldats et de nouvelles forces.

§

Un Laurier, avec ce mot: Je récompense la vertu. Pour dire que les graces qui sortent du Tresor Royal sont la récompense utile des belles actions, comme le laurier en est la récompense honorable.

[30v] Hercule avec sa peau de Lion, ayant à ses piés l'Hydre abatuë, le Sanglier

d'Erimante assommé et Gerion étoufé, avec ce mot, Mundo sic otia fecit {*additional underlining*}: Pour dire que ç'a été en abatant toutes les forces que la jalousie de ses ennemis lui a opposées, que le Roi a donné la paix à toute l'Europe en l'année 1682.[13]

Dans le [sic] devises qu'on a faites pour le Tresor Royal, on n'a pas toujours observé qu'elles regardassent son usage; et souvent on a pris pour sujet des devises, quelque évenement memorable arrive dans l'année, ou l'état florissant des affaires, ainsi qu'on le peut voir dans les Devises qui suivent.

[31] Hercule assommant l'Hydre; avec ces mots: Malgré sa force et son venin. L'Hydre représentoit les Puissances étrangères qui s'étoient liguées contre la France, que le Roi a terrassées,[14] malgré toutes leurs forces, toutes leurs intrigues, et toute leur jalousie.

Autre sur le même sujet, avec le même Corps, mais avec des paroles différentes: Plus grande en sera la victoire {*additional underlining*}. Pour dire que plus le nombre des ennemis ligués est grand, plus le Roi aura de gloire de les avoir vaincus.
Autre.
Un Arc-en-Ciel. Terras jubet esse quietas. Cette Devise fut faite après que le Roi eut donné la paix à l'Europe. [31v] Pour dire que quand le Roi le veut, il faut que tout demeure en paix, sans qu'on ait à craindre, ni trouble, ni aucune guerre; comme on ne doit point apprehender qu'il vienne de deluge quand on void l'Arc-en-Ciel.

Pour les Parties Casuelles[15]

Un Cerf qui a quitté son vieux bois qu'on void à ses piés, avec ce mot:
Hæc vires jactura novat {*additional underlining*}
Quand le Cerf quitte son vieux bois, la perte qu'il en fait lui est avantageuse; puisque par ce moyen il acquiert un nouveau bois qui renouvelle ses forces. Ainsi ce que l'Officier paye pour le Droit Annuel, est un gain plus {plutôt, *correction made in the black ink of the original text*} qu'une perte, puisque [32] par là il assure sa Charge.

Un Phare, avec ce mot:
Je montre une route assurée.   ou
Tutum monstrat iter.
Comme le Phare sert à éviter les écueils où les vaisseaux périssent: le Droit Annuel est un moyen qui empêche les Charges de périr.
Un Caducée, avec ce mot.
Superas educit ad oras {*additional underlining*}.
Le Droit Annuel et le Caducée on [sic] la même vertu, qui est de faire revivre ce qui étoit mort.
Le Soleil et des arbres qui commencent
à pousser, avec ce mot.

Appendix B: *Charles Perrault's* Discours Sur l'Art des Devises

Tous les ans je les renouvelle. {§}

Le Soleil donne tous les ans de nouvelles [32v] forces aux arbres: le Droit Annuel fait la même chose à l'égard des Charges qu'il empêche de périr pendant le cours de chaque année où il a été payé.

Devises pour les Bâtimens[1][6]

Le Soleil dans le Zodiaque.
Nobis decor omnis ab illo.

De même que les douze maisons du Zodiaque reçoivent tout leur éclat et toute leur beauté de la présence du Soleil; il en est ainsi des principales maisons royales, qui sont aussi au nombre de douze, et dont la présence du Roi fait la plus grande beauté

Un Arc-en-Ciel.
Solis opus.

[33] Cette devise fut faite et employée dans les jetons de 1673. à l'occasion de l'Arc de Triomphe, pour dire que cet ouvrage devoit être si beau, qu'on verroit bien, que le Roi seul pouvoit l'avoir fait faire, de même que l'Arc-en-Ciel ne peut être l'ouvrage du du [sic] Soleil. Monsieur Clement se servit du même Corps et de la même Legende au sujet de la paix, et fut fort surpris de n'en être pas le premier inventeur.

Un Temple magnifique
<u>Sed minor est domino.</u> {*additional underlining*}

Pour dire que quelques beaux que soient les Bâtimens du Roi, ils ont cela de commun avec les Temples, qu'ils sont toujours inférieurs à la Majesté de ceux pour qui ils ont été faits.

[33v] Les deux grandes pierres du Louvre
<u>Nec pondus obstitit.</u> {*additional underlining*}

Pour dire que comme la pesanteur extraordinaire de ces pierres n'a pas empêché qu'on ne les ait élevées: de même le grand poids des affaires que les ennemis ont suscitées au Roi, n'a pas empêché que Sa Majesté n'en soit venuë à bout glorieusement.

§

Une Ruche environnée de monstres {mouches, 'monstres' *crossed out*}.
<u>Fevet opus, nec bella morantur.</u> {*additional underlining*}

Pour dire que les Bâtimens du Roi continuënt toûjours au milieu de la guerre; de même que les Mouches ne laissent pas de travailler en leurs Ruches, malgré les guerres qu'elles ont continuellement les unes contre les autres.

[34] Un Alcion fesant son nid
Pace datâ ædificat.

Cette devise fût faite l'année de la paix,[1][7] et n'a pas besoin d'explication. Elle agrea tellement, de même que la precedente, que non seulement elles furent employées aux jetons des Bâtimens, chacune en leur année; mais qu'il en a été frapé de grandes médailles en or et en argent.

§

Mineve {Minerve, *black ink correction*} tenant d'une main une lance;
et de l'autre, des instrumens des plus
beaux Arts.
Pugnat, et excitat Artes.

Pour dire que comme Mineve {Minerve, *black ink correction*}, toute armée qu'elle est, ne laisse pas de favoriser les beaux Arts: ainsi le Roi, tout occupé qu'il est aux actions militaires, prend encore [34v] soin de faire fleurir les beaux Arts dans son Royaume.

§

Une Gruë élevant une pierre.
Mens agitat molem.

Comme cette machine donne du mouvement aux pierres, et en forme des édifices, il y a de même dans les Bâtimens un esprit qui les conduit; semblable à cette ame universelle que les Philosophes s'imaginoit [sic] être répanduë dans le monde, et en former toutes les merveilles.

§

Une Colomne.
Fulcit et ornat.   ou
J'en suis la force et l'ornement.

Pour dire que le Roi est la force et l'ornem^t de son Royaume; comme une colomne est [35] le soutien et la beauté d'un bâtiment.

Devises pour la Marine[1] [8]

Un jeune Alcion dans son nid
Et nascens temperat æquor.

C'est la Devise qui a donné occasion à ce discours, et que je rapporte ici, a fin qu'elle soit dans son rang, et que je l'accompagne des vers qui ont été faits pour elle. {§}

Bien qu'il ne vienne que de naître,
La Mer devant ses yeux n'oseroit s'émouvoir
Avec étonnement par-tout on void paraître
Sur l'Empire des flots son absolu pouvoir.
{§}
Une Perle.
Present du Ciel à la Mer. {§}
Toute noble est mon origine.
[35v] Et la Mer où mon sort en naissant me destine,
Me reçoit dans son sein, comme un don precieux,
Le plus grand que jamais elle ait reçû des Cieux.

Appendix B: Charles Perrault's Discours Sur l'Art des Devises

{§}
Une Boussole
<u>Vos ego, me Coelum regit</u> {*additional underlining*}. {§}
Malgré la fureur de l'orage
Et des flots mutinés l'impetueuse rage,
Vaisseaux ne craignez rien, méprisez tout ce bruit,
Je vous conduis, et le Ciel me conduit.
{§}
Un Croissant
Crescit et Imperium. {§}
Au moment que le Ciel à la Mer me fit voir,
Il me donna sur elle un absolu pouvoir,
Que toute la nature admire
Et même plus je crois, plus s'accroît mon Empire.

[36] L'Estoile du Pole
Cœlo manet, et regit {§}
Je découvre aux vaisseaux une route assurée
Sur la plaine azurée
Et du haut du Ciel où je suis
Je les éclaire et les conduis.

Un Timon.
C'est à moi de régir. {§}
Vous par qui les vaisseaux d'une course soudaine
Se meuvent sur l'humide plaine
Vôtre gloire est d'agir
La mienne est de regir.

Une Galère
Obsequio potens
Comme la force d'une galère consiste dans la prompte et pleine obeïssance de la [36v] Chiourme à la voix de celui qui les conduit: de même la puissance du commandement maritime consiste dans l'exacte observation des ordres de Sa Majesté.
{§}
Un Trident
Idem me fulmenque regit
Pour dire que le Roi, qui est maître sur la mer, l'est aussi par-tout ailleurs.
{§}
Pour l'Agenda du Roi touchant la Marine
L'Étoille du Pole.
Me suspicit omnis Navita.
Pour dire qu'il n'y a aucune puissance sur la mer, qui ne révere celle de Sa

Majesté.

[37] Pour l'Ordinaire des Guerres[19]

Un Foudre
Tela sueta Jovis
La {Le} Foudre est l'arme ordinaire de Jupiter, et la plus redoutable de toutes. L'Ordinaire des Guerres prétend la même chose à l'égard de Sa Majesté.
{§}
Une Aigle portant un Foudre
Jovi sua tela ministrat.
C'est, à peu près, le même sens que la precedente.

Une Rose
Floret cincta armis
La Rose fleurit au milieu des épines, qui sont ses armes ordinaires: de même &c.

[37v] Pour les jetons de la Reine.[20]
Une Horloge.
Coelestes sequitur motus.
Pour dire que la piété de la Reine n'est pas moins réglée qu'une horloge, à suivre les mouvemens du Ciel.

Pour une Dame qui se plaignoit que sa destinée l'avoit toujours appelée à des choses où elle n'avoit point d'inclination, et qu'elle avoit neanmoins suivies, parceque la raison le vouloit.

Une Pierre qu'une Gruë éleve, pour
la construction d'un bâtiment.
Non où je veux, mais où je doi. {§}
La raison dispose de moi
Contre ma pente naturelle,
Et je me vois placer par elle,
Non où je veux, mais où je doi. {*additional black ink line*}

[38] Quatre devises pour mettre aux quatre coins d'une Pendule dont Monsieur le Duc de Vermandois fit présent à Monsieur le Duc du Maine[21] Colonel general des Suisses.

Une Hallebarde.
Helveticæ robur gentis.

Un Tambour
Martem accendo.

Appendix B: Charles Perrault's Discours Sur l'Art des Devises

Un Fifre.
Me lætus sequitur miles.

Une coupe pleine de vin.
In prœlia trudit inermem. {§}
 Le {Les} Corps de ces quatre Devises convient {conviennent} [38v] particulièrement aux Suisses; et les mots qui les accompagnent, disent que Monsr. le Duc du Maine est leur principale force, qu'il les anime au combat; qu'ils l'y suivent avec joie; et que son exemple les fait aller à l'occasion, quand même ils ne seroient pas armés.
{§}
Pour mettre sur les Canons

Un Soleil.
Hinc lumen et fulmen
Ekaergss
 Ekaergss, longè jaculans, est {c'est} l'épithète qu'Homere donne à Apollon, qui est le même que le Soleil: pour dire que le Soleil, le Canon, et le Roi atteignent de bien loin.

[39] Pour Monsieur de Turenne[2] [2]
Une Fusée volante.
Je meurs au plus haut de ma gloire. {§}
On admire en tous lieux la splendeur de mon cours,
L'éclat en est si grand qu'on a peine à le croire;
Je ne cesse d'agir, et m'élevant toujours,
Je meurs au plus haut de ma gloire.
{§}
 Ce qui suit, est une médaille pour le même Monsieur de Turenne.
 Un Trophée d'armes, et un Tombeau, avec un Foudre au dessus, qui s'étend et sur l'un et sur l'autre.
Clarus Fulmine quo vicit ceciditque {§}
Turenne a de son nom rempli toute la Terre,
Par les coups affreux du Tonnerre
Dont pour nous, tous les ans, Louïs armoit son bras:
Son extrême valeur, à son Roi si fidèlle,
[39v] Receut encore une splendeur nouvelle
Du Foudre malheureux qui causa son trépas.
{§}

Pour Monsieur le Cardinal de Bouillon[2] [3]
Une Rose
Arma inter purpura surgit {§}
Pour dire que ce Cardinal s'est élevé au milieu d'une infinité de grands Capitai-

nes de la même maison. {§}

Autant que ma Pourpre a de charmes,
Et renferme de doux tresors;
Autant la tige d'où je sors
Est redoutable par ses armes.
{§}

Pour M[rs]. les Secretaires du Roi,[2 4] lorsqu'ils furent réünis en un seul Collège.

Une Grenade dont on void les grains.
Tegit decoràtque corona.

[40] De même que les grains d'une Grenade sont tous réünis sous l'abri d'une Couronne qui les défend, et qui fait toute leur gloire: ainsi M[rs]. les Secretaires du Roi réünis en un seul Collège, ont l'avantage d'avoir Sa Majesté pour leur Chef, qui les protège uniquement, et qui les comble de toute sorte d'honneur, de graces, et de privilèges.

Pour la Chambre des Assûrances[2 5]
Une Anchre
Confiance et Fidélité

Les Matelots ont confiance en l'Anchre, qui de son côté leur est fidèle: ainsi les Marchands doivent se confier en la Chambre des Assûrances, qui leur tiendra ce qu'elle leur a promis.

[40v] Les Feux S[t]. Elme
Tutum iter si splendeant

On n'a plus rien à craindre quand les Feux S[t]. Elme paroissent, et promettent le calme. Ainsi quand la Chambre des Assurances a répondu d'un vaisseau, on n'a plus rien à appréhender.

{§}
Pour M[rs]. les Experts et Greffiers[2 6]
des Bâtimens.
Un Plomb.
Recti irrequieta cupido. {§}

Un plomb ne tend qu'à être droit, et ne se remuë si long tems, que pour y parvenir: Les Experts et Greffiers ne se donnent aussi tant de peine, que pour regler et écrire ce qui est de droit et de justice.

Au revers de cette devise, l'Architecture [41] est représentée tenant une Règle et un Compas; et sur un Pié-d'estail auprès d'elle est une Ecritoire et une plume, avec ces mots autour:

Omnia cum pondere, ñumero, et mensura.
{§}
Pour un Chevalier du Carrousel {§}
Un Soleil dont les rayons donnent sur un lion
Ingenitas geminat vires. {§}

Appendix B: Charles Perrault's Discours Sur l'Art des Devises

De la Nature et de ma Race
Je reçois une noble audace
Une belliqueuse chaleur:
Mais à l'Astre brillant, que tout le monde adore
Je suis plus redevable encore
De ma force et de ma valeur.
{§
Pour dire que la presence du Roy et le Zele qu'Il a pour son service luy donneront encore plus de force et de valeur qu'Il n'en a reçû de La Nature et de sa naissance}

[41v] Devises pour les Jetons de l'Ordre du
Saint-Esprit.²⁷

Une Colombe environnée de flammes, avec les mots qui suivent.

Coelestis origo.	pour l'année 1665.
Candor et ardor	pour 1666.
Qui totum impleat orbem.	pour 1667.
Mens omnibus una.	pour 1668.
Virtus omnis ab illo.	pour 1669.
Ubi vult spirat	pour 1690 {1670}.
Igneus est ollis vigor.	pour 1691 {1671}.
Vis et amor.	pour 1692 {1672}.

Tous ces mots ont été employés en des années différentes, et le sens en est aisé à deviner, par le rapport qu'ils ont au Saint Esprit et à l'Ordre.

[42] Pour la Cornette de Monseigneur
le Dauphin.²⁸
Un Foudre sortant d'une Nuë
Et ipso terret in ortu.

Toutes les choses naturelles sont foibles en leur naissance; le Foudre seul, qui sort du sein de la Nuë avec éclat, et tout entouré de lumière, a de la force et se fait craindre dès le premier moment qu'il paroît. La même chose se peut dire de Moneigneur [sic] le Dauphin, que ses armes rendirent redoutable dès sa premiere enfance. Elle a été employée

Le Ciel qui le forma pour punir les coupables,
L'arma de traits si redoutables,
Que tout tremble ici bas au bruit de son courroux;
Et dès qu'il commence à paraître,
Bien qu'il ne fasse que de naître,
Le cœur le plus hardi n'ose attendre ses coups. {*additional black ink line*}

[42v] Pour une femme vertueuse.
Une Ruche

Ordre, travail, et douceur. {§}
En moi se trouvent ensemble
Ordre, travail, et douceur;
Heureuse qui me ressemble !
Plus heureux son possesseur.
{§}
Pour un homme mort en odeur de sainteté
De l'encens qui brûle.
Totum se reddit olympo.
{§}
Pour une [sic] homme célebre pour sa grande fidélité à son maitre.
Une Boussole
Indefessa fides.
Autre
Un chien ayant les piés sur un coffre [43] si plein de richesses, qu'il en sort de tous côtés.
Non sibi, sed domino.
{§}
Pour un Colonel de Dragons.[29]
Un dragon ayant les aîles éployées
Je vole au combat. {§}
Du Lion, de la Panthere
La valeur a de l'éclat;
A peine cependant, au fort de leur colère,
Courent-ils à l'adversaire,
Et moi Je vole au combat.

Pour Monseigneur, sur la pise [sic] de Philisbourg.[30]
Pallas foudroyant les Titans.
Patris sic fulmina torquet.
C'est ainsi que son bras toujours victorieux
[43v] Pressé d'une juste colère,
Pour punir les audacieux
Lance la [sic] Foudre de son Pere.
§
Pour une Cornette de Cavalerie[31] {§}
Une Bombe enflammée
Peream, modo frangam hostes.

Pour le Roi
Le Soleil.
L'ame et l'amour de l'Univers.
Par-tout où s'étend ma Puissance,

Appendix B: Charles Perrault's *Discours Sur l'Art des Devises*

Je répands mille biens divers;
Et suis par ma douce influence
L'ame et l'amour de l'Univers.

§

Pour une personne dont on aime tendrement la mémoire.
{De l'Encens qui brule, *additional red ink line*}
[44] Magis et post funus amatur

§

Pour les jetons de la Maison du Roi,
pendant la guerre.
Une Ruche.
Paix au dedans, guerre au dehors.

Pendant que les Moûches font la guerre, l'ordre, le travail, et la douceur continuënt dans leurs Ruches comme en pleine paix: Il en est de même de la Maison du Roi.

Pour les quatre Compagnies des Gardes du Corps.[3 2]
Un Bouclier
Servantem servat.
Unus satis omnia contra
Obvius est {it} telis
Peream modò tegam.

[44v] Le même Corps, qui est un Bouclier, devoit servir à chacune des quatre Compagnies, avec un de ces quatre mots.

Trois Devises mises aux trois côtés d'une Illumination en forme de pyramide, que je fis élever sur la terasse de mon jardin {elevée, ', que ... jardin' *has been crossed out*}, pour la Naissance de Monseig^r. le Duc de Bourgogne, le 7. Août 1682.[3 3] {§}
Un Soleil-levant.
Nascitur Orbi

{§}

Un Aiglon suivant deux Aigles
Fortes creantur fortibus.

{§}

Un grand Fleuve
Facit omnia læta.

[45] Devise pour un Auteur qui ne pille point
les autres
Un Ver à soie fesant sa Coque.
Tout est de moi dans mon ouvrage. {§}
Je fais seul, et sans bruit ma tâche toute entière,
J'en fournis la façon, j'en fournis la matière;

S'il est des ouvriers plus sçavans et meilleurs,
J'ai du moins sur eux l'avantage,
De ne rien emprunter d'ailleurs,
Tout est de moi dans mon ouvrage.

§

NOTES

[1] The notes that follow are intended to provide a factual clarification of Perrault's references to persons, institutions and events of his time. No attempt has been made here to provide a critique of the text, nor of the devices to which Perrault refers.
Monsieur le Comte de Vermandois was Louis de Bourbon, the third natural son of Louis XIV and the Duchesse de La Vallière. He was born on October 2, 1667 and named Admiral in 1669. The text is inaccurate, therefore, when it describes him as "n'ayant que cinq ans." The Comte died on November 18, 1683. See also note 21.
The halcyon ("Alcion") of his device is a mythical bird, renowned for its ability to calm the seas during its nesting period.

[2] Perhaps Menestrier, but more likely Bourséis. This, however, is conjection as attempts to find the "longue dissertation" to which Perrault refers have been unfruitful. The *Recueil des harangues prononcées de L'Académie francoise, dans leurs receptions, & en d'autres occasions différentes, depuis l'establissement de l'Académie jusqu'à présent* (2 vols., Amsterdam: Aux Dépans de La Compagnie, 1709) contains no trace of our speech.
Amable de Bourséis, Abbé de Saint-Martin-de-Cores (Autun), was born on the 5, April 1606. He was one of the founding members of the Académie Française and placed at the head of the *Académie des inscriptions* (see below) by Colbert. His erudition and controversial opinions were renowned. He died on the 2 August 1672.

[3] Jean Chapelain (1595-1674), one of the first members of the Académie Française and close associate of Colbert. Worked on the *Devises pour les tapisseries du roy*. Best known for his epic poem "La Pucelle."

[4] François Charpentier (1602-1702), charged by Colbert with the founding of the *Compagnie des Indes*. One of Perrault's main supporters in the *Querelle des anciens et des modernes*, he also composed the inscriptions for the *Grande Galerie* at Versailles, a *Traité de la peinture parlante* (1684, an explanation of certain paintings at Versailles) and some of the *Devises pour les tapisseries du roy*.

[5] Perrault's reference to the meetings in the Louvre tells us that this part of the text must postdate 1683, the year in which meetings were first held there.

[6] Admired by Le Moyne and Conrart, mentioned by Mme. de Sévigné, M. Clément (died 1679) was one of the major emblem theorists of seventeenth-century court life. For his *Regles pour la connoissance des devises*, see D. Russell's edition in *Emblematica* 1 (1986).

[7] Pierre Le Moyne (1602-1672), Jesuit poet and man of letters. One of the main emblem theorists of the century, his works included the *Devises heroiques et morales* (1649), *De l'art de regner, au Roy* (1665) and *De l'art des devises* (1666).

[8] Anne d'Autriche (1601-1666), wife of Louis XIII, mother of Louis XIV and *Régente* from 1643 until 1661. The King of Spain is presumably her father, Philippe III, who died in 1621.

[9] As stated above, the *Devises pour les tapisseries du roy* appeared in luxury manuscript form as well as in various printed editions. The British Library's manuscript version (Harley ms. 4377) bears the date 1669.

Appendix B: Charles Perrault's Discours Sur l'Art des Devises

The text that follows, and continues as far as folio 29, is virtually identical to that of the British Library and Bibliothèque nationale de France (ms. fr. 7819) manuscripts. The general introduction (fols. 13v-14, up to "pour les paroles"), with minor changes in wording, follows that of the London and Paris manuscripts, with the sole omission of a section describing the positioning of the devices on the tapestries themselves. The introduction to the "quatre saisons" (fol. 21v), however, is virtually unique to this manuscript and somewhat shorter than that given in the luxury versions.

The main body of the text contains a few variants from the luxury versions (e. g. fol. 15, line 4 of the luxury manuscripts reads "Quiconque de ma vie observera le cours," fol. 20, "se courber" has replaced "se gauchir"), as well as a spelling system that is generally more modern (e. g. "Roi" replaces "Roy," accents are used more frequently). The order of the devices follows that of the London and not the Paris manuscript: "Terræ amor et decus" precedes "Et tempora læta reducit" (fol. 22), "Miratur natura silens" precedes "Dirigit obliqua" (fols. 24v-25).

[10] The year 1662 saw the peace treaty concluded between France and the United Provinces (dominated by Holland), as well as the buying back of Dunkerque and Mardyck from the English. However, Perrault could possibly be referring to the *Traité des Pyrénées* of 1659, which included the marriage of Louis XIV to Marie-Therèse d'Autriche, daughter of Philippe IV. This brought peace with Spain, with organised celebrations continuing until 1662.

[11] Jacques Cassagnes (1636-1679), *docteur en théologie* and one of the founder members of the *Académie des inscriptions et belles lettres*. He was also elected to the Académie Française at the age of twenty-seven (in 1663). He was above all known for his sermons and for the satirical attacks inflicted upon him by Boileau.

[12] The *Trésor royal* was the name given to the *Trésor de l'epargne* after 1664. It had been reorganised by Colbert after Fouquet's disgrace in 1661. Each year the *Trésor royal* (like the *Ordinaire des guerres* and the *Parties casuelles*) minted, at great expense, a series of golden *jetons*. After 1672 these would carry the inscription "Tresor Royal" or "Aerarium Regium." For a description of the *jetons* of the *Trésor royal* for the years 1693 and 1694, see Jacquiot, vol. 3, pages 652-59.

[13] It is possible that the peace to which Perrault is referring is in fact that of 1678, created by the treaties of Nimègue between France and Holland and between France and Spain. For a discussion of the theme of Louis XIV as Hercules, see Jacquiot, vol. 3, page 655.

[14] The Triple Alliance of La Haye had been signed in 1668 between the United Provinces, England and Sweden, in a bid to halt French military ambitions. However the years that followed saw several important French victories.

[15] Created under Louis XII, the *Parties casuelles* or *Revenus casuels* was the name given to revenue received from the sale of official positions. *Jetons* were minted as from 1616. See Jacquiot, vol. 3, page 692 for the *Parties casuelles*'s rainbow device of 1694.

[16] The administration of the *Bâtiments du roi* minted *jetons* as from the fourteenth century. In the seventeenth century they would normally carry the inscription "Ædificiorum regis" or "Bastimens du roy." The "douze maisons" would include such palaces as Fontainebleau, Versailles and Marly. The theme of human ingenuity as surpassing the weight of the stones (thus "Nec pondus obsulit" fol. 33v and "Mens agitat molem" fol. 34v) was a particularly common one. For the *jetons* of the years 1688 and 1690-1694, see Jacquiot, vol. 3, pages 660-77.

[17] For possibilities see notes 10 and 13 above.

[18] These would be struck in two versions, one bearing the king's portrait, the other that of the *Admiral de France*. Only after 1694 did the word "Marine" feature systematically. For the years 1692-1693, see Jacquiot, vol. 3, pages 684-89.

[19] Essentially the regular corpus of the armed forces, it minted its own *jetons* from the reign of Louis XIII. For those of the years 1686, 1688, 1689 and 1691, see Jacquiot, vol. 3, pages 678-81.

[20] Presumably Anne d'Autriche. As daughter of Philippe III of Spain, much emphasis was placed on the importance of a pious education, although little attention was paid to her intellectual formation. Her final years were given to works of charity and to frequent retreats to the Abbaye du Val-de-Grâce, for the construction of which she had been responsible. See also note 8 above.

[21] Louis-Auguste de Bourbon, duc du Maine (1670-1736), the second son of Louis XIV and the Marquise de Montespan. "Legitimised" in 1673 and made *Colonel général des Suisses et Grison* on February 1, 1674, he was much favoured by Louis XIV. He was, however, according to Saint Simon, very weak in battle.

It seems likely that the clock in question would have been presented in 1674, when the duc du Maine became *Général des Suisses*. In any case, it could not have been any later than 1683, the year when Vermandois, his half-brother (see also note 1), died. We should remember, therefore, that Perrault's claims made below—the duke was an example to his men, their "principale force," "il les anime au combat"—are referring to a child aged between three and thirteen. They are thus highly rhetorical and in keeping with the "culte de l'enfant prodige" of the time.

[22] Henri de la Tour d'Auvergne (1611-1675), son of Henri duc de Bouillon and of Elisabeth, the daughter of William of Orange. After a long and illustrious military career, he died in battle near Salzbach.

[23] Emmanuel-Théodose de la Tour d'Auvergne, Cardinal de Bouillon (1644-1715, appointed cardinal in 1669). Perrault's comment refers to the fact that he was part of the illustrious Tour d'Auvergne family, which included his father Fréderic-Maurice de la Tour d'Auvergne, duc de Bouillon (1605-1652, renowned above all for his part in the siege of Maestricht of 1632), and his grandfather Henri de la Tour d'Auvergne, duc de Bouillon and *Maréchal de France* (1555-1623). His uncle was Turenne (see note 22). The cardinal himself was disgraced after a letter of his satirising Louis XIV was intercepted by Louvois. He was, however, responsible for Turenne's mausoleum, now in the Invalides.

[24] These were officers charged with the signing of official letters. In practice the post was purely honorific and highly sought after on account of the privileges that it brought. These included exemption from various forms of taxes and hereditary nobility. In 1673 there were 240 *Sécretaires du roi*.

[25] Maritime insurance was known from the fifteenth century, but became highly developed in the seventeenth century. In 1686 a *Compagnie générale des assurances et grosses aventures* was created in Paris by edict. Fire and life insurances, by contrast, did not appear until the eighteenth century.

[26] The *Greffiers* had the task of receiving, making known and administering the records of legal judgements. They existed for various forms of legal documentation (e.g. appeals, births and marriages) as well as for the *Bâtiments*. Taxes were raised on their services, of which a portion went to the king and a portion was retained by the *Greffier*.

[27] The *Ordre du Saint-Esprit* was founded by Henri III in 1578 as part of the celebrations in honour of his accession to the throne in 1574. The order brought together the king and leaders of the Catholic church. For the *Médailles de la promotion des Chevaliers du Saint-Esprit* of 1689 (with reference to those of 1662), see Jacquiot, vol. 3, pages 482-86.

[28] Louis, duc de Bourgogne, grandson of Louis XIV, father of Louis XV and Dauphin de France. He was born on the 6 August 1682 and died on the 18 February 1712. A "Cornette" was a military banner often bearing a device. In his *Mémoires de ma vie* (quoted by Jacquiot,

Appendix B: Charles Perrault's Discours Sur l'Art des Devises

vol. 1, page XCVI), Perrault refers to this device as follows:

> Mr. Colbert demanda une Devise pour Monseigneur le Dauphin qui n'avoit encore que trois ou quatre ans. Jeus le bonheur d'en faire une qui fut agréée preferablement à plusieurs autres Le corps est un esclat de Tonnerre qui sort de la nüe avec ce mot *Et ipso terret in ortu*. Elle fut mise sur les enseignes du Regiment de Monseigneur le Dauphin et sur les casaques de ses gardes.

The abrupt halt in our text at this point ("Elle a été employée") suggests the passage is unfinished. One might speculate that Perrault was to point out, as in the *Mémoires de ma vie*, that the device was used as military decoration. Monseigneur le Dauphin was given the charge of the army in Germany from 1701–1703, but he met with little success.

[29] The *Dragons* were a troupe of mounted armed infantrymen. They were infamous for their aggressive conversion of the Protestants who were forced to lodge them in times of war.

[30] Louis de France (1661–1711), the Grand Dauphin, son of Louis XIV (thus "Lance la Foudre de son Pere," fol. 43v) and father of the duc de Bourgogne. It was for Monseigneur that Bossuet, his tutor, wrote the *Discours sur l'histoire universelle*. He followed a distinguished military career, including the successful taking of Philippsburg in 1688, to which Perrault refers here. For further information on medals commemorating Philippsburg, see Jacquiot, vol.1, pages 44–47 and vol. 3, pages 461–65.

[31] A "Cornette" is a military banner often bearing a device (see also fol. 42). The term could also refer to the officer charged with carrying the banner.

[32] The personal guards of the king. The first company was supposedly Scottish, the others French. All members belonged to the nobility. Their banners and buttons also bore the king's "Nec pluribus impar" device.

[33] It is generally accepted that he was born at Versailles on the 6 August 1682. See also note 28.

Bibliography

Quotations of the works of the four primary authors are taken from the following editions:

RENÉ DESCARTES
Discours de la méthode:
Descartes, René. *Discours de la méthode*. Ed. Geneviève Rodis-Lewis. Paris: Flammarion, 1966.
Meditationes de prima philosophia:
Descartes, René. *Œuvres philosophiques*. Ed. Ferdinand Alquié. Vol. 2. Paris: Garnier, 1963-73. 3 vols.
All other works:
Descartes, René. *Œuvres de Descartes*. Ed. Charles Adam and Paul Tannery. 12 vols. Paris: Vrin, 1964-76.

TRISTAN L'HERMITE
Les Amours
Tristan L'Hermite. *Les Amours et autres poésies choisies*. Ed. Pierre Camo. Paris: Garnier, 1925.
"Enfin guery de la folie…"
Poem that originally appeared in Toussainct de Bray's *Recueil des plus beaux vers* (1626-[27]). I have followed Jean-Pierre Chauveau's edition in "Les Débuts poétiques de Tristan," *Cahiers Tristan L'Hermite* 5 (1983), 40-46.
La Lyre
Tristan L'Hermite. *La Lyre*. Ed. Jean-Pierre Chauveau. Geneva: Droz, 1977.
Les Plaintes d'Acante
Tristan L'Hermite. *Les Plaintes d'Acante et autres œuvres*. Ed. Jacques Madeleine. Paris: Cornélie, 1909.
Les Vers héroïques
Tristan L'Hermite. *Les Vers héroïques*. Ed. Catherine Grisé. Geneva: Droz, 1967.
All other works:
Quotations are taken from the original editions as cited.

JEAN DE LA FONTAINE
Les Amours de Psyché et de Cupidon:

La Fontaine, Jean de. *Les Amours de Psyché et de Cupidon*. Ed. Michel Jeanneret. Paris: Livre de Poche, 1991.

Contes et nouvelles en vers:

La Fontaine, Jean de. *Contes et nouvelles en vers*. Ed. Georges Couton. Paris: Garnier, 1985.

Fables:

La Fontaine, Jean de. *Fables choisies mises en vers*. Ed. Georges Couton. Paris: Garnier, 1990.

All other works:

La Fontaine, Jean de. *Œuvres complètes: II: Œuvres diverses*. Ed. Pierre Clarac. Paris: Gallimard, 1991.

CHARLES PERRAULT

Les Contes

Perrault, Charles. *Les Contes*. Ed. Georges Rouger. Paris: Bordas, 1991.

Discours sur l'art des devises

See Appendix B. This edition of the *Discours* first appeared in my "*Discours Sur l'Art des Devises*: An Edition of A Previously Unidentified and Unpublished Text by Charles Perrault," *Emblematica* 7.1 (1993), 99-144.

Mémoires de ma vie

Perrault, Charles. *Mémoires de ma vie*. Ed. Antoine Picon. Paris: Macula, 1993.

La Peinture

Perrault, Charles. *La Peinture*. Ed. Jean-Luc Gautier-Gentès. Geneva: Droz, 1992.

All other works:

Quotations are taken from the original editions as cited.

OTHER SOURCES

Abraham, Claude. *Tristan L'Hermite*. Boston: Twayne, 1980.

Abregé de l'histoire des Roys de France avec leurs effigies, depuis Pharamond jusques au Roy Louys XIII à present regnant. Rouen: David Ferrand, 1636.

Adam, Charles and Paul Tannery. Introduction and Notes. *Œuvres de Descartes*. By René Descartes. 12 vols. Paris: Vrin, 1964-76.

Adams, Alison. "Glasgow University Library SMAdd.392 and the Printed Versions of Tristan L'Hermite's Poetry." *Emblems and the Manuscript Tradition*. Ed. Laurence Grove. Glasgow: Glasgow Emblem Studies, 1997. 141-57.

—. Introduction. *L'Hecatongraphie*. By Gilles Corrozet. Geneva: Droz, 1997. ix-lxvii.

Adams, Alison, Stephen Rawles and Alison Saunders. *A Bibliography of French Emblem Books to 1700*. Geneva: Droz, 1999.

Æsop. *Fables of Æsop*. Trans. S. A. Handford. London: Penguin, 1964.

Alciato, Andrea. *Emblematum libellus*. Paris: Chrestien Wechel, 1536.

—. *Emblematum libellus*. Venice: Aldus, 1546.

—. *Emblematum liber*. Augsburg: Heinrich Steyner, 1531.

Alquié, Ferdinand. Introduction and Notes. *Œuvres philosophiques*. By René Descartes. 3 vols. Paris: Garnier, 1963-73. Vol.1 1-19 and passim, vol. 2 1-4 and passim, vol. 3 1-3 and passim.

Aneau, Barthélemy. *Décades de la description, forme et vertu naturelle des animaulx, tant raisonnables que brutz*. Lyons: B. Arnoullet, 1549.

—. *Imagination poétique*. Lyons: Macé Bonhomme, 1552.

—. *Picta poesis*. Lyons: Macé Bonhomme, 1552.

Annuæ litteræ Societatis Iesu Anni CI>. I>C. X. Ad Patres et fratres eiusdem societatis. Dillingen: Veuve Ioannes Mayer, 1610.

Annæ litteratæ Societatis Iesu, Anni CI>. I>C. XI. Ad Patres et fratres eiusdem societatis. Dillingen: Melchior Algeyer, 1611.

Apuleius. *Metamorphoses*. Ed. J. Arthur Hanson. 2 vols. Cambridge MA: Harvard UP, 1989.

Arias Montano, Benedito. *Humanae salutis monumenta*. Antwerp: Plantin, 1571.

Baillet, Adrien. *La Vie de Monsieur Descartes*. 2 vols. Paris: Daniel Horthemels, 1691.

Bagley, Ayers. "Some Pedagogical Uses of the Emblem in Sixteenth- and Seventeenth-Century England." *Emblematica* 7.1 (1993): 39-60.

Barchilon, Jacques and Peter Flinders. *Charles Perrault*. Boston: Twayne, 1981.

Bassan, Fernande. "La Fontaine héritier d'Esope et de Pilpay." *Comparative Literature Studies* 7 (1970): 161-78.

Bassy, Alain-Marie. *Les Fables de La Fontaine: Quatre siècles d'illustration*. Paris: Promodis, 1986.

Bath, Michael. "The Iconography of Time." *The Telling Image: Explorations in the Emblem*. Eds. Ayers Bagley, Edward Griffin and Austin McLean. New York: AMS, 1996. 29-68.

—. *The Image of the Stag: Iconographic Themes in Western Art*. Baden-Baden: Verlag Valentin Koerner, 1992.

—. "Weeping Stags and Melancholy Lovers: The Iconography of *As You Like It*, II, i." *Emblematica* 1.1 (1986): 13-52.

Baudoin, Jean. *Recueil d'emblèmes divers*. Paris: Jacques Villery, 1638-39.

Bayley, Peter. *French Pulpit Oratory 1598-1650: A Study of Themes and Styles*. Cambridge: Cambridge UP, 1980.

Bergal, Irene. "Discursive Strategies in Early French Emblem Books." *Emblematica* 2.2 (1987): 273-91.

—. "Word and Picture: Erasmus' *Parabolae* in La Perrière's *Morosophie*." *Bibliothèque d'Humanisme et Renaissance* 47.1 (1985): 113-23.

Bernadin, N.-M. *Un Précurseur de Racine: Tristan L'Hermite, sieur du Solier (1601-1655): Sa Famille, sa vie, ses œuvres*. Paris: Picard, 1895.

Bèze, Théodore de. *Icones*. Geneva: J. Laon, 1580.

Bible [*La Sainte Bible*]. Amsterdam: P. and J. Blaeu, 1687.

Bibliothèque nationale de France (Département des Estampes). *Pièce Te 120*. Bibliothèque nationale de France, Paris.

—. *Série Qb 1 in folio*. Bibliothèque nationale de France, Paris.

Bibliothèque nationale de France (Département des Manuscrits, Cabinet des Titres).

"Reçu" (thought to be in the hand of Tristan L'Hermite). Pièces Originales 1711. Bibliothèque nationale de France, Paris.

Birberick, Anne L. *Reading Undercover: Audience and Authority in Jean de La Fontaine*. Lewisburg: Bucknell UP, 1998.

Bordonove, Georges. *Fouquet: Coupable ou victime?* Paris: Pygmalion, 1976.

Bossuet, Jacques Bénigne. *Œuvres*. Ed. Abbé Velat and Yvonne Champaillet. Paris: Gallimard, 1961.

Bouhours, Dominique. *Les Entretiens d'Ariste et d'Eugene*. Paris: Sebastien Mabre-Cramoisy, 1671.

Bourgoin, Auguste. *Un Bourgeois de Paris lettré au XVIIe siècle: Valentin Conrart, premier secrétaire perpetuel de l'Académie Française et son temps, sa vie, ses écrits, son rôle dans l'histoire littéraire de la première partie du XVIIe siècle*. Paris, 1883. Geneva: Slatkine, 1971.

British Museum. *A Catalogue of the Harleian Manuscripts, in the British Museum: With Indexes of Persons, Places and Matters*. Vol. 3. [London]: British Museum, 1808. 4 vols.

Brody, Jules. "La Fontaine, *Les Vautours et les pigeons* (VII, 8): An Intertextual Reading." *Convergences: Rhetoric and Poetic in Seventeenth-Century France*. Eds. David L. Rubin and Mary B. McKinley. Colombus: Ohio State UP, 1989. 143-60.

Camo, Pierre. Préface. *Les Amours et autres poésies choisies*. By Tristan L'Hermite. Paris: Garnier, 1925. v-xxvi.

Carriat, Amédée. *Tristan L'Hermite: Choix de pages*. Limoges: Rougerie, 1960.

—. *Tristan ou l'éloge d'un poète*. Limoges: Rougerie, 1955.

Cats, Jacob. *Proteus*. Rotterdam: Pieter Van Waesberge, 1627.

Charpentier, Françoise. "De Colonna à La Fontaine: Le Nom de Poliphile." *L'Intelligence du passé: Les faits, l'écriture et les sens: Mélanges offerts à Jean Lafond*. Eds. Pierre Aquilon, Jacques Chupeau and others. Tours: Université François Rabelais, 1988. 369-78.

Chatelain, Jean-Marc. *Livres d'emblèmes et de devises: Une Anthologie (1531-1735)*. Paris: Klincksieck, 1993.

Chauveau, Jean-Pierre. "Les Débuts poétiques de Tristan." *Cahiers Tristan L'Hermite* 5 (1983): 40-46.

—. Introduction. *La Lyre*. By Tristan L'Hermite. Geneva: Droz, 1977. ix-lxxvi.

—. "L'Ode à Olympe: Est-elle de Tristan." *Cahiers Tristan L'Hermite* 1 (1979): 36-46.

Chomsky, Noam. *Cartesian Linguistics: A Chapter in the History of Rationalistic Thought*. New York: Harper & Row, 1966.

Clarac, Pierre. Introduction and Notes. *Œuvres complètes: II: Œuvres diverses*. By Jean de La Fontaine. Paris: Gallimard, 1991. ix-l and 795-1098.

Clément, [M.]. "Regles pour la connoissance des devises, par M. …, Conseiller en la Cour des Aydes." Ed. Daniel Russell. "Two Seventeenth-Century Treatises on the Art of the Device." *Emblematica* 1 (1986): 79-106.

Clère, Jules. *Histoire de l'Ecole de La Flèche*. La Flèche: E. Jourdain, 1853.

Colletet, Francois, ed. *Les Muses illustres*. Paris: Louis Chamhoudry, 1658.
Collinet, Jean-Pierre. "La Fontaine et ses illustrateurs." *Œuvres complètes: I: Fables: Contes et nouvelles*. By Jean de La Fontaine. Ed. Jean-Pierre Collinet. Paris: Gallimard, 1986. lxiii-cxlviii.
—. *Le Monde littéraire de La Fontaine*. Paris: Presses Universitaires de France, 1970. Geneva: Slatkine, 1989.
Colonna, Francesco. *Hypnerotomachia Poliphili*. Venice: Aldus Manutius, 1499. New York: Garland, 1976.
Conan, Michael. Postface. *Le Labyrinthe de Versailles*. By Charles Perrault. Paris: Du Moniteur, 1982.
Conrart, Valentin, ed. *Recueil Conrart*. Arsenal ms. 3131. Bibliothèque de l'Arsenal, Paris.
—. *Recueil Conrart*. Arsenal ms. 3135. Bibliothèque de l'Arsenal, Paris.
—. *Recueil Conrart*. Arsenal ms. 3307. Bibliothèque de l'Arsenal, Paris.
—. *Recueil Conrart*. Arsenal ms. 4171. Bibliothèque de l'Arsenal, Paris.
—. *Recueil Conrart*. Arsenal ms. 5131. Bibliothèque de l'Arsenal, Paris.
—. *Recueil Conrart*. Arsenal ms. 5132. Bibliothèque de l'Arsenal, Paris.
—. *Recueil Conrart*. Arsenal ms. 5414. Bibliothèque de l'Arsenal, Paris.
—. *Recueil Conrart*. Arsenal ms. 5417. Bibliothèque de l'Arsenal, Paris.
—. *Recueil Conrart*. Arsenal ms. 5418. Bibliothèque de l'Arsenal, Paris.
—. *Recueil Conrart*. Arsenal ms. 5420. Bibliothèque de l'Arsenal, Paris.
Corrozet, Gilles. *Les Fables du très ancien Esope*. Paris: D. Janot, 1542.
—. *Hecatomgraphie*. Paris: Janot, 1540.
Coustau, Pierre. *Pegma cum narrationibus philosophicis*. Lyons: Macé Bonhomme, 1555. Ed. Stephen Orgel. New York: Garland, 1979.
—. *Le Pegme*. Trans. Lanteaume de Romieu. Lyons: Macé Bonhomme, 1555.
Couton, Georges. *Écritures codées: Essais sur l'allégorie au XVIIe siècle*. Paris: Aux Amateurs de Livres, 1990.
—. Introduction and Notes. *Contes et nouvelles en vers*. By Jean de La Fontaine. Paris: Garnier, 1985. i-lii and 381-435.
—. Introduction and Notes. *Fables choisies mises en vers*. By Jean de La Fontaine. Paris: Garnier, 1990. i-xliv and 403-560.
—. *La Poétique de La Fontaine: Deux études: La Fontaine et l'art des emblèmes: Du Pensum aux* Fables. Paris: Presses Universitaires de France, 1957.
Covarrubias, Sebastián de. *Emblemas morales*. Madrid: Por Luis Sanchez, 1610. Ed. Carmen Bravo-Villasante. Madrid: Fundación Universitaria Espagñola, 1978.
Culpin, David. "Perrault as Moralist: *Les Hommes illustres*." *French Studies* 52.2 (1998): 142-51.
Dalla Valle, Daniela. "A Propos de *La Maison d'Astrée*." *Cahiers Tristan L'Hermite* 6 (1984): 31-37.
Daly, Peter M. *Literature in the Light of the Emblem: Structural Parallels Between the Emblem and Literature in the Sixteenth and Seventeenth Centuries*. Toronto: U of Toronto P, 1979.
Danner, Richard. "La Fontaine's *Fables*, Book X: The Labyrinth Hypothesis." *L'Es-*

prit Créateur 21.4 (1981): 90-98.

—. *Patterns of Irony in the* Fables *of La Fontaine*. Athens: Ohio UP, 1985.

Dandrey, Patrick. "De l'Art des devises à la poétique de l'apologue: La Préface des *Fables* de La Fontaine (1668) à la lumière du traité des *Devises* du P. Le Moyne (1666)." *Le Fablier* 7 (1995): 105-23.

David, Ioannes. *Duodecim specula Deum aliquando videre desideranti concinnata*. Antwerp: Plantin, 1610.

—. *Typus occasionis in quo receptae commoda neglectae vero incommoda, personato schemate propantur*. Antwerp: Plantin, 1605.

DeJean, Joan. "La Fontaine's *Psyché*: The Reflecting Pool of Classicism." *L'Esprit Créateur* 21.4 (1981): 99-109.

Demetz, Peter. "The Elm and the Vine: Notes towards the History of a Marriage Topos." *Publications of the Modern Language Association* 73 (1958): 521-32.

Descartes, René. *Discours de la méthode*. Ed. Geneviève Rodis-Lewis. Paris: Flammarion, 1966.

—. *Œuvres de Descartes*. Ed. Charles Adam and Paul Tannery. 12 vols. Paris: Vrin, 1964-76.

—. *Œuvres philosophiques*. Ed. Ferdinand Alquié. Vol. 2. Paris: Garnier, 1963-73. 3 vols.

Desprechins, Anne. "Images de «L'Astrée»: Etude de la réception du texte à travers les tapisseries." *Revue de l'Histoire Littéraire de la France* 81.3 (1981): 355-66.

Devises pour les tapisseries du roi. Eds. Marc Fumaroli and Marianne Grivel. Paris: Herscher, 1988.

Devises pour les tapisseries du roy. Bibliothèque nationale de France (Département des Manuscrits), Paris. Ms. fr. 7819.

Devises pour les tapisseries du roy. British Library, London. Harley ms. 4377.

Devises pour les tapisseries du roy. National Library, Vienna. Series-nova 24204.

Devises pour les tapisseries du roy. Paris: C. Blageart, 1668.

Dexter, Greta. "Guillaume de La Perrière." *Bibliothèque d'Humanisme et Renaissance* 17 (1955): 56-73.

—. Introduction. *Le Théâtre des bons engins*. By Guillaume de La Perrière. Gainesville: Scholars' Facsimiles & Reprints, 1964. i-xx.

Dieckmann, Liselotte. *Hieroglyphics: The History of a Literary Symbol*. Saint Louis: Washington UP, 1970.

Dimler, Richard. "A Short Title Listing of Jesuit Emblem Books." *Emblematica* 2 (1987): 138-87.

Donné, Boris. *La Fontaine et la poétique du songe: Récit, rêverie et allégorie dans Les Amours de Psyché*. Paris: Champion, 1995.

Du Bray, Toussainct, ed. *Recueil des plus beaux vers*. Paris: Toussainct Du Bray, 1626-[27].

Dundas, Judith. "Emblems and the Art of Painting: *Pictura* and Purpose." *Emblems and Art History*. Eds. Alison Adams and Laurence Grove. Glasgow: Glasgow Emblem Studies, 1996. 69-96.

Emblemes Politiques: Presenté a son Eminence. Paris: n.p., 1649.
Erasmus. *Adagiorum opus*. Basle: Froben, 1528.
—. *Enchiridion militis christiani*. [Strasbourg]: Apud Felicem Argentinam, [1522].
Faene, Gabriel. *Cent Fables*. Trans. Charles Perrault. Paris: J.-B. Coignard, 1699.
—. *Cent Fables*. Trans. Charles Perrault. London: Darres et Du Bosc, 1743.
Félibien, André. *Description de la Grotte de Versailles*. Paris: Imprimerie Royale, 1676.
Flores mei fructus honoris et honestatis. La Flèche: n.p., 1620.
Fontaine, Nicolas. *Dictionnaire chretien où sur differens tableaux de la nature, l'on apprend par l'ecriture et les Saints Peres a voir Dieu peint dans tous ses ouvrages et a passer des choses visibles aux invisibles*. Paris: Elie Josset, 1691.
Fumaroli, Marc. "Un Art royal." *Devises pour les tapisseries du roi*. Ed. Marianne Grivel and Marc Fumaroli. Paris: Herscher, 1988. 7-17.
—. *Le Poète et le roi: Jean de La Fontaine en son siècle*. Paris: Falloir, 1997.
Furetière, Antoine. *Dictionnaire universel*. 3 vols. The Hague and Rotterdam: A. and R. Leers, 1690.
Gardien, [M.] "Discours sur les devises, emblesmes, et revers de medailles." Ed. Daniel Russell. "Two Seventeenth-Century Treatises on the Art of the Device." *Emblematica* 1 (1986): 79-106.
Gaudini, Claire. "La Lumière cartésienne: Métaphore et phénomène optique." *Biblio 17: Actes de New Orleans*. Ed. Francis L. Lawrence. Paris: Biblio 17, 1982. 319-36.
Gaudriault, Raymond. *Filigranes et autres caractéristiques des papiers fabriqués en France aux XVIIe et XVIIIe siècles*. Paris: CNRS, 1995.
Gautier-Gentès, Jean-Luc. Introduction. *La Peinture*. By Charles Perrault. Geneva: Droz, 1992. 9-80.
Giard, Lucy. "Le Système éducatif des jésuites à l'époque de Descartes." *René Descartes (1596-1650): Célébrations nationales du quadricentaire de sa naissance: Actes du colloque universitaire: La Formation de Descartes*. Ed. Jean Petit. La Flèche: Prytanée National Militaire, 1997. 199-225.
Gibson, Boyce. "La «Géométrie» de Descartes au point de vue de sa méthode." *Revue de Métaphysique et de Morale* 4 (1896): 386-98.
Gomberville, Marin Le Roy de. *La Doctrine des mœurs*. Paris: Sevestre, 1646.
Graham, David. "De la haine de l'autre à l'horreur de soi: Conception et représentation du corps dans les *Devises et emblesmes d'amour moralisez* d'Albert Flamen." *Biblio 17: Le Corps au XVIIe siècle*. Ed. Ronald W. Tobin. Paris: Biblio 17, 1995. 161-76.
—. "Pour une rhétorique de l'emblème: *l'Art des emblèmes* du Père Claude-François Menestrier." *PFSCL* 14.26 (1987): 13-36.
—. "'Voiez icy en ceste histoire…': Cross-Reference, Self-Reference and Frame-Breaking in some French Emblems." *Emblematica* 7.1 (1993): 1-24.
Grimm, Jürgen. "Stratégies de désorientation dans les 'Fables' de La Fontaine." *Ouverture et dialogue: Mélanges offerts à Wolfgang Leiner à l'occasion de son soixantième anniversaire*. Eds. Ulrich Döring, Antiopy Lyroudias and Rainer Zaiser.

Tübingen: Narr, 1988. 175-91.
Grisé, Catherine. Introduction. *Les Vers héroïques*. By Tristan L'Hermite. Geneva: Droz, 1967. 7-27.
—. *The Poetry of Tristan L'Hermite*. Diss. U. Toronto, 1964.
—. "Towards a New Biography of Tristan L'Hermite." *Revue de l'Université d'Ottawa* 36 (1966): 295-316.
Grove, Laurence. "*Discours sur l'Art des Devises*: A Previously Unidentified and Unpublished Text by Charles Perrault." *Emblematica* 7.1 (1993): 99-144.
—. "Les *Fables* et les emblèmes: L'Influence de Guillaume Guéroult." *Fabuleux La Fontaine*. Eds. Kees Meerhoff and Paul J. Smith. Amsterdam: Rodopi, 1996. 64-71.
—. "La Fontaine, Emblematics and the Plastic Arts: *Les Amours de Psyché* and *Le Songe de Vaux*." *Emblems and Art History*. Eds. Alison Adams and Laurence Grove. Glasgow: Glasgow Emblem Studies, 1996. 23-39.
—. "Reading Scève's *Délie*: The Case of the Emblematic Ivy." *Emblematica* 6.1 (1992): 1-15.
—. "Tristan L'Hermite, Emblematics and Early-Modern Reading Practices in the Light of Glasgow University Library SMAdd.392." *Emblems and the Manuscript Tradition*. Ed. Laurence Grove. Glasgow: Glasgow Emblem Studies, 1997. 159-92.
—. "The Use and Re-Use of Jesuit Emblematics in Seventeenth-Century France." Forthcoming in *Emblematica*.
Grove, Laurence and Daniel Russell. *The French Emblem: Bibliography of Secondary Sources*. Geneva: Droz, 2000.
Guéroult, Guillaume. *Description des animaux.*. Lyons: Balthazar Arnoullet, 1549.
—. *Le Premier livre des emblemes*. Lyons: Balthazar Arnoullet, 1550. Ed. De Vaux de Lancey. Rouen: Lainé, 1937.
—. *Second livre de la description des animaux, contenant le blason des oyseaux*. Lyons: Balthazar Arnoullet, 1550.
Hall, H. Gaston. "*Contaminatio* in a Fable by La Fontaine (1,3)." *PFSCL* 11 (1979): 91-106.
Haudent, Guillaume. *Trois centz soixãnte & six apologues d'Esope*. Rouen: Iehan Leprest, 1547. Ed. Charles Lormier. Rouen: Société des Bibliophiles Normands, 1877.
Henkel, Arthur and Albrecht Schöne. *Emblemata: Handbuch zur Sinnbildkunst des XVI und XVII Jahrhunderts*. 2 vols. Stuttgart: J.B. Metzlersche, 1967.
History of Abraham Tapestries. c. 1540. Hampton Court Palace, Hampton Court.
Holbein, Hans. *The Ambassadors*. 1533. National Gallery, London.
Horapollo. *De Sacris notis et sculpturis libri duo, ubi ad fidem vetusti codicis manu scripti restituta sunt loca permulta corrupta ante ac deplorata*. Paris: Kerver, 1551.
—. *De la signification des notes hiéroglyphiques des Ægyptiens, c'est à dire des figures par les quelles ilz escripvoient leurs mystères secretz et les choses sainctes et devines*. Paris: Kerver, 1543.

Hugo, Hermann. *Pia desideria*. Antwerp: Heinrich Aertssen, 1624.

Imago primi saeculi Societatis Iesu. Antwerp: Balthazar Moretus, 1640.

In anniversarium Henrici Magni obitus diem lacrymæ collegii flexiensis regii societatis Iesu. La Flèche: Rexe, 1611.

Jacquiot, Josèphe. *Medailles et jetons de Louis XIV d'après le manuscrit de Londres, Add. 31908*. 4 vols. Paris: Klincksieck, 1968.

Jeanneret, Michel. Introduction and Notes. *Les Amours de Psyché et de Cupidon*. By Jean de La Fontaine. Paris: Livre de Poche, 1991. 5-42 and 223-310.

Johnson, L. W. "*Amorum emblemata*: Tristan L'Hermite and the Emblematic Tradition." *Renaissance Quarterly* 21 (1968): 429-41.

Jouvancy, Joseph de. *Magistris scholarum inferiorum societatis Jesu de ratione discendi et dociendi Congregationis Generalis XIV*. Paris: C. Jombert and J. Mongé, 1711.

Junius, Hadrianus. *Emblemata*. Antwerp: Plantin, 1565.

Jurèn, Vladimir. "Le Jeton français et la littérature emblématique." *XVIIe Siècle* 158 (1988): 21-40.

Klein, Robert. "La Théorie de l'expression figurée dans les traités italiens sur les imprese 1555-1612." *Bibliothèque d'Humanisme et Renaissance* 19 (1957): 320-42.

La Bruyère, Jean de. *Œuvres complètes*. Ed. Julien Benda. Paris: Gallimard, 1951.

La Fontaine, Jean de. *Les Amours de Psyché et de Cupidon*. Ed. Michel Jeanneret. Paris: Livre de Poche, 1991.

—. *Contes et nouvelles en vers*. Ed. Georges Couton. Paris: Garnier, 1985.

—. *Fables*. Ed. Georges Couton. Paris: Garnier, 1990.

—. *A Hundred Fables of La Fontaine with Pictures by Percy J. Billinghurst*. Carnegie Library of Pittsburgh copy. London: John Lane, 1900.

—. *Œuvres complètes: II: Œuvres diverses*. Ed. Pierre Clarac. Paris: Gallimard, 1991.

Lancey, De Vaux de. Introduction. *Le Premier livre des emblèmes*. By Guillaume Guéroult. Rouen: Lainé, 1937. ix-xlv.

Landwehr, John. *Emblem books in the Low Countries 1554-1949: A Bibliography*. Utrecht: Haentjens Dekker and Gumbert, 1970.

—. *French, Italian, Spanish and Portuguese Books of Devices and Emblems 1534-1827: A Bibliography*. Utrecht: Haentjens Dekker and Gumbert, 1976.

—. *German Emblem Books 1531-1888: A Bibliography*. Utrecht: Haentjens Dekker and Gumbert, 1972.

La Perrière, Guillaume de. *La Morosophie*. Lyons: Macé Bonhomme, 1553. Ed. Alison Saunders. Aldershot: Scolar, 1993.

—. *Le Théâtre des bons engins*. Paris: D. Janot, 1540 ns. Ed. Greta Dexter. Gainesville: Scholars' Facsimiles & Reprints, 1964. Ed. Alison Saunders. Aldershot: Scolar, 1993.

—. *Le Théâtre des bons engins*. Lyons: J. de Tournes, 1545.

La Rochefoucauld, François de. *Œuvres complètes*. Ed. L. Martin-Chauffier. Paris: Gallimard, 1964.

Laurens, Pierre. *L'Abeille dans l'ambre: Célébration de l'épigramme alexandrine à la fin de la Renaissance*. Paris: Belles Lettres, 1989.

Lecoq, Anne-Marie. *François Ier imaginaire: Symbolique et politique à l'aube de la Renaissance française*. Paris: Macula, 1987.

Le Jay, Gabriel-François. *Le Triomphe de la religion sous Louis le Grand*. Paris: G. Martin, 1687.

Le Moyne, Pierre. *De l'Art des devises*. Paris: Sebastien Mabre-Cramoisy, 1666.

—. *Saint Louys ou la sainte couronne reconquise: Poeme heroique*. Paris: Augustin Courbé, 1668.

LePage, Raymond G. "The 1668 Edition of the *Fables*: An Iconographic Interpretation." *L'Esprit Créateur* 21.4 (1981): 66-77.

Loach, Judi. "Architecture and Emblems: Issues in Interpretation." *Emblems and Art History*. Eds. Alison Adams and Laurence Grove. Glasgow: Glasgow Emblem Studies, 1996. 1-21.

—. "Emblematics Within Mainstream Education." *Abstracts*. Glasgow: Glasgow International Emblem Conference, 1990. 75.

—. "Jesuit Emblematics and the Opening of the School Year at the Collège Louis-Le-Grand." *Emblematica* 9.1 (1995): 133-76.

—. "Menestrier's Emblem Theory." *Emblematica* 2 (1987): 317-36.

Lorgues-Lapouge, Christine. "Banished to Bussy." *FMR* 34 (1988): 89-106.

Lyons, John D. "*Camera Obscura*: Image and Imagination in Descartes's *Méditations*." *Convergences: Rhetoric and Poetic in Seventeenth-Century France*. Eds. David L. Rubin and Mary B. McKinley. Colombus: Ohio State UP, 1989. 179-95.

—. "The Cartesian Reader and the Methodic Subject." *L'Esprit Créateur* 21.2 (1981): 37-47.

Mabille de Poncheville, André. *Valentin Conrart, le père de l'Académie Française*. Paris: Mercure de France, 1935.

Madeleine, Jacques. Introduction. *Les Plaintes d'Acante et autres œuvres*. By Tristan L'Hermite. Paris: Cornélie, 1909. vii-xxxi.

Malarté, Claire-Lise. *Perrault à travers la critique depuis 1960: Bibliographie annotée*. Paris: PFSCL Biblio 17, 1989.

Malherbe, François de. *Œuvres*. Ed. Antoine Adam. Paris: Gallimard, 1971.

Mannich, Johann. *Sacra emblemata*. Nuremberg: J. F. Sartorius, 1625.

Marchant de Burbure, F. *Essais historiques sur la ville et le college de La Flèche*. Angers: Veuve Pavie, 1803.

Marin, Louis. "Préface-Image: le Frontispice des contes de Perrault." *Europe* 68.739-40 (1990): 114-22.

Martin, Henri. *Catalogue des manuscrits*. Paris: Bibliothèque de l'Arsenal, 1887.

Martin, Jean. *Le Paradis terrestre*. Paris: Jean Henault, 1655.

Martinet, [Le Sieur]. *Emblemes royales a Louis le Grand*. Paris: Claude Barbin, 1673.

Massing, Jean Michel. "Erasmus and the Origin of the Emblem." *Abstracts*. Glasgow: Glasgow International Emblem Conference, 1990. 76.

McGowan, Margaret M. "Moral Intention in the Fables of La Fontaine." *Journal of the Warburg and Courtauld Institutes* 29 (1966): 264-81.

McStewart, William. "Descartes and Poetry." *Romanic Review* 29 (1938): 212-42.

Menestrier, Claude-François. *L'Art des emblemes*. Lyons: B. Coral, 1662. Ed. Stephen Orgel. New York: Garland, 1979.

—. *L'Art des emblèmes, où s'enseigne la morale par les figures de la fable, de l'histoire et de la nature*. Paris: La Caille, 1684. Ed. Stephen Orgel. New York: Garland, 1979.

—. *Description de la decoration funebre de Saint Denis pour les obseques de la Reine*. Paris: La Caille, 1683.

—. *Devise du roy, justifiée*. Paris: Michalet, 1679.

—. *Histoire du roy Louis le Grand par les médailles, emblèmes, devises, jettons, inscriptions, armoiries & autres monumens publiques, recueillis et expliquéz*. Paris: Nolin, 1689.

—. *Lettre sur l'usage d'exposer des devises dans les églises pour les décorations funèbres*. Paris: R. Pepie, 1687.

Le Mercure françois ou, la suitte de l'histoire de la paix: Commençant l'an MDCV pour suitte du Septenaire du D. Cayer, & finissant au Sacre du Tres-Chrestien Roy de France & de Navarre Loys XIII. Paris: Jean Richer, 1619.

Moderna, Nicoletto de. *The Birth of Christ*. 1510. National Museum, Vienna.

Montenay, Georgette de. *Emblemes, ou devises chrestiennes*. Lyons: Jean Marcorelle, 1571. Ed. C. N. Smith. Menston: Scolar, 1973.

Morand, Paul. *Fouquet, ou le soleil offusqué*. Paris: Gallimard, 1961. Paris: Le Grand Livre du Mois, 1996.

Morgan Zarucchi, Jeanne, see Zarucchi, Jeanne Morgan.

Mourey, Gabriel. *Le Livre des fêtes françaises*. Paris: Librairie de France, 1930.

Musæ Flexienses Ludovico XIII regi christianissimo justo pioque principi de rebellione et perfidia triumphanti canunt: Epicinium. La Flèche: n.p., 1629.

Nelson, Robert J. "Night Unto Day Unto Night: Racianian Tragedy." *La Cohérence intérieure: Etudes sur la littérature française du dix-septième siècle présentées en hommage à Judd D. Hubert*. Eds. Jacqueline Van Baelen and David Lee Rubin. Paris: Place, 1977. 95-112.

Nelson, Theodor Holm. *Literary Machines 93.1*. Sausalito CA: Mindful Press, 1993.

Nicolich, Robert N. "The Triumph of Language: The Sister Arts and Creative Activity in La Fontaine's *Songe de Vaux*." *L'Esprit Créateur* 21.4 (1981): 10-21.

Orationes variæ funebres latinæ et gallicæ, item Poemata in Depositione Corde Henrici Magni. La Flèche: n.p., 1612.

Ovid. *Tristia*. Ed. Jacques André. Paris: Les Belles Lettres, 1968.

Pace, Claire. "'La Vie des champs est la vie des héros': Images of Landscape and Rural Life and Gomberville's *La Doctrine des moeurs*." *Emblems and Art History*. Eds. Alison Adams and Laurence Grove. Glasgow: Glasgow Emblem Studies, 1996. 41-68.

Panofsky, Erwin. *Meaning in the Visual Arts*. New York: Doubleday, 1955. Harmondsworth: Penguin, 1970.

—. *Studies in Iconology*. New York: Oxford UP, 1939.

Paradin, Claude. *Devises héroïques*. Lyons: J. de Tournes and G. Gazeau, 1557. Ed.

Alison Saunders. Aldershot: Scolar Press, 1989.

—. *Devises héroïques et emblêmes de M. Claude Paradin, reveuës & augmentées de moytie.* Paris: J. Millet, 1614.

—. *Devises héroïques: Reveuës & augmentées de moitié par messire Francois d'Amboise.* Paris: Rolet Boutonne, 1622.

Pascal, Blaise. *Pensées.* Ed. Philippe Sellier. Paris: Bordas, 1991.

Passe-Temps poetiques, historiques et critiques. 2 vols. Paris: Duchesne, 1757.

Pastoureau, Michel. "Aux Origines de l'emblème: La Crise de l'héraldique européenne aux XVe et XVIe siècles." *Emblèmes et devises au temps de la Renaissance.* Ed. M.-T. Jones-Davies. Paris: Touxot, 1981. 129-36.

Paultre, Roger. *Les Images du livre: Emblèmes et devises.* Paris: Hermann, 1991.

Pederson, John. "«Les Yeux de la pensée»: A Propos d'une métaphore." *Cahiers Tristan L'Hermite* 5 (1983): 25-29.

Perrault, Charles. *Courses de testes et de bagues faittes par le roy et par les princes et seigneurs de sa cour, en l'année 1662.* Paris: Imprimerie Royale, 1669.

—. "Devise: Un Lys sur sa tige." *Passe-Temps poetiques, historiques et critiques.* Vol. 1. Paris: Duchesne, 1757. 270-71. 2 vols.

—. *Discours sur l'art des devises.* Arsenal ms. 3328 pièce 1. Bibliothèque de l'Arsenal, Paris. Ed. Laurence Grové. "*Discours Sur l'Art des Devises*: An Edition of A Previously Unidentified and Unpublished Text by Charles Perrault." *Emblematica* 7.1 (1993): 99-144.

—. "Emblème ingenieux d'un peintre." *Passe-Temps poetiques, historiques et critiques.* Vol. 1. Paris: Duchesne, 1757. 268-69. 2 vols.

—. *Histoires ou Contes du temps passé.* Paris: Claude Barbin, 1697. Ed. Jacques Barchilon. Geneva: Slatkine, 1980. Ed. Georges Rouger. Paris: Bordas, 1991.

—. *Les Hommes illustres qui ont paru en France pendant ce siècle, avec leurs portraits au naturel.* 2 vols. Paris: Antoine Dezaillier, 1696-1700.

—. *Le Labyrinthe de Versailles.* Paris: Imprimerie Royale, 1677. Ed. Michael Conan. Paris: Du Moniteur, 1982.

—. "Lettre à Monsieur Charpentier." Eds. William Brooks, Bedford Norman and Jeanne Morgan Zarucchi. *Alceste, suivi de La Querelle d'Alceste.* By Philippe Queneau. Geneva: Droz, 1994. 113-22.

—. *Mémoires de ma vie.* Ms. fr. 23991. Bibliothèque nationale de France (Département des Manuscrits), Paris. Ed. Paul Bonnefon. Paris: H. Laurens, 1909. Ed. and Trans. Jeanne Morgan Zarucchi. Columbia: U of Missouri P, 1989. Ed. Antoine Picon. Paris: Macula, 1993.

—. *La Peinture.* Ed. Jean-Luc Gautier-Gentès. Geneva: Droz, 1992.

Perrault, Charles, trans. *Cent Fables.* By Gabriel Faene. Paris: J.-B. Coignard, 1699.

—. *Cent Fables.* By Gabriel Faene. London: Darres et Du Bosc, 1743.

Perrier, Simone. "La Circulation du sens dans les *Emblemes chrestiens* de G. de Montenay (1571)." *Nouvelle Revue du XVIe Siècle* 9 (1991): 73-89.

Petit, Jean, ed. *René Descartes (1596-1650): Célébrations nationales du quadricentenaire de sa naissance: Actes du colloque universitaire: La Formation de Descartes.* La Flèche: Prytanée National Militaire, 1997.

Phaedrus. *Fabulae aesopiae quum veteres tum novae atque restituatae*. Ed. Christian Timothy Dressler. Leipzig: Teubner, 1856.
Philostratus. *Les Images ou tableaux de platte peinture*. Ed. Blaise de Vigenère. Paris: Veuve Abel L'Angelier, 1615.
Picon, Antoine. "Un Moderne paradoxal." *Mémoires de ma vie*. By Charles Perrault. Paris: Macula, 1993. 1-108.
Pièce Te 120, see Bibliothèque nationale de France (Département des Estampes).
Porteman, Karel. *Emblematic Exhibitions (Affixiones) at the Brussels Jesuit College (1630-1685): A Study of the Commemorative Manuscripts (Royal Library, Brussels)*. Brussels: Brepols, 1996.
Poussin, Nicolas. *Les Bergers d'Arcadie*. c. 1638-40. Louvre, Paris.
Pozzi, Giovanni. "Les Hiéroglyphes de l'*Hypnerotomachia Poliphili*." *L'Emblème à la Renaissance*. Ed. Yves Giraud. Paris: Société d'Education et d'Enseignement Supérieur, 1982. 15-27 and 139-41.
Praz, Mario. *Studies in Seventeenth-Century Imagery*. 2nd ed. 2 vols. Rome: Edizione di Storia et Letteratura, 1975.
Quartier, Philibert. *Ludovico Magno pro extincta hæresi panegyricus dictus*. Paris: G. Martin, 1687.
Queneau, Philippe. *Alceste, suivi de La Querelle d'Alceste*. Eds. William Brooks, Buford Norman and Jeanne Morgan Zarucchi. Geneva: Droz, 1994.
Racine, Jean. *Phèdre*. Ed. Jean Salles. Paris: Bordas, 1967.
Ratio atque institutio studiorum societatis Iesu. Tours: Claude Michael, 1603.
Rawles, Stephen. "The Bibliographic Context of Glasgow University Library SMAdd.392: A Preliminary Analysis." *Emblems and the Manuscript Tradition*. Ed. Laurence Grove. Glasgow: Glasgow Emblem Studies, 1997. 105-17.
"Reçu" (thought to be in the hand of Tristan L'Hermite), see Bibliothèque nationale de France (Département des Manuscrits, Cabinet des Titres).
Recueil Conrart, see Conrart, Valentin, ed.
Recueil de devises données à Marie de la Tour, duchesse de La Trémoille. Arsenal ms. 5217. Bibliothèque de l'Arsenal, Paris.
Recueil de divers rondeaux. Paris: Courbé, 1639.
Recueil des harangues prononcées de L'Académie francoise, dans leurs receptions, & en d'autres occasions différentes, depuis l'establissement de l'Académie jusqu'à présent 2 vols. Amsterdam: Aux Dépans de La Compagnie, 1709.
Recueil de pièces en prose. 4 vols. Paris: Charles de Sercy, 1658.
Reusner, Nicolas. *Emblemata*. Frankfurt: Joannus Feyer, 1581.
Rochemonteix, Camille de. *Un College de Jesuites au XVIIe et XVIIIe siècles*. 4 vols. Le Mans: Leguicheux, 1889.
Rodis-Lewis, Geneviève. "Un Elève du collège jésuite de La Flèche: René Descartes." *René Descartes (1596-1650): Célébrations nationales du quadricentenaire de sa naissance: Actes du colloque universitaire: La Formation de Descartes*. Ed. Jean Petit. La Flèche: Prytanée National Militaire, 1997. 25-36.
—. Introduction and Notes. *Discours de la méthode*. By René Descartes. Paris: Flammarion, 1966. 5-27 and passim.

Romanowski, Sylvie. *L'Illusion chez Descartes: La Structure du discours cartésien.* Paris: Klincksieck, 1974.

Rousset, Jean. *L'Intérieur et l'extérieur: Essais sur la poésie et sur le théâtre au XVIIe siècle.* Paris: Corti, 1968.

Royaumont, [Le Sieur de]. *L'Histoire du Vieux et du Nouveau Testament représentée avec des figures et des explications édifiantes tirées des Saints Pères pour régler les moeurs dans toutes sortes de conditions.* Paris: Pierre Le Petit, 1671.

Rubin, David Lee. *A Pact with Silence: Art and Thought in the* Fables *of Jean de La Fontaine.* Columbus: Ohio State UP, 1991.

—. "Triple Calculus: Notes Towards a Poetic and Rhetoric of La Fontaine's *Fables*, Book 7." *The Ladder of High Designs: Structure and Interpretation of French Lyric Sequence.* Eds. Doranne Fenoaltea and David Lee Rubin. Charlottesville VA: UP of Virginia, 1991. 91-109.

Russell, Daniel. *The Emblem and Device in France.* Lexington: French Forum, 1985.

—. *Emblematic Structures in Renaissance French Culture.* Toronto: U of Toronto P, 1995.

—. "Emblematic Structures in Sixteenth-Century French Poetry." *Jahrbuch für Internationale Germanistik* 14 (1982): 54-100.

—. "Emblème et mentalité symbolique." *Littérature* 78 (1990): 11-21.

—. "Emblems and Devices in Seventeenth-Century French Culture" *EMF: Studies in Early Modern France: Volume 1: Word and Image.* Ed. David Lee Rubin. Charlottesville VA: Rookwood, 1994. 9-30.

—. "M. de Montplaisir and his Emblems." *Neophilologus* 67 (1983): 503-16.

—. "Thoughts on a Newly-Discovered Manuscript Version of Gomberville's *Doctrine des moeurs* (1646)." *Emblems and the Manuscript Tradition.* Ed. Laurence Grove. Glasgow: Glasgow Emblem Studies, 1997. 1-18.

—. "Two Seventeenth-Century Treatises on the Art of the Device." *Emblematica* 1 (1986): 79-106.

Sainéan, Lazare. "Le Songe de Poliphile." *Problèmes littéraires du seizième siècle.* Paris: Boccard, 1927. 251-60.

Saint-Amant, Marc-Antoine de Girard, sieur de. *Oeuvres complètes.* Ed. Ch.-T. Livet. Paris, 1855. Nendeln: Kraus Reprint, 1972.

Sandt, Maximilian Van der. *Aviariam marianum.* Mainz: J. T. Schonwetterus, 1627.

—. *Maria flos mysticus.* Mainz: G. Schonwetterus, 1629.

—. *Maria, gemma mystica.* Mainz: J. T. Schonwetterus, 1631.

Saunders, Alison. *The Sixteenth-Century French Emblem Book: A Decorative and Useful Genre.* Geneva: Droz, 1988.

Scève, Maurice. *Délie.* Lyons: Sabon, 1544. Ed. I. D. McFarlane. Cambridge: Cambridge UP, 1966. Ed. D. Wilson. Menston: Scolar, 1972.

Schöne, Albrecht. *Emblematik und Drama im Zeitalter des Barock.* Munich: Beck, 1964.

Schoonhoven, Florent. *Emblemata.* Gouda: Andreas Burier, 1618.

Schwartz, Jerome. "Emblematic Theory and Practice: The Case of the Sixteenth-Century French Emblem Book." *Emblematica* 2.2 (1987): 293-315.

Scott, J. F. *The Scientific Work of René Descartes: (1596-1650)*. London: Taylor and Francis, 1976.

Scudéry, Madeleine de. *Clélie: Histoire romaine*. 10 vols. Paris: Augustin Courbé, 1660-61. Geneva: Slatkine Reprints, 1973.

Sébillet, Thomas. *Art poétique françoys*. Ed. Félix Gaiffe. Paris: Droz, 1932.

Seneca. *Thyestes*. Ed. R. J. Tarrant. Atlanta: Scholars Press, 1985.

Série Qb 1 in folio, see Bibliothèque nationale de France (Département des Estampes).

Sider, Sandra and Barbara Obrist. *Bibliography of Emblematic Manuscripts*. Montreal: Queens-McGill UP, 1997.

Siguret, Françoise. "'Le Ciel avec horreur voit ce monstre sauvage': Genèse de textes d'images." *PFSCL* 14.26 (1987): 83-102.

—. *L'Œil surpris: Perception et représentation dans la première moitié du XVIIe siècle*. 1985. Paris: Klincksieck, 1993.

Soriano, Marc. *Le Dossier Perrault*. Paris: Hachette, 1972.

Soto, Hernando de. *Emblemas moralizades*. Madrid: Por los Herederos de Iuan Iniguez de Lequerica, 1599.

Spica, Anne-Elisabeth. *Symbolique humaniste et emblématique: L'Evolution et les genres (1580-1700)*. Paris: Champion, 1996.

Spitzer, Leo. *Etudes de style*. Paris: Gallimard, 1970.

—. "The 'Récit de Théramène'." *Linguistics and Literary History: Essays in Stylistics*. Princeton: Princeton UP, 1948. 87-134.

Stengel, Georg. *Ova Paschalia sacro emblemate inscripta descriptaque*. Munich: n.p., 1634.

Strosetzki, Christoph. "Hieroglyphentradition und Devisenkunst als Hintergrund der Maximen von La Rochefoucauld." *Romanistisches Jahrbuch* 36 (1985): 104-21.

Symbolorum selectorum centuria. Arsenal ms. 1172. Bibliothèque de l'Arsenal, Paris.

Tapisseries du roy, où sont representez les quatre elemens et les quatre saisons: Avec les devises qui les accompagnent, et leur explication. Paris: Sebastien Mabre-Cramoisy, 1679.

Thuillier, Jacques. "Poètes et peintres au XVIIe siècle: L'Exemple de Tristan." *Cahiers Tristan L'Hermite* 6 (1984): 5-23.

Tiemann, Barbara. *Fabel und Emblem: Gilles Corrozet und die französische Renaissance-Fabel*. Munich: Fink, 1974.

Le Triomphe des Saints Ignace et François Xavier, au College Royal de la Flèche, contenant le Sommaire de ce qui s'y est faicte, en la solemnité de leur canonization: Depuis le Dimanche 24 Juillet 1622 iusques au dernier jour dudit mois. La Flèche: Louis Hebert, 1622.

Tristan L'Hermite. *Les Amours et autres poésies choisies*. Ed. Pierre Camo. Paris: Garnier, 1925.

—. *La Folie du sage*. Paris: Toussaint Quinet, 1645.

—. *La Lyre*. Ed. Jean-Pierre Chauveau. Geneva: Droz, 1977.

—. *La Mariane*. Paris: Augustin Courbé, 1645.
—. *Les Plaintes d'Acante et autres œuvres*. Ed. Jacques Madeleine. Paris: Cornélie, 1909.
—. [*Poems*]. Manuscripts interleaved on *Amorum emblemata*. By Otto Van Veen. Antwerp: Verdussen, 1608. SMAdd.392. Glasgow University Library.
—. *Poésies galantes et héroïques*. Paris: Loyson, 1662.
—. "Reçu" (thought to be in the hand of Tristan L'Hermite), see Bibliothèque nationale de France (Département des Manuscrits, Cabinet des Titres).
—. *Les Vers héroïques*. Ed. Catherine Grisé. Geneva: Droz, 1967.
Typus mundi. Antwerp: Apud Ioannem Cnobbarum, 1627.
Urfé, Honoré d'. *L'Astrée: Extraits choisis*. Ed. Maxime Gaume. Saint Etienne: Le Hénaff, 1981.
Valdor, Jean. *Triomphes de Louis le Iuste, XIII du nom, avec des vers de MM. Beys et de Corneille*. Paris: Antoine Estienne, 1649.
Vanuxem, Jacques. "Le Carrousel de 1612 sur la Place Royale et ses devises." *Les Fêtes de la Renaissance*. Vol. 1. Paris: CNRS, 1956. 191-203.
Vauzelles, Jean de. *Les Simulachres & historiees faces de la Mort, autant elegamment pourtraictes, que artificiellement imaginees*. Lyons: Melchior and Gaspard Trechsel, 1538.
Veen, Otto Van. *Album amicorum*. Ms. II 874. Bibliothèque Royale de Belgique, Brussels. Ed. J. Van den Gheyn. Brussels: Société des Bibliophiles, 1911.
—. *Amorum emblemata*. Antwerp: Verdussen, 1608.
—. *Emblemata horatiana*. Antwerp: Verdussen, 1607.
Verdizotti, Giovanni Mario. *Cento favole bellissime dei più illustri antichi, e moderni autori Greci, e Latini*. Venice: Giovanni Pietro Brigonei, 1661.
Vermeer, Jan. *Lady Standing at the Virginals*. 1670. National Gallery, London.
Vigenère, Blaise de, ed., see Philostratus.
Vincent, Michael. *Figures of the Text: Reading and Writing (in) La Fontaine*. Amsterdam: John Benjamins, 1991.
Visscher, Roemer. *Zinnepoppen*. Amsterdam: n.p., [c. 1620].
Voiture, Vincent. *Œuvres*. Ed. A. Ubicini. Paris: Charpentier, 1855. Geneva: Slatkine Reprints, 1967.
Vulson, Marc de. *Les Portraits des hommes illustres françois qui sont peints dans la galerie du palais Cardinal de Richelieu avec leurs principales actions, armes, devises, & eloges latins, desseignez & gravez par les sieurs Heince et Bignons, peintres et graveurs ordinaires du Roy*. Paris: Sara, 1650.
—. *Les Portraits des hommes illustres françois qui sont peints dans la galerie du palais Cardinal de Richelieu avec leurs principales actions, armes, devises, & eloges latins, desseignez & gravez par les sieurs Heince et Bignons, peintres et graveurs ordinaires du Roy*. Paris: Pepingué, De Sercy et De Luynes, 1655.
Weinberg, Kurt. "The Lady and the Unicorn, or M. de Nemours à Coulomiers: Enigma, Device, Blazon and Emblem in *La Princesse de Clèves*." *Euphorion* 71 (1977): 306-55.
Wierix, Antonius. *Cor Iesu amanti sacrum*. [Antwerp]: n.p., [c. 1586].

Wilhelm, Jacques. "Un Décor disparu: Les Peintures de la gallerie du château de Berny illustrant la vie d'Henri IV et la première année du règne de Louis XIII." *Bulletin de la Société de l'Histoire de l'Art Français* (1983): 29-45.

Zarucchi, Jeanne Morgan. "Charles Perrault et l'éloquence de la devise." *Merveilles et Contes* 5.2 (1991): 167-78.

—. *Perrault's Morals for Moderns*. New York: Peter Lang, 1985.

Zarucchi, Jeanne Morgan, ed. and trans. *Memoirs of my life*. By Charles Perrault. Columbia: U of Missouri P, 1989.

INDEX OF PRIMARY MATERIAL, SECONDARY SOURCES AND PRINCIPAL EMBLEMATIC TOPOI

Individual works, unless anonymous, and fictional characters are included in their authors' classification.

Abraham, Claude, 76, 104
Abraham, History of, Tapestries, 74
Abregé de l'histoire des Roys…, 17, 165
Abstemius, 121-23, 150
Académie des devises et inscriptions, See *Petite académie*
Académie Française, 2, 19, 21, 106, 164, 165, 171, 179, 229, 233, 256, 257
Adam, Charles, 68
Adams, Alison, 23, 25, 83, 100, 104, 105, 160, 206-28
Aesop, 21, 111, 115-17, 123, 151, 152, 156, 160, 162, 183, 200
Album amicorum, 100-01, 105
Alciato, Andrea, 8, 10, 15, 36, 57, 58, 62, 109, 111, 159, 195
Alexander, Sir William, 26
Alquié, Ferdinand, 68
Aneau, Barthélemy, 8, 9, 24, 63, 199
Angiviller, [Comte de], 186
Anne d'Autriche, 234-35, 250-51, 256, 258
Annuæ litteræ Societatis Iesu, 36
Apuleius, 134
Aquilon, Pierre, 161
Architecture, 49-51, 53, 54, 72-73, 137-39, 252-53
Aristotle, 61-67
Arnauld, Antoine, 164, 193

Arnoullet, Balthazar, 112
Arsenal, Bibliothèque de, 3, 18, 27, 75, 102, 105, 143-54, 158, 162, 163, 166-78, 187-88, 201-02, 204, 229-59
Ashman, John, 80
Assûrances, Chambre des, 252, 258
Astronomy, 39
Bagley, Ayers, 11, 72-73, 190
Baillet, Adrien, 32, 43, 44, 69, 72
Bailly, Jacques, 19, 152, 178
Ball, 54-55
Barbiche, Bernard, 189
Barchilon, Jacques, 165, 190
Bassan, Fernande, 162
Bassy, Alain-Marie, 110, 111, 125-26, 160
Bath, Michael, 161, 190
Bâtiments du roi, 247-48, 257
Baudoin, Jean, 2, 9, 10, 109, 160
Bayley, Peter, 14, 15
Bee, 19, 41, 146, 162, 237, 253-54, 255
Benserade, Isaac de, 202-03
Bergal, Irene, 23, 72, 129
Bernadin, N.-M., 75, 103, 104, 105
Bernini, Gian Lorenzo, 129
Berny, Château de, 75, 78, 80-81, 83-84, 86, 100, 101, 104, 204, 206
Bertaut, Jean, 14, 15
Bèze, Théodore de, 9, 58
Bible, 174, 189, 192-94
Bibliothèque nationale de France, 34-37, 41-43, 69, 70, 71, 81, 82, 104, 150-54, 163, 166, 169-70, 178-79, 183, 187, 190, 203, 257

Billinghurst, Percy J., 163
Binet, Etienne, 1
Biographies, 16-17
Birberick, Anne L., 160-61, 162
Bivero, Pedro, 14
Blasons du corps, 107
Bléchet, Françoise, 81
Blindman, 47, 50, 61
Blois, Château de, 8, 17
Bodleian Library, Oxford, 100
Boel, Cornelis, 100
Boileau, Nicolas, 153, 165, 179, 257
Bois-le-Vicomte, 18, 163
Boissard, Jean-Jacques, 9
Bonnefon, Paul, 170
Bordonove, Georges, 161
Bose, Guillaume de, 112
Bossuet, Jacques Bénigne, 203, 259
Bouhours, Dominique, 21, 33, 188
Bouillon, [Cardinal de], 251-52, 258
Bouillon, [Duc de], 102, 258
Bouillon, [Duc de, father of above], 258
Bourbon, Antoine de, 53, 55
Bourgogne, [Duc de], 170-71, 253, 255, 258-59
Bourgoin, Auguste, 162
Bourséis, [Abbé de], 164, 171, 256
Boutet de Monvel, Maurice, 126
Bravo-Villasante, Carmen, 205
British Library, 151, 154, 178, 256-57
Brody, Jules, 162
Brooks, William, 189-90
Brussels, Royal Library, 26, 100
Bussy-le-Grand, Château de, 8, 27
Bussy Rabutin, [Comte de], 18
Calvin, Jean, 112
Camerarius, Joachim, 9, 195
Camo, Pierre, 103, 206
Candle, 15
Carnegie Library of Pittsburgh, 156-57
Carriat, Amédée, 3, 4, 75-76, 104
Carrousels, 15, 164, 180
Cassagnes, Jacques, 163, 164, 244-45, 257

Cats, Jacob, 59
Caussin, Nicolas, 32, 141
Cebes, 8, 34
Chadel, Jules, 126
Chagall, Marc, 125
Champaillet, Yvonne, 205
Chantilly, Musée Condé, 179
Chanut, Pierre, 43
Chapelain, Jean, 164, 170, 229, 243-44, 256
Charlet, [le Père], 32
Charpentier, François, 106, 163, 170, 177, 229, 241-43, 256
Charpentier, Françoise, 1, 4, 161
Chastellier, Jean, 33
Chatelain, Jean-Marc, 25, 26, 27
Chaulnes, [Duchesse de], 75
Chauveau, François, 104, 108, 125-27, 158, 160, 164, 242-43
Chauveau, Jean-Pierre, 94, 100, 101-02, 103, 104, 105
Chertablon [M. de], 198-99, 205
Chomsky, Noam, 31
Christ, 57-58, 60, 145, 200
Chupeau, Jacques, 161
Clarac, Pierre, 107, 136
Clément, [M.], 19, 21, 27, 150, 154, 171, 172-74, 177-78, 187, 233, 256
Clère, Jules, 69
Clock, 50, 60, 250-51
Cochin, Charles-Nicolas, 125
Colbert, Jean-Baptiste, 18, 131, 144-45, 152-53, 164, 165, 179, 256, 257, 259
Colletet, François, 103
Collinet, Jean-Pierre, 1, 3, 4, 108, 120, 125, 127, 154-55, 160, 161
Colonna, Francesco, 1, 8, 136-37, 159, 161
Conan, Michael, 183, 190
Condé, [Princesse de],
    See, Montmorency, Charlotte-Marguerite de
Conrart, Valentin, 106, 143-44, 152-53, 162, 256

Index

Conrart, Valentin, ed (*Recueil Conrart*), See Arsenal, Bibliothèque de
Corneille, Pierre, 1, 155, 203
Corrozet, Gilles, 5, 6, 8, 23, 55, 59, 63, 66, 109, 111, 112, 116-18, 162, 182
Coustau, Pierre, 9, 10, 25, 59
Couton, Georges, 1, 4, 108, 109, 110, 111, 112, 158, 159, 160, 163, 194, 198-99, 203, 205
Covarrubias, Sebastián de, 195
Crashaw, Richard, 28
Culpin, David, 190
Daly, Peter, 1, 3, 23, 28, 194
Dandrey, Patrick, 1, 4, 110
Dalla Valle, Daniela, 78, 86
Danner, Richard, 108, 120-21
David, Ioannes, 12, 13, 14, 26, 30, 54-55, 56, 135-36, 199
Davidson, Hugh M., 74
Debeaune, Florimond, 29
DeJean, Joan, 3, 4, 134-35, 161
Demetz, Peter, 63
Desargues, Gérard, 29
Descartes, Jeanne, 32
Descartes, Joachim, 32
Descartes, René, 1, 2, 3, 21, 29-74, 120, 155, 178, 191-92, 200, 201, 204
Desprechins, Anne, 202
DeTournes, Jean, 8
Devises pour les tapisseries du roy, 19, 20, 149, 151-54, 163, 164, 165, 170, 171, 178-79, 187-88, 190, 235-45, 256, 257
Dexter, Greta, 8, 24
Dieckmann, Liselotte, 112, 141, 161
Dimler, Richard, 11, 14
Dinet, Jacques, 29
Donné, Boris, 1, 3, 160, 161
Doré, Gustave, 125
Dragons, 254, 259
Dreaming Sleeper, 56-57
Du Bray, Toussainct, 75, 92, 94
Dundas, Judith, 73
Eagle, 18, 36, 233-34, 237, 255

Education, 11, 32-46, 69
Eisen, Charles, 127
'Embleme representant L'Estat de la...', 39
Emblemes Politiques: Presenté a son Eminence, 16, 27
Entries, Royal, 15, 16, 193
Epigrams, 38-39
Erasmus, 33, 44, 72, 174-75, 189
Estienne, Henri, 21, 77, 141, 187
Etampes-Valençay, Charlotte de, 86
Faene, Gabriel, 182, 190
Félibien, André, 131-32, 165, 179
Fermat, Pierre de, 29
Flamen, Albert, 161
Flinders, Peter, 165
Flores mei fructus..., 71
Fontaine, Nicolas, 192-93, 200
Fortune, 18
Fotiade, Ramona, 105
Fouquet, Nicolas, 3, 8, 18, 19, 23, 27, 102, 106, 131, 133, 137-38, 143-54, 158, 161, 163, 164, 202, 204, 257
Fragonard, Jean-Honoré, 127
François I, 8, 17, 23
François-Xavier, Saint, 40
Franqué, Catharine, 100
Fumaroli, Marc, 152-53, 158, 161, 163, 190
Furetière, Antoine, 111, 162
Galilei, Galileo, 39, 43, 67
Gallows, 19
Ganymede, 36
Gardening, Landscape, 137-39
Gardes du corps, 255
Gardien, [M.], 172
Gaston, Duc d'Orléans, 75, 77-78
Gaudini, Claire, 74
Gaudriault, Raymond, 166
Gautier-Gentès, Jean-Luc, 165, 186, 190
Geometry, 68
Getty Museum, 179
Giard, Lucy, 69
Gibson, Boyce, 68, 74

Giovio, Paolo, 17
Girard, Yves, 161
Glasgow Emblem Group, 24
Glasgow University Library, 2, 78, 80-103, 104, 150, 202, 204, 206-28
Globes, 41
Gobelins, Tapestries, 19, 151, 164, 178
Golius, 29, 68
Gomberville, Marin Le Roy de, 9, 10, 25, 75, 77, 102
Gordian Knot, 44
Graham, David, 23, 28, 53, 68, 105, 129, 160, 161, 189, 205
Greffiers, 252-53, 258
Greiffenberg, Catherina Regina von, 23
Griffin, Edward, 190
Grimm, Jürgen, 3, 4, 108, 111, 118-19, 159, 161, 163
Grimmelshausen, Hans J. C. von, 23
Grisé, Catherine, 76, 103, 104, 206
Grivel, Marianne, 163, 165, 190
Grove, Laurence, 24, 69, 70, 74, 103, 159, 160
Guérard, Nicolas, 125
Guéroult, Guillaume, 2, 8, 9, 24, 109, 110, 111-24, 158, 159, 182
Guichon, Marie, 164
Guise, Henri de, 75
Halcyon, 171, 229-31, 242, 247-48, 256
Hall, H. Gaston, 2, 4, 159
Hals, Frans, 72
Hare, 147, 149
Harvard University Library, 179
Haudent, Guillaume, 111, 116, 117
Heinsius, Daniel, 63
Heliotrope, 27
Henkel, Arthur, 25, 63, 73, 195
Henri III, 258
Henri IV, 17, 32, 34-41, 64-65, 84, 86, 102, 104
Henriette d'Angleterre, 203
Heraldry, 8
Hercules, 95, 105, 149-50, 209, 245-46, 257

Hippolytus, 195-97
Holbein, Hans, 59
Höltgen, Karl-Josef, 105
Hooch, Rommyn de, 127
Horapollo, 8, 17, 45, 73, 111, 112, 141-43, 156, 158, 161, 162
House,
    See, Architecture
Hugo, Hermann, 11
Ignatius, Saint, 40, 41, 45, 50
Imago primi saeculi Societatis Iesu, 11, 62, 64, 69
Imprese, 8, 27, 96
Ivy, 2, 5, 23, 50, 51, 55, 61-67, 74, 193, 204
Jacquin, [le Père], 34
Jacquiot, Josèphe, 188, 257-59
Janin, Pierre, 81
Janot, Denis, 8
Jansenism, 192-94, 198-201
Jeanneret, Michel, 133
Jesuit,
    See, Society of Jesus
Jetons, 33, 39, 170, 229, 253, 255, 257-58
Jewelry Box, 137-38
Johnson, Leonard, 1, 2, 4, 75, 81, 84
Jonson, Ben, 28
Jouvancy, Joseph de, 11, 21, 26, 32, 33, 34, 62
Joy, 52
Junius, Hadrianus, 9, 57, 200
Jurèn, Vladimir, 10
Justice, 78
Klein, Robert, 27
La Bruyère, Jean de, 200-01
Lacroix, Paul, 163
Lacrymæ collegii..., 38-39, 62, 71
La Fayette, [Mme. de], 1, 201
La Flèche, 2, 3, 26, 32-46, 52, 61-67, 69, 70, 71, 150
La Fontaine, Jean de, 1, 2, 3, 21, 22, 27, 28, 106-63, 183, 191, 200, 201, 202, 204

280

Index

Lagarde et Michard, 101
La Hyre, Laurent de, 78
Lancret, Nicolas, 127
Lancy, De Vaux de, 112, 159
Landwehr, John, 25
La Perrière, Guillaume de, 8, 24, 47, 48, 53, 55, 58, 63, 66, 74, 129, 195, 199
La Rochefoucauld, François de, 156, 193, 200-01
La Trémoille, Marie de La Tour, [Duchesse de], 201
Laurens, Pierre, 71, 73
La Vallière, [Duchesse de], 256
Le Brun, Charles, 22, 129, 131, 138, 164, 186, 194
Le Clerc, Sébastien, 178
Le Compte, Hippolyte, 125
Le Coq, Anne-Marie, 23
LeFevre, Jean, 8
Lefèvre, Roger, 30
Le Fort de La Morinière, Adrien-Claude, 102
Leibniz, Gottfried Wilhelm, 44
Le Jay, Gabriel-François, 14, 26, 51-52, 64, 70, 102, 150, 203
Le Moyne, Pierre, 19, 21, 77, 110, 125, 159, 163, 171, 172-74, 177-78, 201-02, 233, 234, 256
Le Nôtre, André, 22, 131
LePage, Raymond, 1, 3, 108, 109, 126, 160
Le Tellier, Michel, 18, 131, 144-45
Le Vau, Louis, 22, 131, 138
Lizard, 18
Loach, Judi, 11, 15, 26, 28, 160, 189
Lorgues-Lapouge, Christine, 27
Lormier, Charles, 159
Lorraine, [Cardinal de], 5, 23, 63
Louis de France, 254, 259
Louis le Grand, Collège, 15, 51
Louis, Saint,
    See, Saint Louis
Louis XII, 5, 17, 257
Louis XIII, 16, 38, 41, 64, 71, 77, 104, 231, 256
Louis XIV, 16, 18, 21, 22, 52, 102, 129-36, 144-45, 148-54, 161, 171-72, 178, 179, 180, 197-98, 229, 235-53, 255, 256-59
Louis XV, 258
Louvois, [Marquis de], 165, 179, 258
Louvre, 179, 233, 247, 256
Lute, 58-59
Lyons, John, D., 3, 4, 30, 31, 45, 50, 51, 56
Mabille de Poncheville, André, 162
Madeleine, Jacques, 103, 206
Maggs Bros. Ltd., London, 80
Maine, [Duc du], 250-51, 258
Malarte, Claire-Lise, 189
Malherbe, François de, 203
Malleville, Claude de, 81, 101, 105
Mannich, Johann, 57
Manning, John, 69
Mansard, François, 81
Marchant de Burbure, F., 32
Marguerite de Navarre, 8, 27
Marie-Thérèse d'Autriche, 15, 16, 257
Marin, Louis, 165
Martin, Henri, 166
Martin, Jean, 14
Martinet, [le Sieur], 16
Massing, Jean-Michel, 72
Maucroix, François de, 106
Maulevant, Jacques de, 53, 55, 129
Mazarin, [Cardinal], 16
McGowan, Margaret, 1, 4, 109-10, 111, 159
McLean, Austin, 190
McStewart, William, 30, 72
Meerhoff, Kees, 159
Mellan, Claude, 78
Ménard, Jean-Claude, 69
Menestrier, Claude-François, 1, 15, 16, 21, 22, 26, 27, 28, 68, 108-09, 126, 141, 156, 163, 171-72, 174, 187, 189, 202, 203, 256
Mercure françois, 36

Mercure galant, 172
Mersenne, Marin, 32, 43
Meyer [illustrator], 125
Mirror, 14, 54-55, 135-36
Moderna, Nicoletto de, 62
Molière, 22, 111, 131, 201
Monnet, Charles, 125
Montaigne, Michel de, 72
Montano, Benedito Arias, 25
Montenay, Georgette de, 9, 14, 59-60, 175-76, 200
Montespan, [Marquise de], 258
Montglas, [Mme. de], 18
Montmorency, Charlotte-Marguerite de, 201, 202
Montplaisir, René de Bruc, [Marquis de], 11, 25
Moon, 234-35
Morand, Paul, 161
Moreau, Gustave, 125
Moreau, Jean-Michel, 127
Morgan, Jeanne,
    See, Zarucchi, Jeanne Morgan
Mosaic, 120, 159, 204
Mourey, Gabriel, 16, 27
Musæ Flexienses…, 71
Muses illustres, Les, 75
Nadal, Jeronimo, 14
Nashe, John, 26
Navy, 248-49, 257
Nelson, Robert J., 198, 205
Nelson, Theodor Holm, 28
Nicholich, Robert N., 4, 28, 161
Norman, Buford, 189-90
Obrist, Barbara, 178-79
Orationes variæ funebres…, 71
Ordinaire des guerres, 250, 258
Orgel, Stephen, 24, 28
Oudry, Jean-Baptiste, 125
Ovid, 9, 72
Pace, Claire, 25
Painting, 46-48, 137-39, 186
Panofsky, Erwin, 28, 190
Paradin, Claude, 5, 7, 10, 17, 63

Paris, Ville de, 16
Parties casuelles, 246-47, 257
Pascal, Blaise, 175, 193, 198-200
Passe-Temps poetiques…, 187
Pastoureau, Michel, 8
Paul, Saint, 174-75
Paulmy, [Marquis de], 166
Paultre, Roger, 12
Pedersen, John, 104
Pelican, 15, 34
Pellisson, Paul, 106
Perrault, Charles, 2, 3, 15, 17, 19, 21, 27, 68, 106, 151-53, 164-90, 191, 204, 229-59
Perrault, Charles, Jr., 164
Perrault, Charles-Senvel, 164
Perrault, Claude, 164, 171
Perrault, Nicolas, 164
Perrault, Pierre, 164
Perrier, Simone, 23
Petau, Noël, 32
Petit, Jean, 69
Petite académie, 19, 21, 106, 164, 165, 179, 188, 233, 256, 257
Phaedrus, 117, 140-41, 182
Philippe III of Spain, 256
Philippe IV of Spain, 257
Phoenix, 34, 150, 166
Picon, Antoine, 170, 189
Pièce Te 120,
    See, Bibliothèque nationale de France
Pierpont Morgan Library, 179
Piety, 52, 78
Pilpay, 111, 162
Pithou, [M.], 182
Place Royale, Paris, 15
"Planche que les Iesuites ont fait graver", 40-43, 64-65, 67, 72
Plantin, Christopher, 78
Plutarch, 199
Poetry, 137-39, 186
Pomegranate, 40, 151-53, 242-43, 252
Porcupine, 5, 23, 245

Porteman, Karel, 26, 69
Port Royal,
 See, Jansenism
Poussin, Nicolas, 22, 28, 124, 129
Pozzi, Giovanni, 161
Praz, Mario, 1, 3, 26, 27, 54
Puisieux, [Marquis de], 86
Quartier, Philibert, 14, 26, 51-52, 53, 203
Querelle des anciens et des modernes, 165, 177-78, 182, 256
Quinault, Philippe, 164, 177
Rabelais, François, 160
Racine, Jean, 177, 179, 193-98, 203, 205
Rambouillet, [Mme. de], 201
Ratio studiorum, 11, 26, 32, 33, 34, 36, 62, 65
Rawles, Stephen, 25, 104, 105
Recueil Conrart,
 See Arsenal, Bibliothèque de
Recueil de divers ouvrages en prose et en vers, 190
Recueil de divers rondeaux, 81, 101
Recueil de pièces en prose, 104
Recueil de poésies chretiennes..., 152
Recueil des harangues..., 256
Recueil des meilleurs dessins..., 107
Recueil des plus beaux vers..., 92, 94
Reed, 200
Reusner, Nicolas, 9, 60
Richelieu, [Cardinal de], 17, 18, 19, 102, 149-50, 154, 163, 234
Richelieu, [Mlle. de], 19
Ripa, Caesare, 112, 203
Rochemonteix, Camille de, 69
Rodis-Lewis, Geneviève, 68-69
Rollenhagen, Gabriel, 57
Romanowski, Sylvie, 50
Rouger, Georges, 188
Rousset, Jean, 136
Royaumont, [le Sieur de], 192
Rubens, Peter Paul, 194
Rubin, David Lee, 3, 4, 108, 113, 116, 120-21, 123, 143, 147, 155-56

Ruscelli, Girolamo, 17
Russell, Daniel, 1, 4, 10, 23, 24, 25, 26, 27, 28, 63, 101, 145, 151, 189, 203, 256
Sacy, Louis-Isaac Le Maitre de, 194
Sainéan, Lazare, 161
Saint-Amant, [Sieur de], 203
Saint Denis, Basilica of, 15, 203
Saint-Esprit, Ordre du, 253, 258
Saint Germain, Château de, 17
Saint Louis, 41, 64
Saint Louis, Maison Professe de, 34, 69
Saint Paul Saint Louis, Eglise,
 See, Saint Louis, Maison Professe de
Saint Simon, [Duc de], 258
Salamander, 8, 23
Salles, Jean, 205
Sambucus, Ioannes, 9
Sandt, Maximilian Van der, 54
Saunders, Alison, 23, 24, 25
Scarron, Paul, 202-03
Scève, Maurice, 9, 66
Schöne, Albrecht, 25, 63, 73, 195, 205
Schoonhoven, Florent, 59
Schouls, Peter, 30
Schwartz, Jerome, 23
Scott, J. F., 68
Scudéry, Madeleine de, 78, 153, 201-02
Sea Monster, 194-95, 197
Sébillet, Thomas, 159
Sécretaires du roi, 252, 258
Seguiran, Gaspar de, 15
Sellier, Philippe, 189
Seneca, 72
Série Qb 1 in folio,
 See, Bibliothèque nationale de France
Sermons, 14, 15
Servet, Michel, 112
Sévigné, [Mme. de], 144, 256
Shakespeare, William, 26, 28
Ship, 16, 59-60, 200, 204, 249
Sider, Sandra, 178-79
Siguret, Françoise, 1, 4, 194

Silkworm, 146-49, 154, 255-56
Silvestre, Israël, 130, 164
Smith, C. N., 25
Smith, Paul J., 159
Snake, 19
Society of Jesus, 3, 11, 12, 14, 21, 26, 32-46, 54-55, 56, 61-67, 69, 135-36, 191-92, 199, 201, 207
Soriano, Marc, 165-66
Soto, Hernando de, 195-97
Soul, 12
Spica, Anne-Elisabeth, 24
Spitzer, Leo, 155, 194
Squirrel, 8, 18, 23, 145, 152-53, 163
Stag, 139-43, 156, 161, 190, 204, 209, 219, 246
Stars Viewed from Afar, 46, 48, 49
Stella, Jacques, 78
Stengel, Georg, 54
Strosetzki, Christoph, 200-01
Suffren, Jean, 15
Sun, 18, 52, 53, 131, 133-34, 146, 148-49, 154, 162, 171-72, 180, 197-98, 231, 234, 245, 246-47, 251, 254-55, 259
Symbolorum selectorum centuria, 105, 149-50, 154
Tannery, P., 68
Taurellus, Nicolaus, 195
Terence, 2
Thou, [M. de], 182
Thuillier, Jacques, 78
Tiemann, Barbara, 116-17, 162, 182
Time, 186-87, 190
Trésor royal, 245-46, 257
Triangle, 41, 67
Triomphe des Saints, Le, 40-41
Tristan L'Hermite, 1, 2, 3, 75-105, 119, 150, 166, 191, 202, 204, 206-28
Tuileries, Jardins des, 15
Turenne, [M. de], 251, 258
Urfé, Honoré de, 202
Val-de-Grâce, Abbaye de, 258

Valdor, Jean, 75-76, 102
Valeriano Bolzani, Giovanni Pierio, 112
Valour, 78
Van den Gheyn, J., 105
Vanuxem, Jacques, 27
Van Vaeck, Marc, 69
Van Veen, Otto, 2, 10, 57, 63, 75, 77, 80-103, 105, 204, 206-28
Vaux-le-Vicomte, Château de, 2, 18, 22, 106, 131, 133, 138-39
Vauzelle, Jean de, 9
Velat, [Abbé], 205
Venus, 133-34
Verdizotti, Giovanni Marie, 111, 112, 115-18
Vermandois, [Comte de], 170, 171, 229-31, 250-51, 256, 258
Vermaulen d'Anvers, Corneille, 107
Vermeer, Jan, 96, 105
Versailles, Palace and Gardens of, 15, 22, 129-36, 158, 180, 183, 186, 197-98, 204, 256
Vienna National Library, 151, 178
Vienne, 11
Vigenère, Jean de, 9, 199
Vincent, Michael, 163
Vine, 63, 74
Visscher, Roemer, 47
Voiture, Vincent, 81, 101, 105, 144, 202
Vulson, Marc de, 17, 27, 39, 165, 177, 179
Warin, Jean, 129
Weinburg, Kurt, 1, 4, 201
Weston, David, 104
Wierix, Antonius, 54
Wilhelm, Jacques, 104, 105
Wilson, D., 74
Wings, 57-58
Wisdom, 52
Wygant, Amy, 194
Zarucchi, Jeanne Morgan, 165-66, 189-90
Zincgref, Julius Wilhelm, 9

OHIO UNIVERSITY LIBRARY
Please return this book as you have
finished using it must

Printed in the United States
1583